CONTENTS

FROMMER'S

COMPREHENSIVE TRAVEL GUIDE

LONDON '94

by Darwin Porter
Assisted by Danforth Prince

PRENTICE HALL TRAVEL

NEW YORK • LONDON • TORONTO • SYDNEY • TOKYO • SINGAPORE

FROMMER BOOKS

Published by Prentice Hall General Reference
A division of Simon & Schuster Inc.
15 Columbus Circle
New York, NY 10023

ISBN 0-671-84900-X
ISSN 0899-2886

Design by Robert Bull Design
Maps by Geografix Inc.

FROMMER'S EDITORIAL STAFF
Editorial Director: Marilyn Wood
Editorial Manager/Senior Editor: Alice Fellows
Senior Editor: Lisa Renaud
Editors: Charlotte Allstrom, Thomas F. Hirsch, Peter Katucki, Sara Hinsey
     Raveret, Theodore Stavrou
Assistant Editors: Margaret Bowen, Christopher Hollander, Ian Wilker
Editorial Assistants: Gretchen Henderson, Bethany Jewett
Managing Editor: Leanne Coupe

Special Sales
Bulk purchases (10+ copies) of Frommer's Travel Guides are available to
corporations at special discounts. The Special Sales Department can produce custom editions to be used as premiums and/or for sales promotion
to suit individual needs. Existing editions can be produced with custom
cover imprints such as a corporate logo. For more information write to:
Special Sales, Prentice Hall Travel, 15 Columbus Circle, New York, New
York 10023.

Manufactured in the United States of America

LIST OF MAPS

INTRODUCING LONDON

London has never quite made up its mind about its size. The City of London is merely 1 square mile of very expensive real estate around the Bank of England. All the rest is made up of 32 boroughs, each governed by a directly elected council. Together they add up to a mammoth metropolis, one of the largest on the globe.

The heart, brick, and mortar core of this giant is one of the most fascinating areas on earth. For about a century, one-quarter of the world was ruled from here. And with every step you take, you'll come across some sign of the tremendous influence this city has had . . . and still wields today.

London is a very old city, even by European standards. The Roman conquerors of Britain founded Londinium in A.D. 43 by settling and fortifying two small hills on the north bank of the River Thames and linking them with the rest of the island by a military network of roads.

More than a thousand years later, another conqueror turned the city into his capital. This was William of Normandy, who defeated the last Saxon ruler of England, Harold, in 1066. There isn't much left of the Roman period, but William the Conqueror left his imprint on London for all time to come.

For a start, he had himself crowned in Westminster Abbey on Christmas Day in 1066. Almost all British monarchs have been crowned there since, right up to the present queen. He also built the White Tower, which today forms part of the Tower of London.

London is a mass of contradictions. On the one hand, it's a decidedly royal city, studded with palaces, court gardens, coats-of-arms, and other regal paraphernalia. Yet London is also the home of the world's second-oldest parliamentary assembly (Iceland has the oldest). And when handsome and rash King Charles I tried to defy its representatives, he found himself swept off his throne and onto a scaffold way back in 1649.

2 · INTRODUCING LONDON

☑ WHAT'S SPECIAL ABOUT LONDON

Historic Buildings
- ☐ The Tower of London, a former palace, prison, mint, and place of execution. A chief attraction today is the Crown Jewels.
- ☐ Westminster Abbey, where English monarchs have been crowned since William the Conqueror in 1066.
- ☐ The Houses of Parliament, the imposing Neo-Gothic "Mother of Parliaments."
- ☐ St. Paul's Cathedral, a beautiful church designed by Sir Christopher Wren after the Great Fire of 1666.

Museums
- ☐ The British Museum, a repository for everything from the Parthenon's Elgin Marbles to an original of the Magna Carta.
- ☐ The Tate Gallery, a fantastic collection of British painting from the 16th to the 20th century.

- ☐ The National Gallery, an unrivaled collection of European painting, expertly displayed.

Parks
- ☐ Hyde Park, some 340 acres of greenery and the famous Speakers' Corner.
- ☐ Regent's Park, with an Open Air Theatre.

For the Kids
- ☐ Madame Tussaud's hauntingly real waxwork effigies of famous and infamous characters.

City Spectacle
- ☐ The Changing of the Guard, a famous daily ceremony at Buckingham Palace.

Evening Entertainment
- ☐ The London theater, a great array from Shakespeare to *Miss Saigon*.

1. GEOGRAPHY, GOVERNMENT & PEOPLE

GEOGRAPHY & GOVERNMENT

London lies in southeast England, about 40 miles from the mouth of the River Thames, which flows through the city from west to east. The great majority of attractions are north of the river.

Among the districts that lie on the northern banks of the Thames are the City of London, Chelsea, Westminster, Fulham, Hammersmith, and—to the north of them—Kensington, Paddington, St. Pancras, Islington, and Hampstead. The area south of the Thames embraces such districts as Battersea, Lambeth, Southwark, Greenwich, and Bermondsey.

Greater London, with a population of about 6.75 million, consists of 32 boroughs, plus the City of London. The boroughs, which range in population between 131,000 and 317,000, are governed by directly elected councils. The City of London has a resident population of just 6,000, but some 320,000 work there. The City is governed by the nonpartisan Corporation of London, which includes the lord mayor.

The West End encompasses the monumental government center of London, Westminster, and Whitehall, but also includes major shopping districts, especially Covent Garden, Kensington High Street, Oxford Street, Knightsbridge, and Piccadilly. Most of what is called "theaterland"—the densest concentration of theaters, and restaurants as well—is around Leicester Square, Shaftesbury Avenue, and Piccadilly Circus. More ethnic restaurants are found in Soho than in any other place of London.

Many of the most important museums are in South Kensington—so many it's often called "museumland." The Tate Gallery, however, is to the east, in Westminster; the British Museum is in Bloomsbury; and the National Gallery and National Portrait Gallery are on Trafalgar Square. The City is the square mile of land that is home to one of the major banking and financial centers of the world, luring most visitors east mainly to see St. Paul's Cathedral and the Tower of London.

PEOPLE

English people, especially Londoners, have a reputation for their "stiff upper lip" and stuffiness. Through most of its long history, however, London has been a distinctly wild and wicked town. Shakespeare, Marlowe, and their roistering, hot-blooded tavern cronies personified London life during the reign of "Good Queen Bess" (Elizabeth I). Seventeenth-century London shocked visiting Frenchmen. A hundred years later, it even managed to shock the visiting Casanova. One look at Hogarth's paintings will tell you just what a boozing, gambling, racy place it was.

For only a relatively short period—from around 1830 to 1950—did Britain's capital don Mrs. Grundy's tight corsets, which had also been worn briefly during Cromwell's earlier, short-lived Puritan Commonwealth. There were various reasons for this: the Industrial Revolution and the rise of the bourgeoisie, the task of building and defending the Empire, the personal morality of Queen Victoria. But 120 years is merely a small interval in the chronicle.

After winning two world wars and losing an empire in the process, the English people have rediscovered the zest for life that characterized their ancestors' "Merrie England."

Nevertheless, the first thing you notice about Londoners is their perpetual air of preoccupation. Don't be put off by this. It's merely a mask, a kind of detachable face they wear in public. Approach them about anything and you'll find them to be courteous and helpful. But . . . you have to approach them first! Londoners are not given to opening casual conversations, even when they sit next to you in a bus or stand alongside you in a bar. This is not through lack of sociability but from a deeply rooted respect for privacy. The reserve often vanishes the moment you start talking.

Remember, though, never to ask anyone if he or she is "English." A person from Ireland, Scotland, or Wales—whose national identities have been fostered since the 1970s—may be deeply insulted. Use the term *Scotch* for the drink but not the people—they are "Scots."

2. HISTORY & POLITICS

DATELINE

- **55 B.C.** Julius Caesar invades England, a short distance from present-day London.
- **43 B.C.** Roman armies defeat Celts, establishing a fortified camp called Londinium.
- **A.D. 61** Celts from East Anglia burn and sack Londinium, but it is repossessed by Romans.
- **410** Romans retreat from London and return to Europe.
- **449** Arrival of Saxons on Kentish coast.
- **886** King Alfred, a Saxon, conquers London but rules from his capital at Winchester.
- **900–1050** Saxons ward off Viking invasions.
- **1066** Norman invasion of England. William the Conqueror defeats Harold at the Battle of Hastings and is crowned in Westminster Abbey.
- **1100s** London asserts its right for some measure of self-government, establishing the office of lord mayor.

(continues)

HISTORY

CELTS, ROMANS, AND THE EARLY MIDDLE AGES

The first artifacts ever discovered, and the first historical reference to the city, date from its occupation by the ancient Romans, who adapted a local Celtic name into the latinized form, Londinium.

Julius Caesar raided England in 55 and 54 B.C., fording the Thames with his armies somewhere downstream from today's London, but the bulk of written history dates from Claudius's military campaigns of A.D. 43, about a century later. Londinium became a thriving port by A.D. 61. That same year a union of Celtic tribes, led by Boadicea, attacked the unprotected rear flank of the Roman armies during one of their northern campaigns and burned the fortified camp of Londinium to the ground. The Romans erected a much larger camp (excavations reveal that it covered about 11 square acres) whose gridwork street plan was later altered into a convoluted form by medieval Londoners. Before they left, the Romans developed the city, but not to the status of a capital. (The heyday of London's excavations of the Roman occupation coincided with the clearing of World War II's rubble, when a Roman temple and statues dedicated to Mithras, Serapis, and Ptolemaic Greek deities were revealed.)

Despite advances into northern England, as far as the site of Hadrian's Wall, the Romans faced continuous rebellion. In the year 410, by which time the seeds of Christianity had been sown within England, the emperor Honorius ordered the Roman legions back to the Continent, cutting off England (and London) from contact with the European mainland.

This isolation lasted for centuries, from which few historical references to London exist. Although a church was erected in the 600s by London's first bishop, Mellitus, in honor of St. Paul, London slumbered and stagnated. The regular Roman street plan was abandoned, and a hodgepodge of medieval houses arose, some reportedly in the middle of thoroughfares. The irregularity of medieval construction and property lines was reinforced by later generations of Londoners, who were usually required to respect the legal claims of earlier owners and builders. Because of this, London developed into a series of independent neighborhoods and private enclaves.

SAXONS, DANES, AND VIKINGS

After the Romans, the next major invaders of London were the Teutonic Saxons and Danes, who arrived on the southeastern (Kentish) coast of England about 449. Depending on who was in power, they either embraced or rejected Christianity. Mellitus, the country's bishop, was banished and London remained rigidly and lustily pagan.

One ruler who emerged from England's early Middle Ages was Alfred, King of the Saxons, who spent much of his career battling the Norse Vikings. In 886, Alfred strengthened London's fortifications: he appointed his son-in-law as governor, continuing to rule his growing kingdom from his capital at Winchester. For a century after Alfred's death (around 900), his heirs were occupied almost exclusively with securing and protecting their holdings against the Viking invaders.

NORMANS Though London was still not defined as the country's capital, more and more treaties, rites of succession, and military conferences were hosted within its walls. The last Saxon king was Harold, who chose London as the site of his election. He ruled for only 9 months before the fateful Battle of Hastings in 1066. There, the politics, bloodlines, language, and destiny of London were to change forever after the victory of the Norman armies, led by William the Conqueror, over the Saxon kingdom.

William the Conqueror might have been the first ruler to recognize fully the political importance of London. His coronation took place in Westminster Abbey, establishing a precedent that has been observed by almost all British monarchs since. He recognized the capital status of London and the power and rights of London's medieval Church. Strengthening his political hold in the process, he acquiesced to the Saxon ecclesiastics by granting them many well-defined rights and privileges. He also constructed the

DATELINE

- **1400s** Trade flourishes in London.
- **1509–47** Reign of Henry VIII. Feud with Rome leads to English Reformation; Church property is confiscated, and English monarch is declared head of Church of England.
- **1558** Elizabeth I ascends throne.
- **1586** William Shakespeare moves to London and buys part of Globe Theatre.
- **1640s** Much fighting between Cromwellians and Royalists. King Charles is beheaded at London's Whitehall (1649).
- **1660** Charles II ascends throne.
- **1665** A plague decimates London.
- **1666** Great Fire demolishes much of the city.
- **1710** St. Paul's Cathedral completed, following design of Sir Christopher Wren.
- **1710–1820** The arts thrive, and London's population increases. Industrial Revolution begins.
- **1837–1901** Reign of Victoria.
- **1901** Edward VII ascends throne.
- **1939–45** World War II. Much of London is damaged.
- **1953** Elizabeth II ascends throne.
  (continues)

DATELINE

- **1987** Conservatives under Margaret Thatcher win third term.
- **1990** John Major becomes prime minister.
- **1992** Royal couple jolted by fire at Windsor Castle and marital troubles of two sons.

White Tower, a fortification incorporated into the Tower of London by later monarchs.

During the 1100s, London asserted its right to some independence from the rest of England, reinforcing the role of its lord mayor. English monarchs, eager for the support of the country's wealthiest and most influential populace, bid for the fealty and allegiance of Londoners in the hopes that holding London was the key to controlling England.

By the 1400s, the banks of the Thames were lined with buildings as depicted in the engravings produced prior to the Great Fire of 1666. London-based merchants built massive residences atop or beside their riverfront warehouses. Ferryboats plied the Thames, and life burgeoned on both banks of the river. The city was dotted with ecclesiastical buildings that were later confiscated by Henry VIII during the Reformation but whose neighborhoods and Catholic images (Blackfriars, Greyfriars, and Whitefriars) still remain as part of modern London.

TUDOR AND ELIZABETHAN LONDON The modern history of London begins with the Tudors. Sadly, Henry VIII's Reformation (1530s) led to the physical destruction of many wonderful medieval buildings, and London—as the centerpiece of the country's political and religious conflicts—was sometimes a willing participant in many of the changes. Tower Hill saw the execution of four of Henry's wives, and two of England's most prominent ecclesiastics (Sir Thomas More and Bishop John Fisher).

The wealth of the medieval churches was confiscated and redistributed to a newly appointed aristocracy willing to comply with Henry's wishes. The medieval gardens, convents, and priories of the Catholic Church were knocked apart and subdivided into narrow streets and courtyards (whose overcrowding led to the increased danger of fire). The cripples and beggars who had been dependent on the Church were unleashed, without resources, on the population of London. Many recalcitrant nuns and monks, refusing to acknowledge the ecclesiastical leadership of the English monarch, were dragged through the streets to the scaffold, hung by the neck, and disemboweled.

From the dissent, bloodshed, and strife of Reformation London sprang the creative juices of Elizabethan England, named after the

---

IMPRESSIONS

Go where we may, rest where we will,
Eternal London haunts us still.
—THOMAS MOORE, *RHYMES ON THE ROAD* (ca. 1820)

By seeing London, I have seen as much of
life as the world can show.
—SAMUEL JOHNSON IN JAMES BOSWELL'S *JOURNAL OF A*
TOUR TO THE HEBRIDES (1773)

great queen who reigned from 1558 to 1603. William Shakespeare, arriving in London in 1586, bought part ownership of the Globe Theatre, which was strategically located a short distance outside the puritanical jurisdiction of the corporation of London. Along with the flowering of the arts, England (and especially London) simultaneously entered a period of mercantile and colonial expansion in the Americas, Asia, and Africa.

PLAGUE, FIRE, AND THE JACOBEAN ERA By the mid-1600s, during the Jacobean era, London was crowded, with half-timbered gabled houses topped by tile roofs. Streets were hopelessly narrow, especially those near the river, a result of reliance on the Thames for transport and commerce.

In the 1640s, London saw much fighting between the Puritan troops of Oliver Cromwell and the Royalist followers of Charles I, which culminated with Charles's execution in 1649 on the scaffold at Whitehall. Not until 1660, the year of Charles II's accession to the throne, was the House of Stuart restored to power.

In 1665, a plague swept through the city's overcrowded slums, claiming an estimated 75,000 lives. A year later, the Great Fire, which began in a bakery on Pudding Lane near London Bridge, destroyed much of the town, including 89 churches and 13,200 homes.

18TH CENTURY Despite the tragedy of fire, urban planners, spearheaded by Sir Christopher Wren, used the disaster to redesign and rebuild London. The beauty of Wren's churches remain unmatched in all Britain. They include St. Mary-le-Bow, one of the most famous, as well as the new St. Paul's Cathedral, both finished by 1710.

By this time the aristocracy had begun migrating westward toward Covent Garden and Whitehall. The most convenient method of transportation was still via the Thames, while the sedan chair allowed aristocrats to be carried over the filthy streets, where dung, sewage, and refuse littered the undrained cobblestones.

Despite the hardships, the arts and sciences flourished in London. In the second half of the century, Joshua Reynolds painted his portraits; James Boswell wrote his reminiscences of lexicographer/critic/poet Samuel Johnson; David Garrick performed his famous Shakespearean roles; and some of the best landscape painting in the history of Europe was about to flower.

The spatial proportions of Georgian and (later) Regency architecture changed the facades of thousands of houses throughout London. For a limited number of citizens, the good life was bountiful, and London was the seat of all that was powerful, beautiful, desirable, intelligent, and witty.

IMPRESSIONS

It is a wonderful place, this London; a nation, not a city; with a population greater than some kingdoms, and districts as different as if they were under different governments and spoke different languages.
—BENJAMIN DISRAELI, *LOTHAIR* (1870)

When it's three o'clock in New York, it's still 1938 in London.
—BETTE MIDLER, QUOTED IN *THE TIMES* (1978)

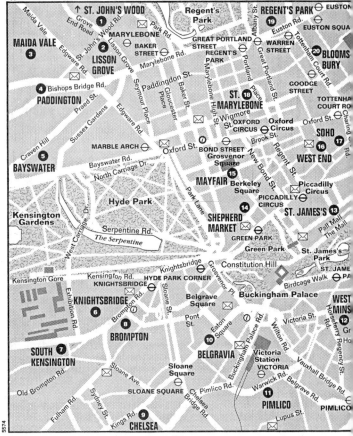

LONDON DISTRICTS

VICTORIAN ERA The most visible progress, as well as the greatest expansion of London, occurred during the Victorian era, when railroad lines and steam engines, sewage systems, cabs, underground trains, and new building techniques transformed London into a modern metropolis and hugely expanded its borders. Massive slums in the city's interior were cleared, but their occupants ended up in newer, more remote slums that remain legendary as examples of the Industrial Revolution's most horrible urban blight. Traffic arteries were rammed through the city's center from west to east. And an

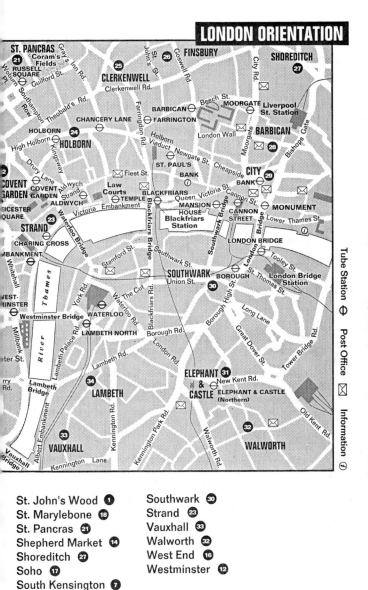

LONDON ORIENTATION

unlikely meadow known as Porridge Island was transformed into Trafalgar Square.

Victorian London was the center of the largest empire the world had ever seen. Londoners left their homes to fill military and administrative posts in such faraway dependencies as Calcutta, Kenya, Singapore, and Hong Kong. The art treasures of the world filled London's museums and private houses. In poorer neighborhoods, died-in-the-wool Londoners evolved a series of dialects and attitudes later identified as cockney; its accents and humor filled the city's music halls and vaudeville houses and subsequently influenced the entertainment industry from Sydney to San Francisco. London thrived, burgeoning into one of the most complicated and diverse capitals of Europe.

EDWARDIAN ERA   During the early 1900s, Victoria's successor, Edward VII, brought elaborate pageantry back to affairs of state (and a welcome laissez-faire attitude to affairs of the heart). Buckingham Palace was enlarged and newly sheathed in a honey-colored layer of stone, and a massive statue to Victoria was erected in front of its newly opened processional avenue leading to the Admiralty Arch. The Neo-Gothic grandeur of the Albert Memorial, though not escaping criticism, helped define the era's architectural style, which permeated vast neighborhoods of London with its eclecticism, ornateness, and high individualism.

WORLD WARS   World War I sent shock waves through Britain, although George V, who ascended the throne in 1910, ruled steadfastly from his London seat. Even if the damage was relatively minor compared to that later inflicted by World War II, 922 incendiary and explosive bombs fell on the financial district (the City), causing great damage and killing or injuring almost 2,500 people. The enraged Londoners poured their national effort into a conflict that was to be idealistically defined as "the War to End All Wars."

During World War II, however, at least 30,000 people died and vast tracts of London were destroyed by aerial bombing. Westminster Abbey (parts of which had stood unmolested since the 11th century) and the magnificent bulk of the Houses of Parliament were seriously damaged over two nights in May 1941. During a period remembered for the indomitable spirit of the people, thousands of Londoners systematically moved their mattresses and bedclothes every night to the city's subway tunnels, considered safe from Nazi bombing.

Although the neighborhood that surrounded it was almost completely destroyed, St. Paul's Cathedral amazingly escaped with only minor damage, rising majestically above the rubble like a beacon of hope for the sorely tested people of London.

Following World War II, vast rebuilding projects replaced London's bombed-out rubble. The transportation system was improved. Then, in 1953, the coronation of Elizabeth II sparked a period of beautification with myriad houses painted and millions of flower beds planted.

TODAY'S LONDON   In the 1970s and 1980s, a revitalized economy led to the revival of some run-down districts (Notting Hill, parts

---

IMPRESSIONS

That tiresome dull place where all people under thirty find so much amusement.
—THOMAS GRAY, LETTER TO NORTON NICHOLLS

You may call it dreary, heavy, stupid, dull, inhuman, vulgar at heart and tiresome in form. . . . But for one who takes it as I take it, London is on the whole the most possible form of life.
—HENRY JAMES (1869)

of Chelsea, the Docklands) into chic and desirable neighborhoods. English wits estimate that at one time or another since the end of World War II, virtually every corner of London has been covered with scaffolding, as builders, homeowners, and real estate moguls add structural support, modernized comforts, and new life to virtually every building.

Prime Minister Margaret Thatcher's reforms of the 1980s created new and modernized financial institutions, including a computerized London Stock Exchange, whose presence has reinforced London's traditional role as a financial, shipping, and insurance center. In 1990, Thatcher was replaced as prime minister by another member of the Conservative party, the less flamboyant but capable John Major. In 1992, it wasn't the prime minister but the House of Windsor that got the boldest headlines. In a year that Elizabeth II labeled *annus horribilis,* a fire swept Windsor Castle; the Queen agreed to pay income taxes for the first time; and the marriages of two sons seemed to crumble as Princes Charles and Andrew separated from their wives, Diana and Sarah. Princess Anne, however, remarried.

Chastened, sadder, and probably wiser after the ruin of the 1940s and the loss of the Empire, not to mention today's racial and economic tensions, London remains one of the most vital, interesting, and influential cities in the world. Its allure to foreigners, be they English-speaking or not, is potent, providing one of the most intriguing, varied and appealing tourist destinations in the world. More true than ever is Samuel Johnson's dictum, uttered over 200 years ago: "When a man is tired of London, he is tired of life."

POLITICS

The United Kingdom of Great Britain and Northern Ireland comprises England, Wales, Scotland, and Northern Ireland. It is a limited monarchy, the present head of state being Elizabeth II. The head of government, however, is the prime minister, selected by a majority in the House of Commons (the lower house of Parliament) and then requested by the monarch to form a government—in other words, to take charge and name cabinet members to head the administrative departments of government. The upper house of Parliament is the House of Lords, which has very limited authority. The monarch's role is mainly ceremonial.

There are two main political parties, Conservative and Labour. The Conservatives, currently led by Prime Minister John Major, believe in free enterprise, private ownership, and membership in the European Community. Labour believes in public ownership of important industries, with a maximum support structure for the individual.

3. FAMOUS LONDONERS

Clement Richard Attlee   (1st Earl Attlee) (1883–1967) A famous 20th-century socialist and a Labour member of Parliament

(1922–55), he served in Churchill's war cabinet. Attlee succeeded him as prime minister in 1945, and in the next six years much social legislation was enacted, major industries were nationalized, and India and Palestine were made independent.

Robert Stephenson Smyth Baden-Powell (1st Baron of Gilwell) (1857–1941) This aggressive soldier is known for establishing the Boy Scout and Girl Guide movements in 1908.

Aubrey Vincent Beardsley (1872–98) The most famous English illustrator of the Victorian era, he's considered a master of the art nouveau movement. His evocative illustrations, often erotic, accompany the texts of Alexander Pope's *Rape of the Lock* and Oscar Wilde's *Salome.*

Sir Cecil Beaton (1904–80) One of the most famous English designers and photographers of his era, he photographed notables, including Wallis Warfield Simpson, who designated him "official photographer" for her celebrated 1936 wedding in France. Americans knew him best for the sets he created for the New York City Ballet and for the costumes he designed for the stage and film productions of *My Fair Lady.*

Sir Thomas Beecham (1879–1961) A great conductor, he was instrumental in introducing London to Russian ballets and the music of Frederick Delius.

Annie Besant (1847–1933) Co-editor of the newspaper *National Reformer,* she was a well-known social reformer, believer in theosophy, and advocate of birth control and free speech. She was also active in politics in India.

William Blake (1757–1827) Artist and mystical poet, he received critical acclaim for his great poetry and his illustrations of *The Book of Job,* Dante's *Divine Comedy,* and Milton's *Paradise Lost.*

Captain William Bligh (1754–1817) This famous seaman was captain of the *Bounty.* The mutiny of his crew (1789) inspired celebrated treatments in fiction and on film.

Anne Boleyn (1507–36) Mistress and second wife of Henry VIII, she was accused of infidelity by the king, tried, declared guilty, and beheaded in the Tower of London. Her daughter eventually ruled as Elizabeth I.

William Booth (1829–1912) Minister and social worker, he founded the Salvation Army in 1878.

James Boswell (1740–95) His *Life of Samuel Johnson* and *London Journal* established him as an ardent and a colorful portrayer of 18th-century London, as well as a devoted biographer.

Benjamin Britten (Baron Britten of Aldeburgh) (1913–76) A celebrated composer, he is famous for operas like *Peter Grimes* and *Death in Venice,* for *A Ceremony of Carols,* and for his great *War Requiem.*

George Bryan Brummell (1778–1840) Beau Brummell was considered the supreme arbiter of fashion in Regency England. He inherited a vast fortune in 1799 but was eventually ruined by gambling and too many enemies; he died a pauper in a French asylum.

Thomas Chippendale (1718–79) He was the most famous cabinetmaker in English history.

John Constable (1776–1837) was one of the finest painters of English landscape. His *View on the Stour* (1819) and *Hay Wain*

(1820) won gold medals at the Paris Salon of 1824 and now hang in London's National Gallery.

Sir Noël Coward (1899–1973) A sophisticated wit and a captivating gossip, he wrote and produced plays that continue to delight, the most famous being *Private Lives.* He also wrote the screenplay for *Brief Encounter,* several novels, and many songs.

Benjamin Disraeli (1st Earl of Beaconsfield) (1804–81) A member of Parliament and author of five novels, he worked closely with Queen Victoria, serving as prime minister. He passed several important reform measures and significantly expanded the British empire.

Sir Arthur Conan Doyle (1859–1930) was the creator of eccentric Sherlock Holmes, who solved more mysteries than anyone else in Victorian London.

Edward FitzGerald (1809–83) A poet in his own right, he is best remembered for his translation (1859) from the Persian of the 16th-century *Rubaiyat* of Omar Khayyam.

Ian Fleming (1908–64) He joined the staff of Reuters and, from Moscow, covered the trials of alleged British spies during the height of the Cold War. Fleming started an international industry when he wrote the first of the "007" books (*Casino Royale*) in two months, naming his suave fictional hero after the author (James Bond) of a standard British ornithological reference work.

David Garrick (1717–79) was a great Shakespearean actor, theatrical producer, and playwright. He's honored with burial in Poets' Corner of Westminster Abbey.

Grinling Gibbons (1648–1721) was the most famous of the brilliant wood-carvers employed by Sir Christopher Wren during the reconstruction of London after the Great Fire. His bronze statue of James II is outside the National Gallery.

William Ewart Gladstone (1809–98), Liberal prime minister, he was noted for important reforms but strongly disliked by both Queen Victoria and rival politican Benjamin Disraeli. He was a superb orator.

William Hogarth (1697–1764) Painter and engraver, Hogarth created works that satirized the social customs, hierarchies, and foibles of his era. His most famous paintings are *The Rake's Progress* and *Marriage à la Mode.*

Edmond Hoyle (1672–1769) was an expert on gaming and the author of the authoritative *Hoyle's Games* (1746).

Jack the Ripper (1857?–88?) The real identity of this truly infamous Londoner, who has captured the imagination of amateur sleuths for more than a century, has never been positively established. He murdered six London women, all found mutilated in the city's impoverished East End in 1888.

John Maynard Keynes (1883–1946) Considered one of the most brilliant economists of the 20th century, he advocated extensive government intervention in the economy, an idea now widely accepted.

Lillie Langtry (1852–1929) The greatest English beauty of her era, she achieved fame as the publicly acknowledged mistress of the son of Queen Victoria (later Edward VII). Born on the Isle of Jersey (and known variously as "The Lily of Jersey" or "Jersey Lillie"), she reigned as an arbiter of taste from her town house near London's Cadogan Square.

W. Somerset Maugham (1874–1965) was the author of novels, short stories, plays, and essays on writing. His most famous works include *Of Human Bondage, The Circle,* and *The Constant Wife.*

John Milton (1608–74) This poet and prose writer, after losing his sight, composed what ranks as the greatest epic poem in the English language, *Paradise Lost.*

Henry Purcell (1659–95) Organist at Westminster Abbey from 1679 until shortly before his death, he is considered the greatest English composer prior to the late 19th century.

Sir Joshua Reynolds (1723–92) The most famous portrait painter in the history of English painting, Reynolds created works that included *The Strawberry Girl* and *The Age of Innocence.*

Sir Arthur Seymour Sullivan (1842–1900) was the musical half of the enormously popular Gilbert and Sullivan team—famous for such operettas as *The Mikado, The Pirates of Penzance,* and *H.M.S. Pinafore.* He also wrote one of the most famous hymns of the Anglican Church, "Onward, Christian Soldiers."

Evelyn Arthur St. John Waugh (1903–66) This London-born author was a master of pessimistic and savage satire, often aimed at the pretensions of the English aristocracy and the institution of war. His most famous works include *Brideshead Revisited* and *The Loved One.*

John Wesley (1703–91) He established the Methodist branch of Protestantism and wrote several works on grammar and history.

Virginia Woolf (1882–1941) Novelist (*To the Lighthouse, Jacob's Room*) and essayist (*The Common Reader*), she founded the Hogarth Press with her husband, social critic Leonard Woolf, and was the center of a brilliant circle of intellectuals, the Bloomsbury Group.

Sir Christopher Wren (1632–1723) is the most famous architect and designer in English history. The appearance of much of London today—including the Royal Hospital in Chelsea, Kensington Palace, Marlborough House, St. Paul's Cathedral, and dozens of London churches—is a direct result of his influence. He is buried in the crypt of what is generally believed to be his finest creation, St. Paul's.

4. ART, ARCHITECTURE, LITERATURE & MUSIC

ART

You can read about English art, but it's better to experience it firsthand in some of London's great galleries. Most noted are the National Gallery and the Tate Gallery, but there are dozens of others.

During the Anglo-Saxon and medieval periods, intricately wrought crosses, religious statuary, and illuminated manuscripts were the major art objects. Ornate tombs with sculpted effigies of the dead marked the resting places of the nobility and the princes of the church, and the cathedrals became art galleries of awesome beauty. By the 13th century, as the Gothic period gathered momentum, embroidered tapestries, metalwork, frescoes, panel painting, and stained glass also served as mediums of religious artistic expression. Inevitably, such ornamentation overflowed into secular life as well.

During the Renaissance, portraiture assumed primacy in secular painting, especially as executed by the great Hans Holbein the Younger, a Swiss-born artist who became painter to Henry VIII. The great miniaturist Nicholas Hilliard and his pupil Isaac Oliver rendered similar service to Elizabeth I. Among the outstanding painters of the Stuart period, neither Sir Anthony Van Dyck nor Sir Peter Lely was English-born.

Native English painters came into their own by the 18th century. Among the great portraitists of the period were Thomas Gainsborough and Sir Joshua Reynolds, and these were supplemented by such remarkable satirists and socially concerned artists as William Hogarth. The Royal Academy of Arts, still flourishing today in Piccadilly, was formed in 1768.

Spanning the 18th and 19th centuries were such great landscape artists as John Constable and J. M. W. Turner, as well as the multitalented William Blake. Later came the Pre-Raphaelites Sir Edward Burne-Jones, Dante Gabriel Rossetti, and Augustus John. Many of their works can be seen in the Tate Gallery, along with those of such famous 20th-century painters as Ben Nicholson, Francis Bacon, and Graham Sutherland.

Most early British sculpture was commissioned by the church. The religious conflicts of the 16th and 17th centuries temporarily ended the lavish ornamentation of churches, but in the late 17th and early 18th centuries, sculpture came back in vogue, producing such artists as Grinling Gibbons. In the 20th century, sculpture became a serious competitor to painting, with Henry Moore, Barbara Hepworth, Sir Jacob Epstein, and Kenneth Armitage all coming to the fore.

ARCHITECTURE

Originally, London was a collection of scattered villages and towns that were unified under the pressure of the Industrial Revolution in the 18th and 19th centuries. A little of the city's original flavor and feeling remains in such places as Whitechapel, Chelsea, Hammersmith, and Hampstead. During the 18th century, when the principles of "picturesque planning" were being evolved for a rapidly expanding London, planners consciously incorporated the best of the greens, riverbank terraces, and small-scale layouts of the original villages. These rural features (rigorously preserved by neighborhood residents today) are now completely enclosed by the bulk and congestion of urban London.

Other than an ancient Roman temple of Mithras, excavated in the 1950s on Queen Victoria Street, and the ruins of a fortified wall discovered near Trinity Place, few architectural remnants of the city's Roman colonization exist.

London's first major architectural style was imported from northern France. Defined as Norman Gothic, it was solid, majestic, and ideal for such defensive structures as gatehouses and castles. Decoration was blunt and geometric, arches were rounded. The style thrived in Britain until about 1190. It can best be admired today in the Tower of London, St. Bartholomew's, and the Temple Church.

EARLY ENGLISH GOTHIC As medieval England grew more

sophisticated, both structural arches and the frames that surrounded windows were designed with pointed ("broken") tops, and exterior buttresses took on more solidity as the windows became larger. Cathedrals grew taller, with roofs and spires angled more steeply. The cathedrals of Ely, York, and Salisbury are the best examples of this Early English Gothic style; in London it was manifested in Westminster Abbey's Chapter House.

During the 1300s, the solid rectilinear lines of English cathedrals gave way to increasing ornateness as vaultings grew more complex and windows became ever larger. Eventually, cathedrals were highlighted with huge expanses of glass and fan-shaped vaulting that resembled the trunks and branches of trees gracefully frozen into stone ribbing. The style became known as Gothic Perpendicular. Its best examples can be seen in the cathedrals of Bath and Gloucester and in St. George's Chapel at Windsor. Its best London manifestation is in Henry VII's chapel in Westminster Abbey.

TUDOR TO JACOBEAN ERAS The true surge in London's building didn't begin until the population explosion and outward urban expansion of the Renaissance. Until the early 1500s, London was contained by the original Roman walls, having only 50,000 inhabitants (about 20% more than it had when occupied by the Romans). By 1600, however, the population had passed the quarter-million mark, with about 75,000 living within the walls.

The main inspirations for Tudor architecture were the Gothic lines and masses that had characterized ecclesiastical building since the 11th century, but this style was now applied to private residences. London's best examples of this style are St. James's Palace and Hampton Court, the home originally built by Henry VIII's Cardinal Wolsey.

By 1660, the population of London had reached half a million, many of whom lived in overcrowded and filthy conditions. London Bridge, until 1739 the only bridge crossing the Thames, today is described as Elizabethan. Picturesque, but highly flammable, they incorporated a framework of oak beams whose open spaces were filled with mud, plaster, chopped straw, and sometimes whitewash. More elaborate houses were constructed of brick and tile or slate in a style eventually identified as Jacobean. Low-ceilinged, with dark paneling and leaded-glass windows, they gave off a richly gorgeous feeling of comfort and carried Elizabethan motifs to a grander and larger scale.

INIGO JONES TO CHRISTOPHER WREN Inigo Jones (1573–1652), considered the first great modern British architect, introduced the airily and mathematically precise designs promoted by Italian Renaissance architect Andrea Palladio. This style opted for strict spatial ratios of windows to doors, plus a balanced symmetry that often combined the three classic Greek orders (Doric, Ionic, and Corinthian) in gracefully symmetrical neoclassical grandeur. In London, two of Jones's most famous buildings are the Banqueting House at Whitehall and the Queen's House at Greenwich.

The Great Fire of 1666, which devastated huge neighborhoods of London, resulted in a revolutionary code of building. Borrowing heavily from construction techniques used in Holland, Sir Christopher Wren did much to replace a city previously built of wood with brick, stone, and (later) stucco. He rebuilt more than 50 churches, dozens of public buildings, and many private homes, making him the most prolific architect in Britain's history. His dignified yet graceful designs have been relentlessly copied throughout the world. The greater part of his work was erected in London, the most famous building being St. Paul's Cathedral. Other examples of his work include Kensington Palace, the Royal Hospital in Chelsea, and portions of Hampton Court Palace.

Wren had submitted a plan to rebuild London on a French baroque-inspired plan of plazas, traffic circles, and panoramic avenues. Fearing the number of land disputes this would have involved, Charles II rejected the plan and the city was rebuilt on a less grand and less coherent scale—one that respected the property lines and medieval layouts that had existed prior to the fire.

London, however, was about to embark on one of its greatest expansions. Where the municipal government failed in imposing a logical order on the city's architectural layout, private speculators created developments that usually included a series of almost identical facades opening onto a plaza, square, or garden.

Covent Garden (designed by Inigo Jones himself in 1631) was the first of the monumental squares. Laden with neoclassical details and grand in their proportions, they led to dozens of imitations, including such famous ones as Portman Square, Soho Square, Grosvenor Square, and Berkeley Square. Later, in the early 19th century, these were copied by private entrepreneurs who created the regular and rhythmic, less monumental neighborhoods of Belgravia, Blooms-bury, Finsbury, and Paddington. The architectural taste of the era (Palladian classical) was endlessly reproduced. This last development partly explains the comparative lack of gargantuan structures in many London neighborhoods, where a sense of privacy and shelter behind walled gardens stems from the British yearning for privacy.

VICTORIAN ERA During the 19th century, the population of London exploded once again, so that by 1902 it had reached almost 4.5 million inhabitants. (The opening of the Underground in 1863 was in part the City Council's attempt to cope with this expansion.) The architecture of this period was eclectic and whimsical, with the Gothic tradition as the main inspiration but adapted in idiosyncratic and clever ways. Today, Victorian architecture seems to dominate the city, but the quintessential example is the memorial erected by Queen Victoria to her departed husband, Albert. Ringed with bronzes of allegorical female figures representing the world's continents, it stands surrounded by greenery in South Kensington.

The English love of gardens, the expansion of London from a series of villages in Europe's biggest metropolis, and the encroachment of urban sprawl on rural areas—all helped to form the concept of the city of gardens, of the "corner of the country within the city."

IMPRESSIONS

London is chaos incorporated.
—GEORGE MIKES, *DOWN WITH EVERYBODY*

In no other city can one so cheerfully enjoy the accidents of bad art.
—V. S. PRITCHETT, *LONDON PERCEIVED*

In 1898, industrial planner Ebeneser Howard conceived of a low-income garden city: an autonomous urban center that contained within its borders outlets both for earning a livelihood and for living within sight of greenery. The first of these developments was Letchworth, a few miles north of London, built in 1903.

EDWARDIAN ERA TO POST-1945 During the early 20th century, Edwardian architects (the most deservedly celebrated of whom was Sir Edwin Lutyens) created what some critics consider the finest examples of domestic architecture in the world. They corrected many of the mistakes of, and improved the designs of, their Victorian predecessors. Often building with earth-colored brick and incorporating elements of Arthurian legend, art nouveau, and the arts-and-crafts movement, they added whimsy and great comfort to thousands of buildings, usually siting and landscaping them gracefully. Inside were oversized bathrooms, extra pantries, and reading nooks. Excellent examples of the Edwardian style include most of the grand hotels of London's Park Lane (most notably the Park Lane, the Ritz, and the somewhat newer art deco Dorchester), as well as the Admiralty Arch.

The blitz that Hitler launched on London during World War II destroyed not only much of the city's great architecture but also the slums of Whitechapel in the East End. This neighborhood—made equally famous by Charles Dickens and Jack the Ripper—had been London's festering sore, having among the worst housing conditions in the Western world. The London City Council rebuilt most of the area into rather drab but infinitely preferable rows of apartment blocks.

This postwar building boom may have made London a little less "quaint," but it also made it a more healthful place in which to live. A consciousness of good modern architecture was much promoted in the 1980s by the articulate efforts of Prince Charles.

LITERATURE

It's hard to know where to begin. From the Old English epic poem *Beowulf* to the works of the post-1945 "angry young men," English literature is much too vast to approach in a limited space. The most outstanding figure of all is William Shakespeare (1564–1616), but if England had had no Shakespeare, its literary tradition would still be richer than most.

Geoffrey Chaucer, the most familiar early English writer, wrote his famous and often bawdy *Canterbury Tales* in a muscular Middle English. He was followed by the 15th century's Sir Thomas Malory, celebrated for his story about King Arthur and his court, *Le Morte d'Arthur*.

During the Tudor and Elizabethan eras, among the literary stars (besides Shakespeare) were Sir Thomas More (*Utopia*), Edmund Spenser (*The Faerie Queen*), and Christopher Marlowe (*The Tragical History of Dr. Faustus*), along with such poets as Sir Philip Sidney.

Seventeenth-century literature tended to reflect the religious, political, and social ferment of the period—the conflict between king and Parliament in particular. Among the Cavalier poets, Robert Herrick heads the list, but the literary giant who strode across the century was John Milton, a pro-Parliamentarian and author of *Paradise Lost*. John Bunyan, a Baptist lay preacher caught up in the Puritan cause, wrote *Pilgrim's Progress,* one of England's early prose works. Other famous figures were the poets John Donne (". . . never send to know for whom the bell tolls . . ."); George Herbert; and Ben Jonson, who also wrote boisterous comedies and who led the group of poets who met regularly at the Mermaid Tavern. The immortal King James Version of the Bible was also completed at this time (1611) under the auspices of James I.

During the Cromwellian period, from 1640 until 1660, the theaters were closed. When Charles II ascended the throne, they reopened and literature took on a lighter, more lively tone, reflected in the plays of William Wycherley. The social life of London was also captured in the *Diary* of Samuel Pepys.

Throughout the 18th century, England's literary world was crowded with the output of geniuses and near-geniuses from the rising middle class. Among these were Joseph Addison and Richard Steele (*Spectator* essays); Daniel Defoe (*Robinson Crusoe* and *Moll Flanders*); Alexander Pope (*An Essay on Man*); Henry Fielding (*Tom Jones*); and a host of other essayists, poets, and novelists. Perhaps most memorable of all during the century, however, was Samuel Johnson, whose *Dictionary of the English Language* made him the nation's premier lexicographer and man of letters. His association with James Boswell (from Scotland) resulted in further fame through Boswell's great biography. Johnson's circle of close friends included another notable writer, Oliver Goldsmith (*She Stoops to Conquer* and *The Vicar of Wakefield*).

19TH AND 20TH CENTURIES To expound on the literary stars of the early 19th century in England in limited space would be impossible, so I'll just mention several of the names known to everyone: William Blake, William Wordsworth, Samuel Taylor Coleridge, Lord Byron, John Keats, Percy Bysshe Shelley, Jane Austen, and Charles Lamb—but there are so many more. As you travel through the country, you will see birthplaces, familiar haunts, residences, and burial places of many such writers. One could spend weeks in London alone, following in the footsteps of such leading lights as Pepys, Johnson, Thackeray, and Dickens.

The mid- to late 19th century, or Victorian era, was the great age of the English novel, the public devouring works of Charles Dickens, William Thackeray, Charlotte Brontë, Emily Brontë, George Eliot, Anthony Trollope, George Meredith, and Thomas Hardy. Also eagerly read were the poetry, prose, and drama of Matthew Arnold, Alfred, Lord Tennyson, the Brownings, Algernon Charles Swinburne, Oscar Wilde, and John Ruskin.

Straddling the turn of the 20th century and ushering in modern literature were such notables as Rudyard Kipling, H. G. Wells, John Galsworthy, W. Somerset Maugham, Walter de la Mare, and Sir Arthur Conan Doyle. Writers of the 20th century include Robert Graves, Stephen Spender, W. H. Auden, Virginia Woolf, D. H. Lawrence, E. M. Forster, Aldous Huxley, Kingsley Amis, Graham Greene, George Orwell, Antonia Fraser, Ted Hughes, William Golding, Muriel Spark, and—not to be forgotten—Winston Churchill.

I could go on and on and on—and I still might well leave out your favorite English writer. In fact, I'm sure someone will ask, "But what about Jonathan Swift? George Bernard Shaw? Sir Walter Scott? Robert Burns? Robert Louis Stevenson? Joseph Conrad? Dylan Thomas?" My only answer is that these novelists, playwrights, and poets were not English-born, though they certainly made their mark in English literature. There's no question about it—London and the British Isles are rich in literary greats, and I've only reminded you of *some* of them.

MUSIC

Although England cannot pretend to possess the musical geniuses that Austria, Germany, and Italy produced, from the time of the Gregorian chant (introduced in 597 by St. Augustine of Canterbury, Pope Gregory's missionary), musical composition and performance have played an important part in the culture. Indeed, today London probably has more orchestras and musical groups than any city in the world. Some of the greatest early music can be heard in the cathedrals of the country, such as Winchester, where the first organ was installed in the 10th century. One of the earliest-written compositions extant is the polyphonic piece (round) *"Summer is icumen in,"* with six parts.

Instruments common in the Middle Ages, besides the organ, were the fiddle, the lute, and the rebeck, all used at court to entertain the monarch and his entourage. Both the Plantagenets and the Tudors had court musicians, and Henry VIII set his own love poems to music, the best known being "Greensleeves"; the British Museum contains 34 manuscripts of Henry's compositions. In the 16th century, music flourished in England to such an extent that Erasmus of Rotterdam commented after one of his visits: "They are so much occupied with music here that even the monks don't do anything else."

Music among the common people of the time may have been less polished but no less enthusiastic, as ditties and rounds were composed and sung in taverns and fields, the richness of the tunes compensating for the frequent vulgarity of the words. Some of the songs Shakespeare had his characters sing attest to the coarseness of the lyrics.

During the Tudor dynasty, English cathedral music came into full flower and so, too, did the masque, a sort of forerunner of opera that combined instrumental and vocal music, dancing, satire, recitations, and elaborate scenic effects.

Musicians were persecuted in the mid-1600s under Cromwell but returned with the Restoration. Henry Purcell wrote the first great English opera, *Dido and Aeneas,* in 1689. From this point on, a veritable galaxy of musical talent was inspired and appreciated in London, and thence in all England. Italian opera became the rage, even as John Gay satirized such productions in *The Beggar's Opera* (1728). George Frideric Handel, who became an English subject, composed many operas and oratorios here, including *Messiah* (first performed in Dublin, however), and other musicians followed (sometimes haltingly) in his train. England produced few if any great opera composers, but in the 19th century Gilbert and Sullivan created their uniquely English operettas.

Many of the great names in 20th-century classical music have been English: Sir Edward Elgar, Ralph Vaughan Williams, Sir William Walton, and Benjamin Britten, to name just a few.

As for popular music, Paul McCartney and John Lennon of the Beatles began what has been called "the British invasion" of America. They were followed by such groups and vocalists as the Rolling

Stones, the Who, Pink Floyd, the Sex Pistols, XTC, Phil Collins, Elton John, David Bowie, Sting, Eric Clapton, George Michael, UB 40, Happy Mondays, and Stone Roses. British rock's influence on Western popular music and culture has been, and is still, tremendous.

5. LANGUAGE, RELIGION & FOLKLORE

LANGUAGE

For many Americans it's a shock to discover that the British in fact speak British English, not American English. Believe it or not, there are enough differences to cause total communication breakdowns. For although the English use words and phrases you think you understand, they often have denotations quite different from their U.S. equivalents.

When the British call someone "mean," they mean stingy. And "homely," meaning ugly or plain in America, becomes pleasant in England. "Calling" denotes a personal visit, not a phone call; however, a person-to-person phone call is a "personal call." To "queue up" means to form a line, which they do at every bus stop. And whereas a "subway" is an underground pedestrian passage, the actual subway system is called "the Underground" or "the tube." The term "theatre" refers only to the live stage; movie theaters are "cinemas," and the films themselves are "the pictures." And a "bomb," which suggests a disaster in America, means a success in England.

In a grocery store, canned goods become "tins," rutabagas become "swedes," eggplants become "aubergines," and endive is "chicory" (while, conversely, chicory is "endive"). Both cookies and crackers become "biscuits," which can be either "dry" or "sweet"— that is, except graham crackers, which are "digestives."

The going gets rougher when you're dealing with motor vehicles. When talking about the actual vehicle, very little means the same except for the word "car," unless you mean a truck, which is called a "lorry." In any case, gas is "petrol," the hood is the "bonnet," the windshield is the "windscreen," and bumpers are "fenders." The trunk is the "boot" and what you do on the horn is "hoot."

Luckily, most of us know that an English apartment is a "flat" and that an elevator is a "lift." And you don't rent a room or an apartment, you "let" it. Although the ground floor is the ground floor, the second floor is the "first floor." And once you set up housekeeping, you don't vacuum, you "hoover."

Going clothes shopping? Then you should know that undershirts are called "vests" and undershorts are "pants" to the English, while long pants are called "trousers" and their cuffs are called "turn-ups." Panties are "knickers" and panty hose are "tights." Pullover sweaters can be called "jumpers," with little girls' jumpers being "pinafores." If you're looking for diapers, ask for "nappies."

The education system offers such varied types of schools, identi- fied by an equally wide variety of terms, that to explain them all to the visitor would be too confusing. Briefly, however, the large English "public schools" (such as Eton) are similar to our large private prep schools (such as Andover). But the English also have other private, or "independent," schools on all levels. And all of the above charge tuition. In addition, there are "state schools," which we would call public schools. These include "primary schools" and secondary "comprehensive schools," "modern schools," and "grammar schools" that are equivalent to our junior and senior high schools.

In school and elsewhere, the letter Z is pronounced "zed," and zero is "nought." And if you want to buy an after-school treat, a Popsicle is called an "iced lolly."

Please note that none of the above terms—except the last—are slang. If you really want a challenge in that arena, you can always take on cockney. The cockneys are indigenous Londoners, although strictly speaking, the label refers only to people born within the sound of the bells of St. Mary-le-Bow in Cheapside.

The exact derivation of the word *cockney* is lost in the mists of antiquity, but it's supposed to have meant an "odd fellow." And the oddest feature about this fellow is undoubtedly the rhyming slang he has concocted over the centuries, based on the rhyme—or the rhyme of a rhyme—that goes with a particular word or phrase. So take my advice and don't try to delve further, unless you happen to be Professor Higgins—pardon me—'iggins.

And—the British spell many words slightly differently than Americans do. Thus, British "colour" equals American "color," "cheque" equals "check," and "centre" equals "center."

RELIGION

England is very different from the United States in that church and state are inextricably intertwined. This relationship dates back to the Reformation, when Henry VIII broke with Rome (1534), proclaimed himself Supreme Head of the Church of England, and confiscated Roman Catholic treasuries and lands and dissolved hundreds of monasteries and convents. After the religious conflicts of the 17th century, which defeated the attempts of the Stuarts to return England to Rome, the Church of England was secured and the law stated that the sovereign not only must be a member of the Church of England but also must swear to uphold its doctrines. Thus today Elizabeth II is the titular head of the Church of England, or Anglican Church, while she reigns over a nation that grants freedom of worship to everyone. (Britain is officially divided into two dioceses—Canterbury and York, the first the more powerful.) Besides these links between church and state, there are still others. The Church of England is not free to change either its doctrines or its form of worship, as originally defined in *The Book of Common Prayer* (compiled in 1549), without the specific assent of Parliament. Despite these legal and historical links, the Church of England is not fiscally subsidized by the state or by the Crown, but rather earns its income from its own capital, real estate, and communal contributions.

Although 60% of the population claim membership in the Church of England, only 8% of its baptized members attend services on Easter Sunday. Contemporary Britain also contains a variety of other Protestant sects—Baptists, Methodists, Quakers, and Congregationalists—as well as Roman Catholics, Jews, and a growing number of Muslims and Hindus.

FOLKLORE

Although it's far too arcane to discuss here, England's history is rich in early myth and mystery—as anyone who has visited Stonehenge will have witnessed. The myth most often associated with England, though, is the Arthurian legend of Camelot, which originated in the southwestern part of the country and in Wales. This story was published in literary form for the first time by Geoffrey of Monmouth around 1135. It recounts the birth of Arthur, his exploits with the knights of the Round Table, the shattering of his idyllic and noble kingdom by the adultery of Queen Guinevere with his favorite knight, Lancelot, and his search for the Holy Grail. Some historians even trace within the Arthurian legend certain exploits that, historically, were achieved by a mixture of Viking, Saxon, and even Roman military leaders. Every era, it seems, has produced its own version of the Arthurian legend—from the medieval version by Sir Thomas Malory; to the Victorian era's rendering by Alfred, Lord Tennyson; to our very own 20th-century tellings by T. H. White and C. S. Lewis.

The other great legend that seems to have wide resonance in England is the legend of Robin Hood and his merry men, who stole from the rich and gave to the poor while resisting the authority of the Sheriff of Nottingham—a prime example, it seems to me, of the British love of justice and the fervor with which they root for the underdog.

6. FOOD & DRINK

FOOD

England's long-standing reputation for soggy cabbage and tasteless dishes—prompting the late humorist George Mikes to write that "the Continentals have good food; the English have good table manners"—is no longer deserved. Contemporary London boasts some very fine restaurants indeed.

MEALS AND DINING CUSTOMS Mealtimes here are much the same as in the United States. England is famous for its enormous breakfast—bacon, eggs, grilled tomato, and fried bread—and although it has largely been replaced by the continental variety, it can still be found at the finer hotels and other places. Kipper, which is the name given to a smoked herring, is also a popular breakfast dish. The finest kippers come from the Isle of Man, Whitby, and Loch Fyne in Scotland. The herrings are split open, placed over oak chips, and smoked slowly to produce a nice pale-brown smoked fish.

Lunch, usually eaten between noon and 2pm, is often taken at the pub—or else consists of a sandwich on the run.

Afternoon tea, still enjoyed by many, may be limited to a simple cup of tea; on the other hand, the formal variety may start with tiny crustless cucumber or watercress sandwiches, proceed through scones or crumpets with jam and possibly cream, and end with cakes and tarts—all accompanied by a proper pot of tea. The tea at Brown's is quintessentially English, while the Ritz tea is an elaborate affair complete with an orchestra and dancing. It is a misconception to believe that "everything" stops for tea. People in Britain drink an average of four cups a day, mainly at work.

Dinner, usually enjoyed around 8pm, may consist of traditional English dishes or any number of the ethnic cuisines that are currently found in London.

Supper is traditionally a late-night meal, usually eaten after the theater.

CUISINE   You don't have to travel around England to experience regional English dishes—you'll find them all over London. On any pub menu you're likely to encounter such dishes as Cornish pasty and shepherd's pie. The first, traditionally made from Sunday-meal leftovers and taken by West Country fisherman for Monday lunch, consists of chopped potatoes, carrots, and onions mixed together with seasoning and put into a pastry envelope. The second is a deep dish of chopped cooked beef mixed with onions and seasoning, covered with a layer of mashed potatoes, and served hot. Another version is cottage pie, which is minced beef covered with potatoes and also served hot. The most common pub meal, though, is the ploughman's lunch—traditional farm-worker's fare—consisting of a good chunk of local cheese, a hunk of homemade crusty white or brown bread, some butter, and a pickled onion or two, washed down with ale. You will now find such variations as pâté and chutney occasionally replacing the onions and cheese. Or you might find Lancashire hotpot, a stew of mutton, potatoes, kidneys, and onions (sometimes carrots). This concoction was originally put into a deep dish and set on the edge of the stove to cook slowly while the workers spent the day at the local mill.

Among appetizers, called "starters" in England, the most typical are potted shrimp (small buttered shrimp preserved in a jar), prawn cocktail, and smoked salmon. You might also be served pâté or "fish pie," which is very light fish pâté. If you're an oyster lover, try some of the famous Colchester variety. Most menus will feature a variety of soups, including cock-a-leekie (chicken soup flavored with leeks), perhaps a game soup that has been flavored with sherry, and many others.

Among the best-known traditional English dishes is, of course, roast beef and Yorkshire pudding—the pudding made with a flour base and cooked under the joint, allowing the fat from the meat to drop onto it. The beef could easily be a large sirloin (rolled loin), which, so the story goes, was named by James I (not Henry VIII, as some claim) when he was a guest at Houghton Tower, Lancashire. "Arise, Sir Loin," he cried, as he knighted the joint with his dagger. Another dish that makes similar use of a flour base is toad-in-the-hole, in which sausages are cooked in batter. Game is also a staple on English tables, especially pheasant and grouse.

On the west coast, you'll find a not-to-be-missed delicacy called Morecambe Bay shrimp, and on any menu you'll find fresh seafood—cod, haddock, herring, plaice, or the aristocrat of flat fish, Dover sole. Cod and haddock are the most popular fish used in the making of a British tradition, fish and chips (chips, of course, are fried potatoes, or thick french fries), which the true Briton covers with salt and vinegar.

The East End of London has quite a few interesting old dishes, among them tripe and onions. Dr. Johnson's favorite tavern, the

Cheshire Cheese on Fleet Street, still offers a beefsteak-kidney-mushroom-and-game pudding in a suet case in winter and a pastry case in summer. East Enders can still be seen on Sunday at the Jellied Eel stall by Petticoat Lane, eating either eel or cockles, mussels, whelks, and winkles—all small shellfish eaten with a touch of vinegar. Eel-pie-and-mash shops can still be found in London purveying what is really a minced-beef pie topped with flaky pastry and served with mashed potatoes and a portion of jellied eel.

The British call desserts "sweets" (although some people still refer to any dessert as "pudding"), with trifle perhaps being the most famous. It consists of sponge cake soaked in brandy or sherry, coated with fruit or jam, and topped with a cream custard. A "fool," such as gooseberry fool, is a light cream dessert whipped up from seasonal fruits.

Cheese is traditionally served after dessert as a savory. There are many regional cheeses, the best known being Cheddar, a good, solid, mature cheese, as is Cheshire. Another is the semismooth-textured Caerphilly from a beautiful part of Wales, and also Stilton, a blue-veined crumbly cheese, often enriched with a glass of port.

DRINK

TEA   Most of the English drink tea in the morning, and it's usually superior to the American tea bag in lukewarm water. It will usually come in a pot, accompanied by milk and sugar.

WATER AND SOFT DRINKS   Tap water is safe to drink. You will usually have to ask for water with your restaurant meal, as it's not served automatically. Neither is ice. Although popular brands of soft drinks are available, you may want to try some of the Schweppes bottled waters, such as "bitter lemon."

BEER, WINE, AND LIQUOR   London pubs serve a variety of cocktails, but their stock in trade is beer—brown beer, or "bitter"; blond beer, or lager; and very dark beer, or stout. The standard English draft beer is much stronger than American beer and is served "with the chill off," because it doesn't taste good cold. Lager is always chilled, while stout can be served either way.

One of the most significant changes in English drinking habits has been the popularity of wine bars, and you will find many to patronize, some turning into discos late at night. Britain is not known for its wine, although it does produce some medium-sweet fruity whites. Its cider, though, is famous—and very potent in contrast to the American variety.

Whisky (spelled without the *e*) refers to scotch. Canadian and Irish whiskey (spelled with the *e*) are also available, but only the very best stocked bars have American bourbon and rye. While you're in England, you may want to try the very English drink called Pimm's, a mixture developed by James Pimm, owner of a popular London oyster house in the 1840s. Though it can be consumed on the rocks, it's usually served as a Pimm's Cup—a drink that will have any number and variety of ingredients, depending on which part of the world (or Empire) you're in. Here, just for fun, is a typical recipe: Take a very tall glass and fill it with ice. Add a thin slice of lemon (or orange), a cucumber spike (or a curl of cucumber rind), and 2 ounces of Pimm's liquor. Then finish with a splash of either lemon or club soda, 7-Up, or Tom Collins mix.

7. RECOMMENDED BOOKS & FILMS

BOOKS

GENERAL HISTORY Anthony Sampson's *The Changing Anatomy of Britain* (Random House, 1982) still gives great insight into the idiosyncracies of English society. *London Perceived* (Hogarth, 1986), by novelist and literary critic V. S. Pritchett, is a witty portrait of the city—its history, art, literature, and life. Virginia Woolf's *The London Scene: Five Essays* (Random House, 1986), a literary gem, brilliantly depicts 1930s London. *In Search of London* (Methusen Publishers, 1988), by H. V. Morton, is filled with anecdotal history and well worth reading even though it was written in the 1950s.

In *London: The Biography of a City* (Penguin, 1980), popular historian Christopher Hibbert paints a very lively portrait. For 17th-century history, you can't beat the *Diary of Samuel Pepys* (1660–1669), and for the flavor of the 18th century, try Daniel Defoe's *Tour Thro' London About the Year 1725.* Winston Churchill's *History of the English-Speaking Peoples* (Dodd Mead, 1956) is a four-volume tour de force, while his *The Gathering Storm* (Houghton-Mifflin, 1986) captures London and Europe on the brink of World War II.

Americans in London (William Morrow, 1986), by Brian N. Morton, is a street-by-street guide to the clubs, homes, and favorite pubs of more than 250 illustrious Americans—Mark Twain, Joseph Kennedy, Dwight Eisenhower, and Sylvia Plath—who made London a temporary home.

Children of the Sun (Basic Books, 1976), by Martin Green, portrays the "decadent" post–World War I period in Britain and the lives of such people as Randolph Churchill, Rupert Brooke, the then Prince of Wales, and Christopher Isherwood.

George Williams's *Guide to Literary London* (Batsford, 1988) charts a series of literary tours through London from Chelsea to Bloomsbury. Peter Gibson's *The Capital Companion* (Webb & Bower, 1985), containing more than 1,200 alphabetical entries, is filled with facts and anecdotes about the streets of London and their inhabitants.

ARCHITECTURE *The Architect's Guide to London* (Reed International, 1990), by Renzo Salvadori, documents 100 landmark buildings with photographs and maps. *Nairn's London* (Penguin, 1988) is Ian Nairn's stimulating, opinionated discourse on London's buildings. Donald Olsen's *The City as a Work of Art: London, Paris, and Vienna* (Yale University Press, 1986) is a well-illustrated text tracing the evolution of these great cities. *London One: The Cities of London and Westminster* (Penguin, 1984) and *London Two: South* (Penguin, 1984) are works of love by well-known architectural writers Bridget Cherry and Nikolaus Pevsner. David Piper's *The Artist's London* (Oxford University Press, 1982) does what the title suggests—captures the city that artists have portrayed. In *Victorian and Edwardian London* (Batsford, 1969), John Betjeman expresses his great love of those eras and their great buildings.

FICTION AND BIOGRAPHY A good feel for English life, both urban and rural, has been created by some of the country's leading exponents of mystery and suspense fiction. Agatha Christie, P. D. James, Dorothy Sayers, and Ruth Rendell are just a few of the familiar names, but, of course, the great London character is Sir Arthur Conan Doyle's Sherlock Holmes. Any of these writers will give pleasure and insight into your London experience.

England's literary heritage is so vast that it's hard to select particular titles, but here are a few favorites. Master storyteller Charles Dickens re-creates Victorian London in such books as *Oliver Twist* (1838), *David Copperfield* (1850), *Great Expectations* (1860), and his earlier, satirical *Sketches by Boz* (1836).

Edwardian London and the 1920s and 1930s are wonderfully captured in any of Evelyn Waugh's social satires and comedies. Any work from the Bloomsbury Group will also prove enlightening— Virginia Woolf's *Mrs. Dalloway* (1925), for example, which peers behind the surface of the London scene. For a portrait of wartime London, there's Elizabeth Bowen's *Heat of the Day* (1949).

For an American slant on England and London, Henry James's *The Awkward Age* (1899) portrays the age of Asquith. Colin MacInnes's novels—*City of Spades* (1957) and *Absolute Beginners* (1959)—focus on more recent social problems. Among contemporaries, Margaret Drabble and Irish Murdoch are both challenging, and there are many more.

The country has produced so many famous figures that it's virtually impossible to choose among biographies. *Life of Samuel Johnson* (1791), by Johnson's friend James Boswell, is a superb examination of the life of this 18th-century writer.

The Wives of Henry VIII, by Antonia Fraser (Knopf, 1992), tells the sad story of the six women foolish enough to marry the Tudor monarch: Catherine of Aragón, Anne Boleyn, Jane Seymour, Anne of Cleves, Katherine Howard, and Catherine Parr. The great Elizabeth I emerges in a fully rounded portrait: *The Virgin Queen, Elizabeth I, Genius of the Golden Age* (Addison-Wesley, 1992) by historian Christopher Hibbert. Another historian, Anne Somerset, wrote *Elizabeth I* (St. Martin's, 1992), which was hailed by some critics as the most "readable and reliable" portrait of England's most revered monarch to have emerged since 1934.

No "man about town" in London became more famous than Shakespeare, and the Bard's life and the English Renaissance are illuminated in Dennis Kay's *Shakespeare: His Life, Work, and Era* (Morrow, 1992). Another interesting portrait emerges in *Shakespeare, the Latter Years,* by Russell Fraser (Columbia University Press, 1992).

An equally famous man about London was Sir Winston Churchill (1874–1965). Although no one told the story of his life more eloquently than did the prime minister and Nobel Prize winner himself, the latest study emerges in *Churchill: A Life* by Martin Gilbert (Hold, 1991). This 1,000-page summary is a distillation of Gilbert's eight-volume official biography.

Richard Ellmann's *Oscar Wilde* (Knopf, 1988) is a masterpiece, revealing the Victorian era and such personalities as Lillie Langtry, Gilbert and Sullivan, and Henry James along the way. Quintessential English playwright Noël Coward and the London he inhabited, along with the likes of Nancy Mitford, Cecil Beaton, John Gielgud, Laurence Olivier, Vivien Leigh, Evelyn Waugh, and Rebecca West, is captured in Cole Lesley's *Remembered Laughter* (Knopf, 1977).

More recently, *The Lives of John Lennon* by Albert Goldman (William Morrow, 1988) traces the life of this most famous of all 1960s musicians.

One of the most talked about biographies of 1992 was *Laurence Olivier: A Biography,* by Donald Spoto (HarperCollins). Spoto details the disappointments and triumphs of the great actor and provides anecdote and analysis for Olivier's most famous roles, including Macbeth.

No one had greater influence on London than did Queen Victoria during her long reign (1837–1901). The Duchess of York ("Fergie") and Benita Stoney, a professional researcher, capture the era in *Victoria and Albert: A Family Life at Osborne House* (Prentice Hall, 1991). Another point of view is projected in *Victoria: The Young Queen,* by Monica Charlot (Blackwell, 1991). Praised for its "fresh information," the book traces the life of Victoria until the 1861 death of her husband, Prince Albert.

In *Elizabeth II, Portrait of a Monarch* (St. Martin's, 1992), Douglas Keay draws on interviews with Prince Philip and Prince Charles to tell a lively story.

FILMS

The British film industry used to be much more important than it is today, enjoying a golden era roughly from 1929 to 1939. The country's foremost director was Alfred Hitchcock, who made his first English talkie, *Blackmail,* in 1929. Other masterpieces followed, such as *The 39 Steps* (1935), *The Lady Vanishes* (1938), and *Jamaica Inn* (1939)—all made before Hitchcock left for Hollywood and even greater glory.

Another famous figure in English cinema was Hungarian Alexander Korda, who settled in London in 1933 and made such memorable movies as *The Private Life of Henry VIII* (1933), starring Charles Laughton, and *The Private Life of Don Juan* (1935), the last film of Douglas Fairbanks, Sr.

In the 1940s David Lean emerged as a major director, making such films as *Blithe Spirit* (1945), an adaptation of Noël Coward's play, and *Brief Encounter* (1946), which some feel is his paramount achievement. His *Great Expectations* (1946) and *Oliver Twist* (1948) are outstanding Dickens adaptations.

After the war, J. Arthur Rank formed the Rank Organisation, but before that he had already produced an array of films, among them Laurence Olivier's acclaimed *Henry V* (1945).

Director Carol Reed is remembered for *Odd Man Out* (1947), with a screenplay by Graham Greene, and also *The Third Man* (1949), a great film starring Joseph Cotten and Orson Welles.

Many movies and British actors have portrayed the British scene. Among some of the great movies you might want to see are *Kind Hearts and Coronets* (1949), in which Alec Guinness played eight parts; *The Ladykillers* (1955); and *The Mouse That Roared* (1959) and *I'm All Right, Jack* (1960), both starring Peter Sellers. In the 1960s, Tony Richardson established himself with such English hits as *A Taste of Honey* and *The Loneliness of the Long Distance Runner* (both 1962). Another movie depicting the intellectual British middle class was *Sunday Bloody Sunday* (1971), starring Glenda Jackson and Peter Finch. Ken Russell came on the scene at the same time with his lustrous *Women in Love* (1970).

Among more recent film portraits of the British at home and abroad are *A Room with a View* (1985) and *Maurice* (1987), both directed by James Ivory. *Antonia & Jane* (1992), the third feature of young English director Beeban Kidron, is a comedy about a friendship between two unhappy Londoners. *Riffraff* (1992), directed by Ken Loach, is an amusing portrait of a nonunion construction worker in London.

A film that generated worldwide excitement is *The Crying Game* (1992), which won the Oscar for original screenplay in 1993. Often compared to *Odd Man Out, The Crying Game,* mainly set in London, is a fearless romantic melodrama, with musings on race, sex, terrorism, and the IRA. James Ivory–directed *Howards End* (1992) won several Oscars, including for best actress (Emma Thompson) and best adapted screenplay (by Ruth Prawer Jhabvala from the novel by E. M. Forster).

PLANNING A TRIP TO LONDON

After people decide where to travel, most have two fundamental questions: What will it cost? and How do I get there? This chapter tackles the hows of your trip to England—all those issues required to get your trip together and take it on the road, whether you're a regular traveler or are disabled, a senior citizen, a single traveler, a student, or a family traveling together. In addition to helping you decide when to take your vacation (climate, events), this chapter discusses what to take, where to gather information, and what documents you need to obtain.

1. INFORMATION, ENTRY REQUIREMENTS & MONEY

SOURCES OF INFORMATION

In the United States and Canada, you can obtain information about Great Britain from the following British Tourist Authority offices: 2580 Cumberland Pkwy., **Atlanta**, GA 30339-3909 (tel. 404/432-9635); 625 N. Michigan Ave., Suite 1510, **Chicago**, IL 60611-1977 (tel. 312/787-0490); World Trade Center, 350 S. Figueroa St., Suite 450, **Los Angeles**, CA 90071 (tel. 213/628-3525); 551 Fifth Ave., **New York**, NY 10176-0799 (tel. 212/986-2200); and 111 Avenue Rd., Suite 450, **Toronto** M5R 3J8, Canada (tel. 416/925-6326).

In London, London Tourist Board's **Tourist Information Centre**, Victoria Station Forecourt, SW1 (tube: Victoria Station), can help you with almost anything which might be of touristic interest to a visitor. Staffed by courteous and patient people, the center deals chiefly with accommodations in all size and price categories, and can handle the whole spectrum of travelers. It also arranges for travel, tour-ticket sales, and theater reservations, and operates a shop offering a wide selection of books and souvenirs. The center is open for personal callers between Easter and October, daily from 8am to 7pm and from November to Easter, Monday to Saturday from 8am to 7pm and Sunday from 8am to 5pm.

The tourist board also maintains an office in the basement of one of London's largest department stores, **Selfridges,** Oxford Street, W1 (tube: Bond Street), Duke Street Entrance, open during store hours. Other offices are at **Heathrow** Terminals 1, 2, and 3, and on the Underground Concourse and at **Liverpool Street Railway Station.**

Telephone inquiries may be made to the board by calling 071/730-3488 for information about London. For tourist information about the rest of England, call 071/824-8000. The board also maintains a 24-hour recorded information service, "Visitorcall" (tel. 0839/123456), which, for a fee of between 36p and 48p ($0.50 to $0.70) per minute, depending on the time you call, will play a recorded message that changes every day and features special events around London.

Written inquiries can be sent to the Correspondence Assistant, Distribution Department, London Tourist Board and Convention Bureau, 26 Grosvenor Gardens, London SW1W ODU.

For riverboat information, phone 071/730-4812. For accommodations reservations (credit-card holders only), call 071/824-8844.

ENTRY REQUIREMENTS

DOCUMENTS U.S. citizens, Canadians, Australians, New Zealanders, and South Africans all require a passport to enter the United Kingdom, but no visa. Some Customs officials will request proof that you have the means to eventually leave the country (usually a round-trip ticket) and visible means of support while you're in Britain. If you're planning to fly to another country from the United Kingdom, it's wise to secure the visa before your arrival in Britain.

CUSTOMS For visitors to England, goods fall into two basic categories—those purchased in a non–European Community (EC) country or bought tax-free within the EC and those purchased tax-paid in the EC. In the former category, limits on imports by individuals (17 and older) include 200 cigarets (or 50 cigars or 250 grams of loose tobacco), 2 liters of still table wine, 1 liter of liquor (over 22% alcohol content) or 2 liters of liquor (under 22%), and 2 fluid ounces of perfume. In the latter category, limits are *much* higher. An individual may import 800 cigarets bought tax-paid in the EC, 200 cigars, *and* 1 kilogram of loose tobacco, 90 liters of wine, 10 liters of alcohol (over 22%), and 110 liters of beer, plus unlimited amounts of perfume.

Foreign vacationers in England may not bring along pets. An illegally imported animal is liable to be destroyed.

If you make purchases in Britain, keep receipts. On gifts, the duty-free limit for U.S. citizens is $50. For more information, see "Taxes" under "Fast Facts: London" in Chapter 3 (which covers England's value-added tax, or VAT) and Section 1 of Chapter 8 (which discusses sending gifts home).

MONEY

POUNDS AND PENCE Britain's decimal monetary system is based on the pound sterling (£), which is made up of 100 pence (written as "p"). There are now £1 coins (called "quid" by Britons), plus coins of 50p, 20p, 10p, 5p, 2p, and 1p. The 0.5p coin has been officially discontinued, although it will be around for a while. Banknotes come in denominations of £5, £10, £20, and £50.

As a general guideline, the price conversions in this book have been computed at the rate of £1 equaling U.S. $1.50. Bear in mind, however, that exchange rates fluctuate daily.

In general, banks in London proper offer the best exchange rates, and you're likely to obtain a better rate for traveler's checks than for cash. There are also branches of the main banks at London's airports, but they charge a small fee. There are in addition Bureaux de Change at the airports and around London that charge a fee for cashing traveler's checks and for changing foreign currency into pounds sterling. Some travel agencies, such as American Express and Thomas Cook, also provide currency-exchange services. It's wise to check around to find the best exchange rate—you usually won't find it in hotels and shops.

THE BRITISH POUND & THE U.S. DOLLAR

£	U.S.$	£	U.S.$
0.05	0.08	15	22.50
0.10	0.15	20	30.00
0.25	0.38	25	37.50
0.50	0.75	30	45.00
0.75	1.15	35	52.50
1	1.50	40	60.00
2	3.00	45	67.50
3	4.50	50	75.00
4	6.00	55	82.50
5	7.50	60	90.00
6	9.00	65	97.50
7	10.50	70	105.00
8	12.00	75	112.50
9	13.50	100	150.00
10	15.00	125	187.50

Note: The above exchange rates prevailed at presstime. Because rates change almost daily, however, check the current value of the pound in a newspaper or at a bank.

TRAVELER'S CHECKS Before leaving home, you can purchase traveler's checks through the following agencies: **American Express** (tel. toll free 800/221-7282 in the U.S. and Canada); **Bank of America** (tel. toll free 800/227-3460 in the U.S., or 415/574-7111, collect, in Canada); **Barclay's Bank** (tel. toll free 800/221-2426 in the U.S. and Canada); **Citicorp** (tel. toll free 800/645-6556 in the U.S. and Canada); and **MasterCard International/Thomas Cook International** (tel. toll free 800/223-9920 in the U.S., or 212/974-5695, collect, from the rest of the world).

When purchasing traveler's checks, ask about refund hotlines. American Express and Bank of America have the greatest number of offices around the world.

Foreign banks may ask a premium of up to 5% to convert your traveler's checks into local currency. Note, also, that you always obtain a better rate if you cash traveler's checks at the banks issuing them: VISA at Barclays, American Express at American Express, and so forth.

PERSONAL CHECKS Some British hotels require an advance deposit in pounds to make reservations. An easy way to obtain a check for this is through **Ruesch International,** 1350 Eye St. NW, Washington, D.C. 20005 (tel. 202/408-1200, or toll free 800/424-2923). To place an order, call and tell them the type and amount of the sterling-denominated check you need. Ruesch will quote a U.S. dollar equivalent, adding a $2 service fee per check. After receiving your dollar-denominated personal check, Ruesch will mail you a sterling-denominated bank draft, drawn at a British bank and payable

WHAT THINGS COST IN LONDON	U.S. $
Taxi from Victoria Station to a Paddington hotel	12.50
Underground from Heathrow Airport to central London	4.70
Local telephone call	0.20
Very expensive double room (at The Dorchester)	322.50
Moderate double room (at Bryanston Court Hotel)	135.00
Inexpensive double room (at Regent Palace Hotel)	100.50
Moderate lunch for one (at Le Sous-Sol)	29.90
Inexpensive lunch for one (at Cheshire Cheese)	14.00
Very expensive dinner for one, without wine (at Le Gavroche)	60.00
Moderate dinner for one, without wine (at Bracewell's)	25.00
Inexpensive dinner for one, without wine (at Porter's English Restaurant)	16.00
Pint of beer	2.50
Coca-Cola in a café	1.50
Cup of coffee	1.20
Roll of ASA 100 color film, 36 exposures	8.00
Admission to the British Museum	Free
Movie ticket	3.75–13.50
Theater ticket	15.00–52.50

to the party you specify. Ruesch will also convert checks in a foreign currency to U.S. dollars, provide the currency in cash of over 120 countries, and sell traveler's checks payable in dollars or six foreign currencies, including pounds. Ruesch also maintains offices in Atlanta, Boston, Chicago, Los Angeles, and New York. It will mail brochures and information packets upon request.

CREDIT CARDS   Credit cards are widely used in London. American Express, VISA, and Diners Club are the most commonly recognized. A Eurocard or Access sign displayed at an establishment means that it accepts MasterCard.

2. WHEN TO GO — CLIMATE, HOLIDAYS & EVENTS

CLIMATE

Charles Dudley Warner (in a remark most often attributed to Mark Twain) once said that the trouble with the weather is that everybody talks about it but nobody does anything about it. Well, Londoners talk about weather more than anyone, but they have also done something about it—air-pollution control, which has resulted in the virtual disappearance of the pea-soup fogs that once blanketed the city.
   A typical London-area weather forecast for a summer day predicts "scattered clouds with sunny periods and showers, possibly heavy at times." Summer temperatures seldom rise above 78° Fahrenheit, nor do they drop below 35°F in winter.
   The British consider chilliness wholesome and usually try to keep room temperatures about 10° below the American comfort level.

London's Average Daytime Temperature & Rainfall

	Jan	Feb	Mar	Apr	May	June	July	Aug	Sept	Oct	Nov	Dec
Temp. (°F)	40	40	44	49	55	61	64	64	59	52	46	42
Rainfall (″)	2.1	1.6	1.5	1.5	1.8	1.8	2.2	2.3	1.9	2.2	2.5	1.9

CURRENT WEATHER CONDITIONS   In the United States, you can dial 1-900-WEATHER, then press the first three letters of the desired English city—LON for London. The cost is 75¢ for the first minute, 50¢ for each minute thereafter.

HOLIDAYS

In England, public holidays include New Year's Day, Good Friday, Easter Monday, May Day (first Monday in May), spring and summer bank holidays (last Monday in May and August, respectively), Christmas Day, and Boxing Day (December 26).

LONDON CALENDAR OF EVENTS

JANUARY

☐ **London International Boat Show,** Earl's Court Exhibition Centre, Warwick Road. The largest boat show in Europe. First 2 weeks in January.

☐ **Charles I Commemoration.** Anniversary of the execution of King Charles I "in the name of freedom and democracy." Hundreds of cavaliers march through central London in 17th-century dress, and prayers are said at the Banqueting House in Whitehall. Free. Last Sunday in January.

FEBRUARY

☐ **Chinese New Year.** The famous Lion Dancers in Soho. Free. February 13.

APRIL

☐ **Easter Parade,** around Battersea Park. Brightly colored floats and marching bands; a full day of Easter Sunday activities. Free. April 3.

MAY

☐ **Chelsea Flower Show,** Chelsea Royal Hospital. The best of British gardening, with displays of plants and flowers of all seasons. Tickets are available abroad from overseas reservations agents; contact your local British Tourist Authority office to find out which agency is handling ticket sales this year, or write to the Chelsea Show Ticket Office, P.O. Box 1426, London W6 OLQ. Late May.

JUNE

☐ **Grosvenor House Antique Fair,** Grosvenor House. A very prestigious antiques fair. 2nd week of June.

✪ *TROOPING THE COLOUR* *The official birthday of the queen. Seated upon a horse for hours, she inspects her regiments and takes their salute as they parade their colors before her. A quintessential British event religiously watched by the populace on TV. The pageantry and pomp are exquisite. Depending on the weather, the young men under the busbies have been known to pass out from the heat. They remain prostrate; nothing is allowed to mar the perfect regimentation of the day.*

Where: Horse Guards Parade, Whitehall. When: June 11. How: Tickets are free but difficult to obtain. Apply in writing in January or February to Brigade Major, HQ

Household Division, Chelsea Barracks, London SW1H 8RF. You can also watch from a distance.

✪ *LAWN TENNIS CHAMPIONSHIPS Ever since the players in flannels and bonnets took to the grass courts at Wimbledon in 1877, this tournament has drawn a socially prominent crowd. Although the courts are now crowded with all kinds of tennis fans, there's still an excited hush at the Centre Court and a certain thrill in being there. Savor the strawberries and cream that are part of the experience.*

Where: Wimbledon, SW London. When: Late June–early July. How: Tickets for Centre and Number One courts obtainable through a lottery. Write in October to Lawn Tennis Association, Church Road, Wimbledon, London SW19 5AE (tel. 081/946-2244). Outside court tickets available daily, but be prepared to wait in line.

JULY

☐ **City of London Festival,** annual arts festival throughout the city. Call 081/377-0540 for information about the various programs and venues. Early to mid-July.

☐ **Royal Tournament,** Earls Court Exhibition Centre, Warwick Road. British armed forces put on dazzling displays of athletic and military skills, which have been called "military pomp, show biz, and outright jingoism." For information and details about performance times and tickets, call 071/373-8141. Late July.

AUGUST

☐ **African-Caribbean Street Fair,** Notting Hill. One of the largest street festivals in Europe, attracting over half a million people annually. Live reggae and soul music combine with great Caribbean food. Free. 2 days in late August.

SEPTEMBER

☾ *OPENING OF PARLIAMENT Ever since the 17th century, when the English cut off the head of Charles I, the British monarch has had no right to enter the House of Commons. Instead, the monarch opens Parliament in the House of Lords, reading an official speech that is written by the government of the day. The monarch rides from Buckingham Palace to Westminster in a royal coach accompanied by the Yeoman of the Guard and the Household Cavalry.*

Where: House of Lords, Westminster. When: 1st Monday in September. How: Strangers' Gallery is open on a first-come, first-served basis.

NOVEMBER

☐ **Fireworks Night.** Commemorating the anniversary of the Gunpowder Plot, an attempt to blow up James I and his Parliament. Huge organized bonfires are lit throughout the city, and Guy Fawkes, the plot's most famous conspirator, is burned in effigy. Free. Early November.

✪ *LORD MAYOR'S PROCESSION AND SHOW* This
*impressive annual event marks the inauguration of the new
lord mayor of the City of London. The queen must ask
permission to enter the City's square mile—a right that has
been jealously guarded by London merchants from the 17th
century to this very day.*
 *Where: From the Guildhall to the Royal Courts of
Justice, in the City. When: 2nd week in November. How:
You can watch the procession from the street; the banquet
is by invitation only.*

3. HEALTH & INSURANCE

HEALTH

Immunization for contagious diseases is required only if a traveler has
been in an infected area within 14 days prior to arrival in London.

Before you leave home, you can obtain a list of physicians in
London from the **International Association for Medical
Assistance to Travelers (IAMAT)**—in the United States at 417
Center St., Lewiston, NY 14092 (tel. 716/754-4883); in Canada at 40
Regal Rd., Guelph, ON N1K 1B5 (tel. 519/836-0102). In Europe,
the address is 57 Voirets, 1212 Grand-Lancy-Geneva, Switzerland.

INSURANCE

Before purchasing additional insurance, check your homeowner's,
automobile, and medical insurance policies. Also check the membership contracts of automobile and travel clubs and credit-card companies. *Note:* U.S. vacationers in England are eligible for free
emergency treatment only under the U.K. National Health Service.
Other health care, such as a hospital stay or a doctor visit, must be
paid.

Among the U.S. companies offering health, accident, trip cancellation, and lost luggage insurance are **Access America,** 6600 W.
Broad St., Richmond, VA 23230 (tel. toll free 800/284-8300);
Mutual of Omaha (Tele-Trip), Mutual of Omaha Plaza, Omaha,
NE 68175 (tel. toll free 800/228-9792); **Travel Guard International,** 1145 Clark St., Stevens Point, WI 54481 (tel. toll free
800/826-1300 in the U.S.); **Travel Insurance PAK,** Travelers
Insurance Co., 1 Tower Sq., Hartford, CT 06183-5040 (tel. toll free
800/243-3174); and **Wallach & Company,** 107 W. Federal St.,
P.O. Box 480, Middleburg, VA 22117-0480 (tel. 705/687-3166, or
toll free 800/237-6615).

4. WHAT TO PACK

Conservative middle-aged Londoners tend to dress up. This is
particularly noticeable in theaters and at concerts. So include at least
one smart suit or dress in your luggage. Better restaurants usually
demand that male diners wear ties and that women not wear shorts.

Of course, if you're under 25 and go to clubs patronized mainly by young people, your attire can be much more informal.

Take at least one outfit for chilly weather and one for warm weather. Even in summer, you may suddenly experience chilly weather. Always take two pairs of shoes, one of them sturdy walking shoes. You may get your feet soaked and need that second pair.

Otherwise, the general rule is to bring four of everything. For men, that means four pairs of socks, four pairs of slacks, four shirts, and four sets of underwear. At least two of these will always be either dirty or in the process of drying.

The most essential items of your wardrobe are a sweater or jersey, a good raincoat, and an umbrella.

5. TIPS FOR THE DISABLED, SENIORS, SINGLES, FAMILIES & STUDENTS

FOR THE DISABLED

Before you go, there are many agencies to check with about information for the disabled.

Travel Information Service, MossRehab, 1200 W. Tabor Rd., Philadelphia, PA 19141-3099 (tel. 215/456-9600), supplies names and addresses of accessible hotels, restaurants, and attractions. It charges a nominal fee for information packets, which include reports from disabled travelers.

Names and addresses of organizations offering tours for travelers with disabilities can be obtained by writing to **Society for the Advancement of Travel for the Handicapped,** 347 Fifth Ave., Suite 610, New York, NY 10016 (tel. 212/447-7284); send a self-addressed stamped envelope. The yearly membership fee of $45 ($25 for senior citizens and students) includes information sources and a quarterly newsletter.

The Federation of the Handicapped, 211 W. 14th St., New York, NY 10011 (tel. 212/727-4200), offers tours for members who pay a yearly fee of $14.

For the blind, the best source is the **American Foundation for the Blind,** 15 W. 16th St., New York, NY 10011 (tel. 212/620-2000, or toll free 800/232-5463).

Many London hotels, museums, restaurants, and sightseeing attractions have wheelchair ramps. Disabled people are often granted special discounts at attractions and, in some cases, nightclubs. These are called "concessions" in Britain. It always pays to ask. Free information and advice is available from **Holiday Care Service,** 2 Old Bank Chambers, Station Road, Horley, Surrey RH6 9HW (tel. 0293/774535). The British Tourist Authority sells *London Made Easy* (£2.50 [$3.80]), a booklet offering advice and describing facilities for the handicapped. Bookstores often carry *Access in London* (£4 [$6]), an even more helpful publication listing facilities for the handicapped, among other things.

London's most visible organization for information about access to theaters, cinemas, subways, buses, and restaurants is **Artsline,** 5

Crowndale Rd., London NW1 1TU (tel. 071/388-2227). Funded by the London Arts Council and staffed for the most part by disabled persons, it offers free information about wheelchair access, hearing aids at theaters, and restaurants and hotels designed with sensitivity for the disabled. Artsline will mail information to North America, but it's most effective when contacted after you arrive in London. Call from 10am to 5:30pm on Monday through Friday. An organization that cooperates closely with Artsline is **Tripscope,** The Courtyard, 4 Evelyn Rd., London W4 5JL (tel. 081/994-9294). It offers advice on travel for disabled persons in Britain and elsewhere.

FOR SENIORS

Many discounts are available for seniors. Be advised, however, that in England you often have to be a member of an association to obtain discounts. Public transportation reductions, for example, are available only to holders of British Pension books. However, many attractions do offer discounts for senior citizens (women 60 or over and men 65 or over). Even if discounts aren't posted, you might ask if they are available. Of course, showing your passport to prove your age is also necessary.

For pretrip information, write for "Travel Tips for Older Americans" (publication #8970), distributed for $1 by the Superintendent of Documents, **U.S. Government Printing Office,** Washington, D.C. 20402 (tel. 202/512-2164). A free booklet, "101 Tips for the Mature Traveler," can be obtained from **Grand Circle Travel,** 347 Congress St., Suite 3A, Boston MA 02210 (tel. 617/350-7500, or toll free 800/221-2610).

Mature Outlook, 6001 N. Clark St., Chicago, IL 60660 (tel. toll free 800/336-6330), is a travel club operated by Sears Roebuck & Co. for people over 50. Annual membership of $9.95 includes a bimonthly newsletter featuring hotel discounts.

SAGA International Holidays, 222 Berkeley St., Boston, MA 02116 (tel. toll free 800/343-0273), is known for all-inclusive tours for seniors (mostly 60 and older). Insurance is included in the tour price.

The best U.S. organization for seniors is **American Association of Retired Persons,** 601 E St. NW, Washington, DC 20049. (tel. 202/434-AARP). Members are offered discounts on car rentals, hotels, and airfares. The association's group travel is provided by the AARP Travel Experience from American Express. Tours may be purchased through any American Express office or travel agent or by calling toll free 800/927-0111. Cruises may be purchased only by telephone through toll free 800/745-4567. Flights to destinations are handled by either of these numbers as part of land arrangements or cruise bookings.

Information is also available from the nonprofit **National Council of Senior Citizens,** 1331 F St. NW, Washington, DC 20005 (tel. 202/347-8800). For $12 per person or couple, you receive a monthly newsletter partly devoted to travel tips and discounts on hotels and auto rentals.

FOR SINGLES

There is one company that has made heroic efforts to match single travelers with like-minded companions, and it is now the largest and best-listed such company in the United States. New applicants desiring travel companions fill out a form stating preferences and needs; they receive a minilisting of potential partners who might be suitable. There is a charge of between $36 and $66 for a six-month listing. A bimonthly newsletter averaging 34 large pages also gives numerous money-saving travel tips of special interest to solo travelers; a sample copy is available for $4. For an application and more information, write to Jens Jurgen, **Travel Companion Exchange,** P.O. Box P-833, Amityville, NY 11701 (tel. 516/454-0880). Another agency to check is **Grand Circle Travel,** 347 Congress St., Boston, MA 02210 (tel. 617/350-7500, or toll free 800/221-2610), which offers escorted tours and cruises for retired people, including singles.

Singleworld, 401 Theodore Fremd Ave., Rye, NY 10580 (tel. 914/967-3334, or toll free 800/223-6490), is a travel agency that operates tours geared to singles. Two basic types of tour are available—a youth-oriented tour for people in their 20s and 30 and jaunts for "all ages." Annual dues are $25.

FOR FAMILIES

If you have a very small child, you will probably want to take along such standard items as children's aspirin, a thermometer, Band-Aids, and similar supplies.

On airlines, you must request a special menu for children at least 24 hours in advance. If baby food is required, however, bring your own and ask a flight attendant to warm it to the right temperature.

Take along a "security blanket" for your child. This might be a pacifier; a favorite toy or book; or, for older children, a baseball cap or favorite T-shirt.

Arrange ahead of time for such necessities as a crib, bottle warmer, and car seat. (In England small children aren't allowed to ride in the front seat.) Find out if the place at which you're staying stocks baby food. If it doesn't, take some with you and plan to buy more abroad in supermarkets.

Babysitters can be found for you at most hotels.

"Family Travel Times" is published ten times a year by TWYCH (Travel With Your Children) and includes a weekly call-in service for subscribers. Subscriptions ($55 a year) can be ordered from TWYCH, 45 W. 18th St., 7th floor, New York, NY 10011 (tel. 212/206-0688). TWYCH also publishes two nitty-gritty information guides, *Skiing with Children* and *Cruising with Children* which sell for $29 and $22, respectively, but are discounted to newsletter subscribers. An information packet, including a sample newsletter, is available for $3.50.

FOR STUDENTS

Council Travel (a subsidiary of the Council on International Educational Exchange) is America's largest student, youth, and budget travel group, with more than 60 offices worldwide. The main office is at 205 E. 42nd St., New York, NY 10017 (tel. 212/661-1414). Council Travel's London Centre is conveniently located at 28A Poland St., W1V 3DB, just off Oxford Circus (tel. 071/287-3337 for European destinations, 071/437-7767 for other destinations). International Student Identity Cards, issuable to all bona fide students for $15, entitle holders to generous travel and other discounts. Discounted international and domestic air tickets are available.

Eurotrain rail passes, YHA passes, weekend packages, overland safaris, and hostel/hotel accommodations are also bookable. Council Travel sells a number of publications for young people, including *Work, Study, Travel Abroad: The Whole World Handbook; Volunteer: The Comprehensive Guide to Voluntary Service in the U.S. and Abroad;* and *The Teenager's Guide to Study, Travel, and Adventure Abroad.*

To keep down costs, I recommend membership in the **International Youth Hostel Federation** (IYHF). Many countries have branch offices, including **American Youth Hostels (AYH)/ Hostelling International,** 733 15th St. NW, Suite 840, Washington, DC 20005 (tel. 202/783-6161). Membership costs $25 annually, except for those under 18, who pay $10, and those over 54, who pay $15.

Several organizations in London specialize in student discounts and youth fares. These include **STA Travel,** 74 Old Brompton Rd., SW7 (tel. 071/937-9921; tube: South Kensington), is open Monday through Friday from 9am to 5:30pm and Saturday from 10am to 4pm.

It's also possible to arrange accommodations in university dormitories from early July to late September. One such place is **Imperial College,** 15 Princes Gardens, London SW7 (tel. 071/589-5111; tube: South Kensington), in the vicinity of London's Royal Albert Hall and Hyde Park. The cost is £24 ($36) per person daily in a shared room, breakfast included.

'6. GETTING THERE

BY PLANE

The deregulation of the airline industry made world headlines in 1979, and since then, any vestige of uniformity in price structures for transatlantic flights has disappeared.

The best strategy for securing the least expensive airfare is to shop around and, above all, to remain as flexible as possible. Keep calling the airlines. If a flight is not fully booked, an airline might discount tickets in an attempt to achieve a full load, allowing you to buy a lower-priced ticket at the last minute.

Most airlines charge different fares according to season. For flights to Europe, the fares are most expensive during midsummer—the peak travel time. The basic season, which falls (with a few exceptions) in the winter months, offers the least expensive fares. Travel during Christmas and Easter weeks is usually more expensive than in the weeks just before or after those holidays. The periods between basic and peak seasons are called shoulder seasons. Also note that prices tend to be higher on the weekend, which is usually defined as Friday, Saturday, and Sunday.

Even within the various seasons, most airlines also offer heavily discounted promotional fares available according to last-minute market plans. But be warned: The less expensive your ticket is, the more stringent the restrictions will be. The most common and frequently used such fare is the APEX, or advance purchase excursion (see below).

MAJOR AIRLINES

Following is a list of several of the airlines that fly the enormously popular routes from North America to Great Britain.

For travelers departing from Canada, **Air Canada** (tel. toll free 800/776-3000) flies daily to London Heathrow nonstop from both Montréal and Toronto. There are nonstop flights from Calgary and Edmonton to Heathrow three to seven times a week, depending on the season. From Vancouver, flights to London either connect through Edmonton or, about once a week, fly directly to London nonstop.

American Airlines (tel. toll free 800/624-6262) offers 12 daily routes to London Heathrow from about a half-dozen U.S. gateways—New York's JFK (four times daily); Chicago's O'Hare (twice daily); Miami International (usually twice daily); and Los Angeles International and Boston's Logan (each once daily).

British Airways (tel. toll free 800/AIRWAYS) offers flights from some 18 U.S. cities to Heathrow and Gatwick airports, as well as many others to Manchester, Birmingham, and Glasgow. Just about all flights are nonstop. With more add-on options than any other airline, BA can make a visit to Britain cheaper than you might have expected. Of particular interest are the "Value Plus," "London on the Town," and "Europe Escorted" packages that include both airfare and hotel accommodations throughout Britain at heavily discounted prices.

Depending on day and season, **Delta** (tel. toll free 800/241-4141) runs either one or two daily nonstops between Atlanta and Gatwick, near London. Delta also offers nonstop daily service from Cincinnati, Detroit, and Miami to Gatwick.

Northwest Airlines (tel. toll free 800/447-4747) flies nonstop from both Minneapolis and Boston to Gatwick.

Under new management, **TWA** (tel. toll free 800/221-2000), flies nonstop to Gatwick every day from its big hub in St. Louis. Connections are possible through St. Louis from most of North America.

United Airlines (tel. toll free 800/241-6522) flies nonstop from New York's JFK to Heathrow two to three times a day, depending on season. United also offers nonstop service twice a day from Dulles International, near Washington, D.C., plus once-a-day service from Newark, NJ; Los Angeles; San Francisco; and Seattle.

USAir (tel. toll free 800/428-4322) flies daily nonstop to Gatwick from Philadelphia; Baltimore/Washington International; and Charlotte, NC.

Virgin Atlantic Airways (tel. toll free 800/862-8621) flies to Gatwick four times a week from Boston, Miami, and Orlando, plus once a day to Heathrow from Los Angeles; New York's JFK; and Newark, NJ.

BEST-VALUE FARES

APEX Generally, your cheapest option on a regular airline is to book an APEX (advance purchase excursion) fare. British Airways, for example, offers three types of APEX fare. The least expensive is a nonrefundable ticket that requires a 30-day advance purchase, plus a delay of between 7 and 21 days before using the return half of your ticket. Passengers who prefer to fly midweek (Monday to Thursday) pay less than those who fly in either direction on a weekend (Friday, Saturday, or Sunday).

A slightly more expensive APEX fare offered by BA allows much greater leeway for changing travel plans. Requiring a 7-day advance booking and a stay abroad that incorporates at least one Saturday night, it allows cancellations or changes of flight dates for a $125 fee. Slight variations in price exist for this type of ticket, depending on whether you'll need a maximum stay abroad of 2 months or 6 months. (The option of staying 6 months costs a bit more than the one requiring an earlier return.)

DISCOUNTS Senior citizens over 60 receive special 10% discounts on British Airways through its Privileged Traveler program. They also qualify for less stringent restrictions on APEX cancellations. The discounts are also granted for BA tours and for intra-Britain air tickets if booked in North America. BA also offers youth fares to anyone 12 to 24.

BUCKET SHOPS [Consolidators] In its purest sense, a bucket shop acts as a clearinghouse for blocks of tickets that airlines discount and consign during normally slow periods of air travel.

Charter operators (see below) and bucket shops used to perform separate functions, but many outfits now perform both functions.

Tickets are sometimes—but not always—priced at around 20% to 35% less than full fare. Terms of payment vary—say, anywhere from 45 days prior to departure to last-minute sales offered in a final attempt by an airline to fill a disturbingly empty craft. Tickets can be purchased through regular travel agents, who usually mark up the ticket 8% to 10%, maybe more, thereby greatly reducing your discount. Use of such a ticket doesn't qualify you for an advance seat assignment, and you are therefore likely to be assigned a less desirable seat at the last minute.

Bucket shops abound from coast to coast, and here are some recommendations. In New York, try **TFI Tours International,** 34 W. 32nd St., 12th floor, New York, NY 10001 (tel. 212/736-1140 in New York State, or toll free 800/825-3834 elsewhere in the U.S.). In Miami, contact **25 West Tours,** 2490 Coral Way, Miami FL 33145 (tel. 305/856-0810 in Miami; toll free 800/423-6954 in Florida, or 800/225-2582 elsewhere in the U.S.). Out West, you can try **Sunline Express Holidays, Inc.,** 607 Market St., San Francisco, CA 94105 (tel. 415/541-7800, or toll free 800/786-5463). In New England, a good possibility is **Travel Management International,** 18 Prescott St., Suite 4, Cambridge, MA 02138 (tel. toll free 800/245-3672), which offers a wide variety of discount fares, including youth fares. Its contract fares are often lower than those offered by rebators (see below).

Since dealing with an unfamiliar bucket shop might be a bit risky, it's wise to call the Better Business Bureau for information about the company.

CHARTER FLIGHTS Strictly speaking, a charter uses an aircraft reserved months in advance for a one-time-only transit to some predetermined point. You may be asked to purchase a tour package and pay far in advance. You'll pay a stiff penalty (or forfeit the ticket entirely) if you cancel, unless you are covered by cancellation insurance. Conversely, some charters are canceled if the plane doesn't fill sufficiently.

Among reliable charter-flight operators is the **Council Charter,** 205 E. 42nd St., New York, NY 10017 (tel. 212/661-0311, or toll free 800/800-8222). This company can arrange "charter seats on regularly scheduled aircraft" to most major European cities.

One of the biggest New York charter operators is **Travac,** 989 Sixth Ave., New York, NY 10018 (tel. 212/563-3303, or toll free 800/TRAV-800). Other Travac offices include 6151 W. Century Blvd., Los Angeles, CA 90045 (tel. 310/670-9692); 166 Geary St., San Francisco, CA 94108 (tel. 415/392-4610); and 2601 Jefferson St., Orlando, FL 32803 (tel. 407/896-0014).

Be warned that some charter companies have proved unreliable in the past.

REBATORS Rebators are companies that pass along to the passenger part of their commission, although many assess a service fee. They are not the same as travel agents but can sometimes offer roughly similar services. A rebator may sell you a discounted travel ticket and also offer discounted land arrangements, including hotels and car rentals. Most rebators offer discounts averaging 10% to 25%, less a $25 handling charge.

Rebators include **Travel Avenue,** 641 W. Lake St., Suite 201, Chicago, IL 60606 (tel. 312/876-1116, or toll free 800/333-3335), and **The Smart Traveller,** 3111 SW 27th Ave., Miami, FL 33133 (tel. 305/448-3338, or toll free 800/448-3338). These companies also discount package tours, cruises, cars, and hotels.

STANDBY **Virgin Atlantic Airways** (tel. toll free 800/862-8621) features both a day-of-departure and a day-prior-to-departure standby fare to London from New York's JFK; Newark, NJ; Orlando; Miami; and Boston—but only from mid-October to late March.

GOING AS A COURIER This cost-cutting technique has lots of restrictions, and tickets may be hard to come by, so it's not for everybody. Basically, you go as both an airline passenger and a courier hired by an overnight air-freight firm. For the service, the courier gets greatly discounted airfare or, in certain very rare instances, flies for free.

You're usually allowed only one piece of carry-on luggage. As a courier, you don't actually handle the merchandise you're accompanying to Europe—you just carry a manifest to present to Customs. Upon your arrival, an employee of the courier service will reclaim the company's cargo. Incidentally, you fly alone, so don't plan to travel with anybody. (A friend may be able to arrange a flight as a courier on a consecutive day.)

Courier services are often listed in the yellow pages or in advertisements in travel sections or newspapers.

To get you started, check with **Halbart Express,** 147-05 176th St., Jamaica, NY 11434 (tel. 718/656-8189 10am–3pm daily). Another firm to try is **Now Voyager,** 74 Varick St., Suite 307, New York, NY 10013 (tel. 212/431-1616 at any time). Now Voyager works with six daily flights to London, one allowing couriers to stay up to 30 days and bring along a modest amount of luggage.

For $35 a year, **International Association of Air Travel Couriers,** P.O. Box 1349, Lake Worth, FL 33460 (tel. 407/582-

8320), will send six issues of its newsletter, "Shoestring Traveler," and about six issues of "Air Courier Bulletin," a directory of worldwide air courier bargains. The organization offers photo identification cards and acts as troubleshooter if a courier runs into difficulties.

BY TRAIN

If you're traveling to London from elsewhere in the United Kingdom, consider buying a **BritRail Pass,** which allows unlimited rail travel during a set time period (8 days, 15 days, or one month).

If you plan to tour Britain and France, you might consider the **BritFrance Railpass,** which includes round-trip catamaran Channel crossings. You may choose a total of any 5 days of unlimited rail travel during a 15-day consecutive period or 10 days during a single month—on both the British and French rail networks.

In Paris at the Gare du Nord, you board a French Turbotrain that will take you to the port of Boulogne. There, at the catamaran terminal, you board a Seacat (a double-hulled catamaran propelled by aircraft-style jet engines) that will take you to Folkestone on England's south coast. From there, you travel by rail to London's Victoria Station. Trip time is 5½ hours.

Americans can secure either pass at **BritRail Travel International,** 1500 Broadway, New York, NY 10036 (tel. 212/575-2667). Canadians can write to P.O. Box 89510, 250 Eglinton Ave. E., Toronto, ON M4P 3E1.

Reaching London from Amsterdam is a frequently exercised option for many travelers visiting Britain as part of a European self-conducted tour. Most travelers buy the complete package from a travel agency. Passengers board at Amsterdam's main railroad station for a train to Hoek van Holland. From there, a ferryboat—usually but not always Sealink Lines—is waiting at a dock adjacent to the train lines and passengers simply cross a platform to the boat. The sea

 FROMMER'S SMART TRAVELER: AIRFARES

1. Take off-peak-season flights—autumn-to-spring and Monday-through-Thursday departures.
2. Avoid last-minute changes of plans to avoid airline penalties.
3. Keep checking the airlines and their fares. One airline discounted a New York–to–London fare by $195 in 7 days.
4. Shop all airlines that fly to your destination.
5. Always ask for the lowest fare, not just for a discount fare.
6. Ask about frequent-flier programs.
7. Check bucket shops for last-minute, even cheaper discount fares.
8. Ask about air/land packages.
9. Check standby fares offered by Virgin Atlantic Airways.
10. Fly free or at a heavy discount as a courier.

crossing takes from 6 to 8 hours. The ferryboat lands at Harwich, from which trains head to London's Liverpool Street Station. The 10-hour journey from Amsterdam to London costs $210 round trip in second class. Passengers can rent a berth during the water section of this transit for a $25 supplement. Berths are not available for the overland sections. There are about two transits every 24 hours, one at night.

Note: The long-awaited Channel Tunnel between Dover and Calais, France, is scheduled to open in early 1994. It will provide a direct train link between the British Isles and the European Continent. Traveling by train to London should be much easier then.

BY BUS

If you're traveling to London from elsewhere in the United Kingdom, consider purchasing a **Britexpress Card,** which entitles you to a 30% discount on National Express (England and Wales) and Caledonian Express (Scotland) buses. Contact a travel agent.

Bus connections to Britain from the Continent are generally not very comfortable, though some lines are more convenient than others. One line with a relatively good reputation is **Euroways Eurolines, Ltd.,** 52 Grosvenor Gardens, London SW1W OUA (tel. 071/730-0202). Their service will book passage on buses traveling once a day between London and Paris (9 hours); Amsterdam (10 hours); Munich (24 hours); and Stockholm (44 hours). On the longer routes, which employ two alternating drivers, the bus proceeds almost without interruption, taking occasional breaks for meals.

BY CAR

If you plan to take a rented car across the Channel, check carefully with the rental company before you leave about license and insurance requirements.

There are many "drive-on, drive-off" car-ferry services across the Channel. The most popular ports in France for frequent Channel crossings are Boulogne and Calais, where you can board Sealink ferries taking you to the English ports of Dover and Folkestone.

BY SHIP
OCEAN LINER

Cunard Line, 555 Fifth Ave., New York, NY 10017 (tel. 212/880-7500, or toll free 800/221-4770), boasts that its flagship, *Queen Elizabeth 2,* is the only five-star-plus luxury ocean liner providing regular transatlantic service—some 27 sailings a year between April and December. Many passengers appreciate its graceful introduction to British mores, as well as the absolute lack of jet lag that an ocean crossing can provide.

Fares are extremely complicated, based on cabin standard and location and the season of sailing. During the thrift/superthrift season—roughly defined as late autumn or early spring—sailings usually cost a minimum of $2,170 in transatlantic class and around $3,515 in first class. These prices are per person, double occupancy. All passengers also pay a $155 port tax. Many packages are promoted, most of which add on relatively inexpensive airfare from your home city to the port of departure plus a return to your home city from London on British Airways.

FERRY & HOVERCRAFT

For centuries, sailing ships and ferryboats have traversed the English Channel bearing supplies, merchandise, and passengers. Today, the major carriers are P&O Channel Lines, Hoverspeed, and Sealink.

P&O Channel Lines maintains a North American sales agency at Scots-American Travel, 26 Rugen Dr., Harrington Park, NJ 07640 (tel. 201/7678-1187). The agency can reserve passage on any P&O ferryboat to Britain and also issue ironclad reservations for portage of autos. Advance reservations, particularly in summertime, are usually necessary for cars.

P&O operates passenger jetfoil service between Dover and Oostende, Belgium, and car and passenger ferries between Portsmouth and Cherbourg, France (3 sailings a day; 4¾ hours each way); between Portsmouth and Le Havre, France (3 sailings a day; 5¾ hours each way); between Dover and Calais, France (sailings every 90 minutes; 75 minutes each way); between Dover and Oostende, Belgium (6 to 8 sailings a day; 4 hours each way); and between Felixstowe and Zeebrugge, Belgium (2 sailings a day; 5¾ hours each way).

P&O's major competitors include **Hoverspeed** and **Sealink,** either of which can carry both passengers and vehicles on all their routes. Both companies are represented in North America by BritRail (tel. 212/595-2667).

By far the most popular route across the Channel is between Calais and Dover. Hoverspeed operates at least 12 daily 35-minute Hovercraft crossings, as well as slightly longer crossings via Seacat (a catamaran propelled by jet engines) between Boulogne and Folkestone. Seacats cross about four times a day and require 55 minutes.

Sealink operates conventional ferryboat service between Cherbourg and Southampton (1 or 2 sailings a day taking 6 to 8 hours) and between Dieppe and Newhaven (4 sailings a day taking 4 hours). Very popular are Sealink's conventional car ferries between Calais and Dover. Departing 20 times a day in either direction, they require 90 minutes for the crossing. The cost is $42 each way for a passenger without a car and $123 to $300 with a car (depending on size and season) and up to five occupants.

FREIGHTER

Passage on a freighter tends to be less expensive than that on a passenger ship, but this requires a little comparison shopping. For example, a budget accommodation aboard the *QE2* can cost less money and require less time than passage on a freighter. For legal reasons, no freighter can carry more than 12 passengers.

In summer, cabins tend to be fully booked for as much as a year in advance. Space is more likely to be available in winter.

For more information on freighter travel, write to **Fords Freighter Travel Guide,** 19448 Londelius St., Northridge, CA 91324 (tel. 818/701-7414).

One company operating freighters is **Mediterranean Shipping Co.,** c/o Sea the Difference, 96 Morton St., New York, NY 10014 (tel. 212/691-3760, or toll free 800/666-9333), offering year-round voyages from Boston and New York ports to Felixstowe in England.

CHAPTER 3

GETTING TO KNOW LONDON

Europe's largest city is like a great wheel, with Piccadilly Circus at the hub and dozens of communities branching out from it. Since London is such a conglomeration of sections—each having its own life (hotels, restaurants, pubs)—first-time visitors may be intimidated until they get the hang of it. Most visitors spend all their time in the West End, where most of the attractions are located, except for the historic part of London known as the City, where the Tower of London stands.

This chapter will help you get your bearings. It provides a brief orientation and a preview of the city's most important neighborhoods and answers questions you need to know about getting around London by transportation or on foot. It also presents a "Fast Facts" section covering everything from babysitters to shoe repairs.

1. ORIENTATION

ARRIVING

BY PLANE   **London Heathrow Airport,** located west of London in Hounslow (tel. 081/759-4321 for flight information), is one of the world's busiest airports, with flights arriving from around the world and throughout Great Britain. It is divided into four terminals, each relatively self-contained. Terminal 4, the newest and most modern, handles the long-haul and transatlantic operations of British Airways. Most transatlantic flights of U.S.-based airlines arrive at Terminals 1 and 2. Terminal 3 receives intra-European flights of several European airlines. Many charter and some scheduled flights land at relatively remote **Gatwick Airport** (tel. 0293/535-353 for flight information), located some 25 miles south of London in West Sussex. **London Stansted** airport, located some 30 miles northeast of central London, mostly handles flights to and from the European Continent. **London City Airport** (tel. 081/474-5555), about six miles east of the City, is primarily used for commuter flights to and from the Continent.

Getting to Central London   from **Heathrow** takes 50 minutes by Underground and costs £3.10 ($4.70) to make the 15-mile trip from the airport to center city. You can also take the Airbus, which gets you into central London in about an hour and costs £5

($7.50) for adults and £3 ($4.50) for children. A taxi is likely to cost around £25 ($37.50). From **Gatwick** express trains leave for Victoria Station in London every 15 minutes during the day and every hour at night. The charge is £8.50 ($12.80). There is also an express bus from Gatwick to Victoria every half hour from 6:30am to 8pm and every hour from 8 to 11pm; this Flightline Bus 777 costs £7 ($10.50) per person. A taxi from Gatwick to central London usually costs £40 to £45 ($60 to $67.50). However, you must negotiate a fare with the driver before you enter the cab; the meter does not apply because Gatwick lies outside the Metropolitan Police District. From **Stansted,** Cambridge Coach Service (tel. 22/344-0640) provides bus service into central London five times daily Monday through Saturday, with service cut to three buses on Sunday. Buses also run to Heathrow and Gatwick if you're making connecting flights. It's also possible to take the Stansted Express, a train that will deliver you from the airport to Liverpool Street Station in the center of London in just 45 minutes. A first-class seat costs £13.50 ($20.30), with a second-class seat priced at £9 ($13.50). Train service is daily from 5:30am to 11pm. From **London City Airport,** there's a free shuttle bus to Canary Wharf Pier, where you can catch the Riverbus service to Charing Cross (with several intermediate stops).

BY TRAIN   Most arrivals of trains originating in Paris are at **Victoria Station** in the center of London. Visitors from Amsterdam arrive at **Liverpool Street Station,** and those journeying south by rail from Edinburgh arrive at **King's Cross Station.** Each station is connected to London's vast bus and Underground (subway) network, and each has phones, restaurants, pubs, luggage-storage areas, and London Regional Transport Information Centres.

BY CAR   If you're taking a car-ferry across the Channel, you can quickly connect with a motorway into London. *Remember to drive on the left* if you're coming from the Continent. London is circled by two roadways—the A406 and A205 combination close in and the M25 farther out. Determine which part of the city you wish to enter and follow signposts. I suggest you confine driving in London to the bare minimum, which means arriving and parking.

Parking is scarce and expensive. Before arrival in London, call your hotel and inquire if it has a garage (and what the charges are) or ask the staff to give you the name and address of a garage nearby.

TOURIST INFORMATION

The **British Travel Centre,** Rex House, 4–12 Lower Regent St., London SW1 4PQ (tel. 071/730-3400; tube: Piccadilly Circus), caters to walk-in visitors who need information about all parts of Britain. (If you need to make only a telephone inquiry, call 071/730-3488 for information about London or 071/824-8000 about the rest of Great Britain.) On the modern premises you'll find a British Rail ticket office, travel and theater-ticket agencies, a hotel-booking service, a bookshop, and a souvenir shop. Hours are 9am to 6:30pm on Monday through Friday and 10am to 4pm on Saturday and Sunday, with extended hours on Saturday during June through September.

CITY LAYOUT

MAIN DISTRICTS, SQUARES, AND STREETS   There is— fortunately—an immense difference between the sprawling vastness of Greater London and the pocket-size chunk north of the River Thames that might be called "Prime Tourist Territory."

This tourist's London begins at **Chelsea**, on the north bank of the river, and stretches for roughly 5 miles north to **Hampstead.** Its western boundary runs through **Kensington**, while the eastern boundary lies 5 miles away at Tower Bridge. Within this 5- by 5-mile square, you'll find all the hotels and restaurants and nearly all the sights that are usually of interest to visitors.

Make no mistake: This is still a hefty portion of land to cover, and a really thorough exploration of it would take a couple of years. But it has the advantage of being flat and eminently walkable, besides boasting one of the best public transportation systems ever devised.

The logical (although not geographical) center of this area is **Trafalgar Square**, which we'll therefore take as our orientation point. If you stand facing the steps of the imposing National Gallery, you're looking northwest. That is the direction of **Piccadilly Circus**—the real core of tourist London—and the maze of streets that make up **Soho**. Farther north is **Oxford Street,** London's gift to moderately priced shopping, and still farther northwest lies Regent's Park with London Zoo.

At your back—that is, south— is **Whitehall,** which houses or skirts nearly every British government building, from the Ministry of Defence to the official residence of the prime minister at no. 10 Downing Street. In the same direction, a bit farther south, stand the Houses of Parliament and Westminster Abbey.

Flowing southwest from Trafalgar Square is the table-smooth **Mall,** flanked by magnificent parks and mansions and leading to Buckingham Palace, residence of the queen. Farther in the same direction lie **Belgravia** and **Knightsbridge,** the city's plushest residential areas, and south of them lies the aforementioned **Chelsea,** with its chic flavor, plus **King's Road,** principally a boulevard for shopping.

Due west of Trafalgar Square stretches the superb and distinctly high-priced shopping area bordered by **Regent Street** and **Piccadilly Street** (as distinct from the Circus). Farther west lie the equally elegant shops and even more elegant homes of **Mayfair.** Then comes **Park Lane.** On the other side of Park Lane is Hyde Park, the biggest park in London and one of the largest in the world.

Charing Cross Road runs north from Trafalgar Square, past **Leicester Square,** and intersects with **Shaftesbury Avenue.** This is London's theaterland. A bit farther along, Charing Cross Road turns into a browser's paradise, lined with shops selling new and secondhand books.

Finally, it funnels into **St. Giles Circus.** This is where you enter **Bloomsbury,** site of the University of London, the British Museum, and some of the best budget hotels, as well as the erstwhile stamping ground of the famed Bloomsbury Group, led by Virginia Woolf.

Northeast of your position lies **Covent Garden,** known for its Royal Opera House and today a major shopping, restaurant, and café district.

Following the **Strand** eastward from Trafalgar Square, you'll come into **Fleet Street.** Beginning in the 19th century, this corner of London became the most concentrated newspaper district in the world. Where the Strand becomes Fleet Street stands Temple Bar, and only here do you enter the actual City of London, or the City. Its focal point and shrine is the Bank of England on **Threadneedle Street,** with the Stock Exchange next door and the Royal Exchange across the street. In the midst of all the hustle and bustle rises St. Paul's Cathedral, a monument to beauty and tranquillity.

At the far eastern fringe of the City looms the Tower of London, shrouded in legend, blood, and history, and permanently besieged by battalions of visitors.

And this, as far as we will be concerned, concludes the London circle.

FINDING AN ADDRESS London's street layout follows no real pattern, and both street names and house numbers seem to have been perpetrated by xenophobes with equal grudges against postal carriers and foreigners. Don't think, for instance, that Southampton Row is anywhere near Southampton Street or that either of these places has any connection with Southampton Road.

London is checkered with innumerable squares, mews, closes, and terraces, which jut into or cross or overlap or interrupt whatever street you're trying to follow, usually without the slightest warning. You may be walking along ruler-straight Albany Street and suddenly find yourself flanked by Colosseum Terrace (with a different numbering system). Just keep on walking and after a couple of blocks you're right back on Albany Street (and the original house numbers) without having encountered the faintest reason for the sudden change in labels.

House numbers run in odds and evens, clockwise and counterclockwise, as the wind blows. *That is, when numbers exist at all, and frequently they don't.* Many establishments in London, such as the Inn on the Park or Langan's Brasserie, *do not use house numbers,* although a building right next door might be numbered. Happily, Londoners are generally glad to assist a bewildered foreigner.

Every so often you'll come upon a square that is called a *square* on the south side, a *road* on the north, a *park* on the east, and possibly a something-or-other *close* on the west. Your only chance is to consult a map or ask your way as you go along.

NEIGHBORHOODS IN BRIEF

Mayfair Bounded by Piccadilly, Hyde Park, and Oxford and Regent streets, this section of London is considered the most elegant, taking in Grosvenor Square and Berkeley Square.

St. James's Royal London begins at Piccadilly Circus, moving southwest. It basks in its associations with royalty, from the "merrie monarch," Charles II, to today's Elizabeth II.

The Strand and **Covent Garden** Beginning at Trafalgar Square, the Strand runs east into Fleet Street and is flanked with theaters, shops, hotels, and restaurants. Covent Garden was until 1970 the fruit, flower, and vegetable market of London. Today it is a major shopping district, seat of dozens of restaurants and cafés, and site of the Royal Opera House on Bow Street.

Holborn The old borough of Holborn takes in the heart of legal

London—home of the city's barristers, solicitors, and law clerks. It contains the ancient Inns of Court.

Westminster/Whitehall This area has been the seat of British government since the days of Edward the Confessor. It is dominated by the Houses of Parliament and Westminster Abbey.

Victoria Not an official district, Victoria takes its name from bustling Victoria Station, known as the "Gateway to the Continent." It lies directly south of Buckingham Palace in Belgravia, just west of Westminster.

Knightsbridge Knightsbridge is a top residential and shopping area, just south of Hyde Park. It is the location of a great department store, Harrods.

Belgravia South of Knightsbridge, this has been the long-time aristocratic quarter of London, rivaling Mayfair in grandness and money. It reached its pinnacle of prestige in the reign of Victoria. It lies near Buckingham Palace Gardens and Brompton Road, and its center is Belgrave Square.

Chelsea A stylish district stretching along the Thames, Chelsea lies south of Belgravia. It begins at Sloane Square, and its best-known and shop-flanked avenue is King's Road.

Kensington Located west of Kensington Gardens and Hyde Park, Kensington is traversed by Kensington High Street and Kensington Church Street.

South Kensington Lying southeast of Kensington Gardens and Earl's Court, South Kensington is primarily residential and is often called "museumland" because of the many museums here.

Paddington/Bayswater The Paddington section is around Paddington Station, north of Kensington Gardens and Hyde Park. It is a center for budget travelers, who fill up the B&Bs at Sussex Gardens and on Norfolk Square. Just south of Paddington is Bayswater, another center of budget B&Bs.

St. Marylebone South of Regent's Park and north of Oxford Street, St. Marylebone is primarily residential. Mayfair is to the south.

Soho This section of narrow lanes and crooked streets, once London's main foreign quarter, has some of the city's best international restaurants. Soho starts at Piccadilly Circus and stretches to Oxford Street.

Bloomsbury To the northeast of Piccadilly Circus, beyond Soho, is Bloomsbury, heart of academic London and site of the British Museum and British Library.

The City In east London, the City was the original walled Roman community and is today the center of financial London.

East End One of London's poorest districts, the East End borders the richer area of the City. Many immigrants have found a home here, but it is most famous for its cockneys.

STREET MAPS If you're going to explore London in any depth, you'll need a detailed street map with an index—not one of those superficial overviews given away free at many hotels or tourist offices. The best ones are published by *Falk,* and they're available at most newsstands and nearly all bookstores, including **W. & G. Foyle Ltd.,** 113–119 Charing Cross Rd., WC2 (tel. 071/439-8501).

2. GETTING AROUND

BY PUBLIC TRANSPORTATION

If you know the ropes, transportation in London can be easy and inexpensive. Both the Underground (subway or tube) and bus systems are operated by London Transport. There are Travel Information Centres in the Underground stations at King's Cross, Oxford Circus, St. James's Park, Liverpool Street Station, and Piccadilly Circus, as well as in the British Rail stations at Euston and Victoria and in each of the terminals at Heathrow Airport. They take reservations for London Transport's guided tours and offer free Underground and bus maps and other information leaflets. A 24-hour telephone information service is available (tel. 071/222-1234). Information is also obtainable by writing London Transport, Travel Information Service, 55 Broadway, London SW1H 0BD.

London Transport offers **Travelcards** for use on bus, Underground, and British Rail services in Greater London. Available in combinations of adjacent zones, Travelcards can be purchased for a minimum of 7 days or for any period (including odd days) from a month to a year. A Travelcard allowing travel in two zones for one week costs adults £8.50 ($12.80) and children £3.45 ($5.20).

To purchase a Travelcard, you must present a **Photocard.** If you're 16 years or older, bring along a passport-type picture of yourself when you buy your Travelcard, and the Photocard will be issued free. Child-rate Photocards for Travelcards are issued only at main post offices in the London area, and in addition to a passport-type photograph, proof of age is required (for example, a passport or a birth certificate). Teenagers (14 or 15) are charged adult fares on all services unless in possession of one of the cards.

For shorter stays in London, you may want to consider the **One-Day Off-Peak Travelcard.** This Travelcard can be used on most bus, Underground, and British Rail services throughout Greater London after 9:30am on Monday through Friday and at any time on weekends and bank holidays. The Travelcard is available from Underground ticket offices, bus garages, Travel Information Centres, and some newsstands. For two zones, the cost is £2.50 ($3.80) for adults and £1.20 ($1.80) for children 5 to 15.

The **Visitor Travelcard,** allowing unlimited travel on almost the entire London Underground and bus system for up to 7 days, can be purchased in North America (but not in the United Kingdom). Contact a British Tourist Authority office.

UNDERGROUND Known as the tube, the Underground is the fastest and easiest (although not the most interesting) way to get from place to place. The tube has a special place in the hearts of Londoners: During the blitz in World War II thousands of people used its subterranean platforms as air-raid shelters, camping all night in reasonable safety from bombs.

All Underground stations are clearly marked with a red circle and blue crossbar. You descend by stairways, escalators, or huge elevators, depending on the depth. Some Underground stations have complete subterranean shopping arcades and several boast high-tech gadgets, such as pushbutton information machines.

You pick the station for which you're heading on the large diagram displayed on the wall, which includes an alphabetical index. You note the color of the line (Bakerloo is brown, Central is red, and so on). Then, by merely following the colored band, you can see at a glance whether and where you'll have to change and how many stops there are to your destination.

If you have British coins, you can purchase your ticket at one of the vending machines. Otherwise, you must buy it at the ticket office. You can transfer as many times as you like so long as you stay in the Underground. The flat fee for one trip within the Central zone is 80p ($1.20). Trips from the Central zone to destinations in the suburbs range from £1.20 to £3.80 ($1.80 to $5.70) in most cases.

Note: Be sure to keep your ticket; it must be presented when you get off. If you owe extra, you'll be asked to pay the difference by the attendant. And if you're out on the town and dependent on the Underground, watch your time carefully; many trains stop running at midnight (11:30pm on Sunday).

BUSES London has just two types of buses, which you can't possibly confuse: the **red** double-decker monsters that bully their way through the inner-city areas, and the **green** single-deckers that link the center with outlying towns and villages.

The first thing you learn about London buses is that nobody just boards them. You "queue up"—that is, form a single-file line at the bus stop. The English do it instinctively, even when there are only two of them. It's one of their eccentricities, and you will grow to appreciate it during rush hours.

The comparably priced bus system is almost as good as the Underground, and you have a better view. To find out about current routes, pick up a free bus map at one of London Regional Transport's Travel Information Centres listed above. The map is available to personal callers only, not by mail.

London still has old-style Routemaster buses, with both driver and conductor. Once on a bus, a conductor will come to your seat. You pay a fare based on your destination, and receive a ticket in return. This type of bus will be replaced by buses having only a driver. You pay the driver as you enter, and exit via a rear door. As with the Underground, the fares vary according to distance traveled. Generally, they cost 10p to 20p (15¢ to 30¢) less than tube fares. If you travel for two or three stops, the cost is 60p (90¢); longer runs within zone 1 cost 80p ($1.20). If you want to be warned when to get off, simply ask the conductor. (See bus map, pages 56–57.)

BY TAXI

London cabs are among the most comfortable and best-designed in the world. You can pick one up either by heading for a cab rank or by hailing one in the street. (The taxi is free if the yellow "Taxi" sign on the roof is lighted.) For a **radio cab,** you can telephone 071/272-

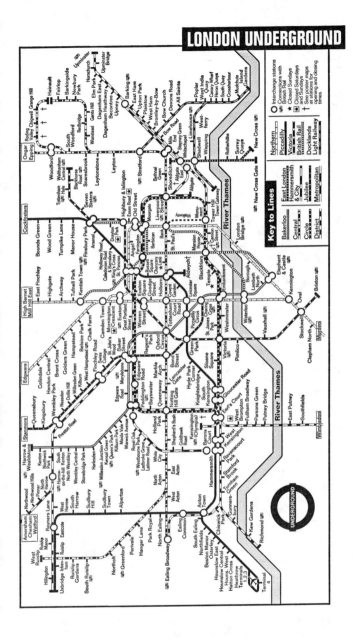

0272, 071/253-5000, or 071/286-0286. The minimum fare is £1 ($1.50) for the first kilometer or 3 minutes and 49.5 seconds, with increments of 20p (30¢) thereafter, based on distance or time. Each additional passenger is charged 20p (30¢). Passengers pay 10p (15¢) for each piece of luggage in the driver's compartment and any other item more than 2 feet long. Surcharges are imposed after 8pm and on

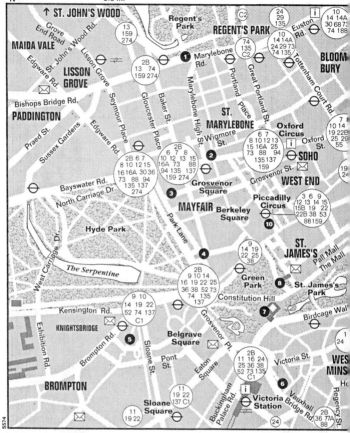

Using the Map

London bus route numbers are shown in circles at places where routes cross. Locate where you are going and then follow the route circles back toward your starting point. This will show if and where you need to change buses and the bus route number or numbers for your trip.

LONDON ATTRACTIONS

Admiralty Arch **9**
Barbican Centre **25**
British Library and British Museum
Buckingham Palace **7**
Downing Street **16**
Harrods **5**
Horse Guards **15**
Houses of Parliament **18**
Imperial War Museum **20**

---

weekends and public holidays. All these tariffs include VAT. Fares usually increase annually. It's recommended that you tip 10% to 15% of the fare.

Warning: If you telephone for a cab, the meter starts running when the taxi receives instructions from the dispatcher. So you could find £1 ($1.50) or more already on the meter when you enter the taxi.

If you have a complaint about taxi service, or if you leave something in a cab, contact the Public Carriage Office, 15 Penton St., N1 (tel. 071/833-0996; tube: Angel Station). If it's a complaint, you

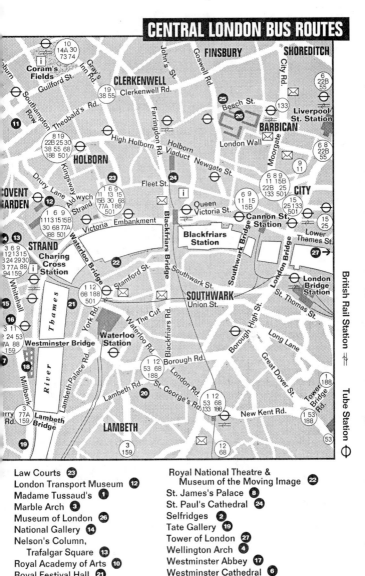

CENTRAL LONDON BUS ROUTES

Law Courts **23**
London Transport Museum **12**
Madame Tussaud's **1**
Marble Arch **3**
Museum of London **26**
National Gallery **14**
Nelson's Column,
   Trafalgar Square **13**
Royal Academy of Arts **10**
Royal Festival Hall **21**

Royal National Theatre &
   Museum of the Moving Image **22**
St. James's Palace **8**
St. Paul's Cathedral **24**
Selfridges **2**
Tate Gallery **19**
Tower of London **27**
Wellington Arch **4**
Westminster Abbey **17**
Westminster Cathedral **6**

British Rail Station ≷

Tube Station ⊖

must have the cab number, which is displayed in the passenger compartment.

Cab sharing is permitted in London, as British law allows cabbies to offer rides for two to five persons. The taxis accepting such riders display a notice on yellow plastic, with the words "Shared Taxi." Each of two riders sharing is charged 65% of the fare a lone passenger would be charged. Three persons pay 55%, four pay 45%, and five (the seating capacity of all new London cabs) pay 40% of the single-passenger fare.

BY CAR

RENTALS   Car rentals are relatively expensive, and London offers a large array of companies to choose from. Most will accept your U.S. driver's license, provided you're over 21 and have held it for more than a year. Don't forget, however, that the car you get will have the steering wheel on the "wrong" side.

Many companies grant discounts to clients who reserve their cars in advance (usually 48 weekday hours) through the toll-free reservations offices in a renter's home country and rent for periods longer than a week. When renting, be sure to ask if the price quoted includes the 17½% value-added tax (VAT), personal accident insurance (PAI), collision damage waiver (CDW), and other insurance options. If not, ask what these will cost because they can make a big difference in your bottom line.

As in the United States, the CDW and some added insurance are offered free by certain credit cards if you use them to rent a car. Check to see if you are covered by the credit card you use, thus avoiding the added expense.

The following are major rental firms.

Avis (tel. toll free 800/331-2112 in the U.S. and Canada) offers a one-day rental of the small but peppy Ford Fiesta with CDW and unlimited mileage for £83 ($124.50) plus taxes. At press time, however, a full week's rental of a similar car, if reserved 14 days in advance, was a much better bargain at £98 ($147). The main Avis downtown office is in Mayfair at 8 Balderton St., London W1 (tel. 071/917-6700; tube: Bond Street).

British Airways (tel. toll free 800/AIRWAYS in the U.S. and Canada) offers a relatively inexpensive way to rent a car in Britain through its reservations service. As the U.K.'s largest car renter, BA can offer heavily discounted rates. Depending on size, horsepower, and amenities, as well as season, cars range in price from $14 to $78 per day, plus VAT and insurance. Child seats are available free. Understandably, these arrangements are offered only to passengers flying into Britain on BA. If hotel nights are also booked through the same toll-free number, booklets of valuable coupons (offering discounts on theaters, restaurants, shops, and museums) are also included.

Budget Rent-a-Car (tel. toll free 800/472-3325 in the U.S. and Canada) maintains eight offices in London, including at the major airports and at Victoria Station, and about 100 others throughout the United Kingdom. The busiest London office is near Marble Arch at 89 Wigmore St., W1 (tel. 071/723-8038; tube: Marble Arch). If you reserve from North America at least 24 hours prior to pickup, cars will cost from £41 ($61.50) per day for short rentals and from £145 ($217.50) per week (less during promotions)—with unlimited mileage, VAT, and CDW included in the net fee.

Hertz (tel. toll free 800/654-3001 in the U.S. and Canada) offers an unlimited-mileage Ford Fiesta for as low as £119 ($178.50) per week, plus VAT, CDW, and PAI. The main Hertz office is at 35 Edgware Rd., Marble Arch, London W1 (tel. 071/402-4242; tube: Marble Arch).

PARKING   Driving around London is a tricky business. The city is a warren of one-way streets, and parking spots are at a premium.

In addition to strategically placed, expensive garages, central

London offers metered parking. But be aware that traffic wardens are famous for issuing substantial fines when the meter runs out. The time limit and the cost of metered parking are posted on the meter. Zones marked "Permit Holders Only" are for local residents. If you violate these sacrosanct places, your vehicle is likely to be towed away. A yellow line along the curb indicates "No Parking"; a double yellow line signifies "No Waiting." However, at night (meters indicate exact times) and on Sunday, you're allowed to park along a curb with a single yellow line.

DRIVING RULES AND REQUIREMENTS In England, as you probably know, you drive on the left and pass on the right. Road signs are clear and the international symbols unmistakable.

Your passport and driver's license must be presented when you rent a car. No special British license is needed. The prudent driver will secure a copy of the *British Highway Code,* available from almost any stationer or newsstand. Wearing seat belts by both front and rear seat occupants is mandatory in the British Isles.

Warning: Pedestrian crossings are marked by striped lines (zebra striping) on the road; flashing lights near the curb indicate that drivers must stop and yield the right of way if a pedestrian has stepped into the zebra zone to cross the street.

ROAD MAPS The best road map of the country, especially if you're trying to locate an obscure village, is *Ordnance Survey Motor Atlas of Great Britain,* revised annually and published by Temple Press. It's available at most bookstores, including W. & G. Foyle Ltd., 113–119 Charing Cross Rd., WC2 (tel. 071/439-8501).

BREAKDOWNS A membership in one of the two major auto clubs in England can be helpful: the **Automobile Association,** Fanum House, Basingstoke, Hampshire RG21 2EA (tel. 0256/20123 for information), and the **Royal Automobile Club,** P.O. Box 700, Spectrum, Bond Street, Bristol, Avon BS99 1RB (tel. 0272/232340 for information). Membership in one of these clubs is usually handled by a car-rental agent. In London, the 24-hour number to call for breakdown service is 0800/887766 for the AA and 0800/828282 for the RAC. Members in either club are entitled to free legal and technical advice on motoring matters, as well as a range of discounts on motor-related products and services. All motorways are provided with special emergency phones connected to police traffic units. The police can also contact an automobile club on your behalf.

GASOLINE Gasoline, called "petrol" by the British, is usually sold by the liter, with 4.5 liters making an imperial gallon. Prices, incidentally, will be much higher than you are accustomed to paying, and you'll probably have to serve yourself. In some remote areas, stations are few and far between, and many are closed on Sunday.

BY BICYCLE

You can rent bicycles by the day or week from a number of firms. One is **On Your Bike,** 52–54 Tooley St., SE1 (tel. 071/378-6669; tube: London Bridge). It is open Monday through Friday from 9am to 6pm and Saturday from 9:30am to 4:30pm. There's an inventory of some 50 bikes, rented by day or week. The 10-speed sports bikes, with high seats and low-slung handlebars, cost £8 ($12) per day or £30 ($45) per week and require a £50 ($75) deposit. Also popular are 18-gear mountain bikes, with straight handlebars and oversize gears. Designed for rough terrain, they are useful on roads of "backstreet London." These cost £15 ($22.50) per day or £60 ($90) per week and require a £200 ($300) deposit. Deposits are payable by MasterCard or VISA. The store also operates a branch near Victoria Station at 22–24 Buckingham Palace Rd., Victoria, SW1 (tel. 071/630-6669; tube: Victoria Station), convenient for cycling through the royal parks.

ON FOOT

London is too vast and sprawling to explore entirely on foot, but if you use public transportation for the long distances and your feet for the narrow crooked lanes, you should do fine. Remember that cars drive on the left. Always look both ways before stepping off a curb. Unlike in some countries, vehicles in London have right of way over pedestrians.

FAST FACTS LONDON

Airport   See "Orientation" earlier in this chapter.

American Express   The main Amex office is 6 Haymarket, SW1 (tel. 071/930-4422; tube: Piccadilly Circus). Full services are available from 9am to 5pm on Monday through Friday and from 9am to noon on Saturday. At other times—Saturday from noon to 6pm and Sunday from 10am to 4pm—only the foreign-exchange bureau is open. The American Express office at the British Travel Centre, Rex House, 4–12 Lower Regent St., SW1 (tel. 071/839-2682; tube: Piccadilly Circus), is open from 9am to 6:30pm on Monday through Friday and from 10am to 4pm on Saturday and Sunday. There are four other London locations.

Area Code   London has two telephone area codes—071 and 081. The **071** area code is for central London within a 4-mile radius of Charing Cross (including the City, Knightsbridge, Oxford Street, and as far south as Brixton). The **081** area code is for outer London (including Heathrow Airport, Wimbledon, and Greenwich). Within London, you will need to dial the area code when calling from one section of the city to the other, but not within a section. The country code for England is **44.**

Babysitters   Your hotel may be able to recommend someone, and advertised in the yellow pages are organizations that provide registered nurses and carefully screened mothers, as well as trained nannies, as sitters. One such is **Childminders,** 9 Paddington St., W1M 3LA (tel. 071/935-9763; tube: Regent's Park). You pay £3.85 ($5.80) per hour in the daytime and £2.65 ($4) per hour at night. There is a 4-hour minimum. You must also pay reasonable transportation costs. Another company is **Universal Aunts,** P.O. Box 304, London SW4 ONN (tel. 071/738-8937), established in 1921 and providing such services as child care, mother's helpers, proxy parents, and nannies. Interviews can be arranged in the Fulham-Chelsea area. You must call first for an appointment or a booking.

Business Hours   Banks are usually open Monday through Friday from 9:30am to 3:30pm. Business **offices** are open Monday through Friday from 9am to 5pm; the lunch break lasts an hour, but most places stay open during that time. **Pubs** and **bars** are allowed to stay open from 11am to 11pm on Monday through Saturday and noon to 3pm and 7 to 10:30pm or 11pm on Sunday. Many pubs observe these extended hours; others prefer to close from 3 to 5:30pm. London **stores** generally open at 9am and close at 5:30pm, staying open until 7pm on Wednesday or Thursday. Most central shops close on Saturday around 1pm. They do not close for lunch earlier.

Car Rentals See "Getting Around" in this chapter.

Climate See "When to Go" in Chapter 2.

Currency See "Information, Entry Requirements & Money" in Chapter 2.

Currency Exchange In general, banks in London provide the best exchange rates, and you're likely to get a better rate for traveler's checks than for cash. There are branches of the main banks at London's airports, but they charge a small fee. There are also Bureaux de Change at the airports and around London that charge a fee for cashing traveler's checks and personal U.K. checks, and for changing foreign currency into pounds sterling. Some travel agencies, such as American Express and Thomas Cook, also have currency-exchange services.

Dentists For dental emergencies, call Emergency Dental Service (tel. **071/752-0133).** The service is available 24 hours a day.

Doctors In an emergency, contact Doctor's Call at **071/351-5312.** Some hotels also have physicians on call. Medical Express, 117A Harley St., W1 (tel. 071/499-1991; tube: Great Portland Street), is a private British clinic; it is not part of the free British medical establishment. For filling the British equivalent of a U.S. prescription, there is a surcharge of £20 ($30) on top of the cost of the medication; a British doctor must validate the U.S. prescription. The clinic is open Monday through Friday from 9am to 5pm and Saturday from 9:30am to 2pm.

Documents Required See "Information, Entry Requirements & Money" in Chapter 2.

Driving Rules See "Getting Around" earlier in this chapter.

Drugstores In Britain they're called "chemist shops." Every police station in the country has a list of emergency chemists (dial "0" [zero] and ask the operator for the local police). One of the most centrally located chemists, keeping long hours, is **Bliss The Chemist,** 5 Marble Arch, W1 (tel. 071/723-6116; tube: Marble Arch). It is open daily from 9am to midnight. Every London neighborhood has a branch of the ubiquitous **Boots,** the leading pharmacist of Britain.

Electricity British current is 240 volts, AC cycle, roughly twice the voltage of North American current, which is 115–120 volts, AC cycle. You will probably not be able to plug the flat pins of your appliance's plugs into the holes of British wall outlets without suitable converters or adapters. Some (but not all) hotels will supply them for guests. Experienced travelers bring their own transformers. An electrical supply shop will also have what you need. Be forewarned that you will destroy the inner workings of your appliance (and possibly start a fire as well) if you plug an American appliance directly into a European electrical outlet without a transformer.

Embassies/High Commissions For passports, visas, whatever your problem, London has official representatives from nearly all countries of the world. The **U.S. Embassy** is at 24 Grosvenor Sq., W1 (tel. 071/499-9000; tube: Bond Street). However, for passport and visa information, go to the **U.S. Passport & Citizenship Unit,** 55–56 Upper Brook St., London, W1 (tel. 071/499-9000, ext. 2563; tube: Marble Arch). Hours are Monday through Friday from 8:30am to noon and from 2 to 4pm. On Tuesday, the office closes at noon. The **Canadian High Commission,** MacDonald House, 1 Grosvenor Sq., W1 (tel. 071/692-9492; tube: Bond Street), handles visa and passport problems for Canada. Hours are Monday through Friday from 9am to 5pm. The **Australian High Commission** is at Australia House, the Strand, WC2 (tel. 071/379-4334; tube: Charing Cross or Aldwych); it's open Monday through Friday from 10am to 4pm. The **New Zealand High Commission** is at New Zealand House, 80 Haymarket at Pall Mall, SW1 (tel. 071/930-8422; tube: Charing Cross or Piccadilly Circus); it's open Monday through Friday from 10am to 4pm. The **Irish Embassy** is at 17 Grosvenor Place, SW1 (tel. 071/235-2171; tube: Hyde Park Corner); it's open Monday through Friday from 9:30am to 5pm.

Emergencies In London, for police, fire, or an ambulance, dial **999.**

Etiquette Be normal, be quiet. The British don't like hearing other people's conversations. In pubs you are not expected to buy a round of drinks unless someone has bought you a drink. Don't talk religion in pubs, and it's best to avoid the subject of politics, especially questions dealing with "the Irish issue."

Eyeglasses If your glasses are lost or broken, try **Selfridges Opticians** on the street level of **Selfridges** department store, 400 Oxford St., W1 (tel. 071/629-1234, ext. 3889; tube: Bond Street or Marble Arch), open Monday through Saturday from 9:30am to 7pm and Thursday until 8pm. Contact lenses are also available on the same day, in most cases. Multifocal lenses sometimes take two to three working days to complete. It's always wise to carry a copy of your eyeglass prescription when you travel.

Hairdressers/Barbers Hairdressers and hairstylists crop up on most major London street corners (a slight exaggeration), and they range from grandly imperial refuges of English dowagers to punk-rock citadels of purple hair and chartreuse mascara. One of the most visible—and one of the best—is a branch of **Vidal Sassoon,** 11 Floral St., WC2 (tel. 071/240-6635; tube: Covent Garden). Unlike some other Sassoon outlets, this one caters to both men and women. The shop is open Monday through Friday from 10am to 7:30pm and Saturday from 8:45am to 5:45pm.

Holidays See "When to Go" in Chapter 2.

Hospitals The following offer emergency care in London 24 hours a day, with the first treatment free under the National Health Service: **Royal Free Hospital,** Pond St., NW3 (tel. 071/794-0500; tube: Belsize Park), and **University College Hospital,** Gower St., WC1 (tel. 071/387-9300; tube: Warren Street). Many other London hospitals also have accident and emergency departments.

Hotlines The **Capital Helpline** (tel. 071/388-7575) can answer almost any question about London. For police or medical emergencies, dial **999** (no coins required). If you're in some sort of legal emergency, call **Release** at 071/729-9904, 24 hours a day. The **Rape Crisis Line** is 071/837-1600, also in service 24 hours a day. **Samaritans,** 46 Marshall St., W1 (tel. 071/734-2800; tube: Oxford

Circus), maintains a 24-hour crisis hotline that helps with all kinds of trouble, even threatened suicides. **Alcoholics Anonymous** (tel. 071/352-3001) answers its hotline daily from 10am to 10pm. The **AIDS** 24-hour hotline is toll-free 0800/567-123.

Information   See "Information, Entry Requirements & Money" in Chapter 2 and "Orientation" earlier in this chapter.

Laundry/Dry Cleaning   Danish Express Laundry, 16 Hinde St., W1 (tel. 071/935-6306; tube: Marble Arch)—open Monday through Friday from 8:30am to 5:30pm and Saturday from 9:30am to 12:30pm—will clean, repair, or alter clothes, even repair shoes. It's one of the best places in London for such services. One of the leading dry-cleaning establishments of London is **Sketchley,** 49 Maddox St., W1 (tel. 071/629-1292), with more than three dozen branches. Check the yellow pages of the London phone book or call 081/300-5552 for a location convenient to your hotel. And if you're in the vicinity of the Bloomsbury B&Bs, you may choose **Red and White Laundries,** 78 Marchmont St., WC1 (tel. 071/387-3667; tube: Russell Square), open daily from 7am to 9pm.

Libraries   London's best collection of periodicals and reference materials is **Westminster Central Reference Library,** St. Martin's St., WC2 (tel. 071/798-2034; tube: Leicester Square). It opens Monday through Saturday at 10am.

Liquor Laws   No alcohol is served to anyone under the age of 18. Children under 16 aren't allowed in pubs, except in certain rooms, and then only when accompanied by a parent or guardian. Don't drink and drive; penalties for drunk driving are stiff, even if you are an overseas visitor. Restaurants are allowed to serve liquor during the same hours as pubs; however, only people who are eating a meal on the premises can be served a drink. A meal, incidentally, is defined as "substantial refreshment." And you have to eat and drink sitting down. In hotels, liquor may be served from 11am to 11pm to both residents and nonresidents; after 11pm, only residents may be served.

Lost Property   To find lost property, first report to the police and they will advise you where to apply for its return. Taxi drivers are required to hand over property left in their vehicles to the nearest police station. The property may also be turned over to the **Taxi Lost Property Office,** 15 Penton St., N1 (tel. 071/833-0996; tube: Angel Station), open Monday through Friday from 9am to 4pm. London Transport's Lost Property Office will try to assist personal visitors only at their office at 200 Baker St., NW1 (tel. 071/486-2496), open from 9:30am to 2pm Monday through Friday. For items lost on British Rail, report the loss as soon as possible to the station on the line where the loss occurred. For lost passports, credit cards, or money, report the loss and circumstances immediately to the nearest police station. For lost passports, you should go directly to your embassy or high commission. The address will be in the telephone book, or see "Embassies/High Commissions," above. For lost credit cards, also report to the appropriate organization; the same holds true for lost traveler's checks.

Luggage Storage/Lockers   Places for renting lockers or storing luggage are widely available in London. Lockers can be rented at airports such as Heathrow or Gatwick and at all major rail stations, including Victoria Station. In addition, there are dozens of independently operated storage companies in the London area. The usual charge is £3 to £5 ($4.50 to $7.50) per week per item. Check the yellow pages in your directory for the closest establishment.

Mail   Letters and parcels may, as a rule, be addressed to you at any post office except a town suboffice. The words "To Be Called For" or "Poste Restante" must appear in the address. When claiming your mail, always carry some sort of identification, preferably your passport. Poste Restante service is provided solely for the convenience of travelers, and it may not be used in the same town for more than 3 months. It can be redirected, upon request, for up to 3 months. An airmail letter to North America costs 39p (60¢), and postcards require a 33p (50¢) stamp. Letters generally take 7 to 10 days to arrive from the United States.

Maps   See "Street Maps" under "Orientation" earlier in this chapter.

Money   See "Information, Entry Requirements & Money" in Chapter 2.

Newspapers/Magazines   *The Times* is tops, then the *Telegraph,* the *Daily Mail,* and the *Guardian,* all London dailies carrying the latest news. The *International Herald Tribune,* published in Paris, and an international edition of *USA Today,* beamed via satellite, are available daily. Copies of *Time* and *Newsweek* are also sold at most newsstands. Small magazines, such as *Time Out* and *City Limits,* contain much useful data about the latest happenings in London, including theatrical and cultural events.

Photographic Needs   The **Flash Centre,** 54 Brunswick Centre, WC1 (tel. 071/837-6163; tube: Russell Square), is considered the best professional photographic equipment supplier in London. You can purchase your film next door at **Leeds Film and Hire,** which has a wide-ranging stock. Kodachrome is accepted for 48-hour processing.

Police   In an emergency, dial **999** (no coin required). You can also go to one of the local police branches in central London, including **New Scotland Yard,** Broadway (without number), SW1 (tel. 071/230-1212; tube: St. James's Park).

Post Office   Post offices and subpost offices are centrally located and open Monday through Friday from 9am to 5:30pm and on Saturday from 9:30am to noon. The **main post office,** at King Edward Street, EC1A 1AA, near St. Paul's Cathedral (tel. 071/239-5047; tube: St. Paul's), is open Monday through Friday from 8:30am to 6:30pm. The **Trafalgar Square Post Office,** 24–28 William IV St., WC2N 4DL (tel. 071/239-5047; tube: Charing Cross), operates as three separate businesses: inland and international postal service and banking, open Monday through Saturday from 8am to 8pm; philatelic postage stamp sales, open Monday through Friday from 10am to 7pm and Saturday from 10am to 4:30pm; and the post shop, selling greeting cards and stationery, open Monday through Friday from 9am to 6:30pm and Saturday from 9:30am to 5pm. Other post offices and subpost offices are open Monday through Friday from 9am to 5:30pm and Saturday from 9am to 12:30pm. Many subpost offices and some main post offices close for an hour at lunchtime.

Radio   There are 24-hour radio channels operating throughout the United Kingdom, including London. They offer mostly pop music and "chat shows" during the night. Some "pirate" radio stations add more spice. So-called legal FM stations are BBC1 (104.8); BBC2 (89.1), BBC3 (between 90 and 92), and the classical station, BBC4 (95). There is also the BBC Greater London Radio (94.9) station, with lots of rock, plus LBC Crown (97.3), with much news and reports of "what's on" in London. Pop/rock U.S. style is heard on Capital FM (95.8), and if you like jazz, Jamaican reggae, or salsa, tune in to Choice FM (96.9). Jazz FM (102.2) also offers blues and big-band music.

Religious Services   Service times are posted outside places of worship. Almost every creed is represented in London. The **American Church in London** is at 79A Tottenham Court Rd., W1 (tel. 071/580-2791; tube: Goodge Street). A worship service is conducted on Sunday from 11am to noon. The London Tourist Board has a fairly complete list of various churches. **Protestants** might want to attend a Sunday morning service at either Westminster Abbey (tel. 071/222-5152), or St. Paul's Cathedral (tel. 071/248-2705). Service times vary at St. Paul's, so it's best to call ahead. At Westminster Abbey, Sunday services are at 8, 10, and 11:15am and 3, 5:45, and 6:30pm. **Roman Catholics** gravitate to Westminster Cathedral (not to be confused with Westminster Abbey), Ashley Place (without number), SW1 (tel. 071/834-7452). Masses are conducted here at 7, 8, 9, and 10:30am and noon and 5:30 and 7pm.

Rest Rooms   They are usually found at signs saying "Public Toilets." Women should expect to pay from 5p (8¢); men usually pay nothing. The English often call toilets "loos." Automatic toilets, found on many streets, are sterilized after each use and cost around 10p (15¢).

Safety   Theft here is not as big a problem, perhaps, as in U.S. cities like Miami, Los Angeles, and New York. Muggings mainly occur in poor areas. As for murder and assault, most are reported within families and kin groups. The best advice is to use discretion and a little common sense and keep to well-lit areas. Be aware of your immediate surroundings. Wear a moneybelt and watch your cameras and purses. These precautions will minimize the possibility of your becoming a victim of crime. Every society has its criminals. It's your responsibility to be aware and alert, even in the most heavily touristed areas.

Shoe Repair   Most major Underground stations, including centrally located Piccadilly Circus, have "heel bars"—British for shoe-repair centers. Mostly, these are for quickie jobs. For major repairs, go to one of the major department stores (see "Department Stores" under "Shopping A to Z," in Chapter 8). Otherwise, patronize **Jeeves Snob Shop,** 7 Pont St., SW1 (tel. 071/235-1101; tube: Knightsbridge).

Smoking   Most U.S. cigaret brands are available in London. Antismoking laws are tougher than ever. Smoking is strictly forbidden in the Underground, including the cars and the platforms. Smoking is not permitted on buses and is increasingly frowned upon in many other places.

Taxes   As part of an energy-saving program, the British government has added a special 25% tax on gasoline (petrol). There is no local sales tax in cities and towns, but a 17½% value-added tax (VAT) is added to all hotel and restaurant bills. The VAT is also included in the cost of many of the items you purchase to take home with you. At shops that participate in the Retail Export Scheme, it is possible to get a refund sent to you at home for the amount of the VAT on your purchases. Ask the salesperson for a Retail Export Scheme form (Form VAT 407) and a stamped preaddressed envelope to return it in; to be eligible, you must have your passport with you when you make the purchase. Save the VAT forms along with your sales receipts to show at British Customs when you leave. You may also have to show the actual purchases to Customs officials at airports or other ports of departure. After the form has been stamped by Customs, mail it back to the shop in the envelope provided—before you leave the United Kingdom.

Here are three organizing tips to help you through the Customs procedures: (1) keep your VAT forms with your passport, as Customs is often located near Passport Control; (2) pack your purchases in a carry-on bag so that you will have them handy after you've checked your other luggage; (3) and allow yourself enough time at your departure point to find a mailbox.

Taxis See "Getting Around" earlier in this chapter.

Telephone/Telex/Fax For directory assistance for London, dial **142;** for the rest of Britain, **192.** To call London from the United States, dial 011 (international code), 44 (Britain's country code), 071 or 081 (London's area codes), and the seven-digit local telephone number.

British TeleCom is carrying out a massive improvement program of its public pay-phone service. During the transitional period, you could encounter four types of pay phones. The old-style (gray) pay phone is being phased out, but there are many still in use. You will need 10p (15¢) coins to operate such phones, but you should not use this type for overseas calls. Its replacement is a blue-and-silver push-button model that accepts coins of any denomination. The other two types of phones require cards instead of coins to operate. The Cardphone takes distinctive green cards specially designed for it. These cards are available in five values—£1 ($1.50), £2 ($3), £4 ($6), £10 ($15), and £20 ($30)—and are reusable until the total value has expired. Cards can be purchased from newsstands and post offices. Finally, the credit-call pay phone operates on credit cards—Access (MasterCard), VISA, American Express, and Diners Club—and is most common at airports and large railway stations.

Phone numbers in Britain outside of the major cities consist of an exchange name plus telephone number. In order to dial the number, you will need the code of the exchange being called. Information sheets on call-box walls give the codes in most instances. If your code is not there, however, call the operator by dialing 100. In major cities, phone numbers consist of the exchange code and number (seven digits or more). These digits are all you need to dial if you are calling from within the same city. If you are calling from elsewhere, you will need to prefix them with the dialing code for the city. Again, you will find these codes on the call-box information sheets. If you do not have the telephone number, call directory assistance (see the numbers above).

Telex and fax are restricted mostly to business premises and hotels. If your hotel has a telex or fax, they will send a message for you but you may have to arrange in advance for the receipt of a reply. Otherwise, go to **Chesham Executive Centre,** 150 Regent St., W1 (tel. 071/439-6288; tube: Piccadilly Circus). They rent offices by the hour and have secretarial and stenographic services; they also accept walk-in business and will send fax messages. The cost of sending a one-page fax from London to anywhere in the world is £2.50 ($3.80), plus VAT and the cost of the phone call. Hours are 9am to 6pm on Monday through Friday and 9am to noon on Saturday. See also Area Code, above.

Television TV starts around 6am with breakfast and educational programs. Lighter entertainment begins around 4 to 5pm, after the children's programs, and continues until around midnight. There are four television channels—two commercial and two BBC without commercials.

Time   England follows Greenwich mean time (5 hours ahead of ET), with British summer time lasting (roughly) from the end of March to the end of October.

Tipping   In restaurants, service charges in the 15% to 20% range are usually added to the bill. Sometimes this is clearly marked; at other times it isn't. When in doubt, always ask. If service is not included, it is customary to add 15% to the bill. Sommeliers (wine stewards) get about £1 ($1.50) per bottle of wine served. Tipping in pubs is not common, although in cocktail bars the server usually gets about 75p ($1.10) per round of drinks. Hotels, like restaurants, often add a service charge of 10% to 15% to most bills. In smaller B&Bs, the tip is not likely to be included. Therefore, tip for special service, such as for the person who served you breakfast. If several persons have served you in a B&B, many guests ask that 10% or 15% be added to the bill and divided among the staff. Otherwise, for chamber service, give about 75p ($1.10) per day or about £4 ($6) per week. Tip porters about 75p ($1.10) per piece of luggage. It's standard to tip taxi drivers 10% to 15% of the fare, although a tip for a taxi driver should never be less than 20p (30¢), even for a short run. Theater ushers are not tipped.

Transit Information   Phone **071/222-1234,** 24 hours a day.

Water   Tap water in London is considered safe to drink. However, because the water is different, you might still experience a stomach upset. If in doubt, order bottled water.

Weather   Phone 071/246-8091.

Yellow Pages   The yellow pages in London are in English, but certainly not American English. Therefore, you'll find drugstores listed under "Chemists" or "Pharmacies."

3. NETWORKS & RESOURCES

FOR STUDENTS

The **University of London Student Union,** Malet Street (without number), WC1 (tel. 071/580-9551; tube: Goodge Street), the largest of its kind in the world, is the best place to go to learn about student activities in the Greater London area. The Union contains a swimming pool, a fitness center, a gymnasium, a general store, a sports shop, a ticket agency, banks, bars, inexpensive restaurants, venues for live events and discos, an office of STA Travel, and many other facilities. It is open Monday through Saturday from 9:30am to 11pm and Sunday from 9:30am to 10:30pm. Bulletin boards at the Union provide a rundown on sponsored events, some of which you might be able to attend; others might be "closed door."

FOR GAY MEN & LESBIANS

The **Lesbian and Gay Switchboard** (tel. 071/837-7324) is open 24 hours a day, providing information about gay-related London activities or advice in general.

The **Bisexual Helpline** (tel. 081/569-7500) offers useful information but only on Tuesday and Wednesday from 7:30 to 9:30pm. Harassment, gay bashing, and other such matters are handled by **Gay and Lesbian Legal Advice** (tel. 071/253-2043) on Monday through Friday from 7 to 10pm.

FOR WOMEN

The **London Rape Crisis Centre,** P.O. Box 69, WC1 (tel. 071/837-1600), operates 24 hours a day. Besides dealing with rape, it also offers women medical or legal advice. It can even arrange to have another woman accompany you to a doctor, clinic, or police station.

The leading feminist bookstore in London is **Silvermoon,** 64–68 Charing Cross Rd., WC2 (tel. 071/836-7906; tube: Leicester Square). Besides stocking literally thousands of titles by and about women, it sells tapes, videos, jewelry, T-shirts, and other items. It is open Monday through Saturday from 10am to 6:30pm.

LONDON ACCOMMODATIONS

London boasts some of the most famous and luxurious hotels in the world—Claridge's, the Dorchester, and the Ritz (where the term *ritzy* originated). It is in this bracket that you get the most in terms of architecture and comfort. Whereas some hotels have gone to no end to modernize their interiors, others have remained virtually unchanged, with built-in drafts and daisy-strewn wallpaper. In between, you come across new structures that seem to have been shifted bodily from Los Angeles.

Within the last decade, a new breed of charming small-scale hotels has emerged. They are known as *bijou* (jewel) or boutique hotels because of their small size and attention to detail. Many pose competition to the larger, stately establishments originally built by the Edwardians. Our selection of London hotels has incorporated as many of these charming but expensive newcomers as possible while retaining a select handful of the grand monuments to the past.

If you've arrived as a first-time visitor and plan to seek low-cost lodgings, you should know that many of central London's bed-and-breakfast establishments and low-budget hotels are in poor condition. In fact, since the last edition of this book was researched, I have received more complaints about B&B hotels in London than in any destination on the continent of Europe. I've listed what I consider adequate B&B lodgings, but I present most of them without any particular enthusiasm. There are a few good ones, but they tend to be booked year round.

My task is to select those hotels that combine maximum comfort with good value, in all price categories.

RATES All hotels, motels, inns, and guesthouses in Britain with four bedrooms or more (including self-catering accommodations) are required to display notices showing minimum and maximum overnight charges. The notice must be displayed in a prominent position in the reception area or at the entrance. The prices shown must include any service charge and may include VAT, and it must be made clear whether or not these items are included; if VAT is not included, then it must be shown separately. If meals are provided with the accommodation, this must be made clear too. If prices are not standard for all rooms, then only the lowest and highest prices need be given.

Classifying London hotels into a rigid price category is a bit tricky. For example, sometimes it's possible to find a moderately priced room in an otherwise "very expensive" hotel or an expensive room in an otherwise inexpensive property. That's because most hotel rooms—at least the older properties—are not standardized; therefore, the range of rooms goes from superdeluxe suites to the "maid's pantry," now converted into a small bedroom.

The following price categories are only for a quick general reference, and note that there will be many exceptions to this quick rule-of-thumb. It should also be noted that London is one of the most expensive cities in the world for hotels. Therefore, what might be viewed as expensive in your hometown could very likely be classified as "inexpensive" in London.

The **very expensive** category includes hotels that charge about £185 ($277.50) and up for a double room. Hotels ranked **expensive** charge from about £120 to £185 ($180 to $277.50) for a double. **Moderate** hotels generally range from £80 to £120 ($120 to $180) for a double. **Inexpensive** refers to doubles under £80 ($120). Unless otherwise noted, prices are for rooms with private bath, breakfast (often continental instead of English), 17½% VAT, and a 10% to 15% service charge. (VAT and service charges are always included in the prices quoted in this guide, unless otherwise indicated in the write-ups.) **Parking** rates are per night.

RESERVATIONS   Most hotels require at least a night's **deposit** before they will reserve a room. Preferably, this can be accomplished with an international money order or, if agreed to in advance, with a personal check. You can usually cancel a room reservation one week ahead of time and receive a full refund. A few hotels will return money three days before the reservation date, but some will take a deposit and never return it, even if you cancel far in advance. Many budget hotel owners operate on such a narrow profit margin that they find just buying stamps for airmail replies too expensive by their standards. Therefore, it's most important that you should enclose a prepaid International Reply Coupon with your payment, especially if you're writing to a budget hotel. Better yet, call and speak to the hotel of your choice, or send a fax.

If you're booking at a chain hotel, such as a Hilton, you can call toll free in North America and easily make reservations over the phone. Whenever such a service is available, toll-free **800 numbers** are indicated in the individual hotel write-ups.

If you arrive without a reservation, begin your search for a room as early in the day as possible. If you arrive late at night, you may have to take what you can get, often in a much higher price range than you'd like to pay.

A FEW REMINDERS   Elevators are called "lifts," and some of them predate Teddy Roosevelt's Rough Riders and act it. They are, however, regularly inspected and completely safe.

As mentioned earlier, hotel rooms are somewhat cooler than you're accustomed to. It's supposed to be more healthful that way.

What is termed continental breakfast consists of coffee or tea and some sort of roll or pastry. An English breakfast is a fairly lavish meal of tea or coffee, cereal, eggs, bacon, ham or sausages, toast, and jam.

If you want to remain undisturbed, don't forget to hang the "Do Not Disturb" sign on your doorknob. English hotel service personnel—most of whom aren't English—have a disconcerting habit of bursting in simultaneously with their knock.

1. MAYFAIR

VERY EXPENSIVE

BROWN'S HOTEL, 29–34 Albemarle St., London W1A 4SW. Tel. 071/493-6020, or toll free 800/435-4542 in the U.S. and Canada. Fax 071/493-9381. 133 rms, 6 suites. A/C MINIBAR TV TEL **Tube:** Green Park.
$ Rates: £193–£205 ($139.50–$307.50) single; £211–£223 ($316.50–$334.50) double; from £393 ($589.50) suite. Breakfast £13.75 ($20.60) extra. AE, DC, MC, V.

Brown's is highly recommended for those who want a fine hotel among the top traditional choices. This upper-crust prestigious establishment was created by James Brown, a former manservant of Lord Byron's. He and his wife, Sarah, who had been Lady Byron's personal maid, wanted to go into business for themselves. Brown knew the tastes of gentlemen of breeding and wanted to create a dignified clublike place for them. His dream came true when the hotel, a former town house at 23 Dover Street, opened in 1837, the year Queen Victoria ascended the throne.

Today, Brown's Hotel occupies some 14 historic houses on two streets just off Berkeley Square. Old-fashioned comfort is dispensed with courtesy. A liveried doorman ushers you to an antique reception desk, where you check in. The street-floor lounges are inviting, including the Roosevelt Room, the Rudyard Kipling Room (the famous author was a frequent visitor here), and the paneled St. George's Bar (for the drinking of "spirits").

The guest rooms vary considerably and are a tangible record of the history of England, showing restrained taste in decoration and appointments. Even the washbasins are semiantiques.

Dining/Entertainment: A good old-fashioned English tea is served in the Albemarle Room. Men are required to wear jackets and ties in the dining room, which has a quiet dignity and unmatched service. Most meals are à la carte, although there is also a set luncheon menu at £28 ($42) and a fixed-price dinner at £32 ($48)—including service and VAT.

Services: 24-hour room service, laundry, dry cleaning, babysitting.

Facilities: Men's hairdresser, car-rental agency.

CLARIDGE'S, Brook St. (without number), London W1A 2JQ. Tel. 071/629-8860, or toll free 800/223-6800 in the U.S. and Canada. Fax 071/499-2210. 109 rms, 56 suites. A/C TV TEL **Tube:** Bond St.
$ Rates: £185–£215 ($277.50–$322.50) single; £235–£280 ($352.50–$420) double; from £470 ($705) suite. Breakfast £15.75 ($23.60) extra. AE, DC, MC, V.

✪ Claridge's has been known from the mid-Victorian era under its present name, although an earlier "lodging house" complex occupied much of the hotel's present area as far back as the reign of George IV. It has cocooned royal visitors in an ambience of discreet elegance since the time of the Battle of Waterloo. Queen Victoria visited Empress Eugénie of France here, and thereafter Claridge's lent respectability to the idea of ladies dining out in public. The hotel took on its present modest exterior in 1898. Inside, art deco decor was added in the 1930s, much of it still existing agreeably along with antiques and TVs. The guest rooms are spacious, many having generous-size baths complete with dressing rooms and numerous amenities. Suites can be connected by private foyers closed away from the main corridors, providing large self-contained units suitable for a sultan and his entourage.

Dining/Entertainment: Excellent food is stylishly served in the intimacy of the Causerie, renowned for its lunchtime smörgåsbord and pretheater suppers, and in the more formal The Restaurant, with its English and French specialties. From The Restaurant, the strains of the Hungarian Quartet, a Claridge's institution since 1902, can be heard in the adjacent foyer during lunch and dinner. Both the Causerie and The Restaurant are open daily from noon to 3pm. The Causerie serves evening meals from 5:30 to 11pm, with dinner offered in The Restaurant from 7 to 11:15pm.

Services: 24-hour room service, valet, laundry, babysitting.

Facilities: Adjacent health club for male guests, hairdresser, car-rental agency.

THE DORCHESTER, 53 Park Lane, London W1A 2HJ. Tel. 071/629-8888, or toll free 800/727-9820 in the U.S. Fax 071/409-0114. 197 rms, 55 suites. A/C MINIBAR TV TEL **Tube:** Hyde Park Corner.

$ Rates: £180 ($270) single; £215–£240 ($322.50–$360) double; from £330 ($495) suite. VAT extra. Continental breakfast £10.50 ($15.80) extra. AE, DC, MC.

✪ In 1929, with an increased demand for hotel space in the expensive Park Lane district, a famous mansion—whose inhabitants had been known for everything from great debauchery to great aesthetic skills—was torn down. In its place was erected the finest hotel London had seen in many years. Breaking from the neoclassical tradition, the most ambitious architects of the era designed a building of reinforced concrete clothed in terrazzo slabs. Throughout the hotel, completely restored in 1990, you'll find a 1930s interpretation of Regency motifs. The flower arrangements and the elegance of the gilded-cage Promenade seem appropriate for a diplomatic reception, yet they convey a kind of sophisticated comfort in which guests from all over the world feel at ease. Those guests used to include General Dwight D. Eisenhower, Marlene Dietrich, and Bing Crosby; today's roster is likely to list Michael J. Fox, Cher, Tom Cruise, or Michael Jackson.

Owned by the sultan of Brunei, who invested $192 million in its makeover, the Dorchester boasts guest rooms featuring linen sheets, all the electronic gadgetry you'd expect from a world-class hotel, and double- and triple-glazed windows to keep out noise. The rooms are filled with plump armchairs, cherrywood furnishings, and, in many cases, four-poster beds. In mottled gray Italian marble with Lalique-style sconces, even the bathrooms are stylish. The best rooms open onto views of Hyde Park.

Dining/Entertainment: Two of the hotel's restaurants—The Terrace and The Grill—are considered among the finest dining establishments in London, and the Dorchester Bar is legendary. The gray-and-green Terrace is a historic room outfitted in a Regency motif with an overlay of chinoiserie—a combination that is especially sumptuous. When referring to its soaring columns capped with gilded palm fronds and mammoth swathes of filigree curtains, one English reviewer referred to it as "pure Cecil B. de Mille." The Terrace still features dancing, a tradition that goes back to the 1930s, when London's "bright young things" patronized the place. Today, unlike yesterday, there is a health-conscious *Menu Léger* to keep waistlines thin. In addition, the hotel also offers Cantonese cuisine in its Asian restaurant, The Oriental.

Services: 24-hour room service, laundry, dry cleaning, medical service.

Facilities: One of the best-outfitted health clubs in London, the Dorchester Spa; exclusive nightclub; business center; barbershop; hairdresser.

INN ON THE PARK, Hamilton Place (without number), Park Lane, London W1A 1AZ. Tel. 071/499-0888, or toll free 800/332-3442. Fax 071/493-1895. 201 rms, 26 suites. A/C MINIBAR TV TEL **Tube:** Hyde Park Corner.

$ Rates: £200 ($300) single; £245–£320 ($367.50–$480) double; from £400 ($600) suite. VAT extra. English breakfast £13.75 ($20.60) extra. AE, DC, MC, V. **Parking:** £12.25 ($18.40).

Inn on the Park, a member of the Four Seasons group, has captured the imagination of the glamour-mongers of the world ever since it was inaugurated by Princess Alexandra in 1970. With its smallish triangular garden and position amid one of the most expensive neighborhoods in the world, it sits behind a tastefully modern facade. Its clientele includes heads of state, superstars, and business executives. (Howard Hughes, who could afford anything, chose it as a retreat.) As you enter the reception area, you'll find that the acres of superbly crafted paneling and opulently conservative decor create the impression that the hotel is far older than it is. A gently inclined grand stairway leads to a symmetrical grouping of Chinese and European antiques flanked by cascades of fresh flowers.

The guest rooms are large and beautifully outfitted with well-chosen chintz patterns, reproduction antiques, and plush upholstery, along with dozens of well-concealed electronic extras. Ten of the largest rooms contain private conservatories.

Dining/Entertainment: The Cocktail Bar—a piano bar—serves drinks in a room where Wellington might have felt at home. Both restaurants create a most alluring rendezvous, especially the highly acclaimed Four Seasons, which is both elegant and stylish, with views opening onto Park Lane. The finest wines and continental specialties dazzle guests at lunch and at dinner, which is served until 11pm. The alternative dining choice is the less expensive Lanes Restaurant, rather popular with many members of London's business community. The coffee shop is open from 9am to 2am.

Services: 24-hour room service, valet, laundry, babysitting.

Facilities: Quality shops, theater desk, health club, garden, car-rental agency.

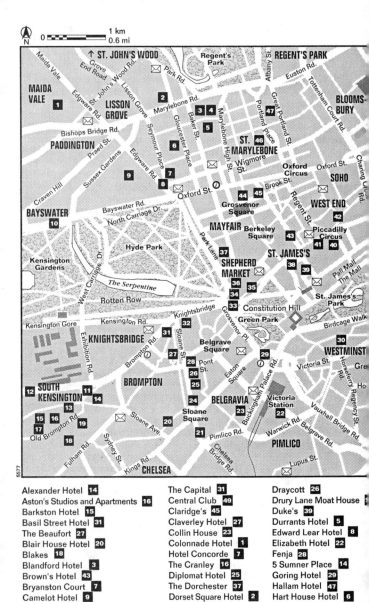

Alexander Hotel **14**	The Capital **31**	Draycott **26**
Aston's Studios and Apartments **16**	Central Club **49**	Drury Lane Moat House ▮
Barkston Hotel **15**	Claridge's **45**	Duke's **39**
Basil Street Hotel **31**	Claverley Hotel **27**	Durrants Hotel **5**
The Beaufort **27**	Collin House **23**	Edward Lear Hotel **8**
Blair House Hotel **20**	Colonnade Hotel **1**	Elizabeth Hotel **22**
Blakes **18**	Hotel Concorde **7**	Fenja **28**
Blandford Hotel **3**	The Cranley **16**	5 Sumner Place **14**
Brown's Hotel **43**	Diplomat Hotel **25**	Goring Hotel **29**
Bryanston Court **7**	The Dorchester **37**	Hallam Hotel **47**
Camelot Hotel **9**	Dorset Square Hotel **2**	Hart House Hotel **6**

**LONDON HILTON ON PARK LANE, 22 Park Lane, London
W1A 2HH. Tel. 071/493-8000,** or toll free 800/445-8667 in
the U.S. or Canada. Fax 071/493-4957. 448 rms, 54 suites. A/C
MINIBAR TV TEL **Tube:** Hyde Park Corner.

$ Rates: £165–£210 ($247.50–$315) single or double; £240
($360) single or double on Executive Floors; from £300 ($450)
suite. Continental breakfast £12.50 ($18.80) extra. AE, DC, MC,
V. **Parking:** £12.50 ($18.80).

The tallest building along Park Lane, and indeed one of the tallest

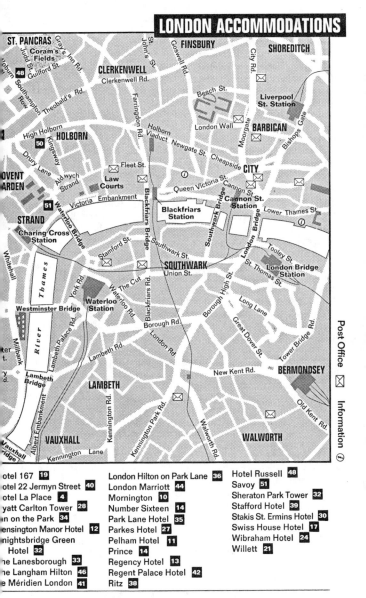

LONDON ACCOMMODATIONS

structures in London, this hotel created an uproar when it was constructed in 1963. There were persistent allegations that residents of its uppermost floors could spy on the boudoirs of faraway Buckingham Palace.

Now considered a linchpin of the London hotel scene and currently owned by Britain's Ladbroke chain, the Hilton is stylish and sophisticated. Graced with large picture windows overlooking London and Hyde Park, the guest rooms are decorated in tastefully restful colors, with fine copies of Georgian furniture. Six Executive

Floors offer private check in and a complimentary continental breakfast.

Dining/Entertainment: The 28th-floor Windows on the World restaurant features French/international cuisine and offers spectacular views over London; reservations are needed far in advance for a window table. There is dancing to a live band every night. Food is also served in the hotel's Café-Brasserie, and you can order Polynesian food at Trader Vic's downstairs. St. George's Bar is a fashionable rendezvous.

Services: 24-hour room service, valet, laundry, babysitting, concierge.

Facilities: Sauna, solarium, massage, business center, Hertz Rent-a-Car desk, theater-ticket booking desk.

LONDON MARRIOTT, Grosvenor Sq. (without number), London W1A 4AW. Tel. 071/493-1232, or toll free 800/524-2000 in the U.S. and Canada. Fax 071/491-3201. 223 rms, 12 suites. A/C MINIBAR TV TEL **Tube:** Bond St.

$ Rates: £160–£200 ($240–$300) single or double; from £300 ($450) suite. English breakfast £10.50 ($15.80) extra. AE, DC, MC, V. **Parking:** £25 ($37.50).

This hotel was first built in a grander era as the very conservative Hotel Europa. After Marriott poured millions into its refurbishment, only the very best elements—and, of course, much of the tradition—remained. This triumph of the decorator's art sits proudly behind a brick-and-stone Georgian facade on one of the most distinguished squares in London, Grosvenor Square. Its battalions of polite porters, doormen, and receptionists wait near the entrance along a side street. The U.S. embassy is just a few doors away.

Throughout the carefully crafted interior, combinations of pink, peach, ivory, and green are consistently in evidence. The breakfast room is a decorator's dream, filled with a cluster of Chippendale antiques and the kind of chintz that goes perfectly with masses of seasonal flowers. The accommodations, decorated in the Georgian style, contain all the electronic extras you'd expect.

Dining/Entertainment: Guests enjoy the Regent Lounge, which is outfitted in English country style. In the Diplomat, meals are served in an elegant yet comfortable setting. A contemporary cuisine, featuring dishes inspired by such places as California, France, Tuscany, and England, are served.

Services: 24-hour room service, valet, laundry, concierge, babysitting.

Facilities: Rooms for nonsmokers, health club facilities accessible from hotel, business center.

EXPENSIVE

PARK LANE HOTEL, Piccadilly (without number), London W1Y 8BX. Tel. 071/499-6321, or toll free 800/223-5652 in the U.S. and Canada. Fax 071/499-1965. 322 rms, 54 suites. MINIBAR TV TEL **Tube:** Hyde Park Corner.

$ Rates: £147 ($220.50) single; £175–£205 ($262.50–$307.50) double; from £230 ($345) suite. Continental breakfast £8.50 ($12.80) extra. AE, DC, MC, V. **Parking:** £25 ($37.50).

One of the long-established Park Lane hotels that has its own loyal clients and keeps winning new converts, this hotel is now the last of this breed to be privately owned by an English family. It was begun in 1913 by an enterprising former member of the Life Guards, who used advanced engineering techniques to construct the foundations and an intricately detailed iron skeleton. When its creator was tragically killed in World War I, residents mockingly referred to the empty shell as "the bird cage." Then, in 1924, one of London's leading hoteliers, Bracewell Smith, completed the construction, and a short time later the Park Lane became one of Europe's leading hotels.

Today you'll enter an intensely English hotel behind a discreet stone-block facade. One of its gateways, the Silver Entrance, is considered such an art deco marvel that its soaring columns have been used in many films, including *Shanghai Surprise,* the U.S. miniseries *The Winds of War,* and the British miniseries *Brideshead Revisited.* Designed in a ∪ shape, with a view overlooking Green Park, the Park Lane Hotel offers luxurious accommodations with double-glazed windows; the rooms are among the least expensive offered by the major Park Lane competitors. Many of the suites have marble fireplaces and the original marble-sheathed bathrooms.

Dining/Entertainment: The hotel's restaurant, Bracewell's, is recommended in Chapter 5. Bracewell's Bar is one of London's most popular cocktail hangouts, with a talented pianist; the chic decor is of Chinese cinnabar lacquer. A less expensive dining choice is the Brasserie on the Park, serving French-inspired cuisine (also recommended in Chapter 5).

Services: 24-hour room service, concierge, valet, laundry, dry cleaning, babysitting.

Facilities: Fitness center, business center, safety-deposit boxes, gift and newspaper shop, barbershop, women's hairdresser.

---

2. ST. JAMES'S & PICCADILLY CIRCUS

ST. JAMES'S

VERY EXPENSIVE

DUKES HOTEL, 35 St. James's Place, London SW1A 1NY. Tel. 071/491-4840. Fax 071/493-1264. 38 rms, 36 suites. TV TEL **Tube:** Green Park.

$ Rates: £180 ($270) single; £215–£275 ($322.50–$412.50) double; from £330 ($495) suite. English breakfast £11.75 ($17.60) extra. AE, DC, MC, V.

The Dukes provides elegance without ostentation. A hotel since 1908, it stands in a quiet courtyard off St. James's Street with its turn-of-the-century gas lamps. A short walk away are Buckingham Palace, St. James's Palace, and the Houses of Parliament. Shoppers will be near Bond Street and Piccadilly, and literature buffs will be interested to note that Oscar Wilde lived and wrote at St. James's Place for a time.

Each well-furnished guest room is decorated in the style of a particular English period, ranging from Regency to Edwardian. In lieu of air conditioning, there are ceiling fans. Renovations are ongoing, covering one floor every year on a never-ending basis.

Dining/Entertainment: Dukes' Restaurant is small, tasteful, and elegant, combining both classic British and continental cuisine with nouvelle cuisine. The fixed-price lunches at £19.95 ($29.90) are an excellent value, although the three-course fixed-price dinner is more expensive, at £28.50 ($42.80) per person. The hotel also has a clublike bar.

Services: 24-hour room service, laundry, babysitting.

LE MÉRIDIEN LONDON, 21 Piccadilly, London W1V 0BH.
Tel. 071/734-8000, or toll free 800/543-4300 in the U.S. Fax 071/437-3574. 222 rms, 41 suites. A/C MINIBAR TV TEL **Tube:** Piccadilly Circus.

$ Rates: £190–£210 ($285–$315) single; £210–£230 ($315–$345) double; from £275 ($412.50) suite. English breakfast £12.75 ($19.10) extra. AE, DC, MC, V. **Parking:** £20 ($30).

At the time of the hotel's 1908 opening, the Ionic arcade capping its arched neoclassical facade was considered the height of Edwardian extravagance. Le Méridien was instantly pronounced the grandest hotel in London, with such guests as Mary Pickford, but its huge expenses bankrupted its creator. New owners continued to make it one of the world's most stylish. After World War II, however, the hotel sank into a kind of musty obscurity until its lavish refurbishment during the revitalization of the Piccadilly theater district.

Today, enjoying its reincarnation, the hotel is considered the European flagship of the Méridien chain. Elaborately detailed plasterwork, stained glass, and limed-oak paneling are notable design elements. Except for the intricate beauty of the skylit reception area, the centerpiece of the hotel is the grand, soaring Oak Room Lounge, where gilded carvings and chandeliers of shimmering Venetian glass re-create Edwardian styles. The guest rooms are tasteful, exuding quality, comfort, and style.

Dining/Entertainment: The formal and very elegant Oak Room is recommended in Chapter 5. The Terrace Restaurant is less formal, a sun-flooded eyrie under the greenhouse walls of the facade's massive Ionic portico. There is, as well, a very British bar sheathed in hardwoods and filled with live piano music.

Services: 24-hour room service, laundry, hairdresser, babysitting.

Facilities: Champney's health club with large pool, saunas, steambaths, aerobic workshops, squash courts; billiard tables; business center.

RITZ, 150 Piccadilly, London W1V 9DG. Tel. 071/493-8181, or toll free 800/544-7570 in the U.S. Fax 071/493-2687. 115 rms, 14 suites. MINIBAR TV TEL **Tube:** Green Park.

$ Rates: £190–£220 ($285–$330) single; £220–£290 ($330–$435) double; from £505 ($757.50) suite. English breakfast £14.50 ($21.80) extra. AE, DC, MC, V. **Parking:** £35 ($52.50).

Built in the French Renaissance style in 1906, overlooking the landscapes of Green Park, the Ritz is synonymous with luxury. The original color scheme of apricot, cream, and dusty rose enhances the gold-leafed molding, marble columns, and potted palms. The gold-leafed statue *La Source* adorns the fountain of the oval-shaped Palm Court.

The guest rooms, each with its own character, are spacious and comfortable; most are air-conditioned. Many have marble fireplaces, elaborate gilded plasterwork, and a decor of soft pastel hues. All have radios and the availability of in-house films.

Dining/Entertainment: The Ritz is still the most fashionable place in London to meet for afternoon tea, at which a selection of finger sandwiches—including cucumber and smoked salmon—and specially made scones, cakes, and French pastries are served. The Ritz Restaurant, one of the loveliest dining rooms in the world, has been faithfully restored to its original splendor. Service is efficient yet unobtrusive, and the tables are spaced to allow the most private of conversations—perhaps the reason Edward and Mrs. Simpson dined here so frequently before they married.

Services: 24-hour room service, valet, laundry, babysitting.

Facilities: News kiosk, boutiques, access to nearby St. James's Health Club.

STAFFORD HOTEL, 16–18 St. James's Place, London SW1A 1NJ. Tel. 071/493-0111, or toll free in the U.S. 800/222-0939. Fax 493-7121. 67 rms, 7 suites. TV TEL **Tube:** Green Park.

$ Rates: £184 ($276) single; £200–£245 ($300–$367.50) double; from £253 ($379.50) suite. English breakfast £10.75 ($16.10) extra. AE, DC, MC, V.

Famous for its American Bar and the warmth of its Edwardian decor, the Stafford was built in the late 19th century as a private home on a cul-de-sac off one of London's most centrally located and busiest neighborhoods. It can be entered by St. James's Place or by a cobble-covered courtyard originally designed as a mews and known today as the Blue Ball Yard. Owned by the Cunard group, the Stafford has retained a country-house atmosphere, with touches of antique charm and modern amenities.

Each of the guest rooms is individually decorated, reflecting the

 FROMMER'S SMART TRAVELER: HOTELS

1. In inexpensive or moderately priced hotels, a room with a shower is cheaper than a room with a private bath. Even cheaper is a room with hot and cold running water and a corridor bathroom.
2. Consider a package tour (or book land arrangements with your air ticket). You'll often pay 30% or more less than individual "rack" rates (off-the-street, independent bookings).
3. If London hotels are not full, a little bargaining can bring down the cost of a hotel room. Be polite: Ask if there's a "businessperson's rate" or if schoolteachers get a discount. The technique works best when the hotel has a 40% vacancy at night and wants to fill those empty rooms.
4. At less expensive hotels that take credit cards, ask if payment by cash will get you a reduction.
5. If you're going to spend at least a week in London, ask about long-term discounts.

hotel's original function as a private home. A handful of the hotel's newest and plushest accommodations require a walk across the Blue Ball Yard.

Dining/Entertainment: The Stafford Restaurant is an elegant dining room lit with handsome chandeliers and wall sconces and accented with flowers, candles, and white napery. Classic international dishes are made from select fresh ingredients. Lunch costs from £19.50 ($29.30), dinner from £25 ($37.50). The previously mentioned American Bar (actually more like the memento-packed library of an English country house) is an especially cozy attraction.

Services: 24-hour room service, babysitting, concierge, secretarial service, laundry.

EXPENSIVE

HOTEL 22 JERMYN STREET, 22 Jermyn St., London SW1Y 6HL. Tel. 071/734-2353, or toll free 800/729-FLAG in the U.S. Fax 071/734-0750. 5 rms, 13 suites. MINIBAR TV TEL **Tube:** Piccadilly Circus.

$ Rates: £165 ($247.50) single or double; from £215 ($322.50) suite. English breakfast £11.50 ($17.30) extra. AE, DC, MC, V. **Parking:** Valet, £20 ($30).

Set behind a facade of gray stone with neoclassical embellishment, this structure was originally built in 1870 as an apartment house for English gentlemen doing business in London. Since 1915, it has been administrated by three generations of the Togna family, whose most recent scion closed it for a radical restoration in 1990. Now reveling in its new role as a chic and upscale boutique hotel, it offers an interior with many plants and the kind of art you might find in an elegant private home. The guest rooms, done in traditional English style, have masses of fresh flowers, chintzes, and furniture.

Services here include 24-hour room service, a concierge, a babysitting service, and a laundry. Guests have free use of Dictaphones and fax machines, and there's a health club nearby.

INEXPENSIVE

REGENT PALACE HOTEL, 12 Sherwood St., near Piccadilly Circus, London W1A 4BZ. Tel. 071/734-7000. Fax 071/734-6435. 887 rms (none with bath). TV TEL **Tube:** Piccadilly Circus.

$ Rates (including English breakfast): £45 ($67.50) single; £67 ($100.50) double. AE, DC, MC, V.

Considered a major focal point since it was built in 1915 at the edge of Piccadilly Circus, this is one of the largest hotels in Europe. Today, it's known for staunch loyalty to its original design: None of the rooms contains a private bath. (Shared facilities in the hallways are adequate, and each room has a sink with hot and cold running water. Some clients believe that this huge hotel's design reflects British life from another era.)

If guests stay for two nights or more, charges are reduced to £33 ($49.50) for a single and £66 ($99) for a double, including breakfast. The hotel's Original Carvery makes a good place to dine, and The Dome bistro is open for pretheater meals. Drinks are served in the Half Sovereign and the Planters bars. Coffee, sandwiches, and snacks are available in Antonio's Coffee Bar.

3. BLOOMSBURY

MODERATE

HOTEL RUSSELL, Russell Sq. (without number), London WC1 B5BE. Tel. 071/837-6470, or toll free 800/435-4542 in the U.S. Fax 071/837-2857. 308 rms, 19 suites. TV TEL **Tube:** Russell Sq.

$ Rates: £105 ($157.50) single; £120 ($180) double; from £150 ($225) suite. English breakfast £10 ($15) extra. AE, DC, MC, V.

A late-Victorian hotel facing the garden of this famous square and within easy reach of theaters and shopping, the Russell is run by Forte Hotels. The guest rooms, in contrast to the overall style of the hotel, are thoroughly modernized and up-to-date, with well-chosen fabrics and immaculately maintained baths.

The refurnished public rooms include an excellent carvery restaurant and a brasserie. A grill restaurant, Virginia Woolf's, specializes in pasta. All the dining establishments offer good value. The Kings Bar serves cocktails in the atmosphere of a London club, and you can enjoy draft beer in the country-pub ambience of the Benjamin's Bar. There are also 24-hour room service, a laundry, and a theater-ticket agent.

INEXPENSIVE

CENTRAL CLUB, 16-22 Great Russell St., London WC1B 3LR. Tel. 071/636-7512. Fax 071/636-5278. 100 rms. TV TEL **Tube:** Tottenham Court Road.

$ Rates: £31 ($46.50) single; £56 ($84) double; £17 ($25.50) per person in triple or quad. Breakfast from £2.50 ($3.80) extra. MC, V.

This large and attractive building was designed by Sir Edwin Lutyens (1869-1944), the famous architect, and built around 1932 as a YWCA. Although still vaguely affiliated with YWCA, it now functions as a hotel that accepts men, women, families, and groups traveling together. Each simple but comfortable guest room contains a radio and beverage-making facilities. Included in the rate is use of the lounges, coin-operated laundry facilities, hair salon, gym, and solarium. There's a coffee shop.

4. THE STRAND & COVENT GARDEN

THE STRAND

VERY EXPENSIVE

SAVOY, The Strand (without number), London WC2R 0EU. Tel. 071/836-4343, or toll free 800/223-6800 in the U.S. and

Canada. Fax 071/240-6040. 156 rms, 48 suites. A/C MINIBAR TV TEL **Tube:** Charing Cross.

$ Rates: £158 ($237) single; £180–£240 ($270–$360) double; from £332 ($498) suite. English breakfast £15.75 ($23.60) extra. VAT extra. AE, DC, MC, V. **Parking:** £20 ($30).

The Savoy is a London landmark, its eight stories of glazed tiles rising majestically between the Strand and the Thames. The hotel was built in 1889 by impresario Richard D'Oyly Carte as an annex to his nearby theater, where many Gilbert and Sullivan operettas were first performed. Today, one of the most vivid memories retained by many guests is of the sculpted frieze surrounding the upper reaches of the soaring lobby.

Through the Savoy's portals have passed famous personages of yesterday and today, everybody from royalty to stars of stage, screen, TV, and rock. Nowadays the hotel has regained the impeccable hospitality, service, and splendor of its early years.

Each guest room has a unique decor, with color-coordinated accessories, solid and comfortable furniture, and large closets. The units—48 with their own sitting rooms—contain an eclectic blend of antiques, such as gilt mirrors, Queen Anne chairs, and Victorian sofas. Guests find fresh flowers and fruit in their rooms on arrival.

Dining/Entertainment: The world-famous Savoy Grill has long been popular with a theatrical clientele, with Sarah Bernhardt among its most celebrated former customers. The even more elegant River Restaurant is in a prime position, with tables overlooking the Thames; a four-person band plays in the evening for dancing.

Services: 24-hour room service, nightly turndown, limousine service, same-day laundry and dry cleaning, babysitting.

Facilities: Hairdresser, news kiosk, unique Health Club built atop historic Savoy Theatre (destroyed by fire, 1990, rebuilt, 1993).

COVENT GARDEN

EXPENSIVE

DRURY LANE MOAT HOUSE, 10 Drury Lane, High Holborn, London WC2B 5RE. Tel. 071/836-6666. Fax 071/831-1548. 146 rms, 7 suites. A/C TV TEL **Tube:** Holborn or Covent Garden.

$ Rates: £128–£148 ($192–$222) single or double; from £200 ($300) suite. English breakfast from £9.50 ($14.30). AE, DC, MC, V. **Parking:** £10 ($15).

A steel-and-glass structure built in 1978 and enlarged in the 1980s, with terraced gardens, its own plaza, and individually controlled central heating, this Covent Garden hotel is elegantly decorated in greens and beiges. The well-appointed guest rooms—many for nonsmokers—have hairdryers, in-house videos, trouser presses, and tea/coffee makers.

Dining/Entertainment: Maudie's Bar makes a good pretheater rendezvous, and Maudie's Restaurant is open daily for lunch and dinner, specializing in French cuisine. Who was the original Maudie? She's Sir Osbert Lancaster's famous arbiter-of-chic cartoon character, Maudie Littlehampton.

Services: 24-hour room service, babysitting, laundry.

5. WESTMINSTER & VICTORIA

WESTMINSTER
EXPENSIVE

STAKIS ST. ERMINS HOTEL, Caxton St. (without number), London SW1H 0QW. Tel. 071/222-7888. Fax 071/222-6914. 290 rms, 7 suites. MINIBAR TV TEL **Tube:** St. James's Park.

$ Rates: £112 ($168) single; £145 ($217.50) double; from £275 ($412.50) suite. Continental breakfast £7.75 ($11.60) extra. AE, DC, MC, V.

A turn-of-the-century red-brick building, enlarged with a modern wing, this hotel is ideally located in the heart of Westminster and only a few minutes' walk from Buckingham Palace, the Houses of Parliament, and Westminster Abbey. Many guest rooms are quite sumptuous, with luxurious furnishings, that are often elegant and ornate. Other rooms are modernized, tastefully furnished, but often rather compact.

Dining/Entertainment: The hotel has two restaurants. The Caxton Grill offers an excellent-value à la carte menu. The Carving Table has a fixed-price lunch and dinner, serving a selection of roast meats, salads, and international dishes. Lunch costs £14.75 ($22.10), dinner costs £15.75 ($23.60). The lounge bar serves light snacks 24 hours a day, as well as an afternoon tea every day from 3 to 5:30pm.

Services: 24-hour room service, laundry, babysitting, guide services.

Facilities: Nearby Queen Mother Sports Centre.

VICTORIA
EXPENSIVE

GORING HOTEL, 15 Beeston Place, Grosvenor Garden, London SW1W 0JW. Tel. 071/396-9000. Fax 071/834-4393. 75 rms, 5 suites. TV TEL **Tube:** Victoria Station.

$ Rates: £120 ($180) single; £150–£170 ($225–$255) double; from £190 ($285) suite. English breakfast £12 ($18) extra. AE, DC, MC, V. **Parking:** £15 ($22.50).

Built in 1910 by O. R. Goring, this was the first hotel in the world to have central heating and a private bath in every guest room. Located just behind Buckingham Palace, it lies within easy reach of the royal parks, Victoria Station, the West London air terminals, Westminster Abbey, and the Houses of Parliament.

Top-quality service is still provided, nowadays by the founding father's grandson, George Goring. The charm of a traditional English country hotel is reflected in the paneled drawing room, where fires burn in the ornate fireplaces on nippy evenings. Nearby is a sunroom overlooking the gardens in the rear, with a bar situated by the window. All the well-furnished guest rooms have been refurbished with marble baths.

Three-course luncheon costs £20 ($30), and dinner begins at £30 ($45). Some of the chef's specialties are a fine duckling pâté, calves' liver with bacon and fried onions, venison, and roast boned best end of lamb.

Services include 24-hour room service, a laundry, valet service.

MODERATE

TOPHAM'S EBURY COURT, 28 Ebury St., London SW1W 0LU. Tel. 071/730-8147. Fax 071/823-5966. 42 rms (23 with bath). TEL **Tube:** Victoria Station.

$ Rates (including English breakfast): £55 ($82.50) single without bath, £85 ($127.50) single with bath; £65–£95 ($97.50–$142.50) double or twin without bath; £115 ($172.50) double or twin with bath. AE, DC, MC, V.

Topham's was created in 1937 when five small row houses were interconnected. With its flower-filled windowboxes, the place has a country-house flavor and is brightly painted in turquoise and white, with railings to match. The little reception rooms are informal and decorated with flowery chintzes and nice antiques. All twin and double rooms have color TVs and facilities for making coffee and tea.

Specializing in traditional English food, Topham's Restaurant offers both lunch and dinner. Services include 24-hour porter service, babysitting, and laundry and dry cleaning.

INEXPENSIVE

COLLIN HOUSE, 104 Ebury St., London SW1W 9QD. Tel. 071/730-8031. 13 rms (8 with bath). **Tube:** Victoria Station.

$ Rates (including English breakfast): £34–£36 ($51–$54) single with bath; £48 ($72) double without bath, £56 ($84) double with bath. No credit cards.

Collin House provides a good, clean B&B under the watchful eye of its resident proprietors, Mr. and Mrs. D. L. Thomas. Everything is well maintained in this mid-Victorian town house. There are a number of family rooms. The main bus, rail, and Underground terminals all lie about a 5-minute walk from the hotel. Knightsbridge, Piccadilly Circus, Leicester Square, and Oxford Street are easily accessible by tube, bus, or taxi, as are the theaters of the West End.

ELIZABETH HOTEL, 37 Eccleston Sq., London SW1V 1PB. Tel. 071/828-6812. 38 rms (20 with bath or shower), 8 studios and apts. **Tube:** Victoria Station.

$ Rates (including English breakfast): £36 ($54) single without bath, £55 ($82.50) single with bath or shower; £58 ($87) double without bath, £70–£84 ($105–$126) double with bath or shower; £75 ($112.50) triple without bath, £93 ($139.50) triple with bath or shower; £80 ($120) quad without bath, £104 ($156) quad with bath or shower; from £195 ($292.50) weekly studio; from £325 ($487.50) weekly 2-bedroom apt. No credit cards.

The Elizabeth, an intimate privately owned establishment overlooking the gardens of Eccleston Square, was built by Thomas Cubitt, Queen Victoria's favorite builder. Located

IMPRESSIONS

Till that day I never noticed one of the worst things about London—the fact that it costs money even to sit down.
—GEORGE ORWELL, *DOWN AND OUT IN PARIS AND LONDON* (1933)

behind Victoria Station, it's an excellent place to stay, convenient to Belgravia and Westminster, not far from Buckingham Palace, and just a few doors away from a house where Sir Winston Churchill once lived. Most of the accommodations are reached by elevator, and each is individually decorated in a Victorian motif, some with TVs. The original atmosphere has been carefully preserved, as reflected in the furnishings, framed prints, and wallpaper. If you're going to be in London for a week, ask about leasing an apartment.

6. KNIGHTSBRIDGE & BELGRAVIA

KNIGHTSBRIDGE
VERY EXPENSIVE

THE BEAUFORT, 33 Beaufort Gardens, London SW3 1PP. **Tel. 071/584-5252,** or 212/682-9191 in New York. Fax 071/589-2834. 21 rms, 7 junior suites. TV TEL **Tube:** Knightsbridge.

$ Rates (including continental breakfast): £110–£120 ($165–$180) single; £150–£220 ($225–$330) double or twin; £250 ($375) junior suite for two. AE, DC, MC, V. **Parking:** Free overnight on street.

The Beaufort, only 100 yards from Harrods, sits behind two Victorian porticoes and an iron fence that was added when the buildings were constructed in the 1870s. The owner combined a pair of adjacent houses, ripped out the old decor, and created a stylishly updated ambience of merit and grace. You register at a small desk extending off a bay-windowed parlor, then climb the stairway used by the queen of Sweden during her stay.

Each guest room features several well-chosen paintings by a London art student, a thoughtfully modern color scheme, and plush carpeting, as well as earphone radios, flowers, and a selection of books. Other advantages of this place are the helpful staff and the inspired direction of owner Diana Wallis, a television producer, who has created the feeling of a private house in the heart of London.

Dining/Entertainment: Meals are available from room service. There's a complimentary 24-hour bar.

Services: 24-hour drink room service, babysitting.

Facilities: Free access to nearby health club.

THE CAPITAL, 22–24 Basil St., London SW3 1AT. Tel. **071/589-5171,** or toll free 800/926-3199 in the U.S. Fax 071/225-0011. 48 rms, 8 suites. A/C MINIBAR TV TEL **Tube:** Knightsbridge.

$ Rates: £175 single; £210–£260 ($315–$390) double; from £300 ($450) suite. English breakfast £12.50 ($18.80) extra. AE, DC, MC, V. **Parking:** £15 ($22.50).

One of the most personalized hotels in the West End and a member of Relais & Châteaux, this small modern place is a stone's throw from Harrods. The proud owner, David Levin, has created a warm town-house ambience, the result of extensive refurbishment. The elegant fin-de-siècle decoration is matched by the courtesy and professionalism of the staff. The corridors and staircase are all treated as an art gallery, with original oil paintings. The guest rooms are tastefully decorated, often with Ralph Lauren designs.

Dining/Entertainment: The Capital Restaurant is among the finest in London, offering exquisitely prepared main dishes. A set lunch costs £20 ($30), a set dinner begins at £25 ($37.50); you can also order à la carte.

Services: 24-hour room service, laundry.

SHERATON PARK TOWER, 101 Knightsbridge, London SW1 X7RN. Tel. 071/235-8050, or toll free 800/325-3535 in the U.S. Fax 071/235-8231. 295 rms, 22 suites. A/C MINIBAR TV TEL **Tube:** Knightsbridge.

$ Rates: £195 ($292.50) single; £230–£280 ($345–$420) double; from £450 ($675) suite. VAT extra. English breakfast £14.05 ($21.10) extra. AE, DC, MC, V. **Parking:** £9 ($13.50).

Rising like a concrete cylinder, the Sheraton Park Tower is not only one of the most convenient hotels in London (virtually at the doorstep of Harrods) but also one of the best. Its unusual circular architecture provides a stark but interesting contrast to the well-heeled 19th-century neighborhood around it. From its windows guests have a magnificent view of Hyde Park. The main door is discreetly placed in the rear, where taxis can deposit guests more conveniently. As this is the flagship for the Sheraton's European enterprises, the management here has tried to make it, in the words of one spokesperson, "a modern version of the Connaught."

The travertine-covered lobby bustles with scores of international businesspeople, diplomats (the French embassy is across the street), and military delegations who congregate on the well-upholstered sofas or amid the Edwardian comfort of the hideaway bar. Back in your room, you'll find such comforts as central heating, soundproof windows, in-house movies, and a radio.

Dining/Entertainment: In the rotunda, near the ground-floor kiosks, afternoon tea is served. The champagne bar offers you the choice of either a glass or a silver tankard filled with the bubbly, along with oysters, dollops of caviar, and iced vodka. The Restaurant 101, with its own entrance onto Knightsbridge, is open daily from 7am to 11pm, offering exceptionally good food; it's ideal for after-theater supper. You can dine on such dishes as roasted sea bass with olives and crabmeat, lobster-stuffed ravioli, or filet of beef with horseradish-béarnaise sauce.

Services: 24-hour room service, laundry, babysitting.

Facilities: Business center, news kiosk, free access to nearby health club.

EXPENSIVE

BASIL STREET HOTEL, 8 Basil St., London SW3 1AH. Tel. 071/581-3311. Fax 071/581-3693. 92 rms (74 with bath or shower), 1 suite. TV TEL **Tube:** Knightsbridge.

$ Rates: £59 ($88.50) single without bath; £110.50 ($165.80) single with bath; £90.50 ($135.80) double without bath, £156.50 ($234.80) double with bath; £238.25 ($357.40) suite. English breakfast £10.50 ($15.80) extra. AE, DC, MC, V. **Parking:** £23 ($34.50).

The Basil, an Edwardian charmer totally unmarred by moderniza-tion, has long been a favorite little hotel for discerning British who make an annual pilgrimage to London to shop at Harrods and perhaps attend the Chelsea Flower Show. There are several spacious and comfortable lounges, appropriately furnished with 18th- and 19th-century decorative accessories. Off the many rambling corridors are smaller sitting rooms. A three-course table d'hôte luncheon costs £15 ($22.50); dinner is à la carte. Candlelight and piano music re-create the atmosphere of a bygone era. The Upstairs Restaurant serves lighter meals and snacks, and the Downstairs Wine Bar offers an excellent selection of wines and inexpensive food.

MODERATE

CLAVERLEY HOTEL, 13–14 Beaufort Gardens, London SW3 1PS. Tel. 071/589-8541. Fax 071/584-3410. 32 rms (29 with bath). TV TEL **Tube:** Knightsbridge.

$ Rates (including English breakfast): £50 ($75) single without bath, £60–£90 ($90–$135) single with bath; £90–£150 ($135–$225) double with bath. MC, V. **Parking:** Free on street (6pm–8am).

Set on a quiet street in Knightsbridge, a few blocks from Harrods, this small, cozy, tasteful place is accented with Georgian-era accessories. The appealing lounge contains 19th-century oil portraits, a Regency fireplace, and a collection of elegant antiques and leather-covered sofas—much like the ensemble you'd find in a private country house. Here, the hotel serves complimentary tea, coffee, hot chocolate, and cookies 24 hours a day. Awarded the British Tourist Authority's Certificate of Distinction for Bed-and-Breakfast Hotels in 1988, the Claverley continues to maintain the high standards that won it the award. Most guest rooms have Victorian-inspired wallpaper, wall-to-wall carpeting, and upholstered armchairs.

KNIGHTSBRIDGE GREEN HOTEL, 159 Knightsbridge, London SW1X 7PD. Tel. 071/584-6274. Fax 071/225-1635. 10 rms, 14 suites. TV TEL **Tube:** Knightsbridge.

$ Rates: £75 ($112.50) single; £100 ($150) double; £125 ($187.50) suite. English breakfast £8.50 ($12.80) extra. AE, MC, V.

In 1966, when this dignified 1890s structure was converted into a hotel, the developers were careful to retain its wide baseboards, cove moldings, high ceilings, and spacious proportions. None of the accommodations has a kitchen, but they nonetheless come close to apartment-style living. The suites are well furnished, with access to an upstairs "club room," where coffee and pastries are available throughout the day. Rooms contain trouser presses and hairdryers.

PARKES HOTEL, 41–43 Beaufort Gardens, London SW3 1PW. Tel. 071/581-9944. Fax 071/225-1442. 4 rms, 29 suites. MINIBAR TV TEL **Tube:** Knightsbridge.

$ Rates (including English breakfast): £90 ($135) single or double; £120–£150 ($180–$225) suite. VAT extra. AE, MC, V. **Parking:** Free on street (6pm–8am); at nearby garage, £12 ($18).

A classy Edwardian-style town house, the Parkes stands in one of the most desirable locations in London, close to Harrods. Facing a quiet and stately square, this place very much resembles a private house, with plenty of charm and style. Except for four standard rooms, each accommodation is a suite, complete with kitchenette. Each unit is individually decorated, sometimes in themes of blue and yellow.

BELGRAVIA
VERY EXPENSIVE

THE LANESBOROUGH, 1 Lanesborough Place, Hyde Park Corner, London SW1X 7TA. Tel. 071/259-5606, or toll free 800/999-1828. Fax 071/295-5606. 49 rms, 46 suites A/C MINIBAR TV TEL **Tube:** Hyde Park Corner.

$ Rates: £165–£190 ($247.50–$285) single; £220–£275 ($330–$412.50) double; £350–£2,500 ($525–$3,750) suite. English breakfast £16 ($24) extra. AE DC MC V. **Parking:** £2 ($3) per hour.

⭐ Only a handful of other locations in London have elicited the kind of curiosity and loyalty as The Lanesborough. Built in 1719, when the neighborhood was relatively uncrowded, as a country house for the second Viscount Lanesborough, it was demolished in 1827. Rebuilt soon after in the neoclassical style as St. George's Hospital, it is famous as the target of a Florence Nightingale crusade for improvement and enlargement. During the darkest days of World War II, St. George's was one of the most visible beacons of hope as bombs fell on London, and many older Londoners were born or "patched up" in the hospital's severe and medicinal-smelling wards.

In 1987, advances in technology had reduced the historic hospital into an inefficient medical antique. The medical facilities were moved to newly built quarters in South London, and the gruelling task of redefining the building began. The Rosewood Group (known for managing top hotels like the Bel-Air in Los Angeles and The Mansion on Turtle Creek in Dallas), received permission from the London Planning Board to upgrade the building into a luxury hotel. Most Georgian details were retained, and the tacked-on machinery necessary for the hospital was demolished. Into the echoing interior were added acres of Regency and neo-Gothic details, ornate plasterwork reminiscent of some of the finest buildings in Britain, yards of mahogany paneling, and a discreet and well-polished aura similar to what you might have expected within a sumptuously decorated country house. The guest rooms are as opulent and antique-drenched as you might expect. Each contains electronic sensors to alert the staff as to when a resident is in or out, a VCR, a CD player and VCR, a personal safe, a fax machine, a 24-channel satellite TV, a bathroom with every conceivable amenity, triple soundproofing, and the services of a personal butler. Security is tight, with the installation of at least 35 surveillance cameras.

Dining/Entertainment: The Conservatory, an elegant coffeeshop whose decor was inspired by the Chinese, Indian, and Gothic motifs of the Brighton Pavilion, is open daily from 7am to midnight. The Library Bar, which opens into a Victorian hideaway charmingly named "The Withdrawal Room," re-creates the atmosphere of an elegant private London Club. Formal meals are served Monday to Saturday at lunch and dinner in The Dining Room.

Services: Personal butlers, concierges.

Facilities: Car rental and newspaper kiosks, exercise equipment (Stairmasters, exercise bicycles) delivered directly to room.

MODERATE

DIPLOMAT HOTEL, 2 Chesham St., London SW1X 8DT.

Tel. 071/235-1544. Fax 071/259-6153. 27 rms. TV TEL **Tube:** Sloane Sq.
$ Rates (including English breakfast buffet): £65–£83 ($97.50–$124.50) single; £99–£135 ($148.50–$202.50) double. AE, DC, MC, V.

Part of the Diplomat's multifaceted allure lies in its status as a small, reasonably priced hotel in an otherwise prohibitively expensive neighborhood filled with privately owned Victorian homes and high-rise first-class hotels. It was built in the 19th century by one of the neighborhood's most famous architects on a wedge-shaped street corner near the site of today's Belgravia Sheraton. The registration desk is framed by the sweep of a partially gilded circular staircase beneath the benign gaze of cherubs looking down from a Regency-era chandelier.

Each high-ceilinged guest room boasts well-chosen wallpaper in Victorian-inspired colors. The staff is very helpful. Each accommodation is named after one of the famous streets in this posh district.

7. CHELSEA & CHELSEA HARBOUR

CHELSEA

VERY EXPENSIVE

DRAYCOTT, 24–26 Cadogan Gardens, London SW3 2RP. Tel. 071/730-6466, or toll free 800/346-7007 in the U.S. Fax 071/730-0236. 24 rms, 5 junior suites. MINIBAR TV TEL **Tube:** Sloane Sq.
$ Rates: £100–£150 ($150–$225) single; £195 ($292.50) double; £250 ($375) junior suite for two. English breakfast £10.50 ($15.80) extra. AE, DC, MC, V.

Located near Sloane Square in the heart of Chelsea, the Draycott opened in 1988 and has remained a well-kept secret among the fanciers of small but elegant hotels around the world. Here you can rest comfortably in a four-poster bed on fresh linen as your champagne cools in a silver bucket. It's that kind of place. Out back, the view opens onto a well-tended English garden; inside, the tone is set by antiques, chintz, and a fire.

The main allure of the place lies in its beautifully furnished guest rooms. In your room you are likely to find a copy of *An Innkeeper's Diary* by John Fothergill, but the Draycott doesn't take all his advice seriously—that is, his belief that boring clients should pay a higher tariff. Although there is no restaurant, 24-hour room service provides perfectly cooked breakfasts. Guests are given a complimentary pass to use a health club nearby.

IMPRESSIONS

London is a roost for every bird.
—BENJAMIN DISRAELI, *LOTHAIR* (1870)

HYATT CARLTON TOWER, 2 Cadogan Place, London SW1 X9PY. Tel. 071/235-5411, or toll free 800/228-9000 in the U.S. Fax 071/235-9129. 164 rms, 60 suites. A/C MINIBAR TV TEL **Tube:** Knightsbridge.
$ Rates: £240 ($360) single or double; £320 ($480) suite. English breakfast £13 ($19.50) extra. AE, DC, MC, V. **Parking:** £20 ($30).

Its location and height made this luxurious hotel a landmark even before Hyatt's decorators, painters, and antiques dealers transformed it into its European flagship—and one of the most plushly decorated and best-maintained hotels in London. It overlooks one of the city's most civilized gardens, which is surrounded by Regency-era town houses. The comfortable and conservatively modern guest rooms feature marble-lined baths, artwork, and in-house movies. Many open onto panoramic views over the rooftops of the neighborhood.

Dining/Entertainment: After the publicity it once received as "Britain's Tea Place of the Year," the hotel has remained one of the most fashionable spots to enjoy a midafternoon pick-me-up. Scones, Devonshire clotted cream, pastries, delicate sandwiches, and music are all part of the experience. The Rib Room offers relatively informal meals in a warmly atmospheric setting. The Chelsea Room, considered one of the great restaurants of London, is described separately in Chapter 5.

Services: 24-hour room service, valet, laundry, hair salon, babysitting.

Facilities: Health club with sauna, solarium.

EXPENSIVE

FENJA, 69 Cadogan Gardens, London SW3 2RB. Tel. 071/589-7333, or toll free 800/544-7570. Fax 071/581-4958. 13 rms. MINIBAR TV TEL **Tube:** Sloane Sq.
$ Rates: £97.75 ($146.60) single; £130–£195 ($195–$292.50) double. English breakfast £11.75 ($17.60) extra. AE, MC, V.
Parking: Free overnight on street; £5 ($7.50) at nearby garage.

Fenja is one of the most luxurious B&Bs in London, located near the Peter Jones Department Store and the fashionable boutiques of King's Road. It was built during the 19th century as a private house and purchased from the estate of Lord Cadogan after World War II. From 1985 to 1987 the building was completely restored and upgraded into a hotel. Rooms are named after famous writers and painters, including, for example, the Turner Room. They are decorated in an intensely traditional English style and furnished in part with antiques.

Light meals are available from the room-service menu, which includes a carefully selected wine list. Drinks can be ordered in the drawing room. Services include laundry and dry cleaning.

INEXPENSIVE

BLAIR HOUSE HOTEL, 34 Draycott Place, London SW3 2SA. Tel. 071/581-2323. Fax 071/823-7752. 17 rms (10 with bath). TV TEL **Tube:** Sloane Sq.
$ Rates (including continental breakfast): £40 ($60) single without bath, £63 ($94.50) single with bath; £60 ($90) double without bath, £73 ($109.50) double with bath. AE, DC, MC, V.

⑤ This comfortable hotel is a good choice in the heart of Chelsea. An older building of some architectural interest, it has been completely refurbished inside, with each room sporting tea- and coffee-making equipment. Breakfast is the only meal served. Babysitting and laundry can be arranged.

WILBRAHAM HOTEL, 1–5 Wilbraham Place, off Sloane St., London SW1X 9AE. Tel. 071/730-8296. Fax 071/730-6815. 53 rms (40 with bath), 5 suites. TV TEL **Tube:** Sloane Sq.

$ Rates: £38.50 ($57.80) single without bath, £52.50 ($78.80) single with bath; £54 ($81) double without bath, £64 ($96) double with bath; from £88 ($132) suite. English breakfast £6 ($9) extra. No credit cards. **Parking:** £18 ($27) nearby.

This is a dyed-in-the-wool British hotel set on a quiet residential street just a few hundred yards from trendy Sloane Square. It occupies three Victorian town houses that are joined. The well-maintained guest rooms are furnished in an uncontroversial traditional style. On the premises is an attractive old-fashioned lounge, The Bar and Buttery, where you can order drinks, a simple lunch, and dinner.

WILLETT, 32 Sloane Gardens, Sloane Sq., London SW1W 8DJ. Tel. 071/824-8415. Fax 071/824-8415. 18 rms (15 with bath). TV TEL **Tube:** Sloane Sq.

$ Rates (including English breakfast): £60.45 ($90.70) single without bath, £65.95 ($98.90) single with bath; £65.95 ($98.90) double without bath, £76.95 ($115.40) double with bath. VAT extra. AE, DC, MC, V.

A 19th-century town house opening onto gardens, the Willett has rapidly become a favorite among English people who like a townhouse address close to the restaurants, attractions, and shops of Chelsea. Its architectural touches include a mansard roof and bay windows. Retaining its traditional charm, the hotel has been fully renovated, with new furnishings in all the well-equipped guest rooms and in the public lounge areas. The breakfast room is especially inviting, with plush red-velvet chairs.

CHELSEA HARBOUR

VERY EXPENSIVE

HOTEL CONRAD, Chelsea Harbour (without number), London SW10 0XG. Tel. 071/823-3000. Fax 071/351-6525. 160 suites. A/C MINIBAR TV TEL **Transportation:** Chelsea Harbour Hoppa Bus C3 from Earls Court and Kensington High St. Mon–Sat. Riverbus from Charing Cross Mon–Fri.

$ Rates: £200–£245 ($300–$367.50) single or double. AE, DC, MC, V. **Parking:** £10 ($15).

One of London's newest five-star deluxe hotels and perhaps the first all-suite hotel in Europe, the Conrad is a stunning modern architectural achievement. It's located in a marina complex of boutiques, restaurants, and some of the most desirable apartments in London. Each elegant room, decorated by the famous designer David Hicks, contains hypoallergenic pillows, a full line of toiletries, a hairdryer, and three phones with two-line capability.

Dining/Entertainment: The hotel's facilities include the

Brasserie, whose stylish and cozy interior overlooks the Thames. The Lounge offers breakfast, light snacks, afternoon tea, and champagne by the glass in the evening (to the accompaniment of live piano music). Drakes Bar, as richly nautical as its name would imply, offers a view of the dozens of neatly moored yachts in the nearby marina.

Services: 24-hour room service, laundry, babysitting, luggage storage.

Facilities: Health club (heated pool, saunas), electronic safety locks, fax machines, personal computers.

8. KENSINGTON & SOUTH KENSINGTON

KENSINGTON

VERY EXPENSIVE

BLAKES, 33 Roland Gardens, London SW7 3PF. Tel. 071/370-6701, or toll free 800/926-3173 in the U.S. Fax 071/373-0442. 43 rms, 9 suites. MINIBAR TV TEL **Tube:** South Kensington or Gloucester Rd.

$ Rates: £135–£155 ($202.50–$232.50) single; £185–£300 ($277.50–$450) double; from £485 ($727.50) suite. English breakfast £14.50 ($21.80) extra. AE, DC, MC, V. **Parking:** £18 ($27).

Blakes, one of the best small hotels in London, is certainly sophisticated (guests might even see Princess Margaret dining in its basement restaurant). The creation of actress Anouska Hempel Weinberg, the hotel's richly appointed lobby boasts Victorian-era furniture, possibly hailing from India. The guest rooms are individually decorated and of various sizes, some with antiques.

Dining/Entertainment: The hotel's restaurant is one of the best in town, with reservations strictly observed. The menu might offer such appetizers as a salad of foie gras with Landais truffles and quail eggs on purée of mushrooms. Main courses include delicious varieties of teriyaki, poached salmon in champagne sauce, and roast partridge with juniper berries. The price of a meal, with wine and service, might come to £170 ($255) for two.

Services: 24-hour room service, laundry, babysitting.

Facilities: Free access to nearby health club, arrange-anything concierge.

INEXPENSIVE

ABBEY HOUSE, 11 Vicarage Gate, London W8 4AG. Tel. 071/727-2594. 15 rms (none with bath). TV **Tube:** Kensington High Street.

$ Rates (including English breakfast): £30 ($45) single; £52 ($78) double; £62 ($93) triple; £72 ($108) quad. No credit cards.

⑤ Some hotel critics have rated this the best B&B in London. Thanks to renovations, Abbey House, built in about 1860 on a typical Victorian square, is modern, though many original features have been retained. The spacious guest rooms have central heating, electrical outlets for shavers, vanity lights, and hot- and cold-water basins. Baths are shared by two units. The rooms are refurbished annually.

SOUTH KENSINGTON
EXPENSIVE

PELHAM HOTEL, 15 Cromwell Place, London, SW7 2LA. Tel. 071/589-8288. Fax 071/584-8444. 35 rms, 2 suites. A/C MINIBAR TV TEL **Tube:** South Kensington.

$ Rates: £115 ($172.50) single; £140–£165 ($210–$247.50) double; from £220 ($330) suite. English breakfast from £7 ($10.50) extra. AE, MC, V.

Privately owned and small, the Pelham is suitable for everyone from a visiting movie star to a discerning traveler. Kit and Tim Kemp, hoteliers extraordinaire, preside over one of the most stunningly decorated establishments in London, formed from part of a row of early 19th-century terrace houses with a white portico facade. Inside, high ceilings and fine moldings create a backdrop for a collection of antiques that embraces Victorian oil paintings and 18th-century paneling (from a bank in Suffolk) in the drawing room. Needlepoint, rugs, and cushions create a homelike warmth.

The Pelham Restaurant is one of the finest in South Kensington (see Chapter 5, "Specialty Dining"). An honor bar in the drawing room creates a clublike atmosphere. Services include 24-hour room service and theater-ticket arrangements.

THE REGENCY HOTEL, 100 Queen's Gate, London SW7 5AG. Tel. 071/370-4595, or toll free 800/328-9898 in the U.S. Fax 071/370-5555. 210 rms, 11 suites. A/C MINIBAR TV TEL **Tube:** Gloucester Rd. or South Kensington.

$ Rates: £115 ($172.50) single; £145 ($217.50) double; £195 ($292.50) luxury suite for two; £235 ($352.50) duplex suite with Jacuzzi. English breakfast £10.50 ($15.80) extra. AE, DC, MC, V.

The Regency—close to museums, Kensington, and Knightsbridge—takes its name from the historical period of the Prince Regent, later George IV. Located on a street lined with Doric porticoes, five Victorian terrace houses were converted into one stylish, seamless whole by an army of construction engineers and decorators. A Chippendale fireplace, flanked by wing chairs, greets guests near the polished hardwood of the reception area. One of the building's main stairwells contains what could be London's most unusual lighting fixture: five Empire chandeliers suspended vertically, one on top of the other. Since its opening, the hotel has hosted everyone from the late Margot Fonteyn to members of the British royal family. The modernized guest rooms are tasteful and elegant.

The Pavilion Restaurant is described under "Specialty Dining" in Chapter 5. Hotel services include 24-hour room service, laundry, and babysitting. At your disposal are the Elysium Health Spa (with steamrooms, saunas, and a sensory-deprivation tank) and a business center.

MODERATE

ALEXANDER HOTEL, 9 Sumner Place, London SW7 3EE. Tel. 071/581-1591, or toll free 800/344-5741 in the U.S. Fax 071/581-0824. 39 rms, 1 cottage suite. TV TEL **Tube:** South Kensington.

$ Rates (including English breakfast): £90.50 ($135.80) single; £116.35 ($174.50) double; £210 ($315) cottage suite for four or five. VAT extra. AE, DC, MC, V.

The Alexander is among the most expensive hotels on Sumner Place, but it is also the best. The four connected town houses, built as a sumptuous private hotel in 1842, are still elegant today thanks to an extensive refurbishment program. The place is filled with much artwork, both modern and antique, making part of the Alexander seem more like a gallery than a hotel and creating an ambience that made American humorist S. J. Perelman return again and again. The guest rooms are elegantly furnished in a country-house style. The most luxurious accommodation is a cottage suite set within the garden. Services include 24-hour room service and valet service.

THE CRANLEY, 10–12 Bina Gardens, London SW5 0LA. Tel. 071/373-0123, or toll free 800/553-2582. Fax 071/373-9497. 27 rms, 5 suites. A/C MINIBAR TV TEL **Tube:** South Kensington.

$ Rates (including continental breakfast): £104–£130 ($156–$195) single or double; £175–£230 ($262.50–$345) suite. AE, DC, MC, V.

A trio of adjacent 1875 town houses became the Cranley when the Michigan-based owners upgraded the buildings into one of the most charming hotels in South Kensington. Today, each high-ceilinged guest room has enormous windows, much of the original plaster-work, a scattering of antiques and plush upholstery, and a vivid sense of the 19th century. The public rooms have been described as a stage set for an ultra-English country house. There is no restaurant on the premises, though light snacks are served in rooms on request. A continental breakfast is served in a public room. All but one of the accommodations contain tiny kitchenettes.

About four blocks away, under the same ownership, is a similar hotel, **One Cranley Place Hotel,** charging the same rates. Originally built in the late 19th century as a private home, it contains a stylish blend of antique and modern decorative accessories, plus 10 rooms with the same amenities, and slightly larger kitchenettes, than its larger sibling.

5 SUMNER PLACE, 5 Sumner Place, London SW7 3EE. Tel. 071/584-7586. Fax 071/823-9962. 14 rms. MINIBAR TV TEL **Tube:** South Kensington.

$ Rates (including English breakfast): £75 ($112.50) single; £89–£98 ($133.50–$147) double. AE, DC, MC, V.

Winner of the British Tourist Authority Best B&B in Central London award in 1991, this carefully restored 1850s Victorian town house is delightful. The experience here is more like staying with friends in a London home than at a hotel. Some of the traditionally furnished rooms contain minibars. Each is immaculately maintained and refreshingly uncluttered. A buffet is served in a 19th-century conservatory overlooking a sun terrace. The owners, John and Barbara Palgan, provide the personal attention that makes visitors want to return.

NUMBER SIXTEEN, 16 Sumner Place, London SW7 3EG. Tel. 071/589-5232. Fax 071/584-8615. 36 rms (34 with bath). MINIBAR TV TEL **Tube:** South Kensington.

$ Rates (including continental breakfast): £55–£75 ($82.50–

$112.50) single without bath, £95 ($142.50) single with bath;
£85–£130 ($127.50–$195) double without bath, £150 ($225)
double with bath; £175 ($262.50) triple with bath. AE, DC, MC, V.
This is an elegant and luxurious pension, composed of four early-
Victorian town houses linked into a dramatically organized whole,
with an elevator. The proportions of the front and rear gardens of
each of the four original buildings were carefully retained, creating
swaths of greenery that today contributes to one of the most idyllic
spots on the street. In 1992, the establishment was awarded a trophy
as the best B&B in London.

The rooms contain an eclectic mixture of English antiques and
modern paintings. There's an honor-system bar in one of the elegant
formal sitting rooms, where a blazing fire is lit to remove the
cold-weather chill. Babysitting is available, as is 24-hour laundry
service on weekdays. Room service is available from 7:30am to 10pm.

INEXPENSIVE

**ASTON'S BUDGET STUDIOS, ASTON'S DESIGNER STU-
DIOS, AND ASTON'S LUXURY APARTMENTS, 39 Ro-
sary Gardens, London SW7 4NQ. Tel. 071/370-0737,**
or toll free 800/525-2810 in the U.S. Fax 071/835-1419. 60
studios and apartments (38 with bath). A/C TV TEL **Tube:**
Gloucester Rd.

$ Rates: Budget Studios £32–£38 ($48–$57) single; £42–£54
($63–$81) double; £60–£72 ($90–$108) triple; £78–£90 ($117–
$135) quad. Designer Studios £75–£95 ($112.50–$142.50) sin-
gle or double. Designer Suites £125–£150 ($187.50–$225)
two-room suite for two to four. AE, MC, V.

A carefully restored row of interconnected Victorian town
houses, this establishment offers comfortably furnished studios
and suites. Weekly rentals are preferred, but daily rentals are
also accepted. Heavy oak doors and 18th-century hunting
pictures give Aston's foyer a rich traditional atmosphere.

Accommodations range in size and furnishings from budget
to luxury. Regardless of its price, however, each unit has a fresh,
colorful decor and a compact but complete kitchenette concealed
behind doors. The Budget Studios have fully serviced bathrooms,
which are shared with only a handful of other guests. The air-
conditioned Designer Studios and two-room Designer Suites are
lavishly decorated with rich fabrics and furnishings and contain
marble-sheathed private showers and bathrooms. Telephones have
answering machines, and there are a host of other electronic
accessories suited for doing business in London. Considering its
amenities and cost, Aston's is an excellent value. It's under the
personal management of Ms. Shelagh King.

Services include laundry, secretarial service, private catering on
request, car and limousine, and daily maid service in the Designer
Studios and Suites. There are also a guests' message line and fax
machines.

**HOTEL 167, 167 Old Brompton Rd., London SW5 0AN.
Tel. 071/373-0672.** Fax 071/373-3360. 19 rms. MINIBAR TV
TEL **Tube:** South Kensington.

$ Rates (including continental breakfast): £51–£61 ($76.50–
$91.50) single, £64–£70 ($96–$105) double. Extra bed in room
£12 ($18). MC, V.

Hotel 167 is one of the more fashionable guesthouses in the area. It occupies a once-private Victorian town house, which, including the basement, has four floors of living space. Although some guest rooms are in the basement, they have large windows for illumination. The decor is quite stylish, with Scandinavian modern and Japanese accents.

KENSINGTON MANOR HOTEL, 8 Emperor's Gate, London SW7 4HH. Tel. 071/370-7516. Fax 071/373-3163. 15 rms, 1 suite. MINIBAR TV TEL **Tube:** Gloucester Rd.

$ Rates (including English breakfast): £55–£59 ($82.50–$88.50) single; £69.95–£80 ($104.90–$120) double; £105 ($157.50) suite. VAT extra. AE, DC, MC, V.

Located in a cul-de-sac, this hotel offers warmth and elegance in a stately late-Victorian building. Personal service of a high standard is the keynote of this place, including room service, laundry service, and dry cleaning. The guest rooms in this small lodging are individually decorated, each named after a county of England. A sumptuous buffet breakfast is served.

PRINCE HOTEL, 6 Sumner Place, London SW7 3AB Tel. 071/589-6488. Fax 071/581-0824. 20 rms (all with shower, 15 with toilet). TV TEL **Tube:** South Kensington.

$ Rates: £47 ($70.50) single with shower (no toilet), £59 ($88.50) single with shower and toilet; £58 ($87) double with shower (no toilet), £71 ($106.50) double with shower and toilet. AE, DC, MC, V.

Prince is the result of a successful conversion of an early-Victorian terrace house of about 1850. Decorated and restored in a classic English style, it opens onto a greenhouse-style conservatory and garden in the rear. All the guest rooms are individually decorated and designed. Breakfast, is served a few doors away at the more elegant (and expensive) Alexander Hotel (above).

9. EARLS COURT & NOTTING HILL GATE

EARLS COURT

INEXPENSIVE

BARKSTON HOTEL, 34–44 Barkston Gardens, London SW5 0EW. Tel. 071/373-7851. Fax 071/370-6570. 80 rms. TV TEL **Tube:** Earls Court.

$ Rates: £54 ($81) single; £72 ($108) double; £85 ($127.50) triple. Continental breakfast £4.50 ($6.80) extra. AE, DC, MC, V. **Parking:** £5 ($7.50) nearby.

The Barkston is close to Earls Court tube stop, which has a direct link to Heathrow. On a historical note, it offered B&B at 5p (10¢) back in 1905; by the 1960s it was the first Forte property in London before that giant went on to become a hotel empire. Nowadays it is privately owned, composed of six harmoniously connected buildings. The Barkston has its own restaurant, and each comfortably furnished room comes with coffee-making equipment and hairdryers.

SWISS HOUSE HOTEL, 171 Old Brompton Rd., London SW5 0AN. Tel. 071/373-2769. Fax 071/373-4983. 16 rms (11 with bath). TV TEL **Tube:** Gloucester Rd.

$ Rates (including continental breakfast): £32 ($48) single without bath, £45 ($67.50) single with bath; £48 ($72) double without bath, £58 ($87) double with bath. MC, V.

Swiss House, one of the more desirable B&Bs in the Earls Court area, is a white-fronted Victorian row house festooned with flowers and vines. The rear windows overlook a communal garden with a view of the London skyline. Like its neighbors, Swiss House has a front-porch portico. Its country-inspired guest rooms are individually designed, some with working fireplaces. Traffic is heavy outside, but windows are double-glazed. Babysitting services are available, and there's room service.

NOTTING HILL GATE

EXPENSIVE

THE ABBEY COURT, 20 Pembridge Gardens, London W2 4DU. Tel. 071/221-7518. Fax 071/792-0858. 22 rms, 3 suites. TV TEL **Tube:** Notting Hill Gate.

$ Rates: £90 ($135) single; £130 ($195) double or twin; £160 ($240) suite with four-poster bed. Breakfast £9 ($13.50) extra. AE, DC, MC, V.

The Abbey Court is a small and rather luxurious choice. Situated in a white-fronted mid-Victorian town house, it has a flowery patio in front and a conservatory in back. The lobby is graciously decorated with a sunny bay window, flower-patterned draperies, and a comfortable sofa and chairs. You'll find fresh flowers in the reception area and the hallways. Each room offers carefully coordinated fabrics and fine furnishings, mostly 18th- and 19th-century country antiques. Bathrooms are equipped with Jacuzzi jets, heated towel racks, and Italian marble–lined baths. Light snacks and drinks are available from room service 24 hours a day. Kensington Gardens is a short walk away, as are the antiques stores along Portobello Road.

10. ST. MARYLEBONE

VERY EXPENSIVE

THE LANGHAM HILTON, 1 Portland Place, London W1V 3AA Tel. 071/636-1000, or toll free 800/932-3322. Fax 071/323-2340. 365 rms, 22 suites A/C MINIBAR TV TEL **Tube:** Oxford Circus.

$ Rates: £165–£240 ($247.50–$360) single or double; £280–£1,000 ($420–$1,500) suite. English breakfast £13.50 ($20.30) extra. **Parking:** £19 ($28.50). AE, DC, MC, V.

When this hotel was inaugurated in 1865 by the Prince of Wales, its accommodations were considered suitable as the full-time London address for dozens of aristocratic squires seeking respite from their country estates. (Its guests included Antonín Dvořák, Arturo Toscanini, Oscar Wilde, Mark Twain, and Arnold Bennett.) After wartime bombing in 1940, it languished as a dusty office space for the BBC until the early 1990s, when Hilton International took over its premises as a historic and extremely well-located hotel.

Today, Langham's public rooms reflect the power and majesty of the British Empire during its 19th-century apex. So visible is this painstaking restoration of a great Victorian hotel that Hilton International now considers this its European flagship. Guest rooms are somewhat less opulent than public rooms, but they're furnished with French provincial furniture and red oak trim—cozy enclaves from the restaurants, cinemas, and commercial bustle of nearby Leicester Square.

Dining/Entertainment: Afternoon tea is served amid the potted palms of the Edwardian-style Palm Court. Vodka, caviar, and champagne flow liberally amid the red velvet of the Tsar's Russian Bar and Restaurant, while drinks are served in the Chukka Bar, a green-toned re-creation of a polo-playing private club. The most upscale restaurant is a high-ceilinged Victorian fantasy, Memories of the Empire, serving patriotic nostalgia and cuisine from the far corners of the British Commonwealth.

Services: 24-hour room service, concierge.

Facilities: Health club (saunas, Jacuzzis), business office.

EXPENSIVE

DORSET SQUARE HOTEL, 39–40 Dorset Sq., London NW1 6QN. Tel. 071/723-7874, or toll free in the U.S. 800/543-4138. Fax 071/724-3328. 37 rms. MINIBAR TV TEL **Tube:** Baker St. or Marylebone.

$ Rates: £85 ($127.50) single; £110–£155 ($165–$232.50) double. English breakfast £10 ($15) extra. AE, MC, V.

Dorset Square is made up of two Georgian Regency town houses. Hotelier Tim Kemp and his wife, Kit, have designed the interior so that the public rooms, luxurious guest rooms, and baths will make you feel that you're in an elegant private home. The rooms are decorated with chintz furniture or other printed fabrics. The furniture is a mix of antiques and reproductions. Half the rooms are air-conditioned.

The menu of the Dorset Square's restaurant changes seasonally and features the best of English cuisine. The hotel's bar contains a grand piano played every evening by a student from the Royal Academy of Music. Services include 24-hour room service, laundry, and babysitting.

MODERATE

BRYANSTON COURT HOTEL, 56–60 Great Cumberland Place, London W1H 7FD. Tel. 071/262-3141, or toll free 800/528-1234 in the U.S. Fax 071/262-7248. 54 rms. TV TEL **Tube:** Marble Arch.

$ Rates: £70 ($105) single; £90 ($135) double; £105 ($157.50) triple. Continental breakfast £6.50 ($9.80) extra. AE, DC, MC, V. **Parking:** £18 ($27).

Three individual houses were joined to form Bryanston about 190 years ago. Today this is one of the most elegant hotels on the street—thanks partly to the decorating efforts of its owners, the Theodore family. There's a gas fire burning in the Chesterfield-style bar, plus a stairway leading up to the comfortably furnished guest rooms.

DURRANTS HOTEL, George St. (without number), London W1H 6BJ. Tel. 071/935-8131. Fax 071/487-3510. 96 rms, 3 suites. TV TEL **Tube:** Bond St.

$ Rates: £65–£90 ($97.50–$135) single; £95–£150 ($142.50–$225) double; from £200 ($300) suite. English breakfast £8.50 ($12.80) extra. AE, MC, V.

Established in 1789, this historic hotel sits behind a sprawling brown-brick facade highlighted with Georgian detailing. During the hundred years of its ownership by the Miller family, several neighboring houses have been incorporated into the original structure, making a walk through the pine-and-mahogany-paneled public rooms a tour through another century. You'll find an 18th-century letter-writing room, as well as a popular neighborhood pub with Windsor chairs, an open fireplace, and a decor that probably hasn't changed very much in two centuries. Accommodations have elaborate cove moldings, very comfortable furnishings, and a solid feeling of well-being.

The in-house restaurant serves full afternoon teas and a satisfying French or traditional English cuisine in one of the most beautiful Georgian rooms in the neighborhood. The less formal breakfast room is ringed with 19th-century political cartoons by a noted Victorian artist. Services include 24-hour room service, laundry, and babysitting.

INEXPENSIVE

BLANDFORD HOTEL, 80 Chiltern St., London W1M 1PS. Tel. 071/486-3103. Fax 071/487-2786. 33 rms. TV TEL **Tube:** Baker St.

$ Rates (including English breakfast): £62 ($93) single; £77 ($115.50) double; £95 ($142.50) triple. AE, DC, MC, V.

Located only a minute's walk from the tube, this family-run hotel is something of a find and definitely one of London's better B&Bs for the price. Each room has a hairdryer and coffee-making equipment. Five rooms rented as triples are suitable for families.

EDWARD LEAR HOTEL, 28–30 Seymour St., London W1H 5WD. Tel. 071/402-5401. Fax 071/706-3766. 31 rms (12 with bath), 4 suites. TV TEL **Tube:** Marble Arch.

$ Rates (including English breakfast): £37.50 ($56.30) single without bath, £55 ($82.50) single with bath; £49.50 ($74.30) double without bath, £62.50 ($93.80) double with bath; from £72.50 ($108.80) suite. MC, V.

S This popular hotel is made all the more desirable by the bouquets of fresh flowers in the public rooms. It's one block from Marble Arch, occupying a pair of brick town houses, both of which date from 1780. The western house was the London home of the 19th-century artist and poet Edward Lear, whose illustrated limericks adorn the walls of one of the sitting rooms. Steep stairs lead up to the cozy rooms, which are fairly small but comfortable.

HALLAM HOTEL, 12 Hallam St., Portland Place, London W1N 5LJ. Tel. 071/580-1166. Fax 071/323-4537. 25 rms. TV TEL **Tube:** Oxford Circus.

$ Rates (including English breakfast): £55–£66 ($82.50–$99) single; £75–£88 ($112.50–$132) double. AE, DC, MC, V.

The Hallam is a heavily ornamented stone-and-brick Victorian house, one of the few on the street to escape World War II bombing. Today, it's the property of the Baker family. Earl and his sons, Grant and David, maintain it well. The guest rooms are comfortably furnished, each with tea- or coffee-making facilities. Some singles are quite small. In addition to 24-hour room service, there are a bar for residents and a bright breakfast room overlooking a pleasant patio.

HART HOUSE HOTEL, 51 Gloucester Place, Portman Sq., London SWH 3PE. Tel. 071/935-8516. 16 rms (10 with bath). TV TEL **Tube:** Marble Arch or Baker St.

$ Rates (including English breakfast): £42 ($63) single without bath, £49 ($73.50) single with bath; £59 ($88.50) double without bath; £72 ($108) double with bath; £75 ($112.50) triple without bath, £80 ($120) triple with bath; £85 ($127.50) quad with bath. AE, MC, V.

This is a well-preserved historic building, part of a group of Georgian mansions occupied by members of the French nobility living in exile during the French Revolution. In the heart of the West End, it lies within easy walking distance of many different theaters, as well as some of the most sought-after concentrations of shops and public parks in London. Cozy and convenient, the hotel is run by Mr. and Mrs. Bowden and son Andrew. All guest rooms are clean and comfortable.

HOTEL CONCORDE, 50 Great Cumberland Place, London W1H 7FD. Tel. 071/402-6169. Fax 071/724-1184. 28 rms. TV TEL **Tube:** Marble Arch.

$ Rates: £62 ($93) single; £72 ($108) double; £85 ($127.50) triple. English breakfast £6.50 ($9.80) extra. AE, DC, MC, V. **Parking:** £18 ($27).

Owned and run by the Theodore family, Concorde was built as a private house in the 1850s and later converted into a small and stylish hotel. Its reception desk, nearby chairs, and a section of the tiny bar area were at one time parts of a London church. A display case in the lobby contains an array of reproduction English silver, which is for sale. The guest rooms are well-maintained. The relatively quiet neighborhood is convenient to the attractions and traffic arteries of Marble Arch.

The owners also maintain 10 apartments in buildings next door and across the street. Each has a kitchen and between one and three bedrooms; in all cases, there is only one bathroom. Decor is old-fashioned and most (but not all) have somewhat dowdy furniture. One-bedroom apartments cost £85 ($127.50), two-bedroom apartments rent for £95 ($142.50), and a three-bedroom apartment goes for £105 ($157.50)—always with breakfast included.

HOTEL LA PLACE, 17 Nottingham Place, London W1M 3FB. Tel. 071/486-2323. Fax 071/486-4335. 24 rms, 4 suites. MINIBAR TV TEL **Tube:** Baker St.

$ Rates (including English breakfast): £55–£65 ($82.50–$97.50) single; £65–£75 ($97.50–$112.50) double; from £85 ($127.50) suite. DC, MC, V. **Parking:** £17 ($25.50).

This Victorian-era building, with a red-brick facade similar to many others on its street, is a refurbished B&B hotel—one of the best of its kind in the area. The guest rooms are clean and comfortable, with

---

Ⓕ FROMMER'S COOL FOR KIDS: HOTELS

Blandford Hotel *(see p. 99)* For families on a budget, this hotel near Baker Street (of Sherlock Holmes fame) has a number of triple and family rooms (suitable for four to five). Kids can walk to Madame Tussaud's waxworks.

Hart House Hotel *(see p. 100)* This is a small family-run B&B right in the center of the West End near Hyde Park. Many of its rooms are triples, and special family suites, with connecting rooms, can be arranged.

Sandringham Hotel *(see p. 103)* Out in Hampstead, where children have plenty of room to play on the heath, this hotel offers both triple and family rooms for four to five.

---

traditional styling. On the premises, doing a healthy neighborhood business, is a chic little wine bar and restaurant.

11. PADDINGTON & BAYSWATER

PADDINGTON
MODERATE

COLONNADE HOTEL, 2 Warrington Crescent, London W9 1ER. Tel. 071/286-1052. Fax 071/286-1057. 49 rms. TV TEL **Tube:** Warwick Ave.
$ Rates (including English breakfast): £60.50–£82.50 ($90.80–$123.80) single; £80–£118 ($120–$177) double. AE, DC, MC, V. **Parking:** £7 ($10.50).
The Colonnade, an imposing town house in a pleasant residential area, just a block from a tube station, has been owned and managed by three generations of the Richards family. There are 16 special rooms with four-poster beds. All rooms have hairdryers and trouser presses; some are air-conditioned and some have Jacuzzis. The hotel has a restaurant and a cocktail bar called Cascades, which is so popular that you sometimes need to make a reservation.

MORNINGTON HOTEL, 12 Lancaster Gate, London W2 3LG. Tel. 071/262-7361, or toll free in the U.S. 800/528-1234. Fax 071/706-1028. 68 rms. TV TEL **Tube:** Lancaster Gate.
$ Rates (including Scandinavian buffet breakfast): £80 ($120) single; £90–£103 ($135–$154.50) double. AE, DC, MC, V.
The Mornington brings a touch of northern European hospitality to the center of London. Just north of Hyde Park and Kensington Gardens, the hotel has a Scandinavian-designed interior and features a genuine Finnish sauna. The modernized guest rooms are tastefully conceived and comfortable. You can wind down in the library, entertaining your friends or making new ones. From the well-stocked bar you can order snacks and, if you're back in time, afternoon tea.

INEXPENSIVE

CAMELOT HOTEL, 45–47 Norfolk Sq., London W2 1RX. Tel. 071/723-9118. Fax 071/402-3412. 44 rms (40 with bath or shower): TV TEL **Tube:** Paddington.

$ Rates (including English breakfast): £36.50 ($54.80) single without bath, £44–£50 ($66–$75) single with bath; £70 ($105) double with bath; £85.50 ($128.30) triple with bath; £110 ($165) quad with bath. MC, V.

Built in 1850 as a pair of adjacent town houses, this simple but comfortable hotel stands at the center of an old tree-filled square, about 2 minutes from Paddington Station. The hotel was refurbished in the late 1980s and now has an elevator. Floral curtains, framed prints, and matching bedspreads create a homelike environment. Families with children are welcome.

BAYSWATER

MODERATE

PEMBRIDGE COURT HOTEL, 34 Pembridge Gardens, London W2 4DX. Tel. 071/229-9977. Fax 071/727-4982. 25 rms. TV TEL **Tube:** Notting Hill Gate.

$ Rates (including English breakfast): £85–£120 ($127.50–$180) single; £110–£150 ($165–$225) double. AE, DC, MC, V.

Built in 1852 as a private house, this hotel presents an elegant cream-colored neoclassical facade to a residential neighborhood that has grown increasingly fashionable. Most guest rooms contain at least one antique, as well as 19th-century engravings and plenty of warmly patterned flowery fabrics. Some of the largest and most stylish rooms are on the top floor, with baths tiled in Italian marble. Others include three exceptionally deluxe rooms overlooking Portobello Road. The Spencer and Church rooms, for example, are tastefully decorated in blues and yellows, while the Windsor room has a contrasting array of tartans.

In Caps, the hotel's brick-lined restaurant, good French and English food and drink, along with a well-chosen array of wines, is served. It's open only in the evening. Services include 24-hour room service, laundry, same-day dry cleaning, and babysitting. A car-rental agency is on the premises.

12. HOLLAND PARK

VERY EXPENSIVE

HALCYON HOTEL, 81 Holland Park Ave., London W11 3RZ. Tel. 071/727-7288, or toll free 800/457-4000. Fax 071/229-8516. 44 rms, 19 suites. A/C MINIBAR TV TEL **Tube:** Holland Park.

$ Rates: £140–£165 ($210–$247.50) single; £185–£295 ($277.50–$442.50) double; from £375 ($562.50) suite. English breakfast £12.50 ($18.80) extra. AE, DC, MC, V.

Only a small brass plaque distinguishes the aptly named Halcyon from other buildings on its street. Called "by far the grandest of London's small hotels," it was formed by uniting a pair of Victorian mansions originally built in 1860. Today, they constitute a hotel of charm, urban sophistication, and much comfort. Since the Halcyon opened in 1985, the clientele has included a bevy of international film and recording stars who like the privacy and anonymity provided by this place: the Rolling Stones, Bruce Willis, Sigourney Weaver.

Nearly half the accommodations are suites, lavishly outfitted with the kinds of furnishings and textiles you might find in an Edwardian country house. Several accommodations boast such whimsical touches as tented ceilings, and all contain the modern luxuries you'd expect in a hotel of this caliber. The public rooms are inviting oases, with trompe l'oeil paintings against backgrounds of turquoise. The designer of the hotel was an American, Barbara Thornhill.

Dining/Entertainment: The hotel's superb restaurant, The Room at the Halcyon, is recommended separately in Chapter 5.

Services: 24-hour room service, 1-hour pressing service, message-paging system (for which beepers are provided) that extends 20 miles from the hotel, complimentary limousine service, baby-sitting, night safes.

Facilities: Business center.

13. HAMPSTEAD

INEXPENSIVE

SANDRINGHAM HOTEL, 3 Holford Rd., London NW3 1AD. Tel. 071/435-1569. Fax 071/431-5932. 19 rms (9 with bath). MINIBAR TEL **Tube:** Hampstead.

$ Rates (including English breakfast): £39 ($58.50) single without bath; £46.50 ($69.80) single with bath; £60 ($90) double without bath; £65 ($97.50) double with bath; £90 ($135) family room with bath. No credit cards.

You'd never guess this is a hotel, because it stands on a residential street in one of the best parts of London. The well-built Sandringham has a pretty breakfast room, enlarged by the addition of a Victorian conservatory that overlooks a walled garden. You'll also find a homelike lounge furnished with color TV. From the upper rooms, you have a panoramic view over the heath to the center of London.

The guest rooms are comfortably furnished and carefully maintained. Laundry service, babysitting, and 24-hour room service are available.

14. AIRPORT HOTELS

NEAR GATWICK

EXPENSIVE

GATWICK HILTON INTERNATIONAL HOTEL, Gatwick Airport, Gatwick, West Sussex RH6 0LL. Tel. 0293/

518080, or toll free 800/HILTONS in the U.S. Fax 0293/
528980. 550 rms, 18 suites. A/C TV TEL

$ Rates: £125–£130 ($187.50–$195) single; £135–£140
($202.50–$210) double; from £210 ($315) suite. Breakfast £10–
£12.95 ($15–$19.40) extra. AE, DC, MC, V. **Parking:** £12.50
($18.80).

Gatwick's most convenient resting place, this deluxe five-floor hotel is
linked to the airport terminal with a covered walkway and offers
trolleys to assist with the transport of luggage. There is also electric
buggy service between the hotel and the airport for the infirm, the
elderly, or anyone with lots of luggage. The most impressive part of
the hotel is the first-floor lobby, whose glass-covered portico rises
through four floors and contains a scale replica of the de Havilland
Gypsy moth airplane *Jason,* used by Amy Johnson on her solo flight
from England to Australia in 1930. The reception desk is nearby, in
an area with a lobby bar and lots of greenery. Rooms are equipped
with soundproofing triple-glazed windows.

Dining/Entertainment: The American-themed restaurant
Amy's serves buffet breakfasts, lunches, and dinners. The Garden
Restaurant, outfitted in an English outdoor theme, serves drinks, full
meals, and snacks as well. There's also the Lobby Bar, open 24 hours
a day, plus a watering hole with a polo-playing theme, The Jockey
Bar.

Services: Same-day laundry and dry cleaning, up-to-date flight
information channel, 24-hour room service, hairdresser, bank, gift
shop.

Facilities: Health club (sauna, steam room, massage room,
swimming pool, gymnasium).

NEAR LONDON HEATHROW
EXPENSIVE

**SHERATON SKYLINE, A-4 Bath Rd. (without number),
Hayes, Middlesex UB3 5BP. Tel. 081/759-2535,** or toll
free 800/325-3535 in the U.S. Fax 081/750-9150. 352 rms, 5
suites. A/C MINIBAR TV TEL

$ Rates: £140–£160 ($210–$240) single; £150–£170 ($225–
$255) double; from £310 ($465) suite. English breakfast £8.25
($12.40) extra. AE, DC, MC, V. **Parking:** Free.

More of a miniature village than a hotel, Sheraton Skyline was voted
in the 1980s as the world's best airport hotel. It was designed around
an atrium where tropical plants and towering palms thrive beneath a
translucent roof. The foundations of a cabana bar are set into the
temperature-controlled waters of a pool. Each guest room sports a
color TV with in-house video movies and a massage-style shower.

Dining/Entertainment: A fireplace flickers late into the night
in the Edwardian Colony Bar and in the adjacent well-upholstered
restaurant, the Colony Room, where well-prepared food is served
beneath massive ceiling timbers and heavy brass chandeliers. A
French café offers light meals and full buffet breakfasts. Diamond
Lil's, a Montana-style cabaret, features showgirls, charbroiled steaks,
and generous drinks.

Services: 24-hour room service, verification and confirmation of
departures from Heathrow.

Facilities: Business center, heated pool.

LONDON DINING

If you want to splurge in a big way, the London "greats" are at your disposal: La Tante Claire, Le Gavroche, Nico at Ninety on Park Lane, and half a dozen other world-class gourmet havens. Usually they serve French cuisine or at least French-inspired cuisine. Many chefs also create remarkable and inventive English dishes with the fresh produce available in the country. Wine tends to be pricey in these establishments.

If star eateries are too expensive for you, there are moderately priced and budget restaurants. Among the latter are public houses. The English public house—also known as the "local," the "watering hole," the "boozer," and the pub—is such a significant national institution that it could merit a separate chapter. Far more than a place in which to drink, the pub is also the regular lunchtime rendezvous for millions of English people. For an even larger number, it also doubles as a club, front parlor, betting office, debating chamber, television lounge, or refuge from the family. It is not, by and large, a good "pickup" spot, but it's very nearly everything else.

There are some 5,000 to 6,000 pubs in metropolitan London, so our suggestions represent no more than a few random samplings. Perhaps you could try an exploration of your own, moving on to another establishment after one drink. If repeated at length, the process becomes a "pub crawl," possibly Britain's most popular national pastime.

Although selections on our list are fine for both women and men, choose your other pubs with care. Some pubs are what the English call "downright grotty"—dirty, often tough drinking places that attract soccer-loving "lager louts." If you're well dressed, a safer bet would be a hotel bar or cocktail lounge.

Once upon a time, London had two traditional dining areas: Soho for Italian and Chinese fare, Mayfair and Belgravia for French cuisine.

Today, you're likely to find any type of eatery anywhere, from Chelsea to Hampstead. The majority of my selections are in the West End, only because this happens to be the handiest for visitors.

SOME DINING NOTES All restaurants and cafés in Britain are required to display the prices of the food and drink they offer, in a place visible from outside the establishment. Charges for service, as well as any minimum charge or cover charge, must also be made clear. The prices shown must include 17½% VAT. Most of the restaurants add a 10% to 15% service charge to your bill, but you'll have to check to make sure of that. If nothing has been added to your bill, leave a 12% to 15% tip.

Nearly all places, except pubs, cafeterias, and fast-food places (often chain-run), prefer or require reservations. Almost invariably, you get a better table if you book in advance. For a few of the really famous places, you might need to reserve a table weeks in advance, even before leaving home, and such reservations should always be confirmed when you land in London.

Restaurants in London keep varied hours, but in general, lunch is offered from noon to 2pm and dinner is served from 7:30 to 9:30pm. Of course, many restaurants open earlier, and others stay open later. Sunday is the typical closing day for London restaurants, but there are many exceptions to that rule.

In this guide restaurants that serve dinner for one without wine that costs roughly £45 ($67.50) and up are listed as **very expensive.** Those charging about £35 to £45 ($52 to $67.50) are grouped as **expensive;** those charging about £15 to £35 ($22.50 to $52), as **moderate;** and those charging less than about £15 ($22.50), as **inexpensive.**

1. MAYFAIR & ST. JAMES'S

MAYFAIR

VERY EXPENSIVE

LE GAVROCHE, 43 Upper Brook St., W1. Tel. 071/408-0881.
   Cuisine: FRENCH. **Reservations:** Required. **Tube:** Marble Arch.
$ Prices: Appetizers £15.50–£28.50 ($23.30–$42.80); main courses £25.50–£34.80 ($38.30–$52.20); fixed-price lunch £29.50 ($44.30); fixed-price dinner £59 ($88.50). AE, DC, MC, V.
   Open: Lunch Mon–Fri noon–2pm; dinner Mon–Fri 7–11pm.

Le Gavroche has long been synonymous with French cuisine, perhaps the finest in Great Britain. It's the creation of two Burgundy-born brothers, Michel and Albert Roux. Service is faultless, the ambience chic and formal without being stuffy. The menu changes constantly, depending on the availability of the seasonal fresh produce and, more important, on the inspiration of the Roux brothers, who began modestly in London at another location and went on to achieve culinary fame.

Their wine cellar is among the most interesting in London, with many quality Burgundies and Bordeaux. While you wait, you can enjoy an apéritif upstairs as you peruse the menu and enjoy the delectable canapés. Try, if featured, stuffed smoked salmon and mousseline of lobster, Bresse pigeon, veal kidneys in a sauce made with three mustards, or baked sea bass served with champagne-cream sauce. Most main courses are served on silver trays covered with domes, which are lifted with great flourish.

EXPENSIVE

NICO AT NINETY, 90 Park Lane, W1. Tel. 071/409-1290.
   Cuisine: FRENCH. **Reservations:** Required (2 days in advance lunch, 10 days dinner). **Tube:** Marble Arch.
$ Prices: Appetizers £12.50–£25 ($18.80–$37.50); main courses £22–£35 ($33–$52.50); fixed-price lunch £26 ($39); fixed-price dinner £42 ($63). AE, DC, MC, V.
   Open: Lunch Mon–Fri noon–2pm; dinner Mon–Sat 7–11pm.
   Closed: 10 days around Christmas/New Year's.

No great restaurant of London has changed locations as often as this one, but dedicated habitués from around the world continue to seek out chef Nico Ladenis, regardless of where he locates. In a new setting, under the umbrella of Grosvenor House, more impressive and stylish than ever before, chef Nico remains one of the most talked about chefs of Great Britain—the only one who is a former oil company executive, an economist, and a self-taught cook.

Dinners are profoundly satisfying and often memorable in the very best gastronomic tradition of "post nouvelle cuisine," in which the tenets of classical cuisine are creatively and flexibly adapted to local fresh ingredients.

The menu, written in French, changes frequently, according to the inspiration of Mr. Ladenis. You might select sole with lobster sauce, delectable quail pie, lobster-stuffed ravioli in truffled butter, or Bresse pigeon with foie gras. Desserts are sumptuous.

OAK ROOM, in Le Méridien, 21 Piccadilly, W1. Tel. 071/734-8000.
   Cuisine: FRENCH. **Reservations:** Required. **Tube:** Piccadilly Circus.
$ Prices: Appetizers £12.50–£18 ($18.80–$27); main courses £17–£23 ($25.50–$34.50); set business lunch £24.50 ($36.80); "menu gourmand" £49 ($73.50). AE, DC, MC, V.
   Open: Lunch Mon–Fri noon–2:30pm; dinner Mon–Sat 7–10:30pm.

The Oak Room, one of the city's finest restaurants, has received numerous culinary awards. The setting alone—said to be the most beautiful dining room in the center of London—is worth the trip. Lavish in its appointments, this splendid period room has been restored to all its gilded splendor, including the ceiling and the original oak paneling. It's no wonder that luminaries continue to dine here.

The decor notwithstanding, the main draw here is the refined cuisine. The menu is the creation of French consultant chef Michel Lorain and resident executive chef David Chambers. You can select from "Cuisine Creative" or "Cuisine Traditionelle" menus, enjoying such dishes as gazpacho served with warm langoustines and zucchini quenelles or lightly smoked sea bass in cream sauce flavored with Sevruga caviar.

MODERATE

BRACEWELL'S, in the Park Lane Hotel, Piccadilly (without number), W1. Tel. 071/499-6321.
Cuisine: BRITISH. **Reservations:** Required. **Tube:** Hyde Park Corner or Green Park.

$ Prices: Appetizers £4.50–£9.50 ($6.80–$14.30); main courses £9–£14.50 ($13.50–$21.80); three-course set-lunch menu £17.50 ($26.30); three-course set-dinner menu £22.50 ($33.80); four-course gastronomique dinner menu £26.50 ($39.80). AE, DC, MC, V.

Open: Lunch Mon–Fri 12:30–2:30pm; dinner Mon–Sat 7–10:30pm.

Sheltered by the thick fortresslike walls of this previously recommended hotel, Bracewell's is one of chic London's better-kept secrets. The cuisine, prepared by highly acclaimed British-born Simon Traynor, is among the best in the capital, and the decor and the five-star service are worthy of its distinguished clientele. You might begin with a drink among the gilded torchères and comfortable armchairs of Bracewell's Bar. Later you will be ushered into an intimately illuminated room whose Louis XVI paneling was long ago removed from the London home of the American banker and philanthropist J. Pierpont Morgan.

The specialties are based on the freshest seasonal ingredients, using British recipes and the best of British produce. The menu throughout the year features an array of such dishes as spinach-and-walnut soufflé with anchovies, terrine of baby leeks and asparagus, lobster and Cornish crab soup, and a variety of fish (mullet, sea bass, salmon, Dover sole). Traditional meat dishes feature prime Scottish filet steak, chateaubriand, and baked lamb saddle. All these traditional ingredients are interpreted creatively and in an attractively contemporary style by chef Traynor. Keep an eye on the three-course table d'hôte, which may feature asparagus, artichoke, and foie gras terrine with a sweet pickled pumpkin, or poached chicken and sweetbreads served on a creamy mushroom sauce with toasted new potatoes. The irresistible desserts include pancake Belmonte, flamed at your table with Armagnac and seasonal berries in an orange sauce, and an array of offerings on the dessert trolley. In the evenings an excellent menu gastronomique is available. Wine is recommended according to your dinner.

GAYLORD MAYFAIR, 16 Albemarle St., W1. Tel. 071/629-9802.
Cuisine: INDIAN. **Reservations:** Not necessary. **Tube:** Green Park.

$ Prices: Appetizers £7.95–£10.75 ($11.90–$16.10); main courses £8.25–£10.95 ($12.40–$16.40); dinner with meat dish £18.25 ($27.40); vegetarian fixed-price lunch or dinner £14.50 ($21.80). AE, DC, MC, V.

Open: Lunch daily noon–3pm; dinner Mon–Sat 6–11:30pm.

Actually, there are two Gaylords in London, but this is the newer one and has established an enviable reputation among local connoisseurs of Indian cuisine. One reason is that Gaylord offers a dazzling variety of several regional cooking styles, so you can feast on Kashmiri and

Mughlai as well as on the usual tandoori delicacies. To sample this variety, it's best to order as many of the smaller dishes as you can; to do this, of course, you will need to go with friends. Try the keema nan (leavened bread stuffed with delicately flavored minced meat) and certainly the spiced vegetable pastries known as samosas. For a main course, you might choose goshtaba (lamb) or murg musallam (diced chicken sautéed with onions and tomatoes). If you don't like curry, the staff will help you select a meal of any size totally devoid of that spice, but flavored with a great many others. You'll find the manager helpful in guiding you through the less familiar Kashmiri dishes.

LANGAN'S BRASSERIE, Stratton St. (without number), W1. Tel. 071/491-8882.
   Cuisine: ENGLISH/FRENCH. **Reservations:** Required. **Tube:** Green Park.
$ Prices: Appetizers £4.50–£11 ($6.80–$16.50); main courses £11.50–£18 ($17.30–$27). AE, DC, MC, V.
   Open: Lunch Mon–Fri 12:30–3pm; dinner Mon–Fri 7–11:45pm, Sat 8pm–12:45am.

This relaxed café-style restaurant is modeled after a Parisian brasserie, and it was *the* place to be in London in the 1970s. It's still going strong. The potted palms and overhead fans create a faded 1930s atmosphere; upstairs, you'll find more formal and intimate, but no more costly, dining rooms. The brainchild of the late restaurateur Peter Langan, in partnership with actor Michael Caine and chef de cuisine Richard Shepherd, Langan's has been a chic spot since it opened in 1976. The menu offers many continental dishes, especially French ones, but it always features English food prepared as the English would, including sausages and "mash" and black pudding. Live music is featured in the evening.

SCOTTS, 20 Mount St., W1. Tel. 071/629-5248.
   Cuisine: SEAFOOD. **Reservations:** Required. **Tube:** Green Park.
$ Prices: Appetizers £5.50–£12 ($8.30–$18); main courses £13.50–£23 ($20.30–$34.50); set lunch £25 ($37.50). AE, DC, MC, V.
   Open: Lunch Mon–Sat 1:30–3pm; dinner Mon–Sat 6–10:45pm, Sun 7–10pm.

In addition to its spacious dining room and cocktail bar, Scotts has a widely noted oyster, lobster, and caviar bar. Its origins were humble, dating back to a fishmonger's in Coventry Street in 1851. However, its fame rests on its heyday, when the proprietors often entertained Edward VII and his guests in private dining rooms. Scotts has been at its present location since 1967, enjoying a chic address in the neighborhood of the swank Connaught Hotel and Berkeley Square. Its decor, with terra-cotta walls, has been called "Assyrian Monumental." The wall panels are hung with English primitive pictures.

Its chef, who believes in British produce, handles the kitchen with consummate skill and authority. You get top-notch quality and ingredients. Lobster, crab, oysters, and perhaps smoked Ellingham eel are featured; the eel comes from Suffolk, where it is "swum" (that is, kept alive) until it's ready for smoking. Dover sole is prepared a variety of ways, although the English prefer it "on the bone," considering filleted fish food for sissies. A favorite appetizer is salad Chloe. More down-to-earth dishes, such as fish cakes, appear regularly (or at least weekly) on the luncheon menu.

VEERASWAMY, 99–101 Regent St., W1. Tel. 071/734-1401.

> **Cuisine:** INDIAN. **Reservations:** Recommended. **Tube:** Piccadilly Circus.
>
> **$ Prices:** Appetizers £3.50–£6 ($5.30–$9); all-vegetarian three-course dinner £17 ($25.50); meat-and-vegetable three-course dinner £20–£29 ($30–$43.50); main dishes £9.95–£18.95 ($14.90–$28.40); three-course lunch buffet £13 ($19.50). AE, DC, MC, V.
>
> **Open:** Lunch Mon–Sat noon–2:30pm; dinner Mon–Sat 6–11:30pm.

When it was established in 1927 as the first Indian restaurant in Europe, Veeraswamy attracted every socialite in London with its exotic cuisine. Founder Edward Palmer, who made a fortune trading spices, was born in 1860 in India. Beautifully restored in the mid-1980s, it is still one of London's leading choices for Indian cuisine.

In the kitchen, each chef specializes in a particular region of the subcontinent. Whether from Gujarat or Goa (try the fiery coconut-flavored chicken), the cuisine is often mouth-tingling. Vegetarians appreciate the thalis, the home-baked breads, and the array of well-seasoned vegetables that some diners order in combinations as a meal. The Regent Street business crowd usually opts for the all-you-can-eat lunchtime buffet, while the evening crowd opts for pre- or posttheater dinners.

INEXPENSIVE

BRASSERIE ON THE PARK, in the Park Lane Hotel, Piccadilly (without number), W1. Tel. 071/499-6321.

> **Cuisine:** INTERNATIONAL. **Reservations:** Recommended. **Tube:** Hyde Park Corner.
>
> **$ Prices:** Appetizers £3.25–£6.50 ($4.90–$9.80); main courses £4.25–£10.75 ($6.40–$16.10); fixed-price menus £11.95 ($17.90) and £14.95 ($22.40). AE, DC, MC, V.
>
> **Open:** Lunch Mon–Fri noon–3pm; dinner Mon–Fri 6–11pm; Sat–Sun noon–11pm.

The Brasserie on the Park in the Park Lane Hotel is bright and breezy, decorated in art deco style to match the hotel's famous ballroom. The standard menu features such appetizers as smoked salmon and sliced avocado served on wholemeal croûton with hollandaise sauce. The main courses include classic brasserie dishes like omelets and more exotic dishes like grilled tiger prawns with chili mayonnaise. A special fixed-price menu changes weekly. It might include stir-fried sea scallops or grilled quail with wild mushrooms. The Brasserie offers a choice of wines (available by the glass) that have been carefully selected to "marry" with your food. The restaurant frequently holds festivals of highlighting specific regions—southwest France, Veneto in northern Italy, and California, for example.

CHICAGO PIZZA FACTORY, 17 Hanover Sq., W1. Tel. 071/629-2669.

> **Cuisine:** AMERICAN. **Reservations:** Recommended for lunch. **Tube:** Oxford Circus.

**FROMMER'S SMART TRAVELER:
RESTAURANTS**

1. Some of London's great restaurants offer fixed-price luncheons at such reasonable prices that the kitchen actually loses money.
2. Order set luncheons or dinners when possible—many represent at least a 30% saving over à la carte menus.
3. Look for the daily specials on any à la carte menu. They're invariably fresh, and often carry a lower price tag than regular à la carte listings.
4. Drink the house wine served in a carafe—it's only a fraction of the price of bottled wine.

$ Prices: Appetizers £2.75–£3.75 ($4.10–$5.60); main courses £6.50–£10 ($9.80–$15); pizza for two £7.50–£12 ($11.30–$18). No credit cards.
Open: Mon–Sat 11:45am–11:30pm, Sun noon–10:30pm.

This restaurant was introduced to London by former advertising executive Bob Payton, an ex-Chicagoan, and is one of the few establishments that provide doggy bags. The 275-seat restaurant is full of authentic Chicago memorabilia, and the waitresses wear *Chicago Sun-Times* newspaper-sellers' aprons. There is a large bar with a wide choice of U.S. beers and cocktails, including a specialty known as St. Valentine's Day Massacre. A television over the bar shows American baseball, football, and basketball games.

The specialty here is deep-dish pizza with toppings in all possible combinations. The regular-size pizza is enough for two or three, and the large one is suitable for four or five. The menu also includes stuffed mushrooms, garlic bread, salads, and homemade cheesecakes. Dress is casual.

HARD ROCK CAFÉ, 150 Old Park Lane, W1. Tel. 071/629-0382.
Cuisine: AMERICAN. **Reservations:** Not accepted. **Tube:** Green Park or Hyde Park Corner.
$ Prices: Appetizers £2.25–£5.25 ($3.40–$7.90); main dishes £5.45–£13.95 ($8.20–$20.90). AE, MC, V.
Open: Sun–Thurs 11:30am–12:30am, Fri–Sat 11:30am–1am.

This is a southern-cum-midwestern American roadside diner with good food, taped music, and service with a smile. It was established on June 14, 1971, and since then more than 12 million people have eaten here. Almost every night there's a line waiting: young people, visiting rock and film stars, and tennis players from America. The portions are generous, and the price of a main dish includes not only a salad but also fries. Specialties include smokehouse steak, filet mignon, and a T-bone special, along with charbroiled burgers and hot chili. The equally tempting dessert menu lists homemade apple pie and thick shakes. There's also a good selection of beer.

PUB

SHEPHERD'S TAVERN, 50 Hertford St., W1. Tel. 071/499-3017.

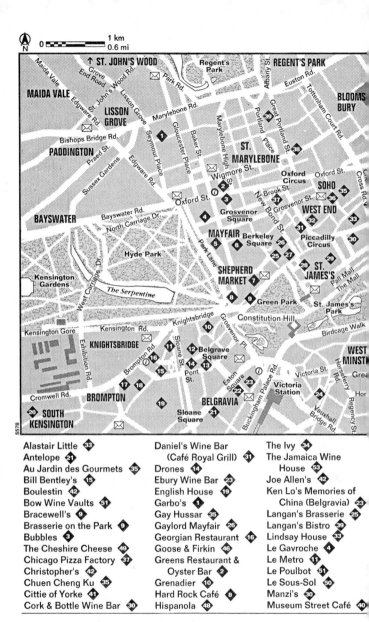

Alastair Little 🔷33	Daniel's Wine Bar (Café Royal Grill) 🔷31	The Ivy 🔷34
Antelope 🔷21		The Jamaica Wine House 🔷53
Au Jardin des Gourmets 🔷35	Drones 🔷14	
Bill Bentley's 🔷15	Ebury Wine Bar 🔷23	Joe Allen's 🔷42
Boulestin 🔷42	English House 🔷19	Ken Lo's Memories of China (Belgravia) 🔷23
Bow Wine Vaults 🔷51	Garbo's 🔷1	
Bracewell's 🔷9	Gay Hussar 🔷45	Langan's Brasserie 🔷25
Brasserie on the Park 🔷9	Gaylord Mayfair 🔷26	Langan's Bistro 🔷39
Bubbles 🔷3	Georgian Restaurant 🔷16	Lindsay House 🔷33
The Cheshire Cheese 🔷49	Greens Restaurant & Oyster Bar 🔷2	Le Gavroche 🔷4
Chicago Pizza Factory 🔷37		Le Metro 🔷11
Christopher's 🔷42	Goose & Firkin 🔷46	Le Poulbot 🔷51
Chuen Cheng Ku 🔷35	Grenadier 🔷10	Le Sous-Sol 🔷50
Cittie of Yorke 🔷41	Hard Rock Café 🔷8	Manzi's 🔷30
Cork & Bottle Wine Bar 🔷30	Hispanola 🔷48	Museum Street Café 🔷40

Cuisine: BRITISH. **Reservations:** Recommended. **Tube:** Green Park.
$ Prices: Appetizers £1.10–£3 ($1.70–$4.50); main courses £2.95–£7.95 ($4.40–$11.90). AE, DC, MC, V.
Open: Lunch Mon–Sat noon–3pm; dinner Mon–Sat 6–11pm, Sun 7–10:30pm; pub Mon–Fri 11am–11pm, Sat noon–3pm and 5:30–11pm, Sun noon–3pm and 7–10:30pm.

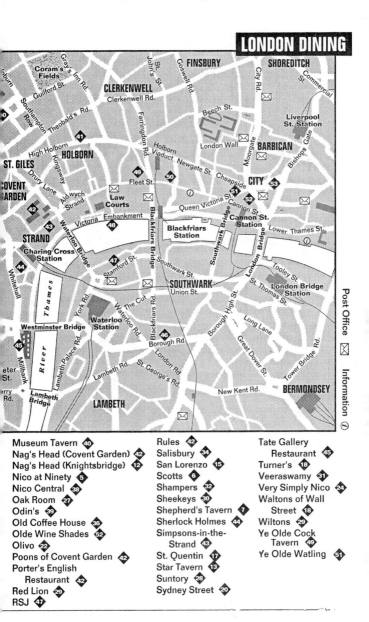

Museum Tavern ◆40
Nag's Head (Covent Garden) ◆42
Nag's Head (Knightsbridge) ◆12
Nico at Ninety ◆5
Nico Central ◆38
Oak Room ◆27
Odin's ◆39
Old Coffee House ◆36
Olde Wine Shades ◆52
Olivo ◆22
Poons of Covent Garden ◆42
Porter's English
  Restaurant ◆42
Red Lion ◆29
RSJ ◆47

Rules ◆42
Salisbury ◆34
San Lorenzo ◆15
Scotts ◆6
Shampers ◆32
Sheekeys ◆30
Shepherd's Tavern ◆7
Sherlock Holmes ◆44
Simpsons-in-the-
  Strand ◆43
St. Quentin ◆17
Star Tavern ◆13
Suntory ◆28
Sydney Street ◆20

Tate Gallery
  Restaurant ◆45
Turner's ◆18
Veeraswamy ◆31
Very Simply Nico ◆24
Waltons of Wall
  Street ◆18
Wiltons ◆29
Ye Olde Cock
  Tavern ◆49
Ye Olde Watling ◆51

This tavern attracts a congenial mix of patrons. There are many luxurious touches, including a collection of antique furniture, chief among which is a sedan chair that once belonged to the son of George III, the Duke of Cumberland. Many of the local habitués recall the tavern's popularity with the pilots of the Battle of Britain. Bar snacks and hot dishes include shepherd's pie and fish pie with vegetables. Upstairs, the owners operate a cozy restaurant—Georgian in style with cedar paneling—serving such classic British dishes as shepherd's pie, steak-and-kidney pie, and Oxford ham.

You can visit just for drinks, of course, with beer prices beginning at £1.65 ($2.50) and wine by the glass at £1.75 ($2.60).

ST. JAMES'S
EXPENSIVE

SUNTORY, 72–73 St. James's St., SW1. Tel. 071/409-0201.
Cuisine: JAPANESE. **Reservations:** Required. **Tube:** Green Park.
$ **Prices:** Appetizers £3.60–£12.50 ($5.40–$18.80); main courses £22–£42 ($33–$63); set lunch £22–£32 ($33–$48); fixed-price dinner £49.50–£64 ($74.30–$96). AE, DC, MC, V.
Open: Lunch Mon–Sat noon–1:30pm; dinner Mon–Sat 7–9:30pm.

Suntory is the most elite, expensive, and best Japanese restaurant in London. Owned and operated by Japanese distillers and brewers, it offers a choice of dining rooms in a setting evocative of a Japanese manor house. First-time visitors seem to prefer the teppanyaki dining room downstairs, where iron grills are set on each table and you watch the mastery of the high-hatted, knife-wielding chef. You can also dine in other rooms on sukiyaki, tempura, and sushi (especially good is the fresh, delicately sliced raw tuna). You may prefer a salad of shellfish and seaweed or a superb squid. Appetizers are artful and delicate, and even the tea is superior. You can be seated in one of the private dining rooms, but only if you are shoeless. Waitresses in traditional dress serve you with all the highly refined ritualistic qualities of the Japanese, including the presentation of hot towels.

PUB & WINE BARS

BUBBLES, 41 N. Audley St., W1. Tel. 071/491-3237.
Cuisine: ENGLISH/CONTINENTAL/VEGETARIAN. **Reservations:** Recommended. **Tube:** Marble Arch.
$ **Prices:** Appetizers £3–£5 ($4.50–$7.50); main courses £6.50–£12 ($9.80–$18); fixed-price dinner £9.50–£14.50 ($14.30–$21.80); fixed-price vegetarian menu £6.75–£7.50 ($10.10–$11.30); glass of wine from £1.90 ($2.90). MC, V.
Open: Lunch daily 11am–6pm; dinner daily 6–11pm.

Bubbles is an interesting wine bar lying between Upper Brook Street and Oxford Street (in the vicinity of Selfridges). The owners attach equal importance to their food and to their impressive wine list. Some wine selections are sold by the glass. On the ground floor, guests enjoy not only the fine wines but also draft beer and liquor, along with a limited but well-chosen selection of bar food—mussels marinara and meat and fish salads, for example. Downstairs, an à la carte restaurant serves both English and continental dishes, including an appealing vegetarian selection. You might begin with French onion soup, followed by roast rack of English lamb or roast duckling with lemon-and-tarragon sauce.

RED LION, 2 Duke of York St. (off Jermyn St.), SW1. Tel. 071/930-2030.
Cuisine: BRITISH. **Reservations:** Not necessary. **Tube:** Piccadilly Circus.

$ Prices: Sandwiches £1.50 ($2.30); main courses £1.50–£3.75 ($2.30–$5.60). No credit cards.

Open: Restaurant, Mon–Sat noon–2:30pm; pub, Mon–Sat 11am–11pm.

This little Victorian pub with its early 1900s decorations is one of London's few remaining gin palaces, with 150-year-old mirrors. Ian Nairm compared the pub's ambience to that of Edouard Manet's painting *A Bar at the Folies-Bergère.* (See the collection at the Courtauld Institute galleries.) The fare is pub grub: chips, port sausages, cheese-and-onion pie, fish and chips, and chicken pie. The food is prepared in upstairs kitchens and sent down in a century-old dumbwaiter; orders are placed at the bar. Wash down your meal with Ind Coope's fine ales. The house's special beer is Burton's, an unusual brew made of spring water from the Midlands town of Burton-on-Trent.

SHAMPERS, 4 Kingly St., W1. Tel. 071/437-1692.

Cuisine: CONTINENTAL. **Reservations:** Recommended. **Tube:** Oxford Circus.

$ Prices: Appetizers £3.20–£5.50 ($4.80–$8.30); main dishes £5.50–£13.50 ($8.30–$20.30); glass of wine from £2.10 ($3.20). AE, DC, MC, V.

Open: Restaurant, Mon–Sat noon–3pm; wine bar, Mon–Fri 11am–11pm, Sat 11am–3pm. **Closed:** Easter and Christmas.

For a number of years, this has been a favorite of West End wine-bar aficionados who gravitate to its location between Carnaby Street of 1960s fame and Regent Street of shoppers' fame. The basement is exclusively a restaurant, with the wine bar upstairs. In the restaurant you can order braised leg or breast of guinea fowl, and in the bar you can enjoy food as well. The restaurant is closed in the evening, but the bar serves an extended menu, incorporating not only the luncheon menu but also such dishes as grilled calves' liver, grilled pork sausages, and homemade duck sausages with lentils. Salads are especially popular, including tuna and pasta with spicy tomato sauce and chicken with tarragon-cream dressing. A platter of Irish mussels cooked in white wine seems to be everyone's favorite.

2. PICCADILLY, LEICESTER SQUARE & TRAFALGAR SQUARE

PICCADILLY

MODERATE

GREENS RESTAURANT AND OYSTER BAR, 36 Duke St., SW1. Tel. 071/930-4566.

Cuisine: SEAFOOD. **Reservations:** Recommended for dinner. **Tube:** Piccadilly Circus or Green Park.

$ Prices: Appetizers £3.50–£7.25 ($5.30–$10.90); main dishes £8.50–£17.50 ($12.80–$26.30); Sun brunch from £12.50 ($18.80). AE, DC, MC, V.

Open: Lunch Mon–Sat 12:30–2:45pm; dinner Mon–Sat 6–11pm; brunch Sun 11:30am–3:30pm.

A busy place, this restaurant is a good choice due to its excellent menu, charming staff, and central location. A cluttered entrance leads to a crowded bar, where you can stand at what the English call "rat-catcher counters," if the tables are full, to sip fine wines and (from September to May) enjoy oysters. Other foods include quail eggs, king prawns, smoked Scottish salmon, "dressed" crab, and baby lobsters. If you choose to go on into the dining room, you can select from a long menu that lists a number of fish dishes and such grilled foods as calves' liver and bacon, kedgeree, and Greens fish cakes with parsley sauce. Desserts include Duke of Cambridge tart, black-currant sorbet, and banana fritters.

WILTONS, 55 Jermyn St., SW1. Tel. 071/629-9955.
   Cuisine: BRITISH. **Reservations:** Required. **Tube:** Green Park or Piccadilly Circus.
$ Prices: Appetizers £4–£14.50 ($6–$21.80); main courses £13.50–£20 ($20.30–$30). AE, DC, MC, V.
   Open: Lunch Mon–Fri 12:30–2:30pm; dinner Mon–Sat 6–10:30pm. **Closed:** 2 weeks in Aug.

Wiltons is one of the leading exponents of cookery called "as British as a nanny." In spite of its move into new quarters, the restaurant has retained the lush ambience of its original premises. You might be tempted to have an apéritif or a drink at the bar near the entrance, where photos of the royal family alternate with oil portraits of the original owners. One of them, the legendary Jimmy Marks, supposedly used to "strike terror into the hearts of newcomers if he took a dislike to them." However, those days, still fondly recalled by some, are gone forever, and today a wide array of international guests are warmly welcomed.

The thoroughly British menu of this restaurant, which opened in 1941, is known for its fish and game. You might begin with an oyster cocktail and follow with Dover sole, plaice, salmon, or lobster, prepared in any number of ways. In season, you can choose among such delights as roast partridge, roast pheasant, roast grouse, and roast widgeon, a wild fish-eating river duck. The chef might ask you if you want it "blue" or "black," a reference to roasting times. Game is often accompanied by bread sauce (made of milk thickened with breadcrumbs). To finish, if you want something truly British, order a savory such as Welsh rarebit or soft roes, even anchovies. But if that's too much, try the sherry trifle or syllabub.

WINE BAR

DANIEL'S WINE BAR [CAFÉ ROYAL GRILL], 68 Regent St., W1. Tel. 071/437-9090, ext. 277.
   Cuisine: BRITISH. **Reservations:** Not necessary. **Tube:** Piccadilly Circus.
$ Prices: Appetizers £2.50–£2.80 ($3.80–$4.20); main courses £5 ($7.50); glass of wine from £2 ($3). AE, DC, MC, V.
   Open: Lunch Mon–Fri noon–2:30pm; wine bar, Mon–Fri noon–3pm and 5:30–11pm.

The deliberately unpretentious annex to the chillingly expensive Café Royal Grill, Daniel's dates from 1865. Both are accessible from the marble-floored lobby, where the literary greats of 19th-century England have trod, including Oscar Wilde. Despite its opulent design—art nouveau moldings, oaken half-paneling, and abundant framed cartoons and illustrations—the bar is very informal and has a

IMPRESSIONS

London's the dining-room of Christendom.
—THOMAS MIDDLETON, *CITY PAGEANT* (1617)

---

resident pianist whose melodies seem to make the wine ever so much more drinkable. Platters of food such as beef Stroganoff are served at lunchtime. The rest of the day until late into the night, only wine and drinks are served.

LEICESTER SQUARE
MODERATE

MANZI'S, 1–2 Leicester St. (off Leicester Sq.), WC2. Tel. 071/734-0224.
   Cuisine: SEAFOOD. **Reservations:** Required for dinner. **Tube:** Leicester Sq.
$ Prices: Appetizers £4.50–£6 ($6.80–$9); main courses £10.50–£18 ($15.80–$27). AE, DC, MC, V.
   Open: Lunch Mon–Sat noon–2:30pm; dinner Mon–Sat 5:30–11:30pm, Sun 6:30–10:30pm.

At Manzi's, London's oldest seafood restaurant, you can dine either in the simply decorated ground-floor restaurant or in the Cabin Room upstairs. Famous for its Whitstable and Colchester oysters, among other specialties, it has a loyal patronage that's drawn to its moderately priced fare and fresh ingredients. If you'd like something less expensive than their legendary oysters, I suggest a prawn cocktail, even fresh sardines. If you come here for lunch, you might happily settle for the crab salad. Main-course specialties include Dover sole and grilled turbot; steaks are also available. The house has a good selection of wines and sherries.

SHEEKEYS, 28–32 St. Martin's Court, WC2. Tel. 071/240-2565.
   Cuisine: SEAFOOD. **Reservations:** Required. **Tube:** Leicester Sq.
$ Prices: Appetizers £5.50–£11 ($8.30–$16.50); main courses £11–£22 ($16.50–$33). AE, DC, MC, V.
   Open: Lunch Mon–Fri 12:30–3pm; dinner Mon–Fri 6–11:15pm, Sat 5:30–11:15pm.

Since it was established in 1896 by an Irish-born vaudevillian, Sheekeys has always been closely associated with London's theater district. Occupying a series of small, intimate dining rooms, it features walls almost completely covered with photographs of British and North American stage and screen stars, many autographed. A formally dressed staff caters to the culinary needs of a conservative and well-heeled clientele who feels comfortable with the restaurant's sense of tradition and good manners. Seafood is the specialty here, one of the few places in London that almost never (only when specifically requested) fries its food. Instead, the delicate fresh ingredients are steamed, grilled, or stewed, then laden with such ingredients as sherry, cream, garlic, lemon, and herbs. The result is usually rich and delicious. Specialties include lobster-and-langoustine bisque, lobster Thermidor, Dover sole prepared in the style of Joseph Sheekey, jellied eels (a British delicacy), fish cakes, and a concoction identified as Sheekeys' fisherman's pie. Desserts include apple tart with Calvados.

PUB & WINE BAR

CORK & BOTTLE WINE BAR, 44–46 Cranbourn St., WC2. Tel. 071/734-7807.
  Cuisine: INTERNATIONAL. **Reservations:** Recommended. **Tube:** Leicester Sq.
  $ Prices: Appetizers £2.95–£4.25 ($4.40–$6.40); main courses £5.50–£8.95 ($8.30–$13.40); glass of wine from £2 ($3). AE, DC, MC, V.
  Open: Mon–Sat 11am–midnight, Sun noon–10:30pm.

Cork & Bottle is just off Leicester Square. The most successful dish is a raised cheese-and-ham pie, which has a cream cheese–like filling and crisp well-buttered pastry—not your typical quiche. (In just one week the bar sold 500 portions of this alone.) The kitchen also offers a spicy chicken salad, smoked chicken with avocado-and-grape salad, tandoori chicken, and lamb in ale. The expanded wine list features an excellent selection of Beaujolais crus and wines from Alsace, some 30 selections from "Down Under," 30 champagnes, and a good selection of California labels.

SALISBURY, 90 St. Martin's Lane, WC2. Tel. 071/836-5863.
  Cuisine: BRITISH. **Reservations:** Not accepted. **Tube:** Leicester Sq.
  $ Prices: Buffet meal £3.50–£4.95 ($5.30–$7.40); beer from £1.76 ($2.60). AE, DC, MC, V.
  Open: Mon–Sat 11am–11pm, Sun noon–3pm and 7–10:30pm.

Salisbury's glittering cut-glass mirrors reflect the faces of English stage stars (and hopefuls) sitting around the curved buffet-style bar. A less prominent place to dine is the old-fashioned wall banquette with its copper-topped tables and art nouveau decor. The light fixtures—veiled bronze girls in flowing robes holding up clusters of electric lights concealed in bronze roses—are appropriate. In the saloon, you'll see and hear the Oliviers of yesterday and tomorrow. But do not let this put you off your food. The pub's specialty, an array of homemade meat and vegetable pies set out on a buffet table with salads, is really quite good and inexpensive. Food is served from noon until 7:30pm.

TRAFALGAR SQUARE

PUB

SHERLOCK HOLMES, 10 Northumberland St., WC1. Tel. 071/930-2644.
  Cuisine: BRITISH. **Reservations:** Recommended for restaurant. **Tube:** Charing Cross or Embankment.
  $ Prices: Appetizers £2.50–£5 ($3.80–$7.50); main dishes £6.95–£12.95 ($10.40–$19.40); ground-floor snacks from £3 ($4.50). AE, DC, MC, V.
  Open: Restaurant, Mon–Sat 9am–9:30pm; Sun lunch noon–2pm, dinner 7–9:30pm. Pub, Mon–Sat 11am–11pm; Sun noon–3pm and 7–10:30pm.

It would be rather strange if the Sherlock Holmes were not the old gathering spot for the Baker Street Irregulars, a once-mighty clan of mystery lovers who met here to honor the genius of Sir Arthur Conan Doyle's most famous fictional character. Upstairs, you'll find a re-creation of the living room at 221b Baker Street and such "Holmesiana" as the serpent of *The Speckled Band* and the head of *The Hound of the Baskervilles.* In the upstairs dining room, you can order complete meals with wine. Main dishes are reliable, including roast beef and Yorkshire pudding as well as Chicken Sherlock Holmes with red-wine-and-mushroom sauce. You select dessert from the trolley. The downstairs is mainly for drinking, but there's a good snack bar with cold meats, salads, cheeses, and wine sold by the glass.

3. SOHO

MODERATE

ALASTAIR LITTLE, 49 Frith St., W1. Tel. 071/734-5183.
Cuisine: BRITISH. **Reservations:** Recommended. **Tube:**
Leicester Sq.
$ Prices: Appetizers £6.50–£12 ($9.80–$18); main courses £14–£18 ($21–$27); fixed-price three-course lunch £18 ($27). AE, MC, V.
Open: Lunch Mon–Fri noon–3pm; dinner Mon–Sat 6–11:30pm.
Tucked in an early 19th-century brick-fronted town house that for a brief period is said to have housed John Constable's art studio, this informal, cozy restaurant serves well-prepared meals. Owned by the British-Danish-Spanish trio of Alastair Little, his wife, Kirsten Pedersen, and Mercedes Downend, it features such main courses as roast baby brill with cèpes (flap mushrooms), filet of red snapper with parsley and grilled vegetable salad, and Chinese-style squab with crispy vegetables. Dessert might consist of a tart with lemon and goat cheese or a prune-and-almond galette served with vanilla ice cream. A full complement of wines (mostly Californian and Australian) might accompany your meal.

AU JARDIN DES GOURMETS, 5 Greek St., W1. Tel. 071/437-1816.
Cuisine: FRENCH. **Reservations:** Required. **Tube:** Tottenham Court Rd.
$ Prices: Appetizers £5–£8.95 ($7.50–$13.40); main courses £14–£19 ($21–$28.50); fixed-price three-course lunch or dinner £19.75 ($29.60). AE, DC, MC, V.
Open: Lunch Mon–Fri 12:15–2:30pm; dinner Mon–Sat 6:15–11:15pm.
Since 1931 this "Ile de France" off Soho Square is where devotees of Gallic cuisine gather to enjoy traditional specialties. The Jardin itself has climbed to a level of hospitality never previously attained, with its new kitchens and wine cellars; lavatories that can be reached without climbing two floors; and, most important of all, air-conditioned restaurant that separates smokers and nonsmokers in the two adjacent rooms on the ground floor. There is a comprehensive à la carte menu with such specialties as feuillette of braised lamb's tongue, sauté of fresh foie gras Aigre-Doux, noisettes of lamb with sauce Riches, and breast of pigeon roasted with cloves of garlic. The masterful selection of vintage Bordeaux and Burgundies is expertly served.

GAY HUSSAR, 2 Greek St., W1. Tel. 071/437-0973.

Cuisine: HUNGARIAN. **Reservations:** Required. **Tube:** Tottenham Court Rd.

$ Prices: Appetizers £4.50–£7.50 ($6.80–$11.30); main courses £12.50–£25 ($18.80–$37.50); fixed-price lunch £15 ($22.50). AE.

Open: Lunch Mon–Sat 12:30–2:30pm; dinner Mon–Sat 5:30–11pm.

Gay Hussar has been called "the best Hungarian restaurant in the world." The "last of the great Soho restaurants," it is an intimate place where diners can begin with a chilled wild-cherry soup or a hot, spicy redfish soup in the style of Szeged, located in Hungary's southern Great Plain. Main courses are likely to include stuffed cabbage; roast saddle of carp; half a perfectly done chicken served in mild paprika sauce with cucumber salad and noodles; and, of course, veal goulash with egg dumplings. For dessert, select either raspberry-and-chocolate torte or lemon-cheese pancakes.

THE IVY, 1–5 West St., WC2. Tel. 071/836-4751.

Cuisine: ENGLISH. **Reservations:** Required. **Tube:** Leicester Sq.

$ Prices: Appetizers £4–£11 ($6–$16.50); main courses £8–£18.50 ($12–$27.80). AE, DC, MC, V.

Open: Lunch daily noon–3pm; dinner daily 5:30pm–midnight (last order).

Effervescent and sophisticated, The Ivy has been intimately associated with the West End theater district since it was established in 1911. Its clientele has included Prime Ministers David Lloyd George and Winston S. Churchill (both of whom knew a lot about viands and wines), Noël Coward, Gracie Fields, Dame Sybil Thorndike, and Rex Harrison. Renovated in the early 1990s, it features near the entrance a tiny bar where guests might be asked to wait until their table is ready; its paneled decor seems deliberately designed to encourage discreet star-gazing. Meals are served till very late, a graceful acknowledgement of the allure of after-theater suppers. Most important, the place, with its ersatz-1930s look, is fun—buzzing and throbbing with the energy of London's glamour.

Menu items appear simple, but show a solid appreciation for fresh ingredients and skillful preparation. They include oysters Rockefeller, sautéed squid with tiger prawns, langoustines mayonnaise, Mediterranean fish soup, a great mixed grill, salads, and such English desserts as sticky toffee pudding and bitter-chocolate ice cream.

LINDSAY HOUSE, 21 Rommily St., W1. Tel. 071/439-0450.

Cuisine: BRITISH. **Reservations:** Required. **Tube:** Leicester Sq. or Tottenham Court Rd.

$ Prices: Appetizers £4–£7.75 ($6–$11.60); main courses £11.50–£15 ($17.30–$22.50); fixed-price lunch £14.75–£16.75 ($22.10–$25.10). AE, DC, MC, V.

Open: Lunch Mon–Sat 12:30–2:30pm, Sun 12:30–2pm; dinner Mon–Sat 6pm–midnight, Sun 7–10pm. **Closed:** Dec 25–26.

Lindsay House bases many of its dishes on 18th-century English recipes, although several platters are designated Tudor or nouvelle. Everyone—from royalty to film stars, from diplomats to regular people—shows up here, including an array of discerning Americans. Since it begins serving dinner early, you might want to consider it for dinner before a stage presentation at a Shaftesbury Avenue theater. Owners Roger Wren and Malcolm Livingston, who already run some of the most fashionable restaurants in London (including Waltons of Walton Street, English House, and the English Garden), decided to open this eating house in the heart of Soho. Fireplaces and fresh flowers give it class and style.

The food lives up to the decor. Appetizers, or "first dishes," include potted spinach with herbs (studded with chicken livers, ham, and tongue, served with Cumberland sauce). To follow, you might try roast rack of Southdown lamb or a traditional fish pie with halibut, salmon, scallops, and quail eggs in a creamy sauce. Summer puddings are often featured; packed with such traditional fruits as strawberries, red currants, and raspberries, they are served with raspberry coulis and Devonshire clotted cream. You might also order a floating island, one of England's best 18th-century confections: light poached meringues floating on a rose-scented custard.

INEXPENSIVE

CHUEN CHENG KU, 17 Wardour St., W1. Tel. 071/437-3281.
  Cuisine: CHINESE. **Reservations:** Recommended on weekend afternoons. **Tube:** Piccadilly Circus or Leicester Sq.
$ Prices: Appetizers £1.85–£9 ($2.80–$13.50); main courses £9.50–£15 ($14.30–$22.50); fixed-price menu from £18 ($27). AE, DC, MC, V.
  Open: Daily 11am–11:45pm. **Closed:** Dec 24–25.

This is one of the finest eateries in Soho's "New China." A large restaurant on several floors, Chuen Cheng Ku is noted for its Cantonese food and is said to have the longest and most interesting menu in London. Specialties are paper-wrapped prawns, rice in lotus leaves, steamed spareribs in black-bean sauce, and shredded pork with cashew nuts—all served in generous portions. Other à la carte dishes include fried oysters with ginger and scallions, sliced duck with chili-and-black-bean sauce, and steamed pork with plum sauce. Dim sum (dumplings) are served from 11am to 6pm.

PUB

OLD COFFEE HOUSE, 49 Beak St., W1. Tel. 071/437-2197.
  Cuisine: BRITISH. **Reservations:** Not accepted. **Tube:** Oxford Circus or Piccadilly Circus.
$ Prices: Main courses £3–£4 ($4.50–$6); beer from £1.70 ($2.60). No credit cards.
  Open: Restaurant, daily noon–3pm; pub, daily 11am–11pm.
Once honored as Soho Pub of the Year, the Old Coffee House takes its name from the coffee-house heyday of 18th-century London. Coffee was called "the devil's brew" back then, and the pub still serves pots of filtered coffee. The place is heavily decorated with bric-a-brac, including such items as old musical instruments and World War I recruiting posters. Have a drink at the long, narrow bar, with a lager costing from £1.80 ($2.70), or retreat to the upstairs restaurant, where you can enjoy good pub food at lunch, including such typically English dishes as steak-and-kidney pie, three vegetarian dishes, and scampi and chips.

4. BLOOMSBURY & FITZROVIA

BLOOMSBURY

MODERATE

MUSEUM STREET CAFÉ, 47 Museum St., W1. Tel. 071/ 405-3211.
   Cuisine: MODERN BRITISH. **Reservations:** Required. **Tube:** Tottenham Court Rd.

$ **Prices:** Lunch appetizers £3.50–£4.50 ($5.30–$6.80); lunch main courses £7–£9 ($10.50–$13.50); lunch three-course fixed-price menu £14 ($21); dinner three-course fixed-price menu £19.50 ($29.30). No credit cards.
   Open: Lunch Mon–Fri 12:30–2:15pm (last order); dinner Mon–Fri 7:30–9:15pm (last order).

A two-minute walk from the British Museum, this small-scale but charming dining room once contained the neighborhood's "greasy spoon" until it was transformed by Boston-born Gail Koerber and her English partner, Mark Nathan. Today, amid a setting of simple furniture and primitive paintings, you can enjoy maize-fed and charcoal-grilled chicken served with pesto sauce or kebabs of salmon and tuna with onion-and-red-wine sauce. Dessert might include crusty tarte tatin (apple pie).

PUB

MUSEUM TAVERN, 49 Great Russell St., WC1. Tel. 071/ 242-8987.
   Cuisine: ENGLISH. **Reservations:** Not accepted. **Tube:** Holborn or Tottenham Court Rd.

$ **Prices:** Bar snacks £3.25–£4.95 ($4.90–$7.40); pint of lager £1.80 ($2.70). AE, DC, MC, V.
   Open: Mon–Sat 11am–11pm, Sun noon–10:30pm.

On a corner opposite the British Museum, Museum Tavern is a pub dating from 1703. However, its Victorian trappings—velvet, oak paneling, and cut glass—are from 1855. It's right in the center of the London University area, very crowded at lunchtime, and frequented by writers and publishers as well as researchers at the museum. It is said that Karl Marx wrote in the pub over his meals. At lunch you can order such authentic low-cost English food as shepherd's pie and beef in beer with two vegetables. There's also a cold buffet, including smoked mackerel, turkey and ham pies, a selection of salads, and English cheeses.

FITZROVIA

MODERATE

NICO CENTRAL, 35 Great Portland St., W1. Tel. 071/436-8846.
   Cuisine: FRENCH. **Reservations:** Required. **Tube:** Oxford Circus.

$ **Prices:** Appetizers £4.60–£12 ($6.90–$18); main courses £7.70–£13 ($11.60–$19.50). AE, MC, V.

Open: Lunch Mon–Fri noon–2pm; dinner Mon–Sat 6:45–11:15pm.

In this brasserie, founded and inspired by London's most legendary chef, Nico Ladenis, who now cooks at Nico at Ninety (see above), this brasserie delivers earthy French cuisine. Of course, everything is handled with considerable culinary urbanity. Guests sit on bentwood chairs at linen-covered tables. Nearly a dozen appetizers—called "starters," the pride of the chef—will tempt you, especially Mediterranean fish soup with rouille and croûtons. Deep-fried squid salad with garlic mayonnaise is another signature dish, but nothing can top the pan-fried foie gras on toasted brioche with caramelized orange. For a main course, try the delightful pot-roasted guinea fowl with white *coco* beans (French white beans). Red mullet with basil-flavored potato purée is yet another temptation. All "puddings" (desserts) cost £5 ($7.50) and range from Armagnac parfait to Bakewell tart.

5. COVENT GARDEN, THE STRAND & HOLBORN

COVENT GARDEN

MODERATE

BOULESTIN, 1A Henrietta St., WC2. Tel. 071/836-7061.
   Cuisine: FRENCH. **Reservations:** Required. **Tube:** Covent Garden.
$ **Prices:** Appetizers £4.50–£15.50 ($6.80–$23.30); main courses £16.75–£18.95 ($25.10–$28.40); set lunch £18.75 ($28.10). AE, DC, MC, V.
   Open: Lunch Mon–Fri 12:30–3pm; dinner Mon–Sat 7:30–11:15pm. **Closed:** Bank holidays, last 3 weeks of Aug.

This famous restaurant was founded more than half a century ago by Marcel Boulestin, the first Fleet Street restaurant critic. It's reached by a side door that leads down into the basement beneath a bank. The chandeliers are still there, and the menu still has many of the old Boulestin dishes. Seared foie gras is served with sliced apples and balsamic vinegar as an appetizer, or you might sample Scottish chanterelles with baby-leek terrine. Poached filet of baby turbot comes with a sauce of white wine and shallots, and breast of pheasant is offered with chestnuts and cranberry-and-Calvados sauce. For dessert, choose from a selection of Boulestin sorbets and ice creams.

CHRISTOPHER'S, 18 Wellington St., WC2. Tel. 071/240-4222.
   Cuisine: AMERICAN. **Reservations:** Recommended. **Tube:** Covent Garden.
$ **Prices:** Appetizers £5–£12 ($7.50–$18); main courses £8–£18 ($12–$27). AE, DC, MC, V.
   Open: Lunch Mon–Fri noon–3pm; dinner Mon–Sat 6–11:30pm.

This is the most stylish, crowded, and sought-after American restaurant in London, favored by everyone from stage and film stars to the youthful and moneyed successes of London's financial district. It is in a Victorian-baroque building constructed in 1820 as a papier-mâché factory. After 1864, it was London's first licensed casino.

Many visitors are tempted to remain in the street-level bar, where steak, hamburger, oysters, and fresh salads are served and no one minds if you while away the time just drinking. More serious diners climb an elaborate corkscrew-shaped stone staircase beneath a lavishly frescoed ceiling to reach a pair of Italianate dining rooms. There, simple but flavorful American-inspired dishes are served, including smoked tomato soup with fresh pesto, rack of lamb, grilled breast of chicken, and stewed red cabbage with onions.

POONS OF COVENT GARDEN, 41 King St., WC2. Tel. 071/240-1743.
   Cuisine: CHINESE. **Reservations:** Recommended. **Tube:** Covent Garden.
$ **Prices:** Appetizers £2.30–£6.90 ($3.50–$10.40); main courses £6.90–£21 ($10.40–$31.50); fixed-price lunch £13.50 ($20.30); set dinner £23.50 ($35.30). AE, DC, MC, V.
   Open: Daily noon–11:30pm.
Run by Bill and Cecilia Poon, this is one of the best Chinese restaurants in London. Mr. Poon's great-great-grandfather cooked for Chinese emperors, and succeeding generations of the family have taken an interest in traditional Chinese cookery. The decor is reminiscent of a 1920s Raffles Hotel in Singapore. Tables surround an island see-through kitchen. Two of the most recommendable courses are Poons special crispy duck and Poons special wind-dried meat, including sausage, which is quite different in flavor from smoked. If you're a serious and dedicated gourmet of Cantonese cuisine, Mr. and Mrs. Poon will arrange for parties of 10 or more special menus featuring dishes not on the à la carte menu—if given at least 24 hours notice.

RULES, 35 Maiden Lane, WC2. Tel. 071/379-0258.
   Cuisine: ENGLISH. **Reservations:** Recommended. **Tube:** Covent Garden.
$ **Prices:** Appetizers £4.25–£9 ($6.40–$13.50); main courses £13–£15.50 ($19.50–$23.30). AE, MC, V.
   Open: Daily noon–midnight.
By anyone's estimate, this might be the most quintessentially British restaurant in London. Established in 1798 as an oyster bar and lined with the framed memorabilia of the British Empire at its height, it rambles through a series of Edwardian dining rooms dripping in patriotic nostalgia. In fact, it lays claim to being the oldest restaurant in London still operating on the site of its original premises. Around the turn of the century, Edward VII, then the portly Prince of Wales, used to arrive here very frequently with his mistress, Lillie Langtry, before heading up to a private red-velvet dining room on the second floor. Their signed portraits still embellish the yellowing walls, along with that of Charles Dickens, who crafted several of his novels here. Brilliant writer and curmudgeon Graham Greene made a visit to Rules an unchangeable condition of each of his birthdays, despite his long-term residence in the south of France. Other artists and actors who have appreciated Rules include William Thackeray, John Galsworthy, H. G. Wells, Evelyn Waugh, John Barrymore, Clark Gable, and Sir Laurence Olivier.

Today, amid cartoons executed by George Whitelaw in the 1920s, you can order such classic dishes as Irish or Scottish oysters, jugged hare, and Aylesbury duckling in orange sauce. Depending on the season, you can also order wild Scottish salmon or wild sea trout; wild Highland red deer; or any of an array of such game birds as grouse, snipe, partridge, pheasant, and woodcock. These might be followed by those unusual British savories called angels on horseback (oysters wrapped in bacon and served on toast).

INEXPENSIVE

PORTER'S ENGLISH RESTAURANT, 17 Henrietta St., WC2. Tel. 071/836-6466.
Cuisine: ENGLISH. **Reservations:** Recommended. **Tube:** Covent Garden or Charing Cross.
$ Prices: Main courses £7.25–£7.70 ($10.90–$11.60); fixed-price menu £15 ($22.50). AE, MC, V.
Open: Mon–Sat noon–11:30pm, Sun noon–10:30pm.

This place is owned by the current Earl of Bradford, who is a frequent visitor. It has a friendly, informal, and lively atmosphere in comfortable surroundings on two floors. Porter's specializes in classic English pies, including steak and kidney, lamb and apricot, and chicken and broccoli. Main courses are so generous that the menu wisely eliminates appetizers. Traditional roast beef with Yorkshire pudding is available on weekends. Served with whipped cream or custard, the puddings come hot or cold, and they include bread-and-butter pudding and steamed-syrup sponge. The English call all desserts "puddings," but at Porter's they are the puddings in the American sense. The bar concocts quite a few exotic cocktails, and you can also order cider by the half pint as well as English wine or traditional English mead. A traditional afternoon tea is also served.

PUB

NAG'S HEAD, 10 James St., WC2. Tel. 071/836-4678.
Cuisine: ENGLISH. **Reservations:** Not accepted. **Tube:** Covent Garden.
$ Prices: Sandwiches £2.50 ($3.80); salads £3.95 ($5.90); main courses £5.50 ($8.30); pint of lager £1.80 ($2.70). No credit cards.
Open: Restaurant, Mon–Sun 11:30am–2:30pm; pub, Mon–Sat 11am–11pm, Sun noon–3pm and 7–10:30pm.

The Nag's Head is one of London's most famous Edwardian pubs. In days of yore, patrons had to make their way through lorries of fruit and flowers for a drink here; elegantly dressed operagoers used to mix with cockney cauliflower peddlers at the bar. With the moving of the market, 300 years of British tradition faded away. Today, the pub is patronized mainly by young people, who seem to fill up all the tables every evening, as well as the drinking space around the bar. Try a draft Guinness for a change of pace. Lunch is typical pub grub: sandwiches, salads, pork cooked in cider, and garlic prawns.

THE STRAND

MODERATE

SIMPSON'S-IN-THE-STRAND, 100 The Strand, WC2. Tel. 071/836-9112.

Cuisine: BRITISH. **Reservations:** Required. **Tube:** Charing Cross or Embankment.

$ Prices: Appetizers £2.75–£14 ($4.10–$21); main courses £9–£18.50 ($13.50–$27.80); fixed-price lunch £21.25 ($31.90); fixed-price dinner £21.25 ($31.90) (6–7pm only). AE, DC, MC, V.

Open: Lunch Mon–Sat noon–3pm, Sun noon–2pm; dinner Mon–Sat 6–11pm, Sun 6–9pm.

Simpson's is more of an institution than a restaurant. Located next to the Savoy Hotel, it has been in business since 1828. This very Victorian place features Adam paneling, crystal, and an army of grandly formal waiters hovering about. Men should wear jackets and ties. Most first-time visitors to London should count on seeing the Changing of the Guard, then lunching at Simpson's.

One food critic wrote that "nouvelle cuisine here means anything after Henry VIII." However, there is one point on which most diners agree: Simpson's serves the best roasts (joints) in London. Huge roasts are trolleyed to your table and slabs of beef are carved off and served with traditional Yorkshire pudding. The classic dishes are roast sirloin of beef; roast saddle of mutton with red-currant jelly; roast Aylesbury duckling; and steak, kidney, and mushroom pie. Remember to tip the coat-tailed carver. For dessert, you might order the treacle roll and custard or Stilton with vintage port.

INEXPENSIVE

JOE ALLEN'S, 13 Exeter St., WC2. Tel. 071/836-0651.

Cuisine: AMERICAN. **Reservations:** Required. **Tube:** Covent Garden or Embankment.

$ Prices: Appetizers £4–£7 ($6–$10.50); main courses £6.50–£12.50 ($9.80–$18.80). No credit cards.

Open: Mon–Sat noon–1am, Sun noon–midnight.

This fashionable American restaurant, which has branches in New York and Paris, attracts mainly theater crowds. It lies north of the Strand in the vicinity of the Savoy Hotel. The decor is inspired by that of the New York branch, with theater posters and gingham tablecloths in red-and-white check. Specialties are black-bean soup, barbecued ribs with black-eyed peas, Cajun chicken breast, chili, and carrot cake.

HOLBORN

PUB

CITTIE OF YORKE, 22–23 High Holborn, WC1. Tel. 071/242-7670.

Cuisine: ENGLISH. **Reservations:** Not accepted. **Tube:** Holborn or Chancery Lane.

$ Prices: Appetizers £2–£3 ($3–$4.50); main courses £2.50–£7 ($3.80–$10.50); fixed-price menu £9.50 ($14.30); glass of wine £1.80 ($2.70). MC, V.

Open: Mon–Fri 11am–11pm, Sat 11:30am–3pm and 5:30–11pm.

Cittie of Yorke stands near the Holborn Bars, the historic entrance to London marked by dragons holding the coat-of-arms of the City between their paws. Persons entering and leaving London were checked and paid tolls here. The pub has stood on this site since 1430. Its principal hall, said to have the longest bar in England, boasts handsome screenwork, comfortable compartments, a row of huge vats, and a high trussed roof. The place is popular with barristers and judges. Lunch is a bar-snack type of affair. You have a choice of four hot platters, plus burgers, goulash, and casseroles. Dinner, slightly more formal, includes ham steak, fresh fish, lasagne, and rumpsteak. Appetizers are served only at dinner.

6. THE CITY & FLEET STREET

THE CITY
MODERATE

LE POULBOT, 45 Cheapside, EC2. Tel. 071/236-4379.
    Cuisine: FRENCH. **Reservations:** Required. **Tube:** St. Paul's.
$ Prices: Appetizers in brasserie £3.60–£5.65 ($5.40–$8.50); main courses £4.65–£9.95 ($7–$14.90); set lunch in restaurant £31.50 ($47.30). AE, DC, MC, V.
    Open: Restaurant, Mon–Fri noon–2:30pm; brasserie, Mon–Fri noon–2:30pm.

Le Poulbot is a French restaurant par excellence. Founded by the Roux brothers of Le Gavroche fame, it was launched in 1969 and ever since has been attracting the movers and shakers of the City's business world. The fixed-price menu is seasonally adjusted depending on what is best at the market; there is no à la carte menu. The new-style continental dishes and longtime favorites include turbot fricassée and lamb cooked in its own juice and flavored with mint.

Upstairs, Le Poulbot offers what the French call a casse-croûte bar, which purveys a limited à la carte menu and French "snacks." This brasserie might be an ideal choice if you're taking a sightseeing tour of the City.

LE SOUS-SOL, 32 Old Bailey, EC4. Tel. 071/236-7931.
    Cuisine: FRENCH. **Reservations:** Required. **Tube:** St. Paul's.
$ Prices: Two-course fixed-price lunch £19.95 ($29.90); three-course fixed-price lunch £24.50 ($36.80). AE, MC, V.
    Open: Mon–Fri noon–3pm.

Acclaimed by some critics as one of the finest restaurants in the City, this spacious air-conditioned establishment serves a creative French cuisine that is prepared with fresh, quality ingredients. It has a pronounced Gallic decor, with impeccable service even when things are rushed. Guests sit down with a glass of Kir and examine the fixed-price luncheon menu, which changes daily. You might begin with game terrine with grapes or crab-and-fennel bisque, then follow with roast guinea fowl with ginger and lime or filet of lamb sautéed with herbs. Each day a traditional plat du jour is offered, evoking memories of old-fashioned Anglo-French cuisine. This featured dish may range from braised pig's trotters to traditional French lamb stew.

PUB & WINE BARS

BOW WINE VAULTS, 10 Bow Churchyard, EC4. Tel. 071/ 248-1121.
    Cuisine: ENGLISH. **Reservations:** Recommended. **Tube:** Bank or St. Paul's.

$ Prices: Appetizers £2.50–£5.95 ($3.80–$8.90); main courses £5.50–£13.50 ($8.30–$20.30); glass of wine from £2 ($3). AE, DC, MC, V.

Open: Restaurant, Mon–Fri 11:30am–3pm; pub, Mon–Fri 11:30am–8pm.

Bow Wine Vaults existed long before the current wine-bar fad that began in the 1970s and is now firmly entrenched in London. It attracts cost-conscious diners and drinkers from the financial district, who head for its vaulted cellars. Menu choices in the Cellar Grill, as it's called, include such traditional fare as deep-fried Camembert, chicken Kiev, and a mixed grill, along with fish. More elegant meals are served in the street-level dining room, called The Restaurant, which offers an English-inspired menu, including mussels in cider sauce, English wild mushrooms in puff pastry, and beef Wellington. Try the steak with brown-butter sauce. Adjacent to The Restaurant is a cocktail bar, popular with City employees after work.

THE JAMAICA WINE HOUSE, St. Michael's Alley (without number; off Cornhill), EC3. Tel. 071/626-9496.
   Cuisine: ENGLISH. **Reservations:** Not accepted. **Tube:** Bank.
$ Prices: Bar snacks £1–£3 ($1.50–$4.50); lager £1.65–£1.95 ($2.50–$2.90). AE, MC, V.
   Open: Restaurant, Mon–Fri 11:30am–3pm; wine bar, Mon–Fri 11:30am–8pm.

The Jamaica Wine House was one of the first coffeehouses opened in England, and, reputedly, in the Western world. For years, London merchants and daring sea captains came here to transact deals over rum and coffee. Nowadays, the two-level house dispenses beer, ale, lager, and fine wine, among them a variety of ports. The oak-paneled bar is on the street level, attracting a jacket-and-tie crowd of investment bankers. You can order game pie and baked potatoes, toasted sandwiches, such old English favorites as Lancashire hot pot and shepherd's pie, and even Créole fish pie and goulash. The basement bar is an even cozier retreat.

OLDE WINE SHADES, 6 Martin Lane, Cannon St., EC4. Tel. 071/626-6876.
   Cuisine: ENGLISH. **Reservations:** Not necessary. **Tube:** Cannon St.
$ Prices: Appetizers £2.50–£4.25 ($3.80–$6.40); main courses £3.50–£12 ($5.30–$18); glass of wine £2.50 ($3.80). MC, V.
   Open: Lunch Mon–Fri 11:30am–3pm. **Closed:** Bank holidays.

Dating from 1663 and a survivor of both the Great Fire of 1666 and Hitler's bombs, this is the oldest wine house in the City. Located near the Monument (a famous London landmark designed by Christopher Wren to commemorate the Great Fire of 1666), Olde Wine Shades is decorated with oil paintings and 19th-century political cartoons. It is also one of the many London bars that Dickens used to patronize. There is a restaurant downstairs, but you can also order light meals upstairs, including Breton pâté, French bread with ham "off the bone," jacket potatoes filled with cheese, venison pie with salad garnish, or a large beef salad. The simple fare notwithstanding, men must wear jackets, collars, and ties.

YE OLDE WATLING, 29 Watling St., EC4. Tel. 071/248-6252.

Cuisine: ENGLISH. **Reservations:** Not accepted. **Tube:** Mansion House.

$ Prices: Fixed-price lunch £3.95–£5 ($5.90–$7.50); bar snacks from £1.60 ($2.40); beer from £1.70 ($2.60). AE, MC, V.

Open: Restaurant, Mon–Fri noon–2:30pm; pub, Mon–Fri 11am–9pm.

Ye Olde Watling was built after the Great Fire of 1666. On the ground level is a mellow pub, and upstairs is an intimate restaurant where, under oak beams and at trestle tables, you can dine on English main dishes for lunch. The menu varies daily, with such choices as beef-and-ale pie, steak-and-kidney pie, seafood Mornay, lasagne, chili con carne, and usually a vegetarian dish. All are served with two vegetables or salad, plus rice or potatoes.

FLEET STREET

INEXPENSIVE

CHESHIRE CHEESE, Wine Office Court, 145 Fleet St., EC4. Tel. 071/353-6170.

Cuisine: ENGLISH. **Reservations:** Not necessary. **Tube:** St. Paul's.

$ Prices: Appetizers £2–£3.50 ($3–$5.30); main courses £6.25–£9 ($9.40–$13.50). AE, DC, MC, V.

Open: Lunch daily noon–2:30pm; dinner daily 6–9:30pm. Drinks and bar snacks available daily 11am–11pm.

Set within a recently remodeled, carefully preserved building whose foundation was laid in the 13th century, this is one of the most famous of the old city chophouses and pubs. Established in 1667, it claims to be the spot where Dr. Samuel Johnson (who lived nearby) entertained admirers with his acerbic wit. Later, many of the ink-stained journalists and scandal-mongers of 19th- and early 20th-century Fleet Street made its four-story premises their "local."

You'll find six bars and three dining rooms here. The house specialties include "ye famous pudding" (steak, kidney, mushrooms, and game) and Scottish roast beef, with Yorkshire pudding and horseradish sauce. Sandwiches, salads, and standby favorites like steak-and-kidney pie are also available.

PUB

YE OLDE COCK TAVERN, 22 Fleet St., EC4. Tel. 071/353-8570.

Cuisine: ENGLISH. **Reservations:** Recommended. **Tube:** Temple or Chancery Lane.

$ Prices: Appetizers £2.50–£5.25 ($3.80–$7.90); main courses £8–£11 ($12–$16.50); buffet lunch £9.95 ($14.90); beer from £1.75 ($2.60). AE, DC, MC, V.

Open: Carvery, lunch Mon–Fri noon–3pm; pub, Mon–Fri 11:30am–10:30pm.

Dating back to 1549, this tavern boasts a long line of literary patrons. Samuel Pepys mentioned the pub in one of his diaries. Dickens frequented it, and Tennyson referred to it in one of his poems, a copy of which is framed and proudly displayed near the front entrance. It is one of the few buildings in London to have survived the Great Fire of

1666. At street level, you can order a pint as well as snack-bar food. You can also order steak-and-kidney pie or a cold chicken-and-beef plate with salad. At the Carvery upstairs, a meal includes a choice of appetizers, followed by roast beef, lamb, pork, or turkey.

7. WESTMINSTER & VICTORIA

WESTMINSTER

INEXPENSIVE

TATE GALLERY RESTAURANT, Millbank, SW1. Tel. 071/ 834-6754.
   Cuisine: ENGLISH. **Reservations:** Required 2 days in advance. **Tube:** Pimlico. **Bus:** 88.
   $ Prices: Appetizers £3.75–£6 ($5.60–$9); main courses £9.25–£14.50 ($13.90–$21.80). MC, V.
   Open: Lunch Mon–Sat noon–3pm.

This restaurant is particularly attractive to wine fanciers, offering what may be the best bargains for superior wines anywhere in Britain. Bordeaux and Burgundies are in abundance, and the management keeps the markup between 40% and 65%, rather than the 100% to 200% added to the wholesale price in other restaurants. In fact, the prices here are even lower than they are in most retail wine shops. Wines begin at £8.50 ($12.80) per bottle or £1.75 ($2.60) per glass. Wine connoisseurs frequently come for lunch, heedless of the paintings.

If you do desire food, the restaurant specializes in English cuisine. You can choose "umbles paste" (a pâté); "hindle wakes" (cold stuffed chicken and prunes); "pye with fruyt ryfshews" (fruit tart topped with meringue); or one of "Joan Cromwell's grand sallets," made of raisins, almonds, cucumbers, olives, pickled beans, and shrimp, among other ingredients. If you prefer more conventional dishes, there are omelets, steak, ham, roasts of beef and lamb, fish, and the traditional steak, kidney, and mushroom pie.

VICTORIA

MODERATE

KEN LO'S MEMORIES OF CHINA, 67–69 Ebury St., SW1. Tel. 071/730-7734.
   Cuisine: CHINESE. **Reservations:** Required. **Tube:** Victoria Station.
   $ Prices: Appetizers £3.65–£8.80 ($5.50–$13.20); main courses £8.40–£26.50 ($12.60–$39.80); fixed-price lunch £18.50 ($27.80); fixed-price dinner £24–£27 ($36–$40.50). AE, DC, MC, V.
   Open: Lunch Mon–Sat noon–2:30pm; dinner Mon–Sat 7–10:45pm.

Considered the finest Chinese eatery in London by many food critics, this restaurant was founded by Ken Lo, whose grandfather was the Chinese ambassador to the Court of St. James's (he was knighted by Queen Victoria in 1880). Mr. Lo has written more than 30 cookbooks and once had his own TV cooking show; his restaurant has been called "a gastronomic bridge between London and China." Against a modern minimalist decor, Cantonese quick-fried beef in oyster sauce, lobster with handmade noodles, pomegranate prawn balls, and "bang bang chicken" (a Szechuan dish) are served.

VERY SIMPLY NICO, 48A Rochester Row, SW1. Tel. 071/630-8061.
  Cuisine: FRENCH. **Reservations:** Required. **Tube:** Victoria Station.
$ **Prices:** Three-course fixed-price lunch £23 ($34.50); three-course fixed-price dinner £25 ($37.50). AE, MC, V.
  Open: Lunch Mon–Fri noon–2pm; dinner Mon–Sat 6:45–11:15pm.

This place was created in a moment of whimsy by Nico Ladenis, owner of the grander and more expensive Nico at Ninety (see above). Run by his sous-chef, Very Simply Nico is, in the words of Nico, "cheap and cheerful." Wood floors seem to reverberate the din of contented diners, who pack in here daily at snug tables. The food is often simply prepared and invariably French inspired, with fresh ingredients handled deftly in the kitchen. The set menu changes frequently.

WINE BAR

EBURY WINE BAR, 139 Ebury St., SW1. Tel. 071/730-5447.
  Cuisine: CONTINENTAL. **Reservations:** Recommended. **Tube:** Victoria Station or Sloane Sq.
$ **Prices:** Appetizers £2.50–£4.75 ($3.80–$7.10); main courses £7.25–£11 ($10.90–$16.50); fixed-price Sun lunch £8.95 ($13.40); glass of wine from £2.20 ($3.30). AE, DC, MC, V.
  Open: Lunch Mon–Sat 11am–3pm, Sun noon–2:45pm; dinner daily 6–10:30pm.
Convenient for dining or drinking, this wine bar and bistro attracts a youthful clientele to its often-crowded though always atmospheric precincts. Wine is sold either by the glass or by the bottle. You can always get an enticing plat du jour, such as traditional beef Wellington or one of the grilled filet steaks.

8. KNIGHTSBRIDGE & BELGRAVIA

KNIGHTSBRIDGE

MODERATE

GEORGIAN RESTAURANT, in Harrods Department Store, 87-135 Brompton Rd., SW1. Tel. 071/581-1656.
  Cuisine: ENGLISH. **Reservations:** Recommended but taken only for lunch. **Tube:** Knightsbridge.
$ **Prices:** Appetizers £3.15–£10.50 ($4.70–$15.80); main courses £10.95–£15.95 ($16.40–$23.90); three-course set lunch £18.50 ($27.80); sandwiches and pastries at teatime £8.95 ($13.40). AE, DC, MC, V.

Open: Lunch Mon–Sat noon–2:45pm; tea Mon–Sat 3:45–5:15pm.

Ⓢ The Georgian Restaurant, lying atop London's fabled emporium, under elaborate ceilings and belle époque skylights, is one of the neighborhood's most appealing places for lunch and afternoon tea. One of the rooms, big enough for a ballroom, features a pianist, whose music trills among the crystals of the chandeliers. A sprawling lunchtime buffet features cold meats and an array of fresh salads. Guests who want a hot meal can head for the carvery section, where a uniformed crew of chefs dish out such offerings as roast beef with Yorkshire pudding, poultry, fish, and pork. First courses and desserts are brought to your table.

SAN LORENZO, 22 Beauchamp Place, SW3. Tel. 071/584-1074.
  Cuisine: ITALIAN. **Reservations:** Required. **Tube:** Knightsbridge.
$ Prices: Appetizers £4.50–£8 ($6.80–$12); main courses £9.50–£17 ($14.30–$25.50). No credit cards.
  Open: Lunch Mon–Sat 12:30–3pm; dinner Mon–Sat 7:30–11:30pm.

Opened in 1987, this fashionable modern place is by now firmly established among not only artists and writers but also models and photographers. It is a favorite of Princess Diana. Reliability is the keynote of the cuisine, along with good-quality produce, often seasoned with fresh herbs. The delectable menu offers homemade fettuccine with salmon, carpaccio, risotto with fresh asparagus, traditional regional Italian dishes such as salt cod with polenta and bollito misto, fried calamari, and partridge in white-wine sauce. The veal piccata is exceptionally good.

WALTONS OF WALTON STREET, 121 Walton St., SW3. Tel. 071/584-0204.
  Cuisine: INTERNATIONAL. **Reservations:** Recommended. **Tube:** South Kensington or Knightsbridge.
$ Prices: Appetizers £6–£16.50 ($9–$24.80); main courses £13.70–£17.50 ($20.60–$26.30); ''Simply Waltons'' fixed-price lunch £14.75 ($22.10); three-course Sun set lunch £16.50 ($24.80); late-night fixed-price supper £22 ($33). AE, DC, MC, V.
  Open: Lunch Mon–Sat 12:30–2:30pm, Sun 12:30–2pm; dinner Mon–Sat 7:30–11pm, Sun 7:30–10:30pm; late-night supper Mon–Sun from 10pm.

A posh and intimate rendezvous, Waltons offers the best-quality fresh produce from local and European markets and serves it with flair amid silk walls and floral decorations. Its chefs prepare a refined international cuisine, featuring such dishes as roast breast of Norfolk duckling and roast filet of Welsh lamb with crab. Specialties include terrine of truffled foie gras, whole roast lobster with coriander and ginger, and orange mousse on white-chocolate sauce. Walton's, long a favorite with the Harrods shopping crowd, also has special-value fixed-price menus. The wide-ranging wine list, encompassing vintages from Australia to California, features the best champagnes in London.

INEXPENSIVE

DRONES, 1 Pont St., SW1. Tel. 071/235-9638.

Cuisine: INTERNATIONAL. **Reservations:** Required. **Tube:** Sloane Sq. or Knightsbridge.

$ Prices: Appetizers £3.80–£5 ($5.70–$7.50); main courses £9.95–£16 ($14.90–$24). AE, DC, MC, V.

Open: Lunch Mon–Sat 12:30–2:45pm; dinner Mon–Sat 7:30–11pm.

Drones was labeled by one newspaper columnist as "the unofficial club for bright people at least half of whom seem to know each other." The late David Niven and his friends launched this two-floor restaurant some years ago, and its reputation for charm and chic has spread. There is no elaborate menu or fancy sauces—just simple, good food. At lunch have the cheese soufflé or salmon fish cakes and parsley sauce. For dinner, the calves' liver with bacon is superb (have it cooked pink if you prefer it). As an appetizer, try the salad of baby leaf spinach and bacon with shaved parmesan or the scallops and frisée salad with garlic oil. Main-dish specialties include veal Pojarsky, roast sea bass with fondue of braised fennel, and Cornish crab salad. For dessert, try steamed ginger-and-treacle pudding or warm mango soufflé. The menu is wisely limited and changes monthly. Two plats du jour are featured. If you linger at the Bar while waiting for a table (a likely possibility), take a look at the baby pictures of famous movie stars and pictures by award-winning young British Artists, all for sale. The decor is that of an Edwardian conservatory.

PUB & WINE BARS

BILL BENTLEY'S, 31 Beauchamp Place, SW3. Tel. 071/589-5080.

Cuisine: ENGLISH. **Reservations:** Recommended. **Tube:** Knightsbridge.

$ Prices: Appetizers £3.50–£7.75 ($5.30–$11.60); main courses £7–£16 ($10.50–$24); glass of wine from £1.80 ($2.70). MC, V.

Open: Lunch Mon–Sat noon–2:30pm; dinner Mon–Sat 6–10:30pm.

Bill Bentley's stands on a fashionable restaurant- and boutique-lined block. Its wine list is varied and reasonable, including a good selection of Bordeaux. Many visitors come here just to sample the wines, including some "New World" choices along with popular French selections. In summer, a garden patio is used. If you don't prefer the formality of the restaurant, you can order from the wine-bar menu that begins with half a dozen oysters, or you can enjoy the chef's fish soup with croûtons and rouille. Main dishes include Bill Bentley's famous fish cakes, served with tomato sauce, and the day's specialties are written on a chalkboard. In keeping with contemporary trends in London dining, the menu has been simplified and is rather less expensive than before. The carte is changed frequently, but typical dishes might include duck-breast salad with beetroot vinaigrette as an appetizer, followed by pan-fried wing of skate with lemon and capers or salmon en croûte with hollandaise sauce. All main dishes are served with a selection of fresh vegetables.

LE METRO, 28 Basil St., SW3. Tel. 071/589-6286.

Cuisine: CONTINENTAL. **Reservations:** Accepted only for large parties. **Tube:** Knightsbridge.

$ Prices: Appetizers £2.75–£4.65 ($4.10–$7); main courses

£5.35–£8.55 ($8–$12.80); glass of wine £1.95 ($2.90). AE, MC, V.

Open: Mon–Fri noon–10:30pm, Sat 7:30am–4pm.

Located around the corner from Harrods, Le Metro draws a fashionable crowd to its basement precincts. You can order special wines by the glass instead of by the bottle. Owned by David and Margaret Levin, the place serves good, solid, and reliable food prepared with flair. The frequently changed menu might include an intriguing squid-and-mussel risotto with pinenuts and basil; grilled *gambas* (shrimp) with garlic, olive oil, and herbs; or spicy baby chicken with turmeric and warm potato salad. Special wines are dispensed from a *cruover* that preserves their freshness.

NAG'S HEAD, 53 Kinnerton St., SW1. Tel. 071/235-1135.
   Cuisine: ENGLISH. **Reservations:** Not necessary. **Tube:** Knightsbridge.
$ **Prices:** Appetizers £1.95–£2.85 ($2.90–$4.30); main dishes £3.50–£3.95 ($5.30–$5.90); beer from £1.80 ($2.70). No credit cards.
   Open: Mon–Sat 11am–11pm, Sun noon–3pm and 7–10:30pm.

Nag's Head, snuggled on a "back street," is a short walk from the deluxe Berkeley Hotel. Previously a jail dating from 1780, it is said to be the smallest pub in London, although others also claim that distinction. In 1921, it was sold for £12 and 6p.

Have a drink up front or wander to the tiny little bar in the rear. For food, you might enjoy "real ale sausage" (made with pork and ale), shepherd's pie, steak-and-mushroom pie, or even the quiche of the day. This warm and cozy pub, with a welcoming staff, is patronized by a cosmopolitan clientele—newspaper people, musicians, and curious tourists.

BELGRAVIA

INEXPENSIVE

OLIVO, 21 Eccleston St., SW1. Tel. 071/730-2505.
   Cuisine: ITALIAN. **Reservations:** Required. **Tube:** Victoria Station.
$ **Prices:** Appetizers £3.50–£5.50 ($5.30–$8.30); main courses £8–£15.50 ($12–$23.30); fixed-price lunch menu £13 ($19.50) and £15 ($22.50). AE, MC, V.
   Open: Lunch Mon–Fri noon–2:30pm; dinner Mon–Fri 7–11pm.
   Closed: Last 3 weeks in Aug.

Located on the periphery of Belgravia, Olivo is the choice of many a discriminating London diner. The artfully simple decor mingles high-tech elements with bright colors, unusual flowers, and imaginative lighting. The menu offers flavorful combinations whose ingredients are impeccably fresh. The vegetables, too often neglected in England, are perfectly cooked and beautifully served by the polite waiters. The restaurant's owners have set for themselves a lofty goal: to become the best Italian restaurant in London.

You might begin with grilled cuttlefish salad or grilled vegetables flavored with basil. Several pasta dishes, including pumpkin ravioli with sage, can be ordered as an appetizer. Main dishes include grilled loin of pork with lentils and pan-fried calves' liver with marsala. For dessert, try the pear cooked in red wine with cinnamon, followed by an espresso.

PUBS

ANTELOPE, 22 Eaton Terrace, SW1. Tel. 071/730-7781.
    Cuisine: ENGLISH. **Reservations:** Recommended for upstairs
dining room. **Tube:** Sloane Sq.

$ **Prices:** Appetizers £1.75–£2.75 ($2.60–$4.10); main courses
£7.85–£9 ($11.80–$13.50); Sun brunch £9.50 ($14.30); glass of
wine £2.20 ($3.30). MC, V.

    Open: Lunch daily 11am–3pm; pub, Mon–Sat 11am–11pm, Sun
noon–3pm and 7:30–10:30pm.

Located on the fringe of Belgravia, at the gateway to Chelsea, this
eatery caters to a hodgepodge of clients, aptly described as "people of
all classes, colours, and creeds." It is also a base for English rugby
aficionados (not to be confused with those who follow soccer). At
lunchtime, the ground-floor bar provides hot and cold pub food, but
in the evening, only drinks are served there. On the second floor
(British first floor), the lunch menu includes principally English
dishes—steak-and-kidney pie, jugged hare, and the like. Steaks are
also served. On Sunday, a two-course carvery meal costs £9.50
($14.30).

GRENADIER, 18 Wilton Row, SW1. Tel. 071/235-3074.
    Cuisine: ENGLISH. **Reservations:** Recommended. **Tube:**
Hyde Park Corner.

$ **Prices:** Appetizers £3.50–£8 ($5.30–$12); main courses £9.95–
£17.55 ($14.90–$26.30); fixed-price lunch or dinner £25
($37.50); glass of wine £2 ($3). AE, DC, MC, V.

    Open: Lunch daily noon–3pm; dinner daily 5:30–11pm.
    Closed: Dec 25–26 and Jan 1.

Tucked away in a mews, Grenadier is one of London's numerous
reputedly haunted pubs. Apart from the poltergeist, the basement
houses the original bar and skittles alley used by the Duke of
Wellington's officers on leave from fighting Napoléon. The scarlet
front door of the one-time officers' mess is guarded by a scarlet sentry
box and shaded by a vine. The bar is nearly always crowded.
Luncheons and dinners are offered daily—even on Sunday, when it is
a tradition to drink Bloody Marys here. In the stalls along the side,
you can order good-tasting fare based on seasonal ingredients. Filet
of beef Wellington is a specialty; other good dishes include pork
Grenadier and chicken and Stilton roulade. Snacks are available at the
bar if you don't want a full meal.

**STAR TAVERN, 6 Belgrave Mews West, SW1. Tel. 071/
235-3019.**
    Cuisine: ENGLISH. **Reservations:** Not accepted. **Tube:**
Knightsbridge or Hyde Park.

$ **Prices:** Lunch pub snacks £2.50–£4 ($3.80–$6); dinner pub
snacks £4.50–£5.50 ($6.80–$8.30); glass of wine £1.75 ($2.60).
No credit cards.

    Open: Lunch Mon–Fri 11:30am–3pm, dinner Mon–Fri 6:30–
8:45pm; pub, Mon–Thurs 11:30am–3pm and 5–11pm, Fri
11:30am–11pm, Sat 11:30am–3pm and 6:30–11pm, Sun noon–
3pm and 7–10:30pm. **Closed:** Dec 25.

Set in a Georgian mews behind a picture-postcard facade, Star Tavern
is one of the most colorful pubs in the West End. Inside are Victorian
walls and banquettes beneath 19th-century Victorian moldings. In
winter it's one of the coziest havens around, with two fireplaces

going. Groups of office workers descend after work, staking out their territory. You can order baby spring chicken, sirloin steak, or vegetable quiche. There is no waitress service; patrons place their orders at the bar.

9. CHELSEA & CHELSEA HARBOUR

CHELSEA

EXPENSIVE

LA TANTE CLAIRE, 68–69 Royal Hospital Rd., SW3. Tel. 071/352-6045.
   Cuisine: FRENCH. **Reservations:** Required. **Tube:** Sloane Sq.
$ Prices: Appetizers £17.50–£19.50 ($26.30–$29.30); main courses £22.50–£26 ($33.80–$39); fixed-price lunch £23.50 ($35.30); minimum charge £45 ($67.50) per person. AE, DC, MC, V.
   Open: Lunch Mon–Fri 12:30–2pm; dinner Mon–Fri 7–11pm. **Closed:** Dec 25 and Jan 1.

The quality of its cuisine is so legendary that La Tante Claire has become, in the eyes of many critics, the leading choice among the capital's gaggle of French restaurants. The ring of a doorbell set discreetly into the facade of Aegean blue and white prompts an employee to usher you politely inside. There, bouquets of flowers, a modernized, vaguely Hellenistic decor, and birchwood-and-chrome trim complement an array of paintings that might have been inspired by Jean Cocteau.

Pierre Koffman is the celebrated chef, creating such specialties as ravioli stuffed with frog meat. Every gastronome in London talks about the pig's trotters stuffed with morels and the exquisite sauces that complement many of the dishes. These include grilled scallops served on a bed of squid-ink sauce, baked filet of turbot with cabbage and fresh vegetables cooked in consommé with preserved duck, and duck in red-wine sauce and confit. For dessert, try a caramelized ice-cream soufflé with hazelnuts and raspberry coulis or the pistachio soufflé.

MODERATE

CHELSEA ROOM, in the Hyatt Carlton Tower, 2 Cadogan Place, SW1. Tel. 071/235-5411.
   Cuisine: FRENCH. **Reservations:** Required. **Tube:** Sloane Sq.
$ Prices: Appetizers £4–£11 ($6–$16.50); main courses £16–£32 ($24–$48); fixed-price lunch £22.50 ($33.80); fixed-price dinner £30.50 ($45.80). AE, DC, MC, V.
   Open: Lunch Mon–Sat 12:30–2:45pm; dinner Mon–Sat 7–11pm, Sun 7–10pm.
The superb Chelsea Room, one of the best restaurants in London, is in one of Hyatt's finest international properties. The dining room's combination of haute cuisine, stylish clientele, and elegant decor

make it a much sought-after place for lunch or dinner. Wedgwood plates with the restaurant's cockerel motif adorn each place setting. The color scheme is tasteful and subdued, in grays, beiges, and soft greens.

The kitchen is run by maître cuisinier de France Bernard Gaume, who has pleased palates at some of the leading hotels of Europe, including L'Abbaye in Talloires in the French Alps, the Savoy in London, and the Hotel des Bergues in Geneva. His portions are large and satisfying, and their presentation shows his extraordinary flair. Highly professional dishes, original offerings, as well as time-tested classics and very fresh ingredients are his forte. The menu changes, but here is an idea of the fare you are likely to be served: baked sea bass in a light sauce with leeks and a garnish of salmon and Russian caviar; roast partridge served on a bed of savoy cabbage; or small filets of venison in game sauce with port, juniper berries, and a medley of multicolored peppercorns. His desserts require a separate menu, ranging from light chestnut mousse with ginger sauce to chilled hazelnut parfait in light Cointreau sauce.

ENGLISH GARDEN, 10 Lincoln St., SW3. Tel. 071/584-7272.
 Cuisine: ENGLISH. **Reservations:** Required. **Tube:** Sloane Sq.
$ **Prices:** Appetizers £3.60–£11.60 ($5.40–$17.40); main courses £12.75–£15.60 ($19.10–$23.40); three-course set lunch £14.75 ($22.10). AE, DC, MC, V.
 Open: Lunch Mon–Sat 12:30–2:30pm, Sun 12:30–2pm; dinner Mon–Sat 7:30–11:30pm, Sun 7–10pm. **Closed:** Dec 25–26.

The decor is pretty and lighthearted in this historic Chelsea town house. The Garden Room on the ground floor is whitewashed brick, with panels of large stylish flowers. Attractive pelmets, in vivid flower colors, contrast with stark-white curtains; rattan chairs in a Gothic theme and candy-pink napery complete the scene. With the domed conservatory roof and banks of plants, the atmosphere is relaxing and pleasant.

The menu includes plenty of salads and fish—offering a checker-board of freshwater fish, including a steamed fish of the day—or roast rack of Welsh lamb with a hazelnut-breadcrumb crust. The chef's daily specials are included in a separate luncheon menu. A comprehensive wine list is available, with an excellent French house wine always obtainable.

ENGLISH HOUSE, 3 Milner St., SW3. Tel. 071/584-3002.
 Cuisine: BRITISH. **Reservations:** Required. **Tube:** Sloane Sq.
$ **Prices:** Appetizers £3.50–£9.75 ($5.30–$14.60); main courses £8.75–£15.60 ($13.10–$23.40); three-course set lunch £14.75 ($22.10). AE, DC, MC, V.
 Open: Lunch Mon–Sat 12:30–2:30pm, Sun 12:30–2pm; dinner Mon–Sat 7:30–11:30pm, Sun 7–10pm. **Closed:** Dec 25–26.

This is another design creation of Michael Smith, who did the English Garden, described above. The English House is a tiny restaurant in the heart of Chelsea where diners feel like a guest in an elegant private home. The decor provides both spectacle and atmosphere. Shades of blue and terra-cotta predominate, and the walls are clad in a printed cotton depicting a traditional English design of autumn leaves and black currants. The fireplace creates a homelike environment, with a collection of interesting, beautiful furniture adding to the background. Attention has been paid to detail, and even the saltcellars are Victorian in origin.

The food is British, with such succulent offerings as roast rack of Welsh lamb with mint-apple jelly, seared breast of duck with spicy plum sauce, or filet of beef with a cream sauce of wild mushrooms and Madeira. Summer berries (in season) predominate on the "pudding" menu, including a bowl of fresh berries laced with Elderflower syrup. Another offering is "A Phrase of Apples," the chef's adaptation of a 17th-century recipe for a delectable apple pancake.

GAVVERS, 61–63 Lower Sloane St., SW1. Tel. 071/730-5983.
Cuisine: FRENCH. **Reservations:** Recommended. **Tube:** Sloane Sq.
$ Prices: Fixed-price lunch £12.50–£14.75 ($18.80–$22.10); fixed-price dinner £22.65–£28.25 ($34–$42.40). DC, MC, V.
Open: Lunch Mon–Fri noon–2:30pm; dinner Mon–Sat 7–11pm.

This was the original location of Le Gavroche (now the premier restaurant of London), which moved to Mayfair in 1981. The owners, the Roux brothers, turned these premises into a winning choice for truly French dining in a chic but inviting atmosphere. Considering the quality of the food, this is one of the best values among London's French restaurants. Fixed-price menus change daily but are likely to include lightly roasted salmon with fresh spring vegetables; breast of duck stuffed with black olives; or rolled, boned, and stuffed quail with braised chicory.

PUBS

FRONT PAGE, 35 Old Church St., SW3. Tel. 071/352-0648.
Cuisine: CONTINENTAL. **Reservations:** Not necessary. **Tube:** Sloane Sq.
$ Prices: Bar snacks £2.50–£5.70 ($3.80–$8.60); main courses £4.70–£5.70 ($7.10–$8.60). MC, V.
Open: Restaurant, daily noon–2:15pm and 7–10:15pm; pub, daily 9am–3pm and 5:30–11pm. **Closed:** Dec 24–26.

Front Page is favored by young professionals who like the mellow atmosphere provided by its wood paneling, wooden tables, and pews and benches. In one section an open fire burns on cold nights. The pub stands in an expensive residential section of Chelsea and is a good place to go for a drink, with lager costing from £1.80 ($2.70). You can also order bottled Budweiser. Check the chalkboard for a listing of the daily specials, which might include ratatouille au gratin, lamb curry, or mackerel with kumquat sauce. You might begin with homemade soup du jour.

KING'S HEAD AND EIGHT BELLS, 50 Cheyne Walk, SW3. Tel. 071/352-1820.
Cuisine: ENGLISH. **Reservations:** Not accepted. **Tube:** Sloane Sq.
$ Prices: Appetizers £2–£4.50 ($3–$6.80); main courses £4–£8 ($6–$12). AE, MC, V.
Open: Pub, Mon–Sat noon–11pm, Sun noon–3pm and 7–10:30pm. Food, Mon–Sat noon–3pm and 7–10pm, Sun noon–2:30pm and 7–10pm.

Many distinguished personalities once lived near this historic Thames-side pub, and a short stroll will take you to the former homes of such personages as Carlyle, Swinburne, and George Eliot. In other days, press gangs used to roam these parts of Chelsea seeking lone travelers to abduct for a life at sea. Today, it's popular with stage and TV celebrities as well as writers.

The best English beers are served here, as well as a good selection of reasonably priced wine. A refrigerated display case holds cold dishes and salads, and a hot counter features the homemade specials of the day, including at least one vegetable main dish.

CHELSEA HARBOUR
INEXPENSIVE

DEAL'S RESTAURANT AND DINER, Harbour Yard (without number), Chelsea Harbour, SW10. Tel. 071/352-5887.
Cuisine: INTERNATIONAL. **Reservations:** Recommended. **Directions:** Chelsea Harbour Hoppa Bus C3 from Earls Court or Kensington High St. Mon–Sat, or riverbus from Charing Cross Pier Mon–Fri. On Sun, take a taxi.
$ Prices: Appetizers £3–£5 ($4.50–$7.50); main courses £5–£14 ($7.50–$21). AE, MC, V.
Open: Mon–Sat 11am–11pm.

After the Queen Mother arrived here on a barge to order a Deal's burger, the success of the place was assured. Deal's is co-owned by Princess Margaret's son, Viscount Linley, and Lord Lichfield. The early 1900s atmosphere includes ceiling fans and bentwood banquettes. The food is American diner style with a strong Eastern influence: Try teriyaki burgers, prawn curry, spareribs, or a vegetarian dish and finish with New England apple pie.

KEN LO'S MEMORIES OF CHINA, Harbour Yard (without number), Chelsea Harbour, SW10. Tel. 071/352-4953.
Cuisine: CHINESE. **Reservations:** Required. **Directions:** Chelsea Harbour Hoppa Bus C3 from Earls Court or Kensington High St. Mon–Sat, or riverbus from Charing Cross Pier Mon–Fri. On Sun, take a taxi.
$ Prices: Appetizers £3.85–£7 ($5.80–$10.50); main courses £5–£10 ($7.50–$15); set lunch £10.85 ($16.30); fixed-price dinner £24 ($36). AE, DC, MC, V.
Open: Lunch Mon–Sat noon–2:30pm; dinner 7–10:45pm; Sun brunch noon–2:30pm; dim sum bar Mon–Fri noon–2:30pm.

This is the far-flung branch of Ken Lo's in the Victoria Station area (see above). Many people like to make an excursion to this modern London "village" with its marina complex. Mr. Lo chose a riverside site for his second restaurant, perhaps remembering his boyhood in Foochow on the banks of the Ming River. The restaurant is decorated in blue and gold, the colors of the Ming dynasty. The cuisine wanders from region to region of China, with an emphasis on fish and seafood. Specialties include steamed sea bass, Mongolian barbecued lamb, and chicken in hot black-bean sauce.

WINE BAR

BOATERS WINE BAR, Harbour Yard (without number), Chelsea Harbour, SW10. Tel. 071/352-3687.

Cuisine: ENGLISH. **Reservations:** Not necessary. **Directions:** Chelsea Harbour Hoppa Bus C3 from Earls Court or Kensington High St. or riverbus from Charing Cross Pier Mon–Fri. On Sun, take a taxi.

$ Prices: Sandwiches, cheese plates, salads £2–£3 ($3–$4.50); main courses £4–£5 ($6–$7.50). AE, MC.

Open: Mon–Fri 11am–11pm, Sun noon–3pm.

Well-heeled locals who own the soaringly expensive apartments in the Chelsea Harbour complex often come here to drink champagne by the bottle while munching complimentary bowls of popcorn on the long wooden bar counter. Visitors from all over the world pour in here as well. Most of the emphasis at the bar is on an impressive array of bottled beer, beer on tap, and wine by either bottle or glass; only a minimum array of liquor is available. Sandwiches, cheese plates, salads, and such main dishes as chili con carne and mushroom-and-leek stroganoff are available throughout the day. An impressive carte offers wine by the glass, costing from £1.95 ($2.90) for the house version.

10. KENSINGTON & SOUTH KENSINGTON

KENSINGTON

MODERATE

TURNER'S, 87–89 Walton St., SW3. Tel. 071/584-6711.
Cuisine: CONTINENTAL. **Reservations:** Required. **Tube:** Knightsbridge.
$ Prices: Weekday set lunch £15.75–£18.50 ($23.60–$27.80); Sun fixed-price lunch £18.50 ($27.80); set dinner £23.50 ($35.30) and £32 ($48). AE, DC, MC, V.
Open: Lunch Mon–Fri and Sun 12:30–2:45pm; dinner Mon–Sat 7:30–11pm, Sun 7:30–10pm. **Closed:** 1 week at Christmas.

This restaurant is named after a native of Yorkshire, Brian J. Turner, the accomplished London chef who gained fame at a number of establishments he didn't own, including the Capital Hotel, before achieving his own place in the culinary sun. As one critic has aptly put it, his food comes not only fresh from the market each day but also "from the heart." He doesn't seem to imitate anyone but sets his own goals and standards. Try, for example, his pigeon breasts in red-wine sauce, English duck with Thai herbs, or roast rack of lamb with herb crust. You might begin with hot crab mousse or cold creamy smoked haddock.

MODERATE

LAUNCESTON PLACE, 1A Launceston Place, W8. Tel. 071/937-6912.
Cuisine: BRITISH. **Reservations:** Required. **Tube:** Gloucester Rd.

ⓕ FROMMER'S COOL FOR KIDS: RESTAURANTS

Chicago Pizza Factory (see p. 110) If your kids are nostalgic for the food back home, they'll find it here, where regular-size pizzas are big enough for two or three.

Deal's Restaurant and Diner (see p. 139) After enjoying the boat ride to Chelsea Harbour, kids will love the food of North America, served here, including Deal's burgers. Reduced-price children's portions are available.

Tall Orders (see p. 149) Food is brought to the table stacked in Chinese-style bamboo steamers. If you're really hungry, you can order a "Skyscraper." The "Fairy Story" is a minitower for the gourmand under 12.

$ Prices: Appetizers £4–£7.50 ($6–$11.30); main courses £12–£14.50 ($18–$21.80); fixed-price lunches £12.50 ($18.80) and £15.50 ($23.30). MC, V.
   Open: Lunch Sun–Fri 12:30–2:30pm; dinner Mon–Sat 7–11:30pm.

Launceston Place is situated in an affluent, almost villagelike neighborhood where many Londoners would like to live if only they could afford it. The architecturally stylish restaurant is a series of uncluttered Victorian parlors illuminated by a rear skylight and decorated with art nouveau lithographs and paintings. Owners Simon Slater and Nicholas Smallwood learned their trade at the world-famous Hard Rock Café, which they ran, but Launceston Place evokes no memory of that. Since its opening in spring 1986, it has been known for its new British cuisine, including such dishes as curried parsnip soup, Lancashire hot pot, roast mallard with cranberries, noisettes of hare with grapes and chanterelles, or stuffed breast of guinea fowl with chestnut purée and celery. Roast grouse is also featured. For an appetizer, try such delights as galette of woodpigeon with leeks, foie gras, and oyster mushrooms or ravioli of braised oxtails, a first for many diners.

INEXPENSIVE

PERSEPOLIS, 39 Kensington High St., W8. Tel. 071/937-3555.
   Cuisine: PERSIAN. **Reservations:** Not necessary. **Tube:** High St. Kensington.
$ Prices: Appetizers £2–£3 ($3–$4.50); main courses £6–£15 ($9–$22.50). AE, DC, MC, V.
   Open: Daily noon–11pm.

Persepolis offers good Iranian cooking, which in some culinary circles is still called Persian. The restaurant is sleek and modern, without the slightest touch of Asian kitsch. The only distinctive Persian features are wall friezes showing winged lions and spade-bearded ancient kings. A small, subtly lit place, it features picture windows with a view of the street. Appetizers include homemade creamy yogurt with either chopped mint-flavored cucumber or chopped spinach flavored with fried onions. For a main dish, you might choose a quarter of chicken cooked with grated walnuts and served with pomegranate purée or finely chopped lamb, eggplant, and split peas cooked with tomato purée. Baklava and halva shekari (a sesame-seed concoction) are among the desserts.

PHOENICIA, 11 Abingdon Rd., W8. Tel. 071/937-0120.
   Cuisine: LEBANESE. **Reservations:** Required. **Tube:** High St. Kensington.
$ **Prices:** Appetizers £2.40–£4.85 ($3.60–$7.30); main courses £6.70–£10.70 ($10.10–$16.10); buffet lunch £8.95 ($13.40); fixed-price dinner £14.50–£26.50 ($21.80–$39.80). AE, DC, MC, V.
   Open: Daily 12:15–11:45pm.

Phoenicia is highly regarded for the quality of its Lebanese cuisine—outstanding in presentation and freshness—and for its moderate prices. For the best value, go for lunch, when you can enjoy a buffet of more than a dozen meze (appetizers), presented in little pottery dishes. Each day, also at lunch, the chef prepares two or three home-cooked dishes to tempt your taste buds, including chicken in garlic sauce or stuffed lamb with vegetables. Many Lebanese patrons begin their meal with the apéritif arak, a liqueur some have compared to ouzo. You can select as an appetizer such classic Middle Eastern dishes as hummus or stuffed vine leaves. In a clay oven the kitchen staff bakes its own bread and makes two types of pizza. Minced lamb, spicy and well flavored, is the eternal favorite. Various charcoal-grilled dishes are also offered.

SOUTH KENSINGTON
MODERATE

BIBENDUM/THE OYSTER BAR, 81 Fulham Rd., SW3. Tel. 071/581-5817.
   Cuisine: MODERN FRENCH/MEDITERRANEAN. **Reservations:** Necessary in Bibendum, not accepted in The Oyster Bar. **Tube:** South Kensington.
$ **Prices:** Appetizers £8.50–£18.50 ($12.80–$27.80); main courses £12–£19 ($18–$28.50); three-course fixed-price lunch £25 ($37.50); cold shellfish platter in Oyster Bar £18.50 ($27.80) per person. MC, V.
   Open: Bibendum, lunch daily 12:30–2:30pm; dinner daily 7–11:30pm. Oyster bar, Mon–Sat noon–10:30pm, Sun noon–3pm and 7–11:30pm.

Considered a top London restaurant, this fashionable eating place occupies two floors of a building that's an art deco masterpiece. Built in 1911, it housed the British headquarters of Michelin Tire. Bibendum, the more visible eatery, lies one floor above street level in a white-tiled art deco room whose stained-glass windows, streaming sunlight, and chic clientele make meals extremely pleasant. Menu items are carefully planned interpretations of seasonal ingredients. The menu might include porcini risotto, deep-fried spinach cakes with anchovy-flavored hollandaise, grilled foccacia, or smoked eel with potato pancakes and horseradish sauce. Simpler meals and cocktails are available at street level, in The Oyster Bar. The bar-style menu and 1930s decor stress fresh shellfish presented in the tradition-al French style, on ice-covered platters occasionally adorned with strands of seaweed.

BOMBAY BRASSERIE, Courtfield Close (without number) (adjoining Bailey's Hotel), SW7. Tel. 071/370-4040.
Cuisine: INDIAN. **Reservations:** Recommended. **Tube:** Gloucester Rd.
$ Prices: Appetizers £3.50–£5.50 ($5.30–$8.30); main courses £10.50–£20.50 ($15.80–$30.80); buffet lunch £13.50 ($20.30). MC, V.
Open: Buffet lunch daily 12:30–3pm; dinner Mon–Sat 7:30pm–midnight, Sun 7:30–11:30pm. **Closed:** Dec 26–27.

By anyone's estimation, this is the finest, most popular, and most talked about Indian restaurant in London. Established in 1982, this cavernous trio of rooms is staffed by one of London's most accommodating teams of Indian-born waiters, each of whom is very able to advise you on the spice-laden delicacies that thousands of years of Indian culinary tradition have developed. Lattices cover the windows, dhurrie rugs cover the floors, cooling is by paddle fans, and sepia Raj pictures of Imperial Britain at its height adorn the walls.

Before heading in to dinner, you might enjoy a drink amid the wicker chairs of the pink-and-white bar. The bartender's special is a mango Bellini. The menu features tandoori scallops, fish with mint chutney, chicken tikka (a dish from the Hindu Kush mountains), sali boti (mutton with apricots, a famous Parsi wedding dish), and vegetarian meals. One corner of the menu is reserved for Goan cookery, representing that part of India seized from Portugal in 1961. The cookery of North India is represented by Mughlai specialties, including chicken biryani, the famous Muslim pilaf dish. Under the category "Some Like It Hot," you'll find such main courses as mirchi korma Kashmiri style, a favorite of a frequent customer, Faye Dunaway.

HILAIRE, 68 Old Brompton Rd., SW7. Tel. 071/584-8993.
Cuisine: FRENCH. **Reservations:** Recommended. **Tube:** South Kensington.
$ Prices: Three-course fixed-price lunch £20 ($30); four-course fixed-price dinner £25.50 ($38.30); dinner appetizers £4–£12.50 ($6–$18.80); dinner main courses £12.50–£18 ($18.80–$27). AE, DC, MC, V.
Open: Lunch Mon–Fri noon–2:30pm; dinner Mon–Sat 7:30–11:30pm. **Closed:** Bank holidays.

Hilaire is a jovially cramped restaurant, housed in what was originally a Victorian storefront. Ceiling fans, apple-green walls, fresh flowers, and twin Corinthian columns provide the setting for the elegant culinary specialties. Chef Bryan Webb prepares a mixture of classical French and cuisine moderne that has made this one of the most stylish restaurants in London. An apéritif bar, extra tables, and a pair of semiprivate alcoves are in the lower dining room. A typical lunch might begin with potato, cêpe, and truffle soup; then follow with pan-fried strips of calves' liver with sweetbreads, cream, and wild mushrooms; and end with plum sorbet. The menu always reflects the best of the season's offerings, and main courses at dinner might include noisettes of venison with polenta, roast grouse with bread sauce, or sea bass with lentils.

ST. QUENTIN, 243 Brompton Rd., SW3. Tel. 071/581-5131.
  Cuisine: FRENCH. **Reservations:** Required. **Tube:** Knightsbridge or South Kensington.
$ **Prices:** Appetizers £3.50–£9.80 ($5.30–$14.70); main courses £10.50–£14.50 ($15.80–$21.80); three-course fixed-price lunch £12.50 ($18.80); four-course fixed-price dinner £15.25 ($22.90). AE, DC, MC, V.
  Open: Lunch Mon–Fri noon–3pm, Sat–Sun noon–4pm; dinner Sun–Fri 7pm–midnight, Sat 6:30pm–midnight.

Founded in 1980, St. Quentin is probably the most authentic-looking French brasserie in London. Modeled after the famous La Coupole in Paris (with its memories of the Lost Generation), it attracts many members of the French community in London (a good sign). The decor of mirrors and crystal chandeliers has been aptly named *glitzy*, a word that might on occasion describe the clientele as well. Try the rack of lamb perfectly roasted and served very pink in the French style, roast quail with truffles and foie gras sauce, or potted duck with mustard sauce. Look also for the plats du jour. For an hors d'oeuvre, you might ask for mixed salad with grilled goat cheese or raw salmon marinated in lime and olive oil.

SYDNEY STREET, 4 Sydney St., SW3. Tel. 071/352-3433.
  Cuisine: AUSTRALIAN. **Reservations:** Recommended. **Tube:** South Kensington.
$ **Prices:** Appetizers £3.50–£8.80 ($5.30–$13.20); main courses £13.80–£17.20 ($20.70–$25.80). AE, DC, MC, V.
  Open: Lunch Mon–Fri noon–2:30pm; dinner Mon–Sat 7–11:30pm (last order).

This restaurant combines the allure of a grand bistro with the earthy colors and Aboriginal theme of the Australian outback. The street level contains an affable bar where an array of whisky, Australian beer, and Australian and New Zealand wine might make an attractive prelude to a meal in the basement-level dining room. There, in an oceanic decor lined with fish tanks, postmodern metal tables, and padded vinyl chairs, you can enjoy some of the most startling specialties in town (many ingredients are imported directly from Sydney, Australia), including kangaroo and Tasmanian crayfish tails. Choices include a spicy version of Australian bouillabaisse made with sea creatures from the Barrier Reef, a quick-seared filet of barramundi (a meaty and aromatic South Pacific seafish) served with braised pineapple chutney, squid-ink noodles, spicy essence of carrots, many preparations of Australian beef, and an Australian version of freshwater crayfish known Down Under as yabbie.

11. WEST BROMPTON

INEXPENSIVE

BLUE ELEPHANT, 4–6 Fulham Broadway, SW6. Tel. 071/385-6595.
  Cuisine: THAI. **Reservations:** Recommended. **Tube:** Fulham Broadway.
$ **Prices:** Appetizers £5.75–£7.50 ($8.60–$11.30); main courses

£6.50–£14.50 ($9.80–$21.80); fixed-price dinners £25–£28 ($37.50–$42). AE, DC, MC, V.

Open: Lunch Sun–Fri noon–2:30pm; dinner daily 7pm–12:30am.

This is the counterpart of the famous L'Eléphant Bleu in Brussels. Located in a converted factory building, London's Blue Elephant has been all the rage since it opened in 1986. In fact, it is the leading Thai restaurant of London, where the competition is growing.

In an almost magical garden setting of lush tropical foliage, diners are treated to an array of ancient and modern MSG-free Thai food. You can begin with a "floating market" (shellfish in clear broth flavored with chili paste and lemongrass), then go on to a splendid and varied selection of main courses, for which many of the ingredients have been flown in from Thailand. You might try roasted duck curry served in a clay cooking pot. The most popular choice is the Royal Thai banquet at £25 ($37.50) a head.

CHAPTER 11, 47 Hollywood Rd., SW10. Tel. 071/351-1683.
  Cuisine: CALIFORNIAN. **Reservations:** Required. **Tube:** Earls Court.
$ Prices: Appetizers £2.20–£5.50 ($3.30–$8.30); main courses £6.50–£10.50 ($9.80–$15.80). AE, DC, MC, V.
  Open: Lunch Mon–Sat noon–3pm; dinner Mon–Sat 6:45–midnight. **Closed:** Dec 24–26.

At one time, the best cuisine you could hope to find in this neighborhood was bangers and mash. But today some of the most fashionable members of young London gravitate here, drawn by shops selling some of the most exclusive and costly goods in town. Chapter 11 has a small garden terrace in back, but in bad weather there is a lower-level dining room. The menu, wisely limited, offers well-prepared dishes based on fresh ingredients. You might select duck breast with rice-wine vinaigrette, roasted red peppers with grilled goat cheese, or red cabbage and pork sausages with Bubble and Squeak (a combination of cabbage and potatoes).

12. EARLS COURT, NOTTING HILL & HOLLAND PARK

EARLS COURT

MODERATE

LA CROISETTE, 168 Ilfield Rd., SW10. Tel. 071/373-3694.
  Cuisine: SEAFOOD. **Reservations:** Required. **Tube:** Earls Court.
$ Prices: Appetizers £4.25–£15 ($6.40–$22.50); main courses £9.50–£15.50 ($14.30–$23.30); fixed-price menu £26 ($39). AE, DC, MC, V.
  Open: Lunch Wed–Sun 1–2:30pm; dinner Tues–Sun 7–11:30pm.

La Croisette lies in an unlikely neighborhood in southwest London, but its French decor might have you believe you're in the south of France. You enter a turn-of-the-century apéritif bar, then descend a wraparound iron staircase into an intimate dining room. The set menu offers an amazingly wide choice of seafood, first courses including five kinds of oysters, three preparations of mussels and five of scallops, frogs' legs Provençale, and six appetizer salads. Most visitors opt for the plateau des fruits-de-mer, where all the bounty of the sea's shellfish is served from a cork platter dripping with garlands of seaweed. A handful of dishes, notably lamb, are offered for meat lovers, but by far the strongest tempters are the imaginative array of red snapper, sea bass, stingray, monkfish, and sole.

NOTTING HILL
MODERATE

CLARKE'S, 124 Kensington Church St., W8. Tel. 071/221-9225.
   Cuisine: BRITISH. **Reservations:** Recommended. **Tube:** Notting Hill Gate or High St. Kensington.
$ **Prices:** Fixed-price lunch £22–£26 ($33–$39); set dinners £22–£37 ($33–$55.50). MC, V.
   Open: Lunch Mon–Fri 12:30–2pm; dinner Mon–Fri 7–10pm.

Named after its owner, Englishwoman Sally Clarke, one of the finest chefs in London, this is one of the hottest restaurants around. Clarke honed her skills at Michaels in Santa Monica and the West Beach Café in Venice (California). In this excellent restaurant, everything is bright and modern, with wood floors; discreet lighting; and additional space in the basement, where tables are more spacious and private. The fixed-price menu offers no choices, but the food is so well prepared "in the new style" that diners rarely object. The menu is changed daily. You might begin with an appetizer such as hot soup of roasted red peppers with parmesan and rosemary breadsticks, then follow with charcoal-grilled lamb sausage with chili mayonnaise. Desserts are likely to include a strawberry-and-vanilla cream trifle.

HOLLAND PARK
MODERATE

THE ROOM AT THE HALCYON, in the Halcyon Hotel, 81 Holland Park Ave., W11. Tel. 071/727-7288.
   Cuisine: INTERNATIONAL/ITALIAN. **Reservations:** Required. **Tube:** Holland Park.
$ **Prices:** Appetizers £4–£6.50 ($6–$9.80); main courses £10.50–£15 ($15.80–$22.50). AE, DC, MC, V.
   Open: Lunch daily 12:30–2:30pm; dinner daily 7–11:30pm.
Part of the Halcyon Hotel (see Chapter 4), this restaurant is worth a detour to visit this pocket of posh. Located on the hotel's lower level, the restaurant attracts the rich and famous, including royalty. You might enjoy an apéritif in the pink-tinted bar before heading for a meal in the tastefully uncluttered dining room. Lattices and a garden view create an image of springtime even in winter.
   Of the sophisticated and highly individualized menu, one food critic wrote it "reads like a United Nations of cuisine," although it leans heavily toward Italy. The daily bill of fare is based on the inspiration of the chef and the freshest ingredients available, along

with minimal sauces. You might begin with ravioli filled with crab, coriander, and ricotta before going on to roast breast of guinea fowl with noodles, prunes, and leeks or salmon baked in pastry with pesto. Desserts are worth saving room for, particularly the ginger parfait with mango coulis or the dark-chocolate pudding with coffee-bean sauce.

13. ST. MARYLEBONE & BAYSWATER

ST. MARYLEBONE

MODERATE

LANGAN'S BISTRO, 26 Devonshire St., W1. Tel. 071/ 935-4531.
   Cuisine: FRENCH/ENGLISH. **Reservations:** Required. **Tube:** Regent's Park.
$ Prices: Appetizers £4–£5.50 ($6–$8.30); main courses £9.50–£10.50 ($14.30–$15.80). AE, DC, MC, V.
   Open: Lunch Mon–Fri 12:30–2:30pm; dinner Mon–Sat 7–11:30pm.

Langan's Bistro has been a busy fixture on the London restaurant scene since the mid-1960s. Like its neighbor, Odin's (see below), it is owned by actor Michael Caine, among others, and is less expensive than the better-known Langan's Brasserie in Mayfair. You'll find it behind a buttercup-yellow storefront in a residential neighborhood. Inside, almost every square inch of the high ceiling is covered with fanciful clusters of Japanese parasols. Rococo mirrors accent the black walls, setting off surrealistic paintings and old photos guaranteed to create a warmly nostalgic kind of excitement.

The French-inspired menu changes frequently, and only the best and freshest seasonal ingredients are used in the tempting specialties. These might include smoked monkfish with tomato, fennel, and Pernod sauce; veal with Pommery mustard and tarragon; and pork with prunes and brandy. On one occasion I enjoyed sautéed calves' liver with cranberries and kumquats. The dessert extravaganza is known as "Langan's chocolate pudding."

ODIN'S, 27 Devonshire St., W1. Tel. 071/935-7296.
   Cuisine: CONTINENTAL. **Reservations:** Required. **Tube:** Regent's Park.
$ Prices: Appetizers £4.25–£6.50 ($6.40–$9.80); main courses £11–£13.50 ($16.50–$20.30). AE, DC, MC, V.
   Open: Lunch Mon–Fri 12:30–2:30pm; dinner Mon–Sat 7–11:30pm.

Odin's is a particularly elegant restaurant owned by actor Michael Caine and others. Amid an eclectic decor of gilt-touched walls, art deco armchairs, Japanese screens, ceiling fans, and evocative paintings, you can enjoy well-prepared specialties of the chef. The menu offers an excellent wine list and selections from many culinary traditions—selections that change every day depending on the availability of fresh ingredients at the market. You might begin with such typical fare as pigeon breast in puff pastry, marinated salmon with lemon, or chicken-liver mousse. Main courses include filet of turbot with prawns from Dublin Bay, steamed Dover sole with ginger and pink peppercorns, wild salmon with sorrel sauce, and Scottish sirloin with garlic and breadcrumbs.

INEXPENSIVE

GARBO'S, 42 Crawford St., W1. Tel. 071/262-6582.
   Cuisine: SWEDISH. **Reservations:** Required. **Tube:** Baker St., Edgware Rd., or Marylebone.
$ **Prices:** Appetizers £2.50–£5.95 ($3.80–$8.90); main courses £5.95–£11.45 ($8.90–$17.20); buffet lunch £8 ($12). AE, MC, V.
   Open: Lunch Mon–Fri noon–3pm; dinner daily 6pm–midnight.

Garbo's is the most engaging and appealing Swedish restaurant in London, taking its theme from that country's celebrated export, the late star herself. Located south of Marylebone Road, it attracts patrons from the Swedish embassy on Montagu Place. The best value—in fact, one of the finest lunchtime values in St. Marylebone—is the "mini-smörgåsbord," which, despite being called "mini," has a range of perfectly prepared hot and cold dishes and is most satisfying and filling. The evening menu might even tempt you to visit Scandinavia. You could begin with gravlax with dill-mustard sauce prepared in the old Viking manner, smoked eel, or Swedish pea soup. Various meat courses are featured, including Swedish meatballs in cream sauce and white cabbage stuffed with beef and pork. Watch also for the specialties of the day. Finish with a dessert from the sweets trolley or else ask for crêpe Garbo, filled with ice cream and coated with Melba sauce.

BAYSWATER

INEXPENSIVE

VERONICA'S, 3 Hereford Rd., W2. Tel. 071/229-5079.
   Cuisine: ENGLISH. **Reservations:** Required. **Tube:** Bayswater or Queensway.
$ **Prices:** Appetizers £3.50–£5.50 ($5.30–$8.30); main courses £5.50–£13.50 ($8.30–$20.30); fixed-price meals £10 ($15). AE, DC, MC, V.
   Open: Lunch Mon–Fri noon–3pm; dinner Mon–Sat 7pm–midnight.

Called the "market leader in café salons," Veronica's offers some of the finest British cuisine in London at tabs you won't mind paying. In fact, it's like a celebration of British food, including some dishes based on recipes used in medieval or Tudor times. For example, your appetizer might be a salad called salmagundy that was enjoyed by Elizabeth I, made with crunchy pickled vegetables. Another concoction might be watersouchy, a medieval stew crammed with mixed seafood. However, each dish is given today's imaginative interpretation by owner Veronica Shaw. One month she'll focus on Scotland, another month on Victorian foods, yet another month on Wales. Many dishes are vegetarian, and everything tastes better when followed with one of the selections of British farmhouse cheeses or a "pudding." The restaurant is brightly and attractively decorated, with service that is warm and ingratiating.

14. AWAY FROM THE CENTER

PIMLICO

MODERATE

POMEGRANATES, 94 Grosvenor Rd., SW1. Tel. 071/828-6560.
Cuisine: INTERNATIONAL. **Reservations:** Required. **Tube:** Pimlico.
$ Prices: Fixed-price lunch £14.50–£20.50 ($21.80–$30.80); fixed-price dinner £17.75–£26.50 ($26.60–$39.80). AE, DC, MC, V.
Open: Lunch Mon–Fri 12:30–2pm; dinner Mon–Sat 7:30–11:15pm.

Patrick Gwynn-Jones, the owner of this basement restaurant by the river in Pimlico, has traveled far and collected recipes throughout the world. Asian and Indonesian delicacies vie for space on the set menus along with European and North American dishes: West Indian curried goat, escargot-and-mushroom pie, Welsh salt duck with a white-onion sauce, Creole-Cajun jambalaya. The decor is fin de siècle, with mirrors and well-laid tables. House wines are reasonably priced, and there is also a good wine list. You have a wide range of choices on the fixed-price menus, which begin with crudités and might end with homemade honey-and-cognac ice cream.

FULHAM

INEXPENSIVE

TALL ORDERS, 676 Fulham Rd., SW6. Tel. 071/371-9673.
Cuisine: MEDITERRANEAN. **Reservations:** Required. **Tube:** Parson's Green.
$ Prices: All dishes £3.50 ($5.30); five-course set menu £15.75 ($23.60). AE, MC, V.
Open: Dinner only, Mon–Fri 6pm–midnight, Sat–Sun noon–midnight.

The decor features a very large, eye-catching mural covering the expanse of one entire wall, showing the crumbs and dregs of a completed and satisfying banquet. Minimalist trappings are in dark blue and beige, and there's a central bar. The Mediterranean-inspired cuisine deliberately blurs the distinctions between appetizer and main course, with food served in dim sum steamers, stacked high on top of one another. Tables are tiny, making a balancing act necessary from time to time. Dishes include salad of smoked chicken with cherry tomatoes and balsamic vinaigrette, quail eggs with freshly poached salmon and new potatoes, polenta with a creamy porcini mushroom sauce, and chargrilled lamb with flageolet beans and a rosemary jus. Four set menus, all consisting of five courses and all costing the same, include a varied assortment called "Multi-Story," with the "Emerald Tower" all vegetarian and the "Pudding Tower" all desserts. The "Fairy Story" set menu at £7.95 ($11.90) is for the gourmet under 12.

HAMPSTEAD HEATH

INEXPENSIVE

KEATS, 3–4 Downshire Hill, Hampstead, NW3. Tel. 071/ 435-3544.
   Cuisine: ENGLISH/CONTINENTAL. **Reservations:** Required. **Tube:** Hampstead.
$ **Prices:** Appetizers £3.50–£5.50 ($5.30–$8.30); main courses £7–£12 ($10.50–$18); three-course fixed-price lunch £9 ($13.50). AE, DC, MC, V.
   Open: Lunch Sun–Fri noon–3pm; dinner daily 7–11:30pm.

Named after poet John Keats's house in Hampstead, which is a three-minute walk away, this pleasant restaurant is the 1992 reincarnation of a famous restaurant, Keats, which used to thrive in the same premises after World War II. Set on the ground floor of a stone-fronted 18th-century house, it offers an elegant pair of dining rooms richly and theatrically outfitted with Victorian-inspired fabrics, furniture, and accessories. Menu items include a frequently changing array of seasonal dishes of the day, such as mussels prepared in the French style with white wine, garlic, and shallots or sauté of wild mushrooms. Items usually available throughout the year include Keats salad (studded with asparagus, artichokes, red peppers, and quail eggs), filet of pepper steak in brandy-and-cream sauce, and Jamaican jerk chicken.

PUBS

JACK STRAW'S CASTLE, North End Way, NW3. Tel. 071/ 435-8885.
   Cuisine: ENGLISH. **Reservations:** Not necessary. **Tube:** Hampstead.
$ **Prices:** Appetizers £1.25–£2.75 ($1.90–$4.10); main courses £9.15–£11.55 ($13.70–$17.30); fixed-price Sun lunch £10.15 ($15.20); beer from £1.80 ($2.70). AE, DC, MC, V.
   Open: Carvery, lunch daily noon–2pm; dinner Mon–Sat 6–10pm, Sun 7–9:30pm. Pub, Mon–Fri 11am–3pm and 5:30–11pm, Sat 11am–11pm, Sun noon–2pm and 7–10:30pm.

This place was named for one of the peasant leaders who, along with Wat Tyler, successfully revolted against what was basically a wage freeze in 1381. The pub, rebuilt on the site of Jack's house, is now a bustling place with a large L-shaped bar and quick-snack counter where there are cold salads, meats, and pies, plus three hot dishes with vegetables served every day. You can eat in the bar or on the large patio overlooking part of the heath.

SPANIARDS INN, Spaniards Lane (without number), NW3. Tel. 081/455-3276.
   Cuisine: ENGLISH. **Reservations:** Not necessary. **Tube:** Hampstead or Golders Green.

$ Prices: Appetizers £2.25–£3.50 ($3.40–$5.30); main courses £4.25–£6.75 ($6.40–$10.10); beer from £1.60 ($2.40). MC, V.
Open: Food bar, Mon–Fri noon–3pm and 6–9:30pm, Sat noon–9:30pm, Sun noon–3pm and 7–9:30pm; pub, Mon–Sat 11am–11pm, Sun noon–3pm and 7–10:30pm.

This Hampstead Heath landmark is located opposite the old toll-house, where people had to pay to enter the country park of the bishop of London. The notorious highwayman Dick Turpin leaped over the gate on his horse when he was in flight from the law. The pub was built in 1585, and the present building dates from 1702; its rooms, with their low beamed ceilings and oak paneling, still contain some antique benches, open fires, and cozy nooks. The pub serves traditional, above-average food. In summer, customers can sit at slat tables on a garden terrace beside a flower-bordered lawn and an aviary. Byron, Shelley, Dickens, and Galsworthy patronized the pub. Even Keats may have quaffed a glass here.

ST. JOHN'S WOOD

PUB

THE CLIFTON HOTEL, 96 Clifton Hill, NW8. Tel. 071/624-5233.
Cuisine: ENGLISH. **Reservations:** Not necessary. **Tube:** St. John's Wood or Maida Vale.
$ Prices: Appetizers £2.25–£7.25 ($3.40–$10.90); main courses £7–£11 ($10.50–$16.50). MC, V.
Open: Restaurant, Mon–Fri noon–2:30pm and 6–10pm, Sat noon–3pm and 6–10pm, Sun noon–3pm; pub, Mon–Fri 11am–3pm and 5–11pm, Sat 11am–11pm, Sun noon–3pm and 7–10:30pm.

One of the most charming pubs in London, the Clifton Hotel stands in an expensive residential area in the northern part of town. Built in 1837, the place was once renowned for its fine ports and wines. Edward VII discovered it and used it as a hideaway with his mistress, Lillie Langtry. Restored in 1984, it is now a pub and restaurant, although it still calls itself a hotel, attracting a lively crowd with its glowing fireplace and mellow atmosphere, enhanced by many Victorian and Edwardian touches. Look for the daily specials, such as beef-and-Guinness stew with dumplings or steak sandwich, perhaps preceded by smoked mackerel pâté.

WATERLOO

MODERATE

RSJ, 13A Coin St., SE1. Tel. 071/928-4554.
Cuisine: ENGLISH/FRENCH. **Reservations:** Required. **Tube:** Waterloo.
$ Prices: Appetizers £4.25–£6.95 ($6.40–$10.40); main courses £11.95–£12.95 ($17.90–$19.40); two-course set lunch or dinner £13.95 ($20.90); three-course fixed-price lunch or dinner £15.95 ($23.90). AE, MC, V.
Open: Lunch Mon–Fri noon–2pm; dinner Mon–Sat 6–11pm.

Set on the traditionally unglamorous South Bank of the Thames, this restaurant has clients so loyal that they travel from many different parts of London to reach it. Others dine here after seeing a program at the South Bank Centre. Named after a type of construction material (rolled structural joists) used during its restoration, the restaurant occupies the 250-year-old premises of what was originally a stable for the Duke of Cornwall. You enter from a nondescript street, then perhaps order a drink from the stand-up apéritif bar before being led upstairs to a table in a room that used to be the hayloft. Nigel Wilkenson, the sophisticated owner, personally selects the French wines (especially Loire Valley) that fill his impressive and reasonably priced wine list. Food, prepared in the tradition of modern British cuisine, includes such specialties as bavarois of salmon, a brace of quail stuffed with smoked ham and sweetbreads, tortellini of shellfish, and French duck marinated in sherry vinegar.

ELEPHANT & CASTLE

PUB

GOOSE & FIRKIN, 47 Borough Rd., SE1. Tel. 071/403-3590.

Cuisine: ENGLISH. **Reservations:** Not accepted. **Tube:** Elephant and Castle.

$ Prices: Sandwiches from £1.90 ($2.90); small pies from £1.60 ($2.40); hot platters £3.15 ($4.70); glass of wine £1.50 ($2.30). No credit cards.

Open: Mon–Fri noon–11pm, Sat–Sun noon–3pm and 7pm–midnight.

Established in 1979 on the premises of a much older, unsuccessful pub, this was the first member of a chain, the Goose & Firken, that later spread throughout the British Isles. The food here is a simple assortment of "big baps" (rolls stuffed with ham, turkey, or tuna), crock pots filled with chili, or platters of such pub staples as lasagne. Most of the clientele comes to drink, converse, and meet with newcomers and other regulars. Goose & Firkin brews its own beer in three special strengths: Goose, Borough Bitter, and the potent Dogbolter. A live guitarist performs three nights a week—usually Wednesday, Friday, and Saturday—from 9 to 11pm.

EAST END

INEXPENSIVE

BLOOM'S, 90 Whitechapel St., E1. Tel. 071/247-6001.

Cuisine: KOSHER. **Reservations:** Required. **Tube:** Aldgate East.

$ Prices: Appetizers £2.75–£4.50 ($4.10–$6.80); main courses £4.50–£9.50 ($6.80–$14.30). AE, DC, MC, V.

Open: Sun–Thurs 11:30am–9:30pm, Fri 11:30am–3pm (until 2pm Dec–Feb).

To reach London's most famous Jewish restaurant, established in 1920, you have to take the tube to the East End near the Tower of London. The large, bustling restaurant is in the back of a delicatessen, and the cooking is strictly kosher. Sunday lunchtime proves to be busy, since many visitors come here after shopping on Petticoat Lane. The cabbage borscht is the traditional opening course, although you may prefer chicken blintzes. Main-dish specialties include sauerbraten and salt (corned) beef. For dessert, the apple strudel is a favorite.

PUB

PROSPECT OF WHITBY, 57 Wapping Wall, E1. Tel. 071/ 481-1095.
Cuisine: ENGLISH/FRENCH. **Reservations:** Required. **Tube:** Wapping.
$ Prices: Appetizers £2.75–£8.95 ($4.10–$13.40); main courses £9.95–£16.50 ($14.90–$24.80). AE, DC, MC, V.
Open: Restaurant, lunch Sun–Mon, noon–2pm; dinner Mon–Sat 7–10pm. Pub, Mon–Sat 11:30am–3pm and 5:30–11pm, Sun noon–3pm and 7–10:30pm.

The Prospect of Whitby was founded in the days of the Tudors, taking its name from a coal barge that made weekly trips from Yorkshire to London. Come here for a tot, a noggin, or whatever it is you drink and soak up the traditional pubby atmosphere. Downstairs you can enjoy beer and snacks. Upstairs you can dine in the Pepys Room, which honors the diarist, who may—just may—have visited the Prospect in rowdier days, when the seamy side of London dock life held sway here. You can enjoy such dishes as veal champagne, Prospect of Whitby pie, and beef Wellington.

ST. KATHARINE'S DOCK
MODERATE

TOWER THISTLE HOTEL, St. Katharine's Way (without number), E1. Tel. 071/481-2575.
Cuisine: ENGLISH. **Reservations:** Not necessary. **Tube:** Tower Hill.
$ Prices: Fixed-price menu £16.75 ($25.10). AE, DC, MC, V.
Open: Lunch Mon–Sat 12:15–2:30pm, Sun 12:15–3pm; dinner Sun–Thurs 5:30–10:30pm, Fri–Sat 5:30–11pm.

In the Carvery Restaurant at this modern hotel overlooking the Thames, you can enjoy unlimited portions of some of the most tempting roasts in the Commonwealth. Everything is served buffet style. Before going to the carving table, you will be served a soup or hors d'oeuvres. Then you can select from ribs of prime beef (rare, medium, or well done), with Yorkshire pudding, horseradish sauce, and the drippings; from tender roast pork with cracklings, accompanied by a spiced-bread dressing and apple sauce; or from the roast spring Southdown lamb, with mint sauce—and help yourself to the roast potatoes, the green peas, and the baby carrots. End your meal with something from the dessert list and a large complimentary cup of American-style coffee.

INEXPENSIVE

DICKENS INN BY THE TOWER, St. Katharine's Way, E1. Tel. 071/488-2208.
Cuisine: ENGLISH. **Reservations:** Recommended. **Tube:** Tower Hill.
$ Prices: Appetizers £2–£5 ($3–$7.50); main courses £5–£19.95 ($7.50–$29.90); snacks £4 ($6), hot dish of the day £5 ($7.50); pizzas £6.50–£18 ($9.80–$27); Sun lunch £11.95 ($17.90). AE, DC, MC, V.
Open: Restaurant Mon–Sat noon–3pm and 6:30–10:30pm, Sun noon–3pm and 7–10pm; bar, Mon–Sat 11am–11pm, Sun noon–3pm and 7–10:30pm.

This three-floor restaurant is within the solid brick walls of an 1830 structure first used as a warehouse for spices pouring into London from afar. Its main decorative allure derives from massive redwood timbers of its original construction. It is deliberately devoid of carpets, curtains, or anything that might conceal its unusual antique trusses. Large windows afford a sweeping view of the nearby Thames and Tower Bridge.

On the ground level, you'll find a bar and the Tavern Room, serving sandwiches, platters of lasagne or smoked mackerel, steaming bowls of soup or chili, and bar snacks. One floor above you'll find a pizza restaurant, serving three sizes of pizzas ranging from 12 inches wide to a much-accessorized 18-inch behemoth known as "The Beast." Above that, you'll find a relatively formal dining room, The Pickwick Grill, serving more elegant meals. Specialties there include roast lamb or roast beef with Yorkshire pudding, fresh seafood, and salads.

BUTLER'S WHARF

MODERATE

LE PONT DE LA TOUR, 36 Shad Thames, Butler's Wharf, SE1. Tel. 071/403-8403.
   Cuisine: INTERNATIONAL. **Reservations:** Not accepted in the Bar and Grill; recommended in The Restaurant. **Tube:** Tower Hill.
$ Prices: Bar & Grill, appetizers £3–£7 ($4.50–$10.50); main courses £7.50–£17.50 ($11.30–$26.30). Restaurant, appetizers £6–£9 ($9–$13.50); main courses £14.50–£19 ($21.80–$28.50); three-course fixed-price lunch £25 ($37.50) per person. AE, DC, MC, V.
   Open: Lunch daily noon–3pm; dinner Sun–Fri 6–11pm, Sat 6pm–midnight. Cold platters and snacks Bar & Grill daily from 3–6pm.

These two restaurants are considered the most interesting and unusual of those contained within a newly developed waterfront complex of shops and cafés near Tower Bridge. Both of them lie on the ground floor of a brick-and-sandstone warehouse (Butler's Wharf), built during the 19th century and gutted and remodeled in 1992. Today, the complex holds condominiums, sophisticated food shops, and a sweeping view of some of the densest river traffic in Europe.

Many visitors prefer the brash hubbub of the Bar & Grill. Its hard surfaces, live entertainment, and widely diverse choice of alchoholic drinks create one of the most animated and convivial places in the neighborhood. Although such dishes as fish and chips, black pudding with sausage, pâté of chicken liver, and grilled pork chops with onion compôte are featured, the culinary star is a heaping platter of flavorful fresh shellfish (fruits de mer). It's perfect when consumed with a friend and a bottle of wine.

In bold contrast is the enormous and more formal room known simply as The Restaurant. Filled with white linen, burl oak, and framed reproductions of French cartoons from the 1920s, it offers excellent food and a polite but undeniable English reserve. Menu items include best end of English lamb in parsley-cream sauce, Bayonne ham with celeriac rémoulade, and lobster à la nage.

15. SPECIALTY DINING

DINING ON THE WATER
MODERATE

MY FAIR LADY, 250 Camden High St., NW1. Tel. 071/485-4433 or 071/485-6210.
   Cuisine: ENGLISH. **Reservations:** Required. **Tube:** Camden Town.
$ **Prices:** Lunch trip £17.95 ($26.90); dinner trip £25.95 ($38.90). MC, V.
   Open: Dinner trip departs at 8pm Tues–Sat; lunch trip departs at 1pm Sun only.

This cruise-while-you-dine establishment, a motor-driven barge, noses through the Regent's Canal for three hours, passing through the zoo, Regent's Park, and Maida Hill tunnel before it reaches Robert Browning's Island at Little Venice, where a popular singer-guitarist joins you for the return journey. The menu, which is based on fresh seasonal ingredients, consists of such traditional English fare as prime roast rib of beef, chicken suprême, and filet of beef.

INEXPENSIVE

HISPANIOLA, Victoria Embankment (without number), Charing Cross, WC2. Tel. 071/839-3011.
   Cuisine: ENGLISH/FRENCH. **Reservations:** Required. **Tube:** Embankment.
$ **Prices:** Appetizers £3–£7 ($4.50–$10.50); main courses £7–£12 ($10.50–$18). AE, DC, MC, V.
   Open: Lunch Mon–Sat noon–2pm; dinner Mon–Sat 6:30–10pm (last order). **Closed:** Mon from Nov–Easter.

This large, luxurious ship was originally built in the 1960s to haul passengers around the islands of Scotland. (Two similar vessels built at the same time still carry passengers between Naples, Italy, and the island of Capri.) Today, stripped of its engine, the ship is permanently moored to the side of the Thames, providing good food and excellent views of the passing river traffic. Tables are set up on two levels, and throughout, a certain elegance prevails. The menu offers many meat, game, and vegetarian dishes, including roasted quail with grapes and chestnuts, Barbary duck with lime-and-honey sauce, and Dover sole meunière. A pianist or harpist provides evening music.

HOTEL DINING
MODERATE

PAVILION RESTAURANT, Regency Hotel, 100 Queen's Gate, SW7. Tel. 071/370-4595.
   Cuisine: INTERNATIONAL. **Reservations:** Not necessary. **Tube:** Gloucester Rd. or South Kensington.
$ **Prices:** Appetizers £3.50–£7.95 ($5.30–$11.90); main courses £9.50–£14.25 ($14.30–$21.40); buffet lunch £15.50 ($23.30). AE, DC, MC, V.
   Open: Lunch Mon–Fri 12:30–2:30pm; dinner daily 5:30–10:30pm.

The Pavilion is a glamorous but reasonably priced choice if you're staying at one of the many hotels in South Kensington and would like to come here for meals and drinks. Menu selections are modern dishes based on prime seasonal produce and include rosemary-flavored lamb roasted to pink perfection and prime beef cut into strips, flavored with spices, and sizzled in butter before a brandy flambé finish. Sea bass, grilled in butter, is served on a bed of beetroot, with lemon on the side. Sole can be grilled or pan-fried to your request, and you can always order tender steaks from the charcoal grill; vegetarian dishes are also available. Care and attention also go into the appetizers, which feature unusual surprises, such as the chef's baked avocado and mango glazed with ginger-wine sabayon or parfait of duck livers and truffles combined with orange and coriander into a salad.

PELHAM RESTAURANT, in the Pelham Hotel, 15 Cromwell Place, SW7. Tel. 071/589-8288.
   Cuisine: FRENCH. **Reservations:** Required. **Tube:** South Kensington.
$ **Prices:** Appetizers £5–£8.50 ($7.50–$12.80); main courses £8–£15 ($12–$22.50); weekday fixed-price lunch £15.50 ($23.30); Sun set lunch £16.50 ($24.80). AE, DC, MC, V.
   Open: Lunch Sun–Fri 12:30–2:30pm; dinner Sun–Fri 6:30–10:30pm.

Located on the ground floor of this previously recommended elegant hotel, the Pelham is decorated with a subtle racing motif, accented with sophisticated lighting, cove moldings, a blue-and-white decor, and a large mahogany bar. It provides uniformed and impeccable French service at its limited number of well-attended tables, which are often filled with London luminaries.

Fashion aside, it is the food that attracts diners. The expertly prepared dishes represent an interpretation of modern French cuisine, including tartlet of sautéed sweetbreads and foie gras, terrine of escargots, and leek quiche with essence of tomatoes. For your main course, your selection might be fricassée of chicken breast with grapes and basil-flavored sauce (the pure essence, with no starchy thickener) or blanquette of lamb. Desserts are sumptuous, often presented like portrait miniatures, including a dark-chocolate mousse on mint sauce and gratiné of exotic fruits.

AFTERNOON TEA

BROWN'S HOTEL, 29–34 Albemarle St., W1. Tel. 071/493-6020. Reservations: Not accepted. **Tube:** Green Park.
$ **Prices:** Afternoon tea £12.95 ($19.40); high tea £15.50 ($23.30). AE, DC, MC, V.
   Open: Daily 3–6pm.

Ranking along with the Ritz Hotel as a chic venue for tea in London, Brown's Hotel offers afternoon tea in its lounge. The room is decorated with English antiques, wall panels, oil paintings, and floral chintz, much like one in a private English country estate. Give your name to the concierge upon arrival. Arrangements will be made for you to be seated on clusters of sofas and settees or at low tables. The regular afternoon tea includes a choice of 10 teas, sandwiches, and pastries that are rolled around on a trolley for your selection. Scones with jam and clotted cream are also included. Some pretheater tea drinkers opt for a high tea, which is more expensive and includes all the ingredients for a regular tea plus a warm dish. This dish might be fish cakes with a medley of relishes or something called a "Brown's griddle," a mixed English grill.

OAK ROOM LOUNGE, in Le Méridien, 21 Piccadilly, W1. Tel. 071/734-8000. Reservations: Recommended. **Tube:** Picadilly Circus or Green Park.
$ Prices: Average tea from £11 ($16.50). AE, DC, MC, V.
Open: Daily 3–6pm.

Restored to its former Edwardian glory, the Oak Room Lounge welcomes nonresidents for the very British tradition of afternoon tea. The soothing elegance of this formal but unstuffy oak-paneled room is augmented by comfortable armchairs and background music by a resident harpist. A complete tea includes a selection of sandwiches and tarts. The menu lists a tempting array of exotic teas, some you may never have tried. Men are required to wear jackets.

PALM COURT, in the Waldorf Hotel, Aldwych (without number), WC2. Tel. 071/836-2400. Reservations: Required. **Tube:** Covent Garden.
$ Prices: Afternoon tea £12.50 ($18.80); tea dance £19.50 ($29.25). AE, DC, MC, V.
Open: Daily 3:30–6:30pm.

Friday through Sunday the Palm Court combines afternoon tea with ballroom dancing. On other days, a pianist entertains as you sip your Earl Grey. The Palm Court is aptly compared to a 1920s movie set, which, in fact, it's been several times. You can order tea on a terrace or in a pavilion lit by skylights. On tea-with-dancing days, the orchestra leader will conduct such favorites as "Ain't She Sweet" and "Yes, Sir, That's My Baby," while a butler in a cutaway inquires if you want a cucumber sandwich. Men must wear jackets and ties.

PALM COURT LOUNGE, in the Park Lane Hotel, Piccadilly (without number), W1. Tel. 071/499-6321.
Reservations: Not necessary. **Tube:** Hyde Park Corner or Green Park.
$ Prices: Average tea menu £9.90 ($14.90); club sandwich £7.80 ($11.70). AE, DC, MC, V.
Open: Daily 24 hours.

One of the great favorites of London for tea, this place has an atmosphere straight from 1927. Restored to its former charm by John Siddeley, one of the world's leading interior designers, the lounge has a yellow-and-white domed glass ceiling, torchères, and palms in Compton stoneware jardinières. A delightful tea of three scones, Devonshire cream and thick jam, sandwiches, and a selection of cakes is served daily. Many guests come here after the theater for a sandwich and a drink, as food is served 24 hours a day. During the week a pianist plays every afternoon and evening. A harpist plays on Sunday afternoons.

RITZ PALM COURT, in the Ritz Hotel, Piccadilly (without number), W1. Tel. 071/493-8181.
Reservations: Required at least a week in advance. **Tube:** Green Park.
$ Prices: Afternoon tea £14.50 ($21.80). AE, DC, MC, V.
Open: Served daily at 3pm and 4:30pm.

✪ This is the most fashionable place in London to order afternoon tea and perhaps the hardest to get into without reservations way in advance. With a setting strictly from the 1920s and 1930s, it would be the most appropriate venue for F. Scott Fitzgerald's Gatsby to entertain if he miraculously appeared in London. The atmosphere is one of marble steps and columns, along with a baroque fountain. You have your choice of the widest possible variety of teas, served with those delectable little sandwiches on white bread and luscious pastries. Gentlemen are required to wear jackets and ties, and ladies are encouraged to wear hats. Jeans and sneakers are not acceptable.

BREAKFAST

FOX AND ANCHOR, 115 Charterhouse St., EC1. Tel. 071/253-4838.
    Cuisine: ENGLISH. **Reservations:** Required. **Tube:** Farringdon or Barbican.
$ Prices: "Full house" breakfast £6.50 ($9.80); steak breakfast £11.50 ($17.30). MC, V.
    Open: Breakfast Mon–Fri 7–10:30am; lunch Mon–Fri noon–2:15pm.

For a breakfast at its best, try this place that has been serving traders from the nearby famous Smithfield meat market since the pub was built in 1898. Breakfasts are gargantuan, especially if you order the "full house," which provides at least eight items on your plate, including sausage, bacon, mushrooms, kidneys, eggs, beans, black pudding, and fried slice of bread, to mention just a few, along with unlimited tea or coffee, toast, and jam. If you want a more substantial meal, you can have a filet steak with mushrooms, chips, tomatoes, and salad. Add a Black Velvet (champagne with Guinness) and the day is yours. Of course, in the modern British view, Guinness ruins champagne, but some people order it anyway—just to be traditional. More fashionable is a Bucks fizz, with orange juice and champagne. The Fox & Anchor is noted for its range of fine English Ales, all available at breakfast. Butchers from the meat market, spotted with blood, still appear, as do nurses getting off their shift and clerks and tycoons from the City who have been working at bookkeeping chores all night. Ale flows freely from 6 to 10:30am.

PICNIC FARE & WHERE TO FIND IT

Because of its "green lungs" (public parks), London is considered a great place for a picnic. Virtually any neighborhood you stay in has a supermarket or a deli where you can purchase cold cuts, cheeses, and soft drinks for a picnic.

    However, if you'd like to do what the queen of England might do if she were inviting guests for a picnic, there is no better place than **Fortnum & Mason,** 181 Piccadilly, W1 (tel. 071/734-8040; tube: Piccadilly Circus or Green Park), the world's most famous grocery store. Here you can find a wide array of foodstuffs to take away to your favorite park. See "Parks & Gardens" in Chapter 6 to decide where you'd like to enjoy your repast.

    Remember, the English disapprove mightily of littering in their public parks, and you could be fined, so clean up afterward.

WHAT TO SEE & DO IN LONDON

- • **SUGGESTED ITINERARIES**
- **1. THE TOP ATTRACTIONS**
- • **DID YOU KNOW . . . ?**
- **2. MORE ATTRACTIONS**
- • **FROMMER'S FAVORITE LONDON EXPERIENCES**
- **3. COOL FOR KIDS**
- **4. SPECIAL-INTEREST SIGHTSEEING**
- **5. ORGANIZED TOURS**
- **6. SPORTS & RECREATION**

The moment you try to categorize the marvels of a sightseer's paradise like London, you find yourself in a predicament. How on earth do you classify the attractions? For instance, Madame Tussaud's is both a museum and a show, and the Commonwealth Institute is an educational, cultural, and entertainment establishment.

This chapter covers the most interesting attractions in all categories. They may all be seen in the daytime. Which ones you elect to see depends on what strikes your fancy and the time you have to spend in London.

Note: As a rule, children's prices apply to persons aged 16 and under.

SUGGESTED ITINERARIES

IF YOU HAVE 1 DAY

Day 1: Even on the most rushed of itineraries, no first-time visitor should leave London without a visit to Westminster Abbey. Afterward, walk over to see Big Ben and the Houses of Parliament. Also see the Changing of the Guard at Buckingham Palace and walk over to 10 Downing Street, home of the prime minister. Dine at one of the little restaurants in Covent Garden.

IF YOU HAVE 2 DAYS

Day 1: Spend Day 1 as above.

Day 2: Devote a good part of the second day exploring the British Museum, considered by many the best in the world. Spend the afternoon visiting the Tower of London and seeing the Crown Jewels (expect slow-moving lines).

IF YOU HAVE 3 DAYS

Days 1–2: Spend Days 1 and 2 as above.

Day 3: Spend the morning at the National Gallery, facing Trafalgar Square. For a change of pace in your sightseeing, enjoy an afternoon at Madame Tussaud's waxworks.

IF YOU HAVE 5 DAYS

Days 1–3: Spend Days 1 to 3 as above.

Day 4: In the morning, head for the City, the financial district of London in the East End. Your major sightseeing goal here will be Sir Christopher Wren's St. Paul's Cathedral. Take our walking tour of the City (see Chapter 7) and visit such attractions as the Guildhall (city hall). Later in the afternoon, head for King's Road in Chelsea for some boutique hopping and dine at one of Chelsea's many restaurants.

Day 5: Explore the Victoria and Albert Museum in the morning, then go to the Tate Gallery for lunch at its restaurant and a look at some of its many masterpieces. Attend the theater this evening, or enjoy as many West End shows as you can on all your evenings in London.

1. THE TOP ATTRACTIONS

BRITISH MUSEUM, Great Russell St. (without number), WC1. Tel. 071/636-1555.

Set in scholarly Bloomsbury, this immense museum grew out of a private collection of manuscripts purchased in 1753 with the proceeds of a lottery. It grew and grew, fed by legacies, discoveries, and purchases, until it became one of the world's largest museums, containing literally millions of objects. It is utterly impossible to take in this museum in one day. You have to choose a particular section to focus on, then move on to another, preferably on another day.

The Egyptian room, for instance, contains the Rosetta Stone, whose discovery led to the deciphering of hieroglyphs; the Duveen Gallery houses the Elgin Marbles (a priceless series of sculptures from the pediments, metopes, and friezes of the Parthenon in Athens); the Nimrud Gallery has the legendary Black Obelisk, dating from around 860 B.C.

Other museum treasures include the contents of Egyptian royal tombs (including mummies); the oldest land vehicle ever discovered (a Sumerian sledge); fabulous arrays of 2,000-year-old jewelry, cosmetics, weapons, furniture, and tools; Babylonian astronomical instruments; and winged lions (in the Assyrian Transept) that once guarded Ashurnasirpal's palace at Nimrud.

The Ethnography Department of the British Museum, showing the art and material culture of the indigenous peoples of many parts of the world, is housed in the **Museum of Mankind,** Burlington Gardens, W1 (tel. 071/437-2224). Hours are the same as at the main museum. (The Café de Colombia within the Museum of Mankind closes half an hour before the museum itself does.)

For information on the great **British Library,** located in the same building as the British Museum, see below.

Admission: Free.

Open: Mon–Sat 10am–5pm, Sun 2:30–6pm. **Closed:** New Year's Day, Good Friday, first Mon in May, Dec 24–26. **Tube:**

Holborn or Tottenham Court Rd.; Piccadilly for Museum of Mankind.

BUCKINGHAM PALACE, at end of The Mall, on road running from Trafalgar Sq.

This massively graceful building is the official residence of the queen, and you can tell whether Her Majesty is at home by the Royal Standard flying at the masthead. For most of the year you can't visit the palace unless you're officially invited. You can, however, peep through the railings into the front yard. Beginning in 1993 you can also tour much of the palace during an eight-week period in August and September, when the royal family usually is vacationing outside London. Elizabeth II agreed to allow visitors to tour her state apartments; the Grand Staircase, Throne Room, and other areas designed by John Nash (1752–1835) for George IV; and the huge Picture Gallery, which displays masterpieces by Van Dyck ("Charles I on Horseback"), Rembrandt ("Shipbuilder and His Wife"), Rubens ("Farm at Laeken"), and others. There's an admission charge, which will help pay for repairing Windsor Castle, badly damaged by fire in 1992.

The red-brick palace was built as a country house for the notoriously rakish Duke of Buckingham. In 1762, it was bought by King George III, who needed room for his 15 children. From then on, the building was expanded, remodeled, faced with Portland stone, and twice bombed (during the Blitz). Located in a 40-acre garden, it stands 360 feet long and contains 600 rooms.

Every morning from early April to mid-August and every other morning the rest of the year, always at 11:30am, Buckingham Palace puts on its most famous spectacle, the Changing of the Guard. This ceremony, which lasts half an hour, is perhaps the finest example of military pageantry extant. The new guard, marching behind a band, comes from either the Wellington or Chelsea Barracks and takes over from the old guard in the forecourt of the palace.

At 11am Monday through Saturday and at 10am on Sunday, another guard-changing takes place a few minutes' walk away, on the far side of St. James's Park, at the Horse Guards Parade, Whitehall, SW1.

Both ceremonies are curtailed between October 1 and March 31. The Changing of the Guard officially takes place on even calendar days in October, December, and February, and on odd calendar days in November, January, and March. Call 071/730-3488 for information on the ceremony if the weather is uncertain. (Two other places in London also get ritual Guards protection: St. James's Palace and the Tower of London.)

Tube: St. James's Park or Green Park.

Admission: Palace tours: £8.30 ($12.45) adults to age 60, £4.40 ($6.60) adults over 60, £4.20 ($6.30) children under 17. Changing of the Guard: Free.

Times: Palace tours: Check tourist information offices, local publications. Changing of the Guard: See above.

HOUSES OF PARLIAMENT, Bridge St. and Parliament Sq., SW1. Tel. 071/219-4272 (House of Commons), 071/ 219-3107 (House of Lords).

The political opposite of the Tower of London, the Houses of Parliament are the stronghold of Britain's democracy, which effectively checked royal power. Both Houses (Commons and

? DID YOU KNOW . . . ?

- A romance between one of the queen's corgis and one of Princess Margaret's dachshunds produced three royal "dorgis."

- Covent Garden once had so many Turkish baths and brothels it was called "the great square of Venus."

- The famous May Fairs launched by Lord St. Albans in 1686 at Shepherd Market became so shocking for their bawdiness that they were eventually suppressed.

- The richest man in the world, the sultan of Brunei, owns the landmark art deco Dorchester and issued orders to restore it until it was "the greatest hotel in the world."

- Future U.S. President Franklin Delano Roosevelt (1882–1945) honeymooned with Eleanor Roosevelt at Brown's Hotel, which had been launched by a manservant of Lord Byron's.

- Nash's Marble Arch (1827), one of the most famous of London landmarks, was moved from Buckingham Palace in 1851 because it was too narrow for the royal coaches to pass through.

Lords) are in the former royal Palace of Westminster, the king's residence until Henry VIII moved to Whitehall.

Although I can't assure you of the oratory of a Charles James Fox or a William Pitt the Elder, the debates are often lively and controversial in the House of Commons (seats are at a premium during crises). The chances of getting into the House of Lords when it's in session are generally better than for the more popular House of Commons, where even the queen isn't allowed. Many political observers maintain that the peerage speak their minds more freely and are less likely to adhere to the party line than their counterparts in the Commons.

The general public is admitted to the Strangers' Gallery in the House of Commons on "sitting days." You have to join a public line outside the St. Stephen's entrance on the day in question, and there is often considerable delay before the public is admitted. You can speed matters up somewhat by applying at the American Embassy or the Canadian High Commission for a special pass, but this is too cumbersome for many people. Besides, the embassy has only four tickets for daily distribution, so you might as well stand in line. It's usually easier to get in after about 6pm. Debates often continue into the night.

The present House of Commons was built in 1840, but the chamber was bombed and destroyed by the German air force in 1941. The 320-foot tower that houses Big Ben, however, remained standing, and the celebrated clock continued to strike its chimes, the signature tune of Britain's news broadcasts. Big Ben, incidentally, was named after Sir Benjamin Hall, a cabinet minister distinguished by his long-windedness.

Except for the Strangers' Galleries, the two Houses of Parliament and Westminster Palace are presently closed to the public. Further information is available by telephone.

Admission: Free.

Open: House of Lords, open to public Mon–Thurs from about 3pm; also some Fridays (check by phone). House of Commons, open to public Mon–Thurs from 4pm, Fri 9:30am–3pm. Join line at St. Stephen's entrance. **Tube:** Westminster.

KENSINGTON PALACE, The Broad Walk (without number), Kensington Gardens, W8. Tel. 071/937-9561.

Once the residence of British monarchs, Kensington Palace has not been the official home of reigning kings since the death of George II in 1760, although it is now the London home of the Princess of Wales. (The Prince of Wales now resides at St. James's Palace.) The palace had been acquired in 1689 by William and Mary as an escape from the damp royal rooms along the Thames. Since the end of the 18th century, the palace has been a residence for various other members of the royal family. It was here in 1837 that a young Victoria was roused from her sleep with the news that her uncle, William IV, had died and that she was now queen of England. You can view a nostalgic collection of Victoriana, including some of her childhood toys and a fascinating dollhouse. Here, too, the late Queen Mary was born.

In the apartments of Queen Mary II, wife of William III, you can admire a striking piece of furniture, a 17th-century writing cabinet inlaid with tortoiseshell. Paintings from the Royal Collection literally line the walls of the apartments.

A special attraction is the Court Dress Collection, a series of room settings with the appropriate court attire of the day, from 1760 to 1950.

Kensington Gardens are open daily to the public for leisurely strolls around the Round Pond. One of the most famous sights here is the controversial Albert Memorial, a lasting tribute not only to Victoria's consort but also to the questionable artistic taste of the Victorian era.

Admission: £4 ($6) adults, £2.75 ($4.10) children.

Open: Mon–Sat 9am–5pm, Sun 11am–4pm. **Tube:** Queensway or Bayswater on north side of gardens; High St. Kensington on south side.

MADAME TUSSAUD'S, Marylebone Rd. (without number), NW1. Tel. 071/935-6861.

Madame Tussaud's is not so much a wax museum as an enclosed entertainment world. A weird, moving, sometimes terrifying collage of exhibitions, panoramas, and stage settings, it manages to be most things to most people, most of the time.

Madame Tussaud attended the court of Versailles and learned her craft in France. She personally took the death masks from the guillotined heads of Louis XVI and Marie Antoinette, which you'll find among the exhibits. Her original museum, founded in Paris, moved to England in 1802. Since then, her exhibition has been imitated in every part of the world, but never with the realism and imagination on hand here. Madame herself molded the features of Benjamin Franklin, whom she met in Paris. All the rest—from George Washington to John F. Kennedy, from Mary Queen of Scots to Sylvester Stallone—are subjects for the same painstaking (and breathtaking) replication.

In the well-known **Chamber of Horrors**—a kind of underground dungeon—there stands a genuine gallows (from Hertford prison) and other instruments of the death penalty, along with figures of their victims. The shadowy presence of Jack the Ripper lurks in the gloom as you walk through a Victorian London street; George Joseph Smith can be seen with the tin bath in which he drowns the last of his three brides; and Christie conceals another murdered body behind his kitchen wall. Dr. Crippen, the poisoner, and his accomplice, Ethel le Neve, stand trial in the dock, and Mrs. Pearcey raises a poker to a crying baby in its pram. Many of their peers are displayed nearby, and present-day criminals are portrayed within the confines of prison.

You'll find a snack bar and gift shops on the premises.

Admission: £6.75 ($10.10) adults, £4.40 ($6.60) children under 16.

Open: Mon–Fri 10am–5:30pm, Sat–Sun 9:30am–5:30pm. **Tube:** Baker St.

NATIONAL GALLERY, northwest side of Trafalgar Sq. (without number), WC2. Tel. 071/389-1785.

This stately neoclassical building contains an unrivaled collection of painting that spans seven centuries and covers every great European school of art. It does not include painting after 1929 (there are other galleries for that), but for sheer skill of display and arrangement, it surpasses counterparts in Paris, New York, Madrid, and Amsterdam.

All the British greats are here—Hogarth, Gainsborough, Reynolds, Constable, Turner—and shown at their finest.

The Italian Renaissance is represented by Leonardo da Vinci's *Virgin of the Rocks;* Titian's *Bacchus and Ariadne;* Giorgione's *Adoration of the Kings;* and unforgettable canvases by Bellini, Veronese, Botticelli, and Tintoretto.

Then there are the Spanish giants: El Greco's *Agony in the Garden,* and portraits by Goya and Velázquez. The Flemish-Dutch school is represented by two Brueghels, Jan van Eyck, Vermeer, and de Hooch; the Rembrandts include two of his immortal self-portraits (at age 34 and 63), while Rubens is represented in adjoining galleries. There is also an immense French collection by late 19th-century impressionists and postimpressionists, including Manet, Monet, Degas, Renoir, and Cézanne. A particularly charming item is the peep-show cabinet by Hoogstraten in one of the Dutch rooms: It's like spying through a keyhole.

The Sainsbury Wing was opened in 1991 by Elizabeth II and designed by noted Philadelphia architects, Robert Venturi and Denise Scott Brown to house the gallery's Early Renaissance collection. Displayed are such masterpieces as Jan van Eyck's *Portrait of Giovanni Arnolfini and his wife Giovanna Cenami,* along with *The Doge* by Bellini, *Christ Mocked* by Bosch, and *Portrait of a Man* by Antonello da Messina. Botticelli's *Venus and Mars* is eternally enchanting. In addition, the Sainsbury Wing is used for large temporary exhibitions. Although admission to the National Gallery is free, a fee is charged for temporary exhibitions.

Admission: Free.

Open: Mon–Sat 10am–6pm, Sun 2–6pm. **Tube:** Charing Cross or Leicester Sq.

ST. PAUL'S CATHEDRAL, St. Paul's Churchyard (without number), EC4. Tel. 071/236-4128 or 071/248-2705.

Partly hidden by nondescript office buildings on Ludgate Hill yet shining through by the sheer power of its beauty, stands London's largest and most famous church. Built by Sir Christopher Wren in place of the cathedral that burned down during the Great Fire of 1666, St. Paul's represents the ultimate masterpiece of this genius.

The golden cross surmounting it is 365 feet above the ground; the golden ball on which the cross rests measures 6 feet in diameter yet looks like a marble from below. Surrounding the interior of the dome is the **Whispering Gallery,** an acoustic marvel in which the faintest whisper can be heard clearly on the opposite side.

Although the interior of the church looks almost bare, it houses a vast number of monuments linked to Britain's history. The Duke of Wellington (of Waterloo fame) is entombed there, as are Lord Nelson and Sir Christopher Wren himself. At the east end of the cathedral is the **American Memorial Chapel,** honoring the 28,000 U.S. service personnel who fell while based in Britain in World War II.

Guided tours, lasting 1½ hours and including the crypt and parts of St. Paul's that are not normally open to the public, take place at 11 and 11:30am and 2 and 2:30pm on Monday through Saturday. In addition, you can climb to the galleries for a spectacular 360-degree view of all of London.

St. Paul's is an Anglican cathedral, with daily services at 7:30am and 5pm (Evensong). Sunday services are at 10:30 and 11:30am and 3:15pm (Evensong).

Admission: Cathedral, £2.50 ($3.80) adults, £1.50 ($2.30) children under 16; galleries, £2.50 ($3.80) adults, £1.50 ($2.30) children under 16. When crypt is closed, entrance charge is reduced by 50p (75¢). Tours, excluding entrance charge but including galleries, £3 ($4.50) adults, £1 ($1.50) children under 16.

Open: Cathedral, daily 7:15am–6pm; crypt and galleries, Mon-Sat 8:45am–4:15pm. **Tube:** St. Paul's.

TATE GALLERY, Millbank (without number), SW1. Tel. 071/821-1313.

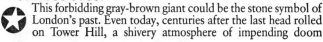

Fronting the Thames near Vauxhall Bridge in Pimlico, the Tate looks like a smaller and more graceful relation of the British Museum. Considered by many the most prestigious gallery in Britain, it houses the national collections, covering British art from the 16th century on, plus an international array of moderns. The Tate's holdings are split between the traditional and the contemporary. Because it is difficult to take in all the exhibits, I suggest that you concentrate on whichever section interests you more.

The older works include some of the best of Hogarth, Stubbs, Gainsborough, Reynolds, Blake, and Constable. The Turner Bequest of more than 19,000 watercolors and nearly 300 oils is housed in the adjoining Clore Gallery, which opened in 1987. Among the moderns, you'll find Picasso, Braque, Matisse, Dalí, Munch, Modigliani, Bacon . . . you name it, it's here. There are also the sculptures—masterpieces by Epstein and Moore.

The wide-ranging exhibits include surrealism and postwar painting in Britain and France, and the most fascinating part of the gallery is frequently the "current exhibition."

Downstairs are a restaurant (see Chapter 5), with murals by Rex Whistler, and a self-service coffee shop.

Admission: Free, except special exhibitions.

Open: Mon-Sat 10am–5:50pm, Sun 2–5:50pm. **Tube:** Pimlico. **Bus:** No. 77A, 88, or C10.

TOWER OF LONDON, Tower Hill (without number), EC. Tel. 071/709-0765.

This forbidding gray-brown giant could be the stone symbol of London's past. Even today, centuries after the last head rolled on Tower Hill, a shivery atmosphere of impending doom

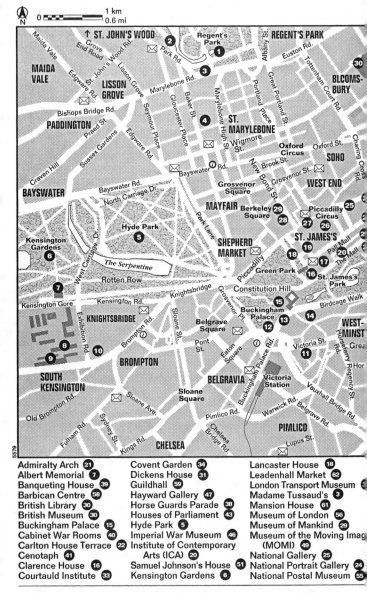

lingers over the mighty walls. The Tower is actually an intricate pattern of different structures built at various times and for varying purposes, mostly as expressions of royal power.

The oldest is the White Tower, begun by William the Conqueror in 1078 to keep the native Saxon population of London in check. Later rulers added other towers, more walls, and fortified gates, until the building became something like a small town within a city. Until the reign of James I, the Tower was also one of the royal residences.

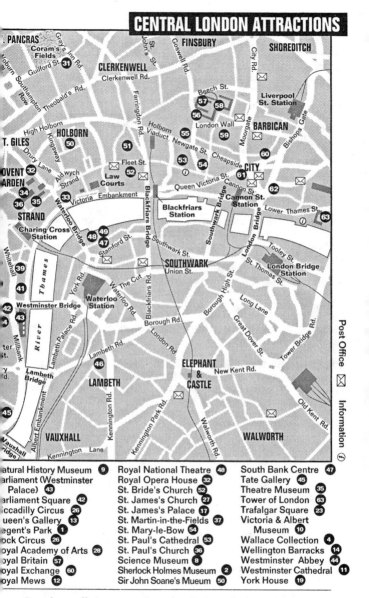

CENTRAL LONDON ATTRACTIONS

But above all, it was a prison for distinguished captives . . . usually their last.

In the **Bloody Tower,** according to the unproved story dramatized by Shakespeare, the two little princes were murdered by the henchmen of Richard III. Here, too, Sir Walter Raleigh spent 13 years before his date with the executioner.

Only one American was ever locked in the Tower—a South Carolina merchant named Henry Laurens, who was also president of the Continental Congress. Captured at sea by the British in 1780, Laurens spent 18 months behind those menacing walls, until he was exchanged for the defeated Cornwallis.

Every stone of the Tower tells a story—usually a gory one. On the walls of the **Beauchamp Tower,** you can actually read the last messages scratched by despairing prisoners.

But the Tower, besides being a royal palace, a fortress, and a prison, was also an armory, a treasury, a menagerie, and—for a few months in 1675—an astronomical observatory.

In the **Jewel House** lie England's Crown Jewels—some of the most precious stones known—set into the robes, sword, scepter, and crowns donned by each monarch at his or her coronation. They've been heavily guarded ever since the daredevil Colonel Blood almost got away with them.

Tours approximately one hour long are given by the Yeoman Warders at frequent intervals, starting at 9:30am from the Middle Tower near the main entrance. The tour includes the Chapel Royal of St. Peter and Vincula. The last guided walk starts about 3:30pm in summer, 2:30pm in winter.

Admission: £6.70 ($10.10) adults, £4.40 ($6.60) children (under 5, free); £19 ($28.50) family ticket for five (but no more than two adults).

Open: Nov–Feb, Mon–Sat 9:30am–5pm; Mar–Oct, Mon–Sat 9:30am–6pm, Sun 10am–6pm. **Closed:** Sun in Nov–Feb, New Year's Day, Good Friday, Dec 24–26. **Tube:** Tower Hill. **Boat:** From Westminster Pier.

VICTORIA AND ALBERT MUSEUM, Cromwell Rd. (without number), SW7. Tel. 071/938-8500.

Located in South Kensington, this museum devoted to fine and decorative art is one of the liveliest and most imaginative in London. It's named after the 19th-century queen and her consort.

There are, for instance, the seven great "cartoons" (in the artistic, non-Disney sense) by Raphael, painted for Pope Leo in 1516, and a large collection of Italian Renaissance sculpture. An entire gallery of medieval art covers everything from carvings in wood and ivory to silver candlesticks and enamel caskets. There are also displays of contemporary design, fashion, and images.

Asian art is represented by stunning carpets from Iran and from every other part of the Muslim world. The museum also has the greatest collection of Indian art outside India. Recently it opened Chinese and Japanese galleries as well. In complete contrast are suites of English furniture, metalwork, and ceramics dating beyond the 16th century, and a superb collection of portrait miniatures, including the one Hans Holbein the Younger made of Anne of Cleves for the benefit of Henry VIII, who was again casting around for a suitable wife.

Other treasures displayed include the Eltenberg Reliquary (Rhenish, second half of the 12th century); the Gloucester Candlestick (Early English); the Veroli Casket (Byzantine); the Syon Cope (early 14th century); a marble group, *Neptune with Triton,* by Bernini; and another rare portrait miniature by Holbein, this one of Mrs. Pemberton.

Admission: Free, donation of £3.50 ($5.30) per adult suggested.

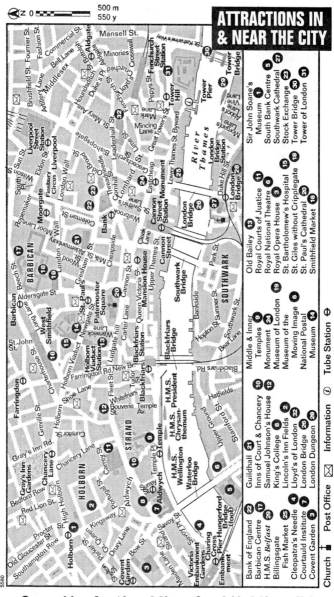

ATTRACTIONS IN & NEAR THE CITY

Z 0 500 m / 550 y

(map labels): Mansell St., Commercial St., Fournier St., Fashion St., Brushfield St., Bell Lane, Artillery Lane, Middlesex St., Aldgate, Minories, Crosswall, Fenchurch Street Station, St. Katharine's Way, Tower Bridge, Tower Pier, Tower Hill, River Thames, London Bridge Station, London Bridge, SOUTHWARK, Barbican, West Smithfield, Farringdon, HOLBORN, STRAND, Covent Garden, Charing Cross, Victoria Embankment Gardens, Waterloo Bridge, Blackfriars Bridge, Southwark Bridge, Bankside

Legend:
- Bank of England 22
- Barbican Centre 17
- H.M.S. Belfast 29
- Billingsgate 25
- Cleopatra's Needle 5
- Courtauld Institute 4
- Covent Garden 3
- Guildhall 21
- Inns of Court & Chancery 10
- Samuel Johnson's House 8
- King's College 2
- Lincoln's Inn Fields 32
- Lloyd's of London 28
- London Bridge 26
- London Dungeon 28
- Middle & Inner Temples 9
- Monument 24
- Museum of London 18
- Museum of the Moving Image 6
- National Postal Museum 14
- Old Bailey 13
- Royal Courts of Justice 11
- Royal National Theatre 7
- Royal Opera House 3
- St. Bartholomew's Hospital 15
- St. Giles without Cripplegate 19
- St. Paul's Cathedral 20
- Smithfield Market 16
- Sir John Soane's Museum
- South Bank Centre 5
- Southwark Cathedral 27
- Stock Exchange 23
- Tower Bridge 30
- Tower of London 31

✝ Church   ■ Post Office   ⊠ [symbol]   ⓘ Information   ⊖ Tube Station

Open: Mon–Sat 10am–5:50pm, Sun 2:30–5:50pm. **Tube:** South Kensington.

WESTMINSTER ABBEY, Broad Sanctuary (without number), SW1. Tel. 071/222-7110.

★ With its square twin towers, superb archways, and Early English Gothic splendors, the abbey is one of the greatest examples of ecclesiastical architecture on earth. But it is far more than that: It is the shrine of a nation, symbol of everything Britain has stood for and stands for, the edifice in which most of her rulers were crowned and many lie buried, along with the nameless bones of the Unknown Warrior.

King Edward the Confessor, whose bones also lie here, rebuilt the abbey in 1065 just before his death. The next year saw both the last of the Saxon kings, Harold, who died at the Battle of Hastings, and the first of the Normans, William the Conqueror, crowned in the church. Little now remains of Edward the Confessor's abbey, as rebuilding in the Gothic style was started by Henry III and completed shortly before the dissolution of the monasteries by Henry VIII, but it has remained the Coronation Church.

Next to the tomb of Edward III is the Coronation Chair, with the ancient Scottish relic known as the Stone of Scone beneath the seat. Just before Elizabeth II's coronation, some Scottish nationalists kidnapped the stone but were persuaded to return it in time for the crowning.

The entire abbey is crammed with treasures, some truly priceless, some curious. There are the strange waxworks, showing images of important personalities that were carried in their funeral processions, including those of Lord Nelson and the Duchess of Richmond (who achieved immortality by posing as the figure of Britannia you see on British pennies).

There is the Poets' Corner, with monuments to the British greats, from Chaucer to Lord Laurence Olivier, and one American, Henry Wadsworth Longfellow. You'll also find the graves of such figures from U.S. history books as Maj. John André and Gen. John Burgoyne. A memorial stone for Sir Winston Churchill was placed in 1965.

The only time photography is allowed in the abbey is Wednesday evening in the Royal Chapels. On Sunday, the Royal Chapels are closed, but the rest of the church is open unless a service is being conducted. For times of services, phone the Chapter Office (tel. 071/222-5152). Up to six super-tours of the abbey are conducted by the vergers Monday through Friday, beginning at 10am.

Admission: Abbey, free; £1.35 ($2) donation suggested. Royal Chapels, Royal Tombs, Coronation Chair, Henry VII Chapel, £3 ($4.50) adults, £1 ($1.50) children. Royal Chapels free Wed evenings.

Open: Mon–Fri 9:20am–4pm, Sat 9:30am–2pm and 3:45–5pm; Royal Chapels, Wed 6–7:45pm. **Tube:** Westminster or St. James's Park.

2. MORE ATTRACTIONS

CEMETERY

HIGHGATE CEMETERY, Swain's Lane (without number), N6. Tel. 081/340-1834.

This 37-acre burial ground is of great attraction for tombstone fanciers. Described in the British press as everything from "walled romantic rubble" to "an anthology of horror," it is the ideal setting for a collection of Victorian sculpture as well as the graves of Karl Marx and others.

Admission: £4 ($6) donation is requested.

Open: Western Cemetery: Apr–Oct, Mon–Fri guided tours only at noon and 2 and 4pm; Sat–Sun hourly 11am–4pm. Nov–Mar, Tues–Fri noon and 2 and 3pm; Sat–Sun hourly 11am–3pm. Eastern Cemetery: Apr–Oct, daily 10am–4:45pm; Nov–Mar, daily 10am–3:45pm. **Tube:** Archway, then walk through Waterlow Park.

HISTORIC BUILDINGS

BANQUETING HOUSE, Whitehall Palace, Horse Guards Ave. (without number), SW1. Tel. 071/930-4179.

The feasting chambers in Whitehall Palace are probably the most sumptuous eateries on earth. Unfortunately, you can't dine there unless you happen to be a visiting head of state. Designed by Inigo Jones and decorated with—among other things—original paintings by Rubens, these banqueting halls are dazzling enough to make you forget about food. Among the historic events that took place here was the beheading of King Charles I (the scaffold stood outside). The restoration ceremony of Charles II, which also took place here, marked the return of monarchy after Cromwell's brief Puritan-republican Commonwealth.

Admission: £2.75 ($4.10) adults, £1.90 ($2.90) children.

Open: Mon–Sat 10am–5pm (last admission 4pm). **Closed:** Good Friday, Easter, Dec 24–Jan 2. **Tube:** Westminster.

CABINET WAR ROOMS, Clive Steps (without number) at end of King Charles St., off Whitehall near Big Ben, SW1. Tel. 071/930-6961.

Visitors today can see the bombproof bunker just as it was left by Winston Churchill in September 1945 at the end of World War II. Many objects were removed only for dusting, and the Imperial War Museum studied photographs to replace things exactly as they were, including notepads, files, and typewriters, right down to pencils, pins, and clips.

You can see the **Map Room** with its huge wall maps, the one of the Atlantic Ocean being a mass of pinholes. Each hole represented at least one convoy. Next door is Churchill's bedroom-cum-office, reinforced with stout wood beams; it has a very basic bed and a desk with two BBC microphones on it for those famous broadcasts that stirred the nation. The **Transatlantic Telephone Room,** to give it its full name, is little more than a broom closet, but it contained the Bell Telephone Company's special scrambler phone called Sig-Saly. From here, Churchill conferred with Roosevelt. The scrambler equipment itself was actually too large to house in the bunker, so it was placed in the basement of Selfridges department store on Oxford Street. All visitors are provided with a step-by-step personal sound guide, providing a detailed account of the function and history of each room.

Admission: £3.80 ($5.70) adults, £1.90 ($2.90) children.

Open: Mon–Sun 10am–6pm. **Closed:** On certain state occasions. **Tube:** Westminster.

FENTON HOUSE, Windmill Hill (without number), NW3. Tel. 071/435-3471.

A National Trust property, Fenton House is in a village area on the west side of Hampstead Grove, just a little north of Hampstead Village. It was built in 1693, and its paneled rooms contain furniture

FROMMER'S FAVORITE LONDON EXPERIENCES

Watching the Sunset at Waterloo Bridge
Waterloo Bridge is the most ideal place in London to watch the sun set over Westminster in the west. The last rays can also be seen bouncing off the City spires in the East End.

Enjoying a Pub Lunch Have lunch in the bustling, overcrowded atmosphere of a London pub, vying for elbow space at the bar as you place your order for a roast-beef sandwich and a mug of lager.

Enjoying a Traditional English Tea Nothing is more typically British. To avoid making advance reservations, try the Hotel Goring, dating from 1910. There, sitting in the lounge, you'll have a view of a small garden as you enjoy "finger" sandwiches (often watercress or cucumber), the hotel's special Ceylon blend tea, scones, and the chef's famous "light fruit cake," offered from a trolley.

Brass Rubbing Re-create all those costumed ladies and knights in armor from England's age of chivalry. One good place for brass rubbings is the crypt of St. Martin-in-the-Fields in Trafalgar Square.

A Night at a West End Theater London is the theatrical capital of the world. The live stage offers a unique combination of variety, accessibility, and economy—and perhaps a look at next year's Broadway hit.

and pictures; English, German, and French porcelain from the 18th century; and the outstanding Benton-Fletcher collection of early keyboard musical instruments.

Admission: £3 ($4.50) adults, £1.50 ($2.30) children.

Open: Mar, Sat–Sun 2–6pm; Apr–Oct, Sat–Sun 11am–6pm, Mon–Wed 1–7pm. **Closed:** Good Friday and Nov–Feb. **Tube:** Hampstead.

INSTITUTES

COMMONWEALTH INSTITUTE, Kensington High St. (without number), W8. Tel. 071/603-4535.

Why come just to London when you can visit the Caribbean, see Canada from a skidoo, climb Mount Kenya, and take a rickshaw across Bangladesh? The history, landscapes, wildlife, and crafts of the Commonwealth of Nations are presented in this tent-shaped building next to Holland Park. Something's always happening here, ranging from special exhibitions, to shows for children, to cultural festivals. The Commonwealth Shop is a source for gifts and items, including food and wine from around the world, and light refreshments are sold at Flags Restaurant.

Admission: Free.

Open: Mon–Sat 10am–7pm, Sun 2–5pm. **Closed:** Jan 1, Good Friday, May Day, Dec 24–26. **Tube:** High Street Kensington, Earl's Court, or Holland Park. **Bus:** 9, 10, 27, 28, 31, or 49.

COURTAULD INSTITUTE GALLERIES, Somerset House, The Strand (without number), WC2. Tel. 071/873-2526.

These galleries contain the following wealth of paintings: the Lee collection of old masters; the Gambier-Parry collection of early Italian painting and sculpture, ivories, majolica, and other works of art; the great collection of French impressionist and postimpressionist paintings (masterpieces by Monet, Manet, Degas, Renoir, Cézanne, van Gogh, Gauguin) brought together by the late Samuel Courtauld; the Roger Fry collection of early 20th-century English and French painting; and the recent bequest of the Princes Gate collection of superb old master paintings and drawings, especially those by Rubens, Michelangelo, and Tiepolo. The galleries are air-conditioned, and some of the paintings are displayed without glass.

Admission: £3 ($4.50) adults, £1.50 ($2.30) children.

Open: Mon–Sat 10am–6pm, Sun 2–6pm. **Tube:** Temple or Covent Garden.

LIBRARY

BRITISH LIBRARY, British Museum, Great Russell St. (without number), WC2. Tel. 071/636-1544.

Some of the treasures from the collections of the British Library, one of the world's greatest libraries, are on display in the exhibition galleries in the east wing of the British Museum building. The Middle Room contains Western illuminated manuscripts. In the Manuscript "Saloon" (yes, that's right), items of historical and literary interest include two of the four surviving copies of King John's *Magna Carta* (1215). Almost every major author—Dickens, Jane Austen, Charlotte Brontë, Keats—is represented in the section devoted to English literature. Also on display are Nelson's last letter to Lady Hamilton and the journals of Captain Cook.

In the King's Library, the history of the book is illustrated by notable specimens of early printing, including the Diamond Sutra of 868, the first dated example of printing, as well as the Gutenberg Bible, the first book ever printed from movable type, 1455. In the center of the library is an exhibition of fine book bindings dating from the 16th century. Beneath Roubiliac's 1758 statue of Shakespeare stands a case of documents relating to the Bard, including a mortgage bearing his signature and a copy of the First Folio of 1623. The library's unrivaled collection of philatelic items, including the 1840 Great British Penny Black and the rare 1847 Post Office issues of Mauritius, are also on view.

Admission: Free.

Open: Mon–Sat 10am–5pm, Sun 2:30–6pm. **Tube:** Holborn or Tottenham Court Rd.

MUSEUMS

APSLEY HOUSE, THE WELLINGTON MUSEUM, 149 Piccadilly, Hyde Park Corner, W1. Tel. 071/499-5676.

This was the mansion of the Duke of Wellington, one of Britain's greatest generals. The "Iron Duke" defeated Napoleon at Waterloo, but later, for a short period while prime minister, he had to have iron shutters fitted to his windows to protect him from the mob outraged by his autocratic opposition to reform. His unpopularity soon passed, however.

The house is crammed with art treasures; military mementos; and a regal silver, china, and porcelain collection. You can admire the duke's medals, the array of field marshals' batons, the battlefield orders, plus three original Velázquez paintings among a score of other greats. One of the features of the museum is a colossal marble statue of Napoleon by Canova in the vestibule. It was a present from the grateful King George IV, who was then Regent.

The museum, closed at press time for restoration, is scheduled to reopen in mid-1994.

Admission: £2 ($3) adults, £1 ($1.50) children.

Open: Daily 11am–6pm. **Closed:** Jan 1, May Day, Dec 24–26. **Tube:** Hyde Park Center.

FREUD MUSEUM, 20 Maresfield Gardens, NW3. Tel. 071/435-2002.

This is the spacious house in which the father of psychoanalysis lived, worked, and died after escaping with his family and possessions from Nazi-occupied Vienna. The rooms contain his furniture (including the famous couch), letters, photographs, paintings, and personal effects, as well as those of his daughter, Anna Freud, also a noted psychoanalyst. Temporary exhibitions and an archive film program are available, plus a shop.

Admission: £2.50 ($3.80) adults; children under 12 free.

Open: Wed–Sun noon–5pm. **Tube:** Finchley Rd.

HAYWARD GALLERY, South Bank Centre (without number), SE1. Tel. 071/928-3144.

Opened by Elizabeth II in 1968, this gallery presents a changing program of major exhibitions. It is part of the South Bank Centre, which also includes the Royal Festival Hall, the Queen Elizabeth Hall, the Purcell Room, the National Film Theatre, and the National Theatre. The gallery is closed between exhibitions, so check the listings before crossing the Thames; for recorded information, phone 071/261-0127.

Admission: £5 ($7.50) adults, £3.50 ($5.30) children; family ticket £12 ($18). Fee varies according to exhibitions; children are often half price.

Open: Thurs–Mon 10am–6pm, Tues–Wed 10am–8pm. **Tube:** Waterloo Station.

IMPERIAL WAR MUSEUM, Lambeth Rd. (without number), SE1. Tel. 071/416-5000.

One of the few sights south of the Thames, this museum occupies one city block the size of an army barracks, greeting you with 15-inch guns from the battleships *Resolution* and *Ramillies*. The large domed building, built in 1815, was the former Bethlem Royal Hospital for the insane, known as Bedlam.

A wide range of weapons and equipment is on display, along with models, decorations, uniforms, posters, photographs, and paintings. You can see a Mark V tank, a Battle of Britain Spitfire, and a German one-man submarine, as well as a rifle carried by Lawrence of Arabia. In the documents room, you can view the famous "peace in our time" agreement that Neville Chamberlain brought back from Munich in 1938. Of his signing the agreement, Hitler later said, "He was a nice old man, so I decided to give him my autograph." Another exhibition is the self-styled "political testament" that Hitler dictated in the chancellery bunker in the closing days of World War II in Europe; it was witnessed by henchmen Joseph Goebbels and Martin Bormann.

Public film shows take place on weekends at 3pm and on certain weekdays during school holidays and on public holidays. Various special exhibitions are displayed at different times.

Admission: £3.50 ($5.30) adults, £1.75 ($2.60) children. Free daily 4:30–6pm.

Open: Daily 10am–6pm. **Closed:** New Year's Day, Good Friday, first Mon in May, Dec 24–26. **Tube:** Lambeth North or Elephant and Castle.

IVEAGH BEQUEST, Kenwood House, Hampstead Lane (without number), NW3. Tel. 081/348-1286.

This structure was built as a gentleman's country home and later enlarged and decorated by the famous Scottish architect Robert Adam, starting in 1764. The house contains period furniture and paintings by Rembrandt, Vermeer, Gainsborough, and Turner, among others.

Admission: Free.

Open: Apr–Sept, daily 10am–6pm; Oct–Mar, daily 10am–4pm. **Closed:** Dec 24–25. **Tube:** Golden Green, then bus 210.

LONDON TRANSPORT MUSEUM, The Piazza (without number), Covent Garden, WC2. Tel. 071/379-6344.

A collection of nearly two centuries of historic vehicles is displayed in a splendid Victorian building that formerly housed the Flower Market at Covent Garden. The museum shows how London's transport system evolved, and a representative collection of road vehicles includes a reconstruction of George Shillibeer's omnibus of 1829. A steam locomotive that ran on the world's first underground railway, a knifeboard horse bus, the "B"-type motor bus, London's first trolleybus, and the Feltham tram are also of particular interest. One of the unique and popular features of the museum is the number of participatory exhibits, which allow visitors to operate the controls of a tube train, a tram, a bus, and full-size signaling equipment.

The museum shop sells a range of souvenirs.

Admission: £4 ($6) adults, £2 ($3) children.

Open: Daily 10am–6pm (last entrance at 5:15pm). **Closed:** Dec 24–26. **Tube:** Covent Garden.

MOMI, Museum of the Moving Image, South Bank underneath Waterloo Bridge, SE1. Tel. 071/401-2636.

MOMI is also part of the South Bank complex. Tracing the history of cinema and television, it takes the visitor on an incredible journey from cinema's earliest experiments to modern animation, from Charles Chaplin to the operation of a TV studio. There are artifacts to handle, buttons to push, and a cast of actors to tell visitors more. Three to four changing exhibitions are presented yearly. Allow two hours for a visit.

Admission: £6 ($9) adults, £4.50 ($6.80) children; £17.50 ($26.30) family ticket.

Open: Daily 10am–6pm (last admission 5pm). **Tube:** Waterloo.

MUSEUM OF LONDON, 150 London Wall, EC2. Tel. 071/600-3699.

In London's Barbican district near St. Paul's Cathedral, overlooking the city's Roman and medieval walls, the museum allows visitors to trace the history of London from prehistoric times to the present through archeological finds; paintings and prints; and social, industrial, and historical artifacts; as well as costumes, maps, and models. On two floors around a central courtyard, exhibits are arranged so that you can begin and end your chronological stroll through 250,000 years at the main entrance to the museum. You can see the death mask of Oliver Cromwell, but the pièce de résistance is the lord mayor's coach, built in 1757 and weighing in at 3 tons. This gilt-and-red horse-drawn vehicle is like a fairy-tale coach. Visitors can also see the Great Fire of London in living color and sound; reconstructed Roman dining rooms, together with the kitchen and utensils; cell doors from Newgate Prison made famous by Charles Dickens; and most amazing of all, a shop counter with pre–World War II prices.

There is a restaurant overlooking a garden.

Admission: £3 ($4.50) adults, £1.50 ($2.30) children.

Open: Tues–Sat 10am–6pm, Sun noon–6pm. **Tube:** St. Paul's, Barbican, or Moorgate.

NATIONAL ARMY MUSEUM, Royal Hospital Rd. (without number), Chelsea, SW3. Tel. 071/730-0717.

The National Army Museum occupies a building adjoining the Royal Hospital, a home for retired soldiers, the Chelsea Pensioners. Whereas the Imperial War Museum is concerned only with wars in the 20th century, the National Army Museum tells the colorful story of British armies from 1485 on. Here you'll find the uniforms British soldiers wore in every corner of the world and many of the items they brought back, as well as weapons and other gear, flags, and medals. Even the skeleton of Napoleon's favorite charger is here. Displayed also is the actual battle order which—through its hazy wording—launched the lunatic but heroic Charge of the Light Brigade at Balaklava.

Admission: Free.

Open: Daily 10am–5:30pm. **Closed:** New Year's Day, Good Friday, first Mon in May, Dec 24–26. **Tube:** Sloane Sq.

NATIONAL PORTRAIT GALLERY, St. Martin's Place (without number), WC2. Tel. 071/306-0055.

In a gallery of remarkable and unremarkable pictures, a few paintings tower over the rest, including Sir Joshua Reynolds's first portrait of Samuel Johnson ("a man of most dreadful appearance"). Among the best are Nicholas Hilliard's miniature of a handsome Sir Walter Raleigh and a full-length Elizabeth I (painted to commemorate her visit to Sir Henry Lee at Ditchley in 1592), along with the Holbein cartoon of Henry VIII (sketched for a family portrait that hung, before it was burned, in the Privy Chamber of Whitehall Palace). There is also a portrait of William Shakespeare (with gold earring, no less) by an unknown artist that bears the claim of being the "most authentic contemporary likeness" of its subject. The John Hayls portrait of Samuel Pepys is here, as is a portrait of Whistler, no mean painter in his own right. One of the most famous pictures in the gallery is the group portrait of the Brontë sisters (Charlotte, Emily, and Anne) painted by their brother, Bramwell. An idealized portrait of Lord Byron by Thomas Phillips is also on display, and you can treat yourself to the likeness of the incomparable Aubrey Beardsley. For a finale, Diana, Princess of Wales, is on the Royal Landing.

Admission: Free. (A fee is charged for certain temporary exhibitions.)

Open: Mon–Fri 10am–5pm, Sat 10am–6pm, Sun 2–6pm. **Tube:** Charing Cross or Leicester Sq.

NATIONAL POSTAL MUSEUM, King Edward Building, King Edward St. (without number), EC1. Tel. 071/239-5420.

This museum attracts philatelists and many others. Actually part of the Post Office, it features permanent exhibitions of the stamps of Great Britain and the world, as well as special displays of stamps and postal history, changing every few months according to certain themes. In 1990, the 150th anniversary of the Penny Black, the world's first adhesive postage stamp, was commemorated by a special exhibition.

Admission: Free.

Open: Mon–Fri 9:30am–4:30pm. **Tube:** St. Paul's or Barbican.

NATURAL HISTORY MUSEUM, Cromwell Rd. (without number), SW7. Tel. 071/938-9123.

This is the home of the national collections of living and fossil plants and animals, minerals, rocks, and meteorites, with many magnificent specimens on display. Exciting exhibitions designed to encourage people of all ages to enjoy learning about natural history include "Human Biology—An Exhibition of Ourselves," "Man's Place in Evolution," "Introducing Ecology," "Origin of the Species," "British Natural History," and "Discovering Mammals." What attracts the most attention is the 13,000-square-feet dinosaur exhibit, displaying 14 complete skeletons. The center of the show depicts a trio of ripping, clawing, chewing, moving full-size robotic Deinonychus having a freshly killed Tenontosaurus for lunch.

Admission: £4 ($6) adults, £2 ($3) children 5–15.

Open: Mon–Sat 10am–6pm, Sun 1–6pm. **Closed:** Jan 1, Dec 23–26. **Tube:** South Kensington.

SCIENCE MUSEUM, Exhibition Rd. (without number), SW7. Tel. 071/938-8000.

This museum traces the development of both science and industry, particularly their application to everyday life. Exhibits vary from models and facsimiles to the actual machines. You'll find Stephenson's original Rocket, the tiny locomotive that won a race against all competitors and thus became the world's prototype railroad engine. See the earliest motor-propelled airplanes, a cavalcade of antique cars, and steam engines from their crudest to their most refined form. Greatest fascinators are the working models of machinery (visitor-operable by push buttons). Galleries include an Exploration of Space, Food for Thought, the Welcome Museum of the History of Medicine and Flight, and a new Aeronautics Gallery. In "Launch Pad," a hands-on gallery, children of all ages can carry out their own fun experiments.

Admission: £3.75 ($5.60) adults, £1.90 ($2.90) children.

Open: Mon–Sat 10am–6pm, Sun 11am–6pm. **Tube:** South Kensington. **Bus:** 14.

SHERLOCK HOLMES MUSEUM, 221b Baker St., NW1. Tel. 071/935-8866.

Where but on Baker Street would there be a museum displaying mementos of this famed fictional detective? Museum officials call it "the world's most famous address," though 10 Downing Street in London is a rival. It was here that mystery writer Sir Arthur Conan Doyle created a residence for Sherlock Holmes and his faithful Doctor Watson. These sleuths "lived" here from 1881 to 1904. In Victorian rooms, visitors examine a range of exhibits, including published Holmes adventures and letters written to Holmes. A gift shop is on the premises.

Admission: £5 ($7.50) adults, £3 ($4.50) children.
Open: Daily 10am–6pm. **Tube:** Baker St.

WALLACE COLLECTION, Manchester Sq. (without number), W1. Tel. 071/935-0687.

Located in a palatial setting (the modestly described "town house" of the late Lady Wallace), the Wallace Collection is a contrasting array of art and armaments. The former (mostly French) includes Watteau, Boucher, Fragonard, and Greuze, as well as such classics as Frans Hals's *Laughing Cavalier* and Rembrandt's portrait of his son Titus. The paintings of the Dutch, English, Spanish, and Italian schools are outstanding. The collection also contains important 18th-century French works of decorative art, including furniture from a number of royal palaces, Sèvres porcelain, and gold boxes.

The European and Asian armaments, shown on the ground floor, are works of art in their own right: superb inlaid suits of armor, some obviously more for parade than battle, together with more business-like swords, halberds, and magnificent Persian scimitars. The crescent sabers were reputedly tested by striking the blade against a stone, then examining it for even the most minute dent; if one was found, the sword was rejected.

Admission: Free.
Open: Mon–Sat 10am–5pm, Sun 2–5pm. **Closed:** New Year's Day, Good Friday, first Mon in May, Dec 24–26. **Tube:** Bond St. or Baker St.

PARKS & GARDENS

London's parks are the greatest, most wonderful system of "green lungs" of any large city on the globe. Although not as rigidly maintained as those of Paris, they are cared for with a loving and lavishly artistic hand that puts their American equivalents to shame.

Battersea Park is a vast patch of woodland, lakes, and lawns on the south bank of the Thames, opposite Chelsea Embankment between Albert Bridge and Chelsea Bridge. Formerly known as Battersea Fields, the present park was laid out between 1852 and 1858 on an old dueling ground. (The most famous duel here was between Lord Winchelsea and the Duke of Wellington in 1829.)

The park, which measures three-quarters of a mile on each of its four sides, has a lake for boating, a deer field with fenced-in-deer and wild birds, and areas for tennis and soccer. There's even a children's zoo, open from Easter to late September, daily from 11am to 5pm. The park's architectural highlight is the **Peace Pagoda**, built by

Japanese craftspeople in cooperation with British architects, who ensured that it would fit gracefully into its surroundings. Built of stone and wood, the pagoda was constructed in 1986 and donated to the now-defunct Council of Greater London by an order of Japanese monks.

Battersea Park can be visited daily from 7:30am to dusk. Tube: Sloane Square in Chelsea on the Right Bank. From there it is a brisk 15-minute walk. If you prefer to ride the bus, take no. 137 from the Sloane Square station, exiting at the first stop after the bus crosses the Thames.

Hampstead Heath is the traditional playground of the Londoner, the "Appy' Ampstead" of cockney legend, the place dedicated "to the use of the public forever" by special Act of Parliament in 1872. Londoners would certainly mount the barricades if Hampstead Heath were imperiled.

Situated on a ridge, Hampstead Heath encompasses 785 acres of wild royal parkland about 4 miles north of the center of London. Its varied landscape encompasses formal parkland, woodland, heath, meadowland, and ponds. There are a wide variety of recreational facilities, ranging from athletics to a small zoo. The heath draws thousands of visitors each year for the walks, views, and traditional bank holiday fairs. Tube: Hampstead.

Largest of the central London parks—and one of the biggest in the world—is **Hyde Park.** With the adjoining Kensington Gardens, it covers 615 acres of central London with velvety lawns interspersed with ponds, flowerbeds, and trees. At the northeastern tip, near Marble Arch, is **Speakers' Corner.**

Hyde Park was once a favorite deer-hunting ground of Henry VIII. Running through its width is a 41-acre lake known as The Serpentine, where you can row, sail model boats, or swim, provided you're not accustomed to Florida water temperatures. **Rotten Row,** a 1½-mile sand track, is reserved for horseback riding and on Sunday attracts some skilled equestrians.

Kensington Gardens, blending with Hyde Park and bordering on the grounds of Kensington Palace, contains the famous **statue of Peter Pan,** with the bronze rabbits that toddlers are always trying to kidnap. It also contains the **Albert Memorial,** that Victorian extravaganza.

East of Hyde Park, across Piccadilly, stretch **Green Park** and **St. James's Park,** forming an almost unbroken chain of landscaped beauty. This is an ideal area for picnics, and you'll find it hard to believe that it was once a festering piece of swamp near the leper hospital. There is a romantic lake, stocked with a variety of ducks and some surprising pelicans, descendants of the pair that the Russian ambassador presented to Charles II back in 1662.

Regent's Park covers most of the district of that name, north of Baker Street and Marylebone Road. Designed by the 18th-century genius John Nash to surround a palace for the prince regent that

IMPRESSIONS

London is enchanting. I step out upon a tawny coloured magic carpet, it seems, & get carried into beauty without raising a finger.
—VIRGINIA WOOLF, *DIARY* (1924)

never materialized, this is the most classically beautiful of London's parks. Its core is a **rose garden** planted around a small lake alive with waterfowl and spanned by humped Japanese bridges; in early summer, the rose perfume in the air is as heady as wine. Regent's Park also contains the **Open Air Theatre** and the **London Zoo.** As at all the local parks, there are hundreds of deck chairs on the lawns in which to sunbathe. The deck-chair attendants, who collect a small fee, are mostly college students on summer vacation.

The hub of England's—and perhaps the world's—horticulture is the **Royal Botanic Gardens,** also known as **Kew Gardens,** at Kew in Surrey (tel. 081/940-1171; tube: Kew Gardens), next to the Thames southwest of the city. These splendid gardens have been a source of delight to visitors, scientific and otherwise, for more than 200 years. The staff deals annually with thousands of inquiries, covering every aspect of plant science. Immense flowerbeds and equally gigantic hothouses grow species of shrubs, blooms, and trees from every part of the globe, from the Arctic Circle to tropical rain forests. Attractions vary with the seasons. There's also the permanent charm of **Kew Palace,** home of George III and his queen, which was built in 1631 and is open for inspection.

Admission to the gardens is £3.50 ($5.30) for adults and £1.30 ($2) for children; a family ticket costs £9 ($13.50). Admission to the palace is £1 ($1.50) for adults and 50p (75¢) for children. The gardens may be visited daily, except Christmas and New Year's Day, from 9:30am; closing varies from 4 to 6:30pm on Monday through Saturday, 8pm on Sunday and public holidays. The palace is open April to September, daily from 11am to 5:30pm.

Syon Park is in Brentford, Middlesex, on the north bank of the Thames between Brentford and Isleworth, just 9 miles from Piccadilly Circus. On 55 acres of the Duke of Northumberland's Thames-side estate, this is one of the most beautiful spots in all of Great Britain. It lies 2 miles west of Kew Bridge and is signposted from A315/310 at Bush Corner. There's always something in bloom. A nation of green-thumbed gardeners is dazzled here, and the park is also educational, showing amateurs how to get the most out of their gardens. The vast flower- and plant-studded acreage still reflect the influence of "Capability" Brown, who laid out the grounds in the 18th century.

Particular highlights include a 6-acre rose garden, a butterfly house, and the **Great Conservatory,** one of the earliest and most famous buildings of its type, built between 1822 and 1829. There is a quarter-mile-long ornamental lake studded with water lilies and surrounded by cypresses and willows, even a large gardening supermarket.

The gardens are open all year (except Christmas and Boxing Day). The gates open at 10am and close at 6pm; in winter (after October 31), the gates close at 4pm. Admission is £2 ($3) for adults and £1.50 ($2.30) for children.

On the grounds is **Syon House,** built in 1431, the original structure incorporated into the Duke of Northumberland's present home. From 1762 to 1769, the house was remade to the specifications of the first Duke of Northumberland, with interior design by Robert Adam. The battlemented facade, however, is that of the original Tudor mansion. Katherine Howard, Henry VIII's fifth wife, was imprisoned in the house before her scheduled beheading in 1542.

The house is open from April until the end of September, Sunday through Thursday from noon to 5pm (last entrance at 4:15pm). Admission is £3 ($4.50) for adults and £2.25 ($3.40) for children. For information, phone 081/360-0881. Tube: Gunnersbury.

3. COOL FOR KIDS

The attractions that follow are general and universal fun places to which you can take youngsters without having to worry about either their physical or moral safety. And—there's nothing to stop you from going to any of them minus a juvenile escort. Other, previously described attractions that hold great interest for kids include Madame Tussaud's, the Science Museum, the London Transport Museum, the Tower of London, and the Commonwealth Institute.

BETHNAL GREEN MUSEUM OF CHILDHOOD, Cambridge Heath Rd. (without number), E2. Tel. 081/980-3204.

This establishment displays toys from past centuries. The variety of dolls alone is staggering, some of them dressed in period costumes of such elaborateness you don't even want to think of the price tags they must have carried. With the dolls go dollhouses, from simple cottages to miniature mansions, complete with fireplaces and grand pianos, furniture, kitchen utensils, household pets, and carriages.

In addition, the museum displays optical toys, toy theaters, marionettes, puppets, and a considerable exhibit of soldiers and warlike toys of both world wars, plus trains and aircraft. There is also a display of children's clothing and furniture related to childhood. Special activities for children are often presented; call for information.

Admission: Free.

Open: Mon–Thurs and Sat 10am–5:50pm, Sun 2:30–5:50pm. **Tube:** Bethnal Green.

LITTLE ANGEL MARIONETTE THEATRE, 14 Dagmar Passage, N1. Tel. 071/226-1787.

This theater, especially constructed for the presentation of puppetry in all its forms, gives between 200 and 300 performances a year. The theater is the focal point of a loosely formed group of about 20 professional puppeteers who work there as occasion demands, sometimes presenting their own shows and often helping with the performances of the resident company.

In the current repertory are 25 programs. These vary in style and content from *The Soldier's Tale,* using 8-foot-high figures, to *Wonder Island* and *Lancelot the Lion,* written especially for the humble glove puppet. Many of the plays, such as Hans Christian Andersen's *The Little Mermaid,* are performed with marionettes (string puppets), but whatever is being presented, you'll be enthralled with the exquisite lighting and the skill with which the puppets are handled.

The theater is beautifully decorated and well equipped. There are a coffee bar in the foyer and an adjacent workshop where the settings and costumes, as well as the puppets, are made.

Admission: Adults £4.50–£6 ($6.80–$9), children £4.50–£5 ($6.80–$7.50).

Open: Show times Sat–Sun 11am and 3pm. **Tube:** Angel Station, Highbury, or Islington Station.

LONDON DUNGEON, 28–34 Tooley St., SE1. Tel. 071/ 403-7221.

The premises simulate a ghoulish atmosphere deliberately designed to chill the blood while reproducing the conditions that existed in the Middle Ages. Set under the arches of London Bridge Station, the dungeon is a series of tableaux that are more grisly than the ones in Madame Tussaud's. The rumble of trains overhead adds to the spine-chilling horror of the place, and tolling bells bring a constant note of melancholy to the background; dripping water and live rats (caged!) make for even more atmosphere. The murder of Thomas à Becket in Canterbury Cathedral is also depicted. Naturally, there's a burning at the stake, as well as a torture chamber with racking, branding, and fingernail extraction.

If you survive, there is a souvenir shop selling certificates that testify you have been through the works.

Admission: £5.50 ($8.30) adults, £3.50 ($5.30) children under 14.

Open: Apr–Sept, daily 10am–5:30pm; Oct–Mar, daily 10am–4:30pm. **Closed:** Dec 24–26. **Tube:** London Bridge.

LONDON ZOO, Regent's Park, NW1. Tel. 071/722-3333.

One of the greatest zoos in the world, the London Zoo is more than a century and a half old. Run by the Zoological Society of London, this 36-acre garden houses about 8,000 animals, including some of the rarest species on earth. Separate houses are reserved for various species: the insect house (incredible bird-eating spiders, a cross-sectioned ant colony); the reptile house (huge dragonlike monitor lizards and a fantastic 15-foot python); and other additions such as the Sobell Pavilion for Apes and Monkeys and the Lion Terraces.

Designed for the largest collection of small mammals in the world, the Clore Pavilion has a basement called the Moonlight World, where special lighting effects simulate night for the nocturnal beasties, while rendering them clearly visible to onlookers. You can see all the night rovers in action.

Many families budget almost an entire day to spend with the animals, watching the sea lions being fed, enjoying an animal ride in summer, and meeting the elephants on their walks around the zoo. On the grounds are two restaurants, one self-service.

Note: Because the zoo is subject to closure, telephone before going there.

Admission: £6 ($9) adults, £3.70 ($5.60) children (under 4 free).

Open: Mar–Sept, daily 10am–5:30pm; Oct–Feb, daily 10am–4pm or dusk, whichever is earlier. **Tube:** Camden Town; then take bus Z1 (summer only) or 274.

NATIONAL MARITIME MUSEUM, Romney Rd. (without number), Greenwich. Tel. 081/858-4422.

Down the Thames at Greenwich, about 6 miles from London, the National Maritime Museum stands in a beautiful royal park along with the Old Royal Observatory. A great many astronomical instruments still mingle with the navigational gadgets; it's easy to see the connection. Otherwise, the building harbors the glory that was Britain at sea. The cannon, relics, ship models, and paintings tell the story of a thousand naval battles and a thousand victories . . . also the price of those battles: Among the exhibits is the uniform that

Lord Nelson wore when he was struck by a French musket ball at the very moment of his triumph at the Battle of Trafalgar.

The **Old Royal Observatory,** also part of the museum, designed by Sir Christopher Wren, overlooks Greenwich from a park laid out to the design of Le Nôtre, the French landscaper. Here you can stand at 0° longitude, where the Greenwich meridian, or prime meridian, marks the first of the globe's vertical divisions. See also the big red time-ball used in olden days by ships sailing down the river from London to set their timepieces by. There is a fascinating array of astronomical and navigational instruments, and time and travel become better understood after a visit here. There is a licensed restaurant in the museum's west wing.

You can also visit **Queen's House,** a 17th-century palace designed by Inigo Jones for the wives of James I and Charles I. The house has been restored in the vibrant colors of 1662, when the place was occupied by Henrietta Maria. A fine art collection of Dutch marine paintings and a treasury complement a tour of the royal apartments.

Admission: Maritime Museum, Old Royal Observatory, and Queen's House, £3.75 ($5.60) adults, £2.75 ($4.10) children 7–16; £13.95 ($20.90) family tickets.

Open: Apr–Sept, Mon–Sat 10am–6pm, Sun 2–6pm; Oct–Mar, Mon–Sat 10am–5pm, Sun 2–5pm. **Closed:** Dec 24–26. **Transportation:** Thames launch downstream from Westminster Charing Cross, or Tower Piers, or train from Charing Cross Station to Maze Hill.

UNICORN THEATRE FOR CHIILDREN, The Arts Theatre, 6–7 Great Newport St., WC2. Tel. 071/379-3280; box office 071/836-3334.

Situated in the heart of London's theater district in the West End, the Unicorn is its only theater just for children. Founded in 1947 and going stronger than ever, it presents a season of plays for 4- to 12-year-olds from September to June each year. The schedule includes specially commissioned plays and adaptations of old favorites, all performed by adult actors. You can also become a temporary member while you are in London and join in an exciting program of workshops every weekend.

Admission: £3.50 ($5.30), £5 ($7.50), and £6.50 ($9.80), depending on seat locations.

Open: Show times Sept–June Sat–Sun and school holidays 2:30pm.

Tube: Leicester Sq.

4. SPECIAL-INTEREST SIGHTSEEING

FOR THE LITERARY ENTHUSIAST

CARLYLE'S HOUSE, 24 Cheyne Row, SW3. Tel. 071/352-7087.

From 1834 to 1881, Thomas Carlyle, author of *The French Revolution,* and Jane Baillie Welsh Carlyle, his noted letter-writing wife, resided in this modest 1708 terraced house. Furnished essentially as it was in Carlyle's day, the house is located about three-quarters of a block from the Thames, near the Chelsea Embankment, along King's Road. It was described by his wife as being "of most antique physiognomy, quite to our humour; all wainscotted, carved and queer-looking, roomy, substantial, commodious, with closets to satisfy any Bluebeard." The second floor contains the drawing room of Mrs. Carlyle, but the most interesting chamber is the not-so-soundproof "soundproof" study in the skylit attic. Filled with Carlyle memorabilia—his books, a letter from Disraeli, personal effects, a writing chair, even his death mask—this is where the author labored on his *Frederick the Great* manuscript.

Admission: £2.50 ($3.80) adults, £1.25 ($1.90) children.

Open: Easter–Oct, Wed–Sun 11am–5pm. **Tube:** Sloane Sq. **Bus:** 11, 19, 22, or 39.

DICKENS HOUSE, 48 Doughty St., WC1. Tel. 071/405-2127.

Here in Bloomsbury stands the simple abode in which Charles Dickens wrote *Oliver Twist* and finished *The Pickwick Papers* (his American readers actually waited at the dock for the ship that brought in each new installment). The place is almost a shrine for a Dickens fan; it contains his study, manuscripts, and personal relics, as well as reconstructed interiors.

Admission: £3 ($4.50) adults, £2 ($3) students, £1 ($1.50) children, £5 ($7.50) families.

Open: Mon–Sat 10am–5pm. **Tube:** Russell Sq.

KEATS'S HOUSE, Wentworth Place, Keats Grove, NW3. Tel. 071/435-2062.

This house was the home of the poet John Keats for only 2 years. But it was here in Hampstead in 1819 that he wrote two famous poems, "Ode to a Nightingale" and "Ode on a Grecian Urn." This well-preserved Regency house contains some of his manuscripts and letters.

Admission: Donations suggested: £1.50 ($2.30) adults, 75p ($1.15) children.

Open: Apr–Oct, Mon–Fri 10am–1pm and 2–6pm, Sat 10am–1pm and 2–5pm, Sun and bank holidays 2–5pm; Nov–Mar, Mon–Fri 1–5pm, Sat 10am–1pm and 2–5pm, Sun 2–5pm. **Closed:** New Year's Day, Easter holidays, first Mon in May, Dec 24–26. **Tube:** Hampstead.

SAMUEL JOHNSON'S HOUSE, 17 Gough Sq., EC3. Tel. 071/353-3745.

Dr. Johnson and his copyists compiled a famous dictionary in this Queen Anne house, where the lexicographer, poet, essayist, and fiction writer lived from 1748 to 1759. Although Johnson also lived at Staple Inn in Holborn and at a number of other places, the Gough Square house is the only one of his residences remaining in London. The 17th-century building has been painstakingly restored, and it's well worth a visit.

Admission: £2 ($3) adults, £1.50 ($2.30) children.

Open: May–Sept, Mon–Sat 11am–5:30pm; Oct–Apr, Mon–Sat 11am–5pm. **Tube:** Blackfriars. Walk up New Bridge St. and turn left onto Fleet. Gough Sq. is tiny and hidden, north of Fleet.

FOR VISITING AMERICANS

Despite the historic fact that they fought wars against each other, no two countries have stronger links than America and Britain. The common heritage cuts right across political and economic conflicts.

In London, mementos of this heritage virtually crowd in on you. Stand in front of the National Gallery and you'll find a bronze **statue of George Washington** gazing at you over Trafalgar Square. Visit **Westminster Abbey** and you'll see a memorial tablet to President Franklin D. Roosevelt, a bust of Longfellow in the Poets' Corner, and the graves of Edward Hyde (Hyde Park, NY, was named for him) and James Oglethorpe, who founded the state of Georgia. **Grosvenor Square,** in the heart of the West End, is known as "Little America." Watched over by a statue of FDR, it contains the modern U.S. embassy and the home of John Adams when he was minister to Britain. **Norfolk House,** St. James's Square, was Gen. Dwight D. Eisenhower's headquarters during World War II, the spot from which he directed the Allies' Normandy landing in 1944. At 36 Craven St., just off the Strand, stands **Benjamin Franklin's London residence.** And in **St. Sepulchre's,** at Holborn Viaduct, is the grave of Capt. John Smith of Pocahontas fame—he had been prevented from sailing on the *Mayflower* because the other passengers considered him an "undesirable character."

The most moving reminder of national links is the **American Memorial Chapel in St. Paul's Cathedral.** It commemorates the 28,000 U.S. service personnel who lost their lives while based in Britain during World War II. The Roll of Honor containing their names was handed over by General Eisenhower on July 4, 1951, and the chapel—with the Roll of Honor encased in glass—has become an unofficial pilgrimage place for visiting Americans.

FOR RIVER THAMES BUFFS

There is a row of fascinating attractions lying on, across, and alongside the **River Thames.** All of London's history and development is linked with this winding ribbon of water. The Thames connects the city with the sea, from which it drew its wealth and its power. For centuries the river was London's highway and main street.

Some of the Thames bridges are household names. **London Bridge,** contrary to the nursery rhyme, never fell down, but it has been dismantled and shipped to the United States. When here, it ran from the Monument (a tall pillar commemorating the Great Fire of 1666) to Southwark Cathedral, parts of which date back to 1207.

Its neighbor to the east is the still-standing **Tower Bridge** (without number or road name), E1 (tel. 071/407-0922; tube: Tower Hill), one of the city's most celebrated landmarks and possibly the most photographed and painted bridge on earth. Its outward appearance is familiar to Londoners and visitors alike, and it is that same bridge that a certain American thought he'd purchased instead of the one farther up the river.

In spite of its medieval appearance, Tower Bridge was built between 1886 and 1894. Its two towers, 200 feet apart, are joined by footbridges that provide glass-covered walkways for the public, who can enter the north tower, take the elevator to the walkway, cross the river to the south tower, and return to street level. It's a photographer's dream, with interesting views of St. Paul's, the Tower of

London, and in the distance, part of the Houses of Parliament. You can also visit the main engine room with its Victorian boilers and steam-pumping engines that used to raise and lower the roadway across the river. Admission to the bridge is £3.50 ($5.30) for adults and £2.50 ($3.80) for children. It's open daily in summer from 10am to 6:30pm (until 4:45pm in winter).

The Thames was London's chief commercial thoroughfare and a royal highway, the only regal one in the days of winding cobblestoned streets. Every royal procession was undertaken by gorgeously painted and gilded barges (which you can still see at the National Maritime Museum in Greenwich; see Section 3 of this chapter). All important state prisoners were delivered to the Tower by water, eliminating the chance of an ambush by their friends in one of those narrow, crooked alleys surrounding the fortress. The royal boats and much of the commercial traffic disappeared when London's streets were widened enough for horse-drawn coaches to maintain a decent pace.

A trip up or down the river today will give you an entirely different view of London from the one you get from dry land. You'll see exactly how the city grew along and around the Thames and how many of its landmarks turn their faces toward the water. It's like Manhattan from a ferry.

There are pleasure launches sailing from Charing Cross and Westminster piers from April to September. You can take them upstream, past the Houses of Parliament, to Kew, Richmond, and Hampton Court; or downstream, ending down at Greenwich. Short-range service from Westminster Pier, to the Tower of London and Greenwich runs all year. The multitude of small companies operating boat services from Westminster Pier have organized themselves into the **Westminster Passenger Service Association,** Westminster Pier, Victoria Embankment, SW1 (tel. 071/930-4097; tube: Westminster). Boats leave the pier for cruises of varying lengths throughout the day and evening.

Since its official opening in 1984, the engineering spectacle known as the **Thames Flood Barrier** has drawn increasing crowds to the site, at a point in the river known as Woolwich Reach (east London), where the Thames is a straight stretch about a third of a mile in width. During the day, visitors can drop in at the **Thames Barrier Visitors Centre,** Unity Way, SE18 (tel. 081/854-1373), if they're seeking information. The center is open Monday through Friday from 10:30am to 5pm and Saturday and Sunday from 10:30am to 5:30pm. Admission to the barrier is £2.25 ($3.40) for adults and £1.40 ($2.10) for children. For centuries, the Thames estuary has from time to time brought tidal surges that have caused disastrous flooding at Woolwich, Hammersmith, Whitehall, Westminster, and elsewhere within the river's flood reaches. The flooding peril has increased during this century from a number of natural causes, which led to the construction, beginning in 1975, of a great barrier; when in use, all parts of it make a solid steel wall (about the height of a five-story building) that completely dams the waters of the Thames, keeping the surge tides from passage up the estuary.

London Launches (tel. 071/930-3373; tube: Waterloo Station to Charleton Station near Thames Flood Barrier; bus: 177 or 180) offers trips up the Thames to the barrier, operating from Westminster Pier to Barrier Pier and back five times daily. Adults pay £5.40 ($8.10) round trip or £3.80 ($5.70) one way; children under 14 are charged £2.75 ($4.10) round trip or £2.20 ($3.30) one way. If you wish to go one way by main line, trains make the 15-minute trip every 30 minutes.

What was a dilapidated wasteland in 8 square miles of property surrounded by water—some 55 miles of waterfront acreage within a sailor's cry of London's major attractions—has been reclaimed, restored, and rejuvenated. **London Docklands** is coming into its own as a leisure, residential, and commercial lure. Included in this complex are **Wapping, the Isle of Dogs,** the **Surrey and Royal Docks,** and more—all with **Limehouse** at its heart.

The former urban wasteland of deserted warehouses and derelict wharves, and the many facilities already completed, can be visited by taking the **Dockland Light Railway,** which links the Isle of Dogs and London Underground's Tower Hill station, via several new local stations. To see the whole complex, take the railway at the Tower Gateway near Tower Bridge for a short journey through Wapping and the Isle of Dogs. You can get off at **Island Gardens** and then cross through the 100-year-old **Greenwich Tunnel** under the Thames to see the attractions at Greenwich.

A visit to the **Exhibition Centre** on the Isle of Dogs gives you an opportunity to see what the Docklands—past, present, and future—include. Already the area has given space to the overflow from the City of London's square mile, and it looks as if the growth and development is more than promising.

An 11,500-ton cruiser, **HMS *Belfast,*** Morgan's Lane (without number), Tooley Street, SE1 (tel. 071/407-6434; tube: Monument, Tower Hill, or London Bridge), is a World War II ship now preserved as a floating naval museum. It is moored opposite the Tower of London, between Tower Bridge and the new London Bridge. During the Russian convoy period and on D-Day, the *Belfast* saw distinguished service, and in the Korean War it was known as "that straight shootin' ship." Exhibitions both above and below deck show how sailors have lived and fought over the past 50 years. The ship can be explored from the bridge right down to the engine and boiler rooms seven decks below. It's open daily from 10am, with last boarding at 5:30pm in summer, 4pm in winter. Admission is £4 ($6) for adults and £2 ($3) for children. Refreshments are available. A ferry runs from Tower Pier (weekends only in winter).

Two other ships, both world famous, are at Greenwich, 4 miles east of London. At Greenwich Pier, now in permanent dry dock, lies the last and ultimate word in sail power—the **Cutty Sark,** King William Walk, Greenwich, SE10 (tel. 081/853-3589; bus: 1, 177, 180, or 188). Named after the witch in Robert Burns's poem "Tam O'Shanter," it was the greatest of the breed of clipper ships that carried tea from China and wool from Australia in the most exciting ocean races ever sailed. The *Cutty Sark*'s record stood at a then-unsurpassed 363 miles in 24 hours. Launched in Scotland in 1869, the sleek black three-master represented the final fighting run of canvas against steam. Although the age of the clippers was brief, they did outpace the steamers as long as there was wind to fill their billowing mountain of sails.

On board the *Cutty Sark* you'll find a museum devoted to clipper lore, plus all the fittings that made it the fastest thing at sea. Admission is £3.25 ($4.90) for adults and £2.25 ($3.40) for children over 7. The vessel may be boarded Monday through Saturday from 10am to 6pm and Sunday (and Good Friday) from noon to 6pm. It closes at 5pm in winter.

Next to the clipper—and looking like a sardine beside a shark—lies the equally famous **Gipsy Moth IV,** King William Walk, Greenwich, SE10 (tel. 081/853-3589; bus: same as above). This, in case you don't remember, was the ridiculously tiny sailing craft in which Sir Francis Chichester circumnavigated the globe . . . solo! You can go on board and marvel at the minuteness of the vessel in which the gray-haired sea dog made his incredible 119-day journey. His chief worry—or so he claimed—was running out of ale before reaching land. The admission to go aboard is 60p (90¢) for adults and 40p (60¢) for children under 16. The *Gipsy Moth IV* keeps the same hours as the *Cutty Sark,* but it's closed November through March.

5. ORGANIZED TOURS

BY BUS

LONDON REGIONAL TRANSPORT SIGHTSEEING TOURS For the first-timer, the quickest and most economical way to bring the big city into focus is to take the almost 2½-hour circular tour of the West End and the City of London on the guided **Original London Transport Sightseeing Tour,** which passes virtually all the major places of interest in central London. Operated by London Coaches, part of the city's official bus company, the journeys leave at frequent intervals daily from Victoria, Piccadilly Circus, Marble Arch, and Baker Street. Tickets cost £9 ($13.50) for adults and £5 ($7.50) for children, and they're available from the conductor. Tickets can also be purchased from London Transport's Travel Information Centres, where you can get a discount of £1 ($1.50) off each. Locations of the Travel Information Centres are listed under "Getting Around" in Chapter 3.

London Transport also offers a 3-hour guided **Royal Westminster Tour,** passing Westminster Abbey, the Houses of Parliament, the Horse Guards, a view of the Changing of the Guard at Buckingham Palace, Trafalgar Square, and Piccadilly Circus. Tickets for this tour cost £12.50 ($18.80) for adults and £11.50 ($17.30) for children under 14.

Another excellent choice would be London Transport's 3-hour **City Tour,** which includes guided trips to the Tower of London and St. Paul's Cathedral. The cost of this tour is £16.50 ($24.80) for adults and £15.50 ($23.30) for children under 14. The City Tour leaves at noon on Monday through Saturday.

The last two tours are also combined to form the **London Day Tour,** which costs £27 ($40.50) for adults and £25 ($37.50) for children under 14, including lunch.

A **London Plus Tour** lets you get off and on as you like, at more than 30 different places around central London. London Plus is operated with traditional "old-fashioned" Routemaster double-deck buses (open top in summer). Buses run every ¼ hour in summer and every ½ hour in winter, daily from about 10am to 5pm—exact times vary from point to point, depending on traffic. Tickets cost £12 ($18) for adults and £6 ($9) for children.

The West End and City tours begin at London Transport's Coach Station, 195 Victoria St., SW1, which lies adjacent to Victoria Railway Station. To reserve seats or for information, phone 071/828-

6449 or go to one of the London Transport Travel Information Centres.

HARRODS SIGHTSEEING BUS A double-decker air-conditioned coach in the discreet green-and-gold livery of **Harrods** (tel. 071/581-3603; tube: Knightsbridge) takes sightseeing tours around London's attractions. The first departure from door eight of Harrods, on Brompton Road, is at 10:30am and there are also tours at 1:30 and 4pm. Tea, coffee, and orange juice are served on board. The tour costs £15 ($22.50) for adults and £7 ($10.50) for children under 12. All-day excursion tours to Bath, Windsor, Stratford-upon-Avon, and the outlying areas of London, are available. You can purchase tickets at Harrods, Sightseeing Department, lower ground floor.

The London canals were once major highways. Since the Festival of Britain in 1951, some of the traditional painted canal boats have been resurrected for Venetian-style trips through these waterways. One of them is *Jason,* which takes you on a 90-minute trip from Blomfield Road in Little Venice through the long Maida Hill tunnel under Edgware Road; through Regent's Park, passing the Mosque, the London Zoo, and Lord Snowdon's Aviary; past the Pirate's Castle to Camden Lock; and finally back to Little Venice.

The season begins on Good Friday and lasts through October. During April, May, and September, the boat runs at 10:30am and 12:30 and 2:30pm. In June, July, and August, there is an additional trip during the afternoon, but always telephone first; in October, the boat runs at 12:30 and 2:30pm only.

At the moorings is a canalside café where lunches and teas are freshly made to order and can be served on the boat or in the courtyard (booking essential for the boat). The round-trip fare is £4.75 ($7.10) for adults and £3.50 ($5.30) for children. To inquire about bookings, contact **Jason's Trip,** opp. 60, Blomfield Road, Little Venice, W9 (tel. 071/286-3428; tube: Paddington Station).

Also offered are one-way trips to Camden Lock with its craft shops and flea market. Every Tuesday, a romantic evening cruise is organized with traditional fish and chips, soft music, and a full bar, costing £13.50 ($20.30) per person, excluding the bar.

ON FOOT

ORGANIZED LONDON WALKS John Wittich, of **J. W. Promotions,** 66 St. Michael's St., W2 (tel. 071/262-9572), started walking tours of London in 1960. A Freeman of the City of London and a member of two of the ancient guilds of London, he is the author of several books on London walks. There is no better way to search out the unusual, the beautiful, and the historic than to take a walking tour. The company concentrates on personal tours for families and groups who have booked in advance. John Wittich conducts all tours. The cost for a 1½-hour walk is £15 ($22.50) minimum for one or two adults.

The **Original London Walks,** 87 Messina Ave., NW6 (tel. 071/624-3978 or 071/794-1764), is London's oldest—and premier—walking tour. Its guides include author Donald Rumbelow, leading authority on Jack the Ripper, the foremost authority on Regent's Canal, the author of a classic guidebook (*London Walks*), and a London Historical Society official, along with prominent actors. Some 50 walks a week are featured year round, ranging from

Ghost Walks to Bloomsbury, from Dickens to the footsteps of the Beatles, even Shakespeare to Soho. Walks cost £4 ($6) for adults and £3 ($4.50) for students and senior citizens; children go free. Call for more information.

6. SPORTS & RECREATION

SPORTS

London can be as exciting for sports enthusiasts as for theater fans.

Soccer (Association Football) is the national winter sport. The London teams that set British pulses racing—Arsenal, Chelsea, Tottenham Hotspurs—sound like so many brands of cheese spread to a Statesider. Various venues are announced in newspapers.

In summer, there is **cricket,** played at Lord's or Oval Cricket Ground, St. John's Wood Road, NW8 (tel. 071/289-1611; tube: Marylebone Station). During the international test matches between Britain and Australia, the West Indies, or India (equivalent in importance to the World Series), the country goes into a collective trance, with everyone glued to the nearest radio or TV describing the event.

At the **All England Lawn Tennis & Croquet Club,** Church Road (without number), Wimbledon, SW19 (tel. 081/946-2244; tube: Southfields, then a special bus), you can see some of the world's greatest tennis players in action. The famous annual championships span roughly the last week in June to the first in July, with matches lasting from about 2pm till dark. (The gates open at 11:30am.) Although the British founded the All England Lawn Tennis & Croquet Club back in 1877, they haven't produced a world champion in ages.

Within easy reach of central London, there are **horse-racing** tracks at **Kempton Park, Sandown Park,** and the most famous of them all, **Epsom,** where the Derby is the main feature of the meeting in early June. Racing takes place both midweek and on weekends, but not continuously. Sometimes during the summer, there are evening race meetings, so you should telephone **United Racecourses Ltd.,** Epsom, Surrey (tel. 0372/464348), for information on the next meeting at Epsom, Sandown Park, or Kempton Park. You can drive yourself or, if you want to travel by rail, phone 071/928-5100 in London for details of train services.

Finally, we come to a spectacle for which it is difficult to find a comprehensive tag—the **Royal Tournament,** which some viewers describe as a series of indoor parades paying homage to the traditions and majesty of the British armed forces. Performed every year in late July, usually for a 2½-week run, it's a long-running spectacle that has been viewed enthusiastically by thousands. The show includes massed bands presenting stirring music, the Royal Navy field-gun competition, the Royal Air Force with their dogs, the Royal Marines in action, the King's Troop Royal Horse Artillery, the Household Cavalry, and a series of visiting military-style exhibitions from throughout the British Commonwealth.

There are two performances Tuesday through Saturday, at 2:30 and 7:30pm, at the Earl's Court Exhibition Centre, Warwick Road, SW5. There are no evening performances on Sunday and no matinees

SPORTS & RECREATION • 191

on Monday. Seats cost from £9 to £23 ($13.50 to $34.50), with discounts of around 40% for children 5 to 14 and senior citizens over 65. For tickets and other information, write to the **Royal Tournament Exhibition Centre,** Warwick Road (without number), London SW5 9TA (tel. 071/373-8141; tube: Earl's Court Station). For any other information, contact the **Royal Tournament Horse Guards,** Whitehall (without number), London SW1 2AX (tel. 071/930-4288; tube: Westminster).

RECREATION

SWIMMING The **Brittania Leisure Centre,** 40 Hyde Rd., N1 (tel. 071/729-4485; tube: Old Street), is a sports-and-recreation center operated and paid for by one of the eastern boroughs of London. It contains a swimming pool with a wave machine, fountains, badminton and squash courts, and soccer and volleyball fields. Admission costs 55p (80¢) for adults and 25p (40¢) for children; the complex is open Monday through Friday from 9am to 8:15pm and Saturday and Sunday from 9am to 5:45pm.

HEALTH AND FITNESS CENTER The **Jubilee Hall Sports Centre,** 30 The Piazza, Covent Garden, WC2 (tel. 071/836-4835; tube: Covent Garden), is the result of a radical 1980s makeover of a Victorian-era fish-and-flower market into a modern gym. Today, it's one of the best and most centrally located sports centers in London, with the capital's largest weight room and an avid corps of body-building regulars. It also offers badminton, basketball, aerobics, gymnastics, martial arts, self-defense training (for women), and tennis. It's maintained by the City of Westminster and is open Monday through Friday from 7am to 10pm and Saturday and Sunday from 8am to 5pm. The cost of admission is £5 ($7.50) for use of the weight room and £4 ($6) for participation in an aerobics class.

CHAPTER 7

STROLLING AROUND LONDON

The best way to discover London is on foot, but unless you are in London for several weeks, it is virtually impossible to visit all of the major attractions. Most people are lucky to see merely the highlights. Your busy itinerary may not allow you to take all of the strolls in this chapter, but try to fit in as many as possible.

The last walking tour, the British Museum, is not, of course, a tour of a district of London, but after going through its monumental block, you'll feel as if you have been on one of the major strolls of your life.

For additional information on many sights mentioned in the Walking Tours, see Chapter 6.

WALKING TOUR 1 —
WESTMINSTER/WHITEHALL

Start: Entrance of the Tate Gallery. *Tube:* Pimlico.
Finish: National Portrait Gallery, Trafalgar Square. *Tube:* Charing Cross or Leicester Sq.
Time: About 3 hours, excluding interior visits.
Best Times: Monday through Thursday, when Parliament is in session.
Worst Times: Evenings and Sunday, when the district becomes almost deserted except for fast-moving traffic.

This tour will take you on a route parallel to the River Thames, past some of London's most visible symbols of both its democracy and its monarchs. Begin your tour in front of the grand Palladian entrance to one of the finest art museums in the world, the:

1. **Tate Gallery.** Built in 1897 and donated to London by the scion of a sugar manufacturer, it is jammed with the works of virtually every great painter in British history. Return to enjoy the collection at your leisure, but for the moment, turn north along the west bank of the Thames (the embankment here is known as Millbank), beside the river that made British history, with the Houses of Parliament looming skyward ahead of you. At the first left turn after the first bridge, you'll see Lambeth Bridge; turn inland onto Dean Stanley Street and after one block you will arrive at:

2. **Smith Square,** whose centerpiece is St. John's Church. Designed with a highly personalized kind of neoclassicism by

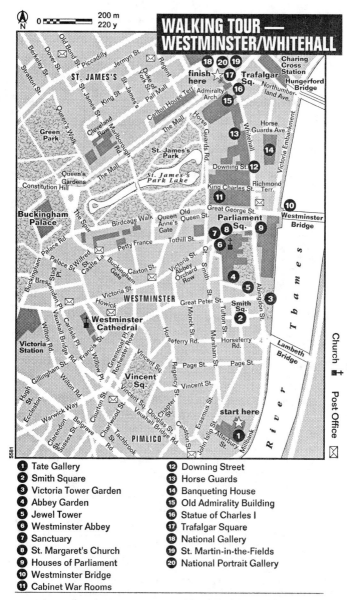

WALKING TOUR — WESTMINSTER/WHITEHALL

1 Tate Gallery
2 Smith Square
3 Victoria Tower Garden
4 Abbey Garden
5 Jewel Tower
6 Westminster Abbey
7 Sanctuary
8 St. Margaret's Church
9 Houses of Parliament
10 Westminster Bridge
11 Cabinet War Rooms

12 Downing Street
13 Horse Guards
14 Banqueting House
15 Old Admiralty Building
16 Statue of Charles I
17 Trafalgar Square
18 National Gallery
19 St. Martin-in-the-Fields
20 National Portrait Gallery

Thomas Archer in 1728, it was heavily damaged by bombs in 1941. Rebuilt (but not reconstructed), it now serves as a concert venue for some of the world's greatest musicians.

Retrace your steps back to the Thames, turn left (northward) toward the Neo-Gothic Houses of Parliament, and enter the verdant triangular-shaped park, Victoria Tower Garden, at its southern entrance. A tranquil oasis rich with sculpture, the:

3. Victoria Tower Garden contains a 1915 replica of Auguste Rodin's 1895 masterpiece, *The Burghers of Calais,* and A. G.

Walker's monument to Emmeline Pankhurst, who was an early 20th-century leader of British woman suffragists frequently imprisoned for her actions and beliefs. Near the northern perimeter of the garden, detour inland by turning left on Great College Street for about a block, noticing on your right the:

4. Abbey Garden. Continuously cultivated over the past 900 years and associated with nearby Westminster Abbey, it is the oldest garden in England, rich with lavender and ecclesiastical ruins. Even if the gate is locked, parts of this charming historic oddity are visible from the street outside.

Retrace your steps along Great College Street to Millbank (which on some maps at this point might be referred to as Abingdon Street), turn left (north), and remain on the side of Millbank opposite from the Houses of Parliament. The tower on your left, completed in 1366 by Edward III for the storage of treasure is the:

5. Jewel Tower. This is all that remains of the domestic portions of the once-mighty Palace of Westminster. It contains a small museum detailing the construction of the Houses of Parliament. Exiting from the Jewel Tower, continue north along Millbank (or Abingdon Street) for two blocks, passing on your left the semicircular apse of the rear side of one of Britain's most densely packed artistic and cultural highlights:

6. Westminster Abbey. The spiritual heart of London, completed in 1245 and steeped in enough tradition, sorrow, majesty, and blood to merit an entire volume of its own, this is one of the most majestic and most visited sights in Europe. Turn left, skirting the building's northern flank, and enter through its western facade.

After your visit, leave the Abbey through the Cloisters, emerging into Dean's Yard, site of Westminster School. Look for an arch straight ahead and on the right. It leads back to the west door of the Abbey and to the:

7. Sanctuary, which consists of two streets, called Broad Sanctuary and Little Sanctuary. In medieval days, the Sanctuary was actually a jumbled mass of buildings and narrow winding lanes. Enclosed by the precinct wall of Westminster, this complex offered a haven for the downcast and the odd political refugee. In time, the Sanctuary was said to shelter a "mire of cutthroats, whores, pickpockets, and murderers." It became so disease-ridden and crime-oriented that James I shut it down. Although the slums here lasted for centuries, urban renewal has been successful in removing the final traces of this once-notorious area.

After a walk around, look to your right, just beyond the Abbey's north transept, to see the much-restored:

8. St. Margaret's Church. Built between 1504 and 1523, it contains the body of the colonizer of Virginia, Sir Walter Raleigh (who was beheaded just outside its front entrance). Both John Milton (1656) and Winston Churchill (1908) were married here. Considered the parish church for the British House of Commons, it contains a noteworthy collection of stained-glass windows.

When you exit from St. Margaret's, you'll see the Neo-Gothic bulk of the:

9. Houses of Parliament, which will almost overwhelm you. Built between 1840 and 1860 as the result of a competition won by architects Sir Charles Barry and Augustus Pugin (both of whom suffered several nervous breakdowns and eventual early deaths as a result of the overwork and stress its creation caused them), Parliament covers eight acres and has what might be the greatest volume of ornate stonework of any building in the world. Your tour of the interior (which you might want to reserve for another day) begins at the base of Big Ben (its clocktower and tallest feature), near the building's northwest corner. One of Parliament's best views can be enjoyed from a position on:

10. Westminster Bridge. Built in 1862 in then-popular cast iron and one of the most ornate bridges in London, it offers, from midway across its span, some of the best views of Parliament anywhere. To reach the bridge, turn right on Bridge Street from your position in front of the very visible Big Ben clocktower. Note at the western base of the bridge, aptly named Westminster Pier, the departure point for many boat trips down the Thames.

Retrace your footsteps along Bridge Street, passing Big Ben, and take the second right turn along the busy thoroughfare of Parliament Street. Take the first left along King Charles Street, where, on the left side, you'll reach the:

11. Cabinet War Rooms, at Clive Steps, King Charles Street. Set 17 feet underground to protect occupants from Nazi air raids, this unpretentious handful of rooms was the meeting place for Churchill's cabinet during World War II and the originating point of many of his most stirring speeches. Half a dozen of the rooms are open to visitors.

Retrace your steps back to Parliament Street, turning left (north). Within two blocks, turn left at:

12. Downing Street. Though security precautions against terrorist activities might prevent you from getting a close look, no. 10 along this street is the much-publicized official residence of the British prime minister; no. 11, the official residence of the chancellor of the exchequer; and no. 12, the office of the chief Government whip, the M.P. responsible for maintaining discipline and cooperation among party members in the House of Commons.

Continue north along Parliament Street, which near Downing Street changes its name to Whitehall. At this point, either side of the street will be lined with the administrative soul of Britain, buildings that influence politics around the world, and whose grandiose architecture is suitably majestic. One of the most noteworthy of these is the:

13. Horse Guards. Completed in 1760 and designed by William Kent, it is one of the most symmetrically imposing of the many buildings along Whitehall, and the location of a ceremony (held Mon–Sat at 11am, Sun at 10am) known as the Mounting of the Guard (which is the first step of an equestrian ceremony that continues, every day at 11:30am, with the Changing of the Guard in front of Buckingham Palace). Across the avenue rises the pure proportions of one of London's most superlative examples of Palladian architecture, the:

14. Banqueting House. Commissioned by James I and designed by Inigo Jones in the early 1600s, it's considered one of the most aesthetically perfect buildings in England. Its facade was the backdrop for what might have been the most disturbing and unsettling execution in British history, the beheading of Charles I by members of Parliament. Inside, there is a mural by Peter Paul Rubens.

Continuing north along Whitehall, after a block you'll come to a:

REFUELING STOP   The Clarence Pub, 53 Whitehall St., W1 (tel. 071/930-4808). One of the most famous pubs of London, beloved of Parliamentarians from throughout England, it was originally opened in the 18th century and has been delighting the taste buds of government administrators ever since. With gaslights, oaken ceiling beams, antique farm implements dangling from the ceiling, and battered wooden tables ringed with churchlike pews, it offers at least half a dozen choices of real ale, as well as pub grub.

After drinnks with members of Parliament, notice the building almost directly across Whitehall from the pub, the:

15. **Old Admiralty Building.** Spring Gardens. Designed in 1725 by Sir Thomas Ripley and strictly closed except for official business, it served for almost two centuries (until replaced by newer quarters between the wars) as the administrative headquarters of the British navy. Continue walking north until you see what might be the finest and most emotive equestrian statue in London, the:

16. **Statue of Charles I.** Isolated on an island in the middle of a sea of speeding traffic, it commemorates one of the most tragic kings of British history and the beginning of:

17. **Trafalgar Square.** Centered around a soaring monument to the hero of the Battle of Trafalgar, Lord Nelson, who defeated Napoleon's navy off the coast of Spain in 1805, it is the grandest plaza in London. Against the square's northern perimeter rises the grandly neoclassical build of the:

18. **National Gallery,** whose collection cannot possibly be cataloged here but which definitely merits a detailed tour of its own. The church that flanks the eastern edge of Trafalgar Square is one of London's most famous:

19. **St. Martin-in-the-Fields.** Designed in the style of Sir Christopher Wren in 1726 by James Gibbs, it has a Corinthian portico and a steeple whose form has inspired the architects of many American churches. It was the christening place of Charles II and the burial place of his infamous but fun-loving mistress, Nell Gwynne. It sponsors a noted orchestra.

Finally, for an overview of the faces that altered the course of Britain and the world, walk to the right (eastern) side of the previously mentioned National Gallery, where the greatest repository of portraits in Europe awaits your inspection at the:

20. **National Portrait Gallery,** 2 St. Martin's Place. They're all here—kings, cardinals, mistresses, playwrights, poets, coquettes, dilettantes, and other names rich in historical connotations. Their assemblage into one gallery means that the subject of each painting is celebrated rather than the individual artists.

WALKING TOUR 2 —— THE CITY

Start: The southern terminus of London Bridge. *Tube:* London Bridge or Monument.
Finish: St. Paul's Cathedral. *Tube:* St. Paul's.
Time: About 3 hours, excluding interior visits.
Best Times: Weekday mornings, when the financial district is functioning but churches are not crowded.
Worst Times: Weekends when the district is almost deserted, unless you prefer the lack of traffic.

Encompassing only a small patch of urban real estate, the area known as the City offers the densest concentration of historic and cultural monuments within Britain. The City is proud of its role as one of the financial capitals of the world. Our tour begins on the southern edge of the Thames, directly to the west of one of the world's most famous bridges. Facing the Thames rises the bulk of:

1. **Southwark Cathedral.** When it was built in the 1200s, it was an outpost of the faraway diocese of Winchester. Deconsecrated after Henry VIII's Reformation, it later housed bakeries and pig pens. Much of what you'll see is a result of a sorely needed 19th-century rebuilding, but a view of its Gothic interior, with its multiple commemorative plaques, gives an idea of the religious power of London's medieval church. After your visit, walk across the famous:

2. **London Bridge.** Originally designed by Henry de Colechurch under the patronage of Henry II in 1176 but replaced several times since, it's probably the most famous bridge in the world. Until as late as 1729, it was the only bridge across the Thames. During the Middle Ages, it was lined with shops, and houses crowded its edges. It served for centuries as the showplace for the severed heads—preserved in tar—of enemies of the British monarchs. (The most famous of these included the head of Sir Thomas More, the highly vocal lord chancellor.) The bridge built from 1825 to 1831 was moved to the United States. The current bridge was built from 1967 to 1973. From Southwark Cathedral, cross the bridge. At its northern end, notice the first street that descends to the right (east), Monument Street. Detour down it a short distance to read the commemorative plaques attached to the:

3. **Monument.** Commemorating the Great Fire of 1666, this soaring Doric column is appropriately capped with a carved version of a flaming urn. The disaster it memorializes erupted from a bakery in nearby Pudding Lane, raged for four days and nights, and destroyed 80% of the City. A cramped and foreboding set of stairs spiral up to the top's view over the cityscape, so heavily influenced after the fire by architect Sir Christopher Wren.

    Retrace your steps toward London Bridge, but before you actually step onto it, detour to the left (south, toward the river) at Monument Street's first intersection, Fish Hill Street. Set near the edge of the water, within its shadow of the bridge, is one of Wren's many churches:

4. **St. Magnus the Martyr.** Completed in 1685 (with a tower

added in 1705), it has a particularly magnificent interior, which at one time was devoted to the neighborhood's many fishmongers. After your visit, continue walking east along Lower Thames Street. At the corner of Idol Lane (the fifth narrow street on your left), turn left to see the bombed-out remains of another of Sir Christopher Wren's churches:

5. St. Dunstan-in-the-East. Its unexpectedly verdant garden, the only part of the complex that regenerated itself after the Nazi blitz of World War II, offers a comforting oasis amid a sea of traffic and masonry. After your visit, continue walking northward. Where Idol Lane dead-ends at Great Tower Street, look straight ahead to the spire of another of Wren's churches, this one in substantially better shape, the church of:

6. St. Margaret Pattens. Built between 1684 and 1689, it has much of its original 17th-century paneling and interior fittings, plus a narrow, slender spire that inspired, in one way or another, the form of many later churches. After your visit, walk to the west side of the church and take Rood Lane north one block to Fenchurch. Go left (west) for two blocks, then right on Gracechurch Street, noting your presence within the dusky and narrow streets of Europe's largest financial capital. Within a very short walk, on your right, you'll reach the Victorian arcades of one of the neighborhood's most densely packed shopping centers:

7. Leadenhall. Designed in 1881 by Horace Jones, it contains the accoutrements you'd need for either a picnic or a full gourmet dinner. Browse at will, but once you've finished, return to Gracechurch Street, walk north about a block, then go right (east) on Leadenhall Street. Take the second right (south) turn on Lime Street, where you can admire the soaring and iconoclastically modern:

8. Lloyd's of London Building. Designed by Richard Rogers in 1986, this is the most recent home of an organization founded in the 1680s as a marine-insurance market. This is the most famous insurer in the world, with a hypermodern headquarters built atop the heart of the ancient Roman community (Londinium) whose builders launched London's destiny over 2,000 years ago. In the early 1990s Lloyd's survival was threatened by immense underwriting losses. (Within a few blocks of your position are the London Metal Exchange, the London Futures and Options Exchange, and many financial institutions whose clout is felt around the world.

Emerge from Lime Street back onto Leadenhall, where you turn left, then take the first right on Bishopsgate, then the second right turn into an alleyway known as Great St. Helen's. Near its end, you'll find the largest surviving medieval church in London:

9. St. Helen Bishopsgate. Built in the 1400s, it was dedicated to St. Helen, the legendary British mother of the Roman emperor Constantine. It was fashionable during the Elizabethan and Jacobean periods, and its interior monuments, memorials, and grave markers are especially interesting. Exit back onto Bishopsgate, turning right (north). Two blocks later, turn left onto Wormwood Street. Turn at the first left (Old Broad Street). Towering above you—the most visible building on its street—rises the modern bulk of the tallest building in Britain and the second-tallest building in Europe, the:

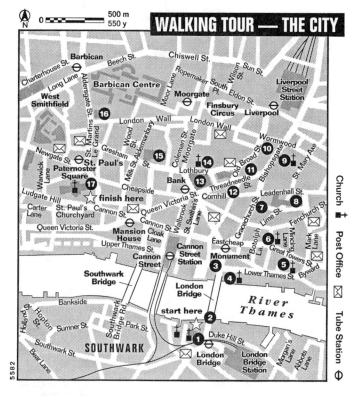

0 |———| 500 m
 |———| 550 y

N

Barbican

Chiswell St.

Charterhouse St.

Beech St.

Sun St.

Long Lane

Ropemaker

South

Wilson St.

Eldon St.

Liverpool Street Station

Barbican Centre

Moor Lane

Moorgate

West Smithfield

Aldersgate St.

London Wall

Finsbury Circus

Liverpool

Walking Tour Area

LONDON

Church ■ ✝

Post Office ⊠

Tube Station ⊖

① Southwark Cathedral
② London Bridge
③ Monument
④ St. Magnus the Martyr

⑤ St. Dunstan-in-the-East
⑥ St. Margaret Pattens
⑦ Leadenhall
⑧ Lloyd's of London Building
⑨ St. Helen Bishopsgate
⑩ NatWest Tower
⑪ London Stock Exchange
⑫ Royal Exchange
⑬ Bank of England
⑭ St. Margaret, Lothbury
⑮ Guildhall
⑯ Museum of London
⑰ St. Paul's Cathedral

---

10. NatWest Tower. Housing the headquarters of National Westminster Bank, it was designed in 1981 by Richard Seifert. Built upon massive concrete foundations above a terrain composed mostly of impervious clay, it was designed to sway gently in the wind. Unfortunately, there is no publicly accessible observation tower in the building, so most visitors admire it from afar.

Continue south along Old Broad Street, noticing on your right the bulky headquarters of the:

11. London Stock Exchange. The center was built in the early

1960s to replace its outmoded original quarters. Its role has become much quieter since 1986, when the nature of most of the City's financial operations changed from a face-to-face agreement between brokers to a computerized clearinghouse conducted electronically.

Continue southwest along Old Broad Street until it merges with Threadneedle Street. Cross over Threadneedle Street, walk a few paces to your left, and head south along the narrow confines of Finch Lane. Cross the busy traffic of Cornhill to the south side of the street. Follow it east to St. Michael's Alley for a:

REFUELING STOP   Jamaica Wine House, St. Michael's Alley, EC3 (tel. 071/626-9496) claims to be one of the first coffeehouses in the Western world. It has been favored by London merchants and the sea captains who imported their goods. From its historic precincts, it today dispenses beer, ale, lager, wine, and other refreshments, including bar snacks and soft drinks.

After you tipple, explore the labyrinth of narrow alleyways that shelter you within an almost medieval maze from the district's roaring weekday traffic. Eventually, however, head for the major boulevard (Cornhill), which lies a few steps north of the site of your earlier refueling stop. There, near the junction of five major streets, rises the:

12. Royal Exchange. Designed by William Tite in the early 1840s, its imposing neoclassical pediment is inset with Richard Westmacott's sculpture of *Commerce*. Launched by a partnership of merchants and financiers during the Elizabethan Age, the Royal Exchange's establishment was a direct attempt to lure European banking and trading functions from Antwerp (then the financial capital of northern Europe) to London. Separate markets and auction facilities for raw materials were conducted in frenzied trading here until 1982, when the building became the headquarters of the London International Financial Futures Exchange (LIFFE).

On the opposite side of Threadneedle Street rises the massive bulk of the:

13. Bank of England. Originally established "for the Publick Good and Benefit of Our People" in a charter granted in 1694 by William and Mary, it is a treasure trove both of gold bullion, British banknotes, and historical archives. The only part of this massive building open to the public is the Bank of England Museum, whose entrance is on a narrow side street, Bartholomew Lane (tel. 071/601-4878; open Mon–Fri 10am–5pm; admission free).

From the Bank of England, walk northwest along Prince's Street to the intersection of Lothbury. From the northeast corner of the intersection rises another church designed and built by Sir Christopher Wren between 1686 and 1690:

14. St. Margaret, Lothbury. Filled with statues of frolicking cupids, elaborately carved screens, and a soaring eagle near the altar, it's worth a visit inside. After you exit, cross Prince's Street and head west on Gresham Street. After traversing a handful of alleyways, you'll see on your right the gardens and the grandly historical facade of the:

15. Guildhall. The power base for the lord mayor of London since the 12th century (and rebuilt, adapted, and enlarged many times since), it was the site of endless power negotiations throughout the Middle Ages between the English kings (headquartered outside the City at Westminster) and the guilds, associations, and brotherhoods of the City's merchants and financiers. Today, the rituals associated with the lord mayor are almost as elaborate as those of the monarchy itself. The medieval crypt of the Guildhall is the largest in London, and its east facade was rebuilt by Sir Christopher Wren after the Great Fire of 1666.

After your visit to the Guildhall, continue walking westward on Gresham and take the second right turn onto Wood Street. Walk two blocks north to London Wall, go left for about a block, where you'll see the modern facade of the:

16. Museum of London. Located in new quarters built in 1975, it contains an assemblage of London memorabilia gathered from several earlier museums, as well as one of the best collections of period costumes in the world. Built on top of the western gate of the ancient Roman colony of Londinium, it is especially strong on archeological remnants unearthed during centuries of London building. There are also tableaux portraying the Great Fire and Victorian prison cells.

After your visit to the museum, head south on Aldersgate, whose name is soon changed to St. Martins-le-Grand. After you cross Newgate Street, the enormous and dignified dome of one of Europe's most famous and symbolic churches will slowly loom in front of you:

17. St. Paul's Cathedral. Considered the masterpiece of Sir Christopher Wren and the inspiration for the generation of Londoners who survived the bombings of World War II, it was the scene of the state funerals of Nelson, Wellington, and Churchill as well as the wedding celebration of Prince Charles and Princess Diana. It is the only church in England built with a dome, the country's only church in the English baroque style, and the first English cathedral to be designed and built by a single architect.

WALKING TOUR 3 — ST. JAMES'S

Start: Admiralty Arch. *Tube:* Charing Cross.
Finish: Buckingham Palace. *Tube:* St. James's Park or Green Park.
Time: About 2 hours, not including stops.
Best Time: Before 3pm.
Worst Time: After dark.

Incorporating neighborhoods reserved almost since their original development for the British aristocracy, this walking tour includes many of the grandest sights of imperial England of the 18th and 19th centuries. Begin your tour near the southwest corner of Trafalgar Square, at the monumental eastern entrance of the:

1. Admiralty Arch. Commissioned by Queen Victoria's son, King Edward VII (who died before it was completed), it was designed in 1911 by Sir Aston Webb. Piercing its center are a quintet of arches faced with Portland stone whose assemblage marks the first (and widest) stage of a majestic processional route leading from Buckingham Palace eastward to St. Paul's Cathedral. The centermost of the five arches is opened only for ceremonial occasions, the two side arches are for vehicular traffic, and the two smallest arches are for pedestrians.

Pass beneath the arch and enter the wide panoramic thoroughfare, which will eventually lead to Buckingham Palace. With your back to the Admiralty Arch, the wide and verdant expanse of:

2. The Mall will stretch out ahead of you. The only deliberately planned avenue in London, it was designed in 1910 as a memorial to the recently departed Queen Victoria by Sir Aston Webb. Lined with even rows of plane trees, it was originally the garden of the nearby St. James's Palace and used for the aristocratic game of *paille maille* (a precursor of croquet) by the courtiers of Charles II. On Sunday, The Mall is often closed to traffic and becomes a pedestrian extension of the adjacent expanse of St. James's Park. The Mall's wide boundaries are a favorite exercise area for London's equestrians and their mounts. Immediately to your left (keeping your back to the Admiralty Arch) are the interconnected buildings of the:

3. New and **Old Admiralties.** Considered very important nerve centers of the British military, they have seen their share of drama since the early 18th century.

As you stroll southwest down The Mall, on your right will be one of the most regal ensembles of town houses in London:

4. Carlton House Terrace. These buildings replaced the once-palatial home of the 18th-century Prince Regent, a man who later became George III. He built (and subsequently demolished) at staggering expense what was considered the most beautiful private home in Britain. Only the columns were saved and later recycled into the portico of Trafalgar Square's National Gallery. The subsequent row of ivory-colored neoclassical town houses was designed as one of architect John Nash's last works before he died, much maligned, at the center of a financial scandal in 1835. Today, in addition to art galleries and cultural institutions, Carlton House Terrace houses the headquarters of one of the most highly reputed scientific bodies in the world, the Royal Society.

Midway along the length of Carlton House Terrace, its evenly symmetrical neoclassical expanse is pierced with:

5. The Duke of York Steps and **the Duke of York Monument.** Built in honor of the second son of George III, the massive sculpture was funded by withholding one day's pay from every soldier within the British Empire. The resulting column was chiseled from pink granite, and the statue was created by Sir Richard Westmacott in 1834. Contemporary wits, knowing that the duke died owing massive debts to his angry creditors, joked that placing his effigy on a column was the only way to keep him away from their grasp. This soaring column and monument (the statue weighs seven tons) dominates the square it prefaces:

6. Waterloo Place. Considered one of the most prestigious

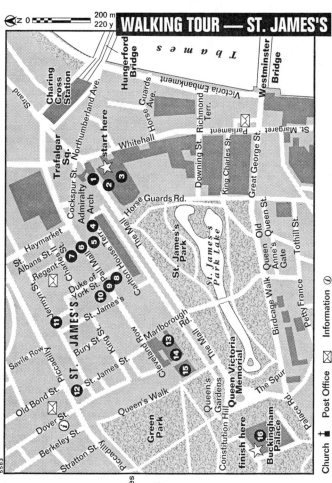

WALKING TOUR — ST. JAMES'S

start here ☆

finish here ☆

Church ✝ Post Office ■ Information ⓘ

LONDON

St. James's Area

1. Admiralty Arch
2. The Mall
3. New and Old Admiralties
4. Carlton House Terrace
5. Duke of York Steps and Monument
6. Waterloo Place
7. Statue of Edward VII
8. No. 4 Carlton House Gardens
9. Pall Mall
10. St. James's Square
11. Jermyn Street
12. St. James's Street
13. St. James's Palace
14. Clarence House
15. Lancaster House
16. Buckingham Palace

pieces of urban planning in London, it contains both aristocratic elegance and nostalgia for England's grand military victories over Napoleon. No. 107 (designed in 1830 and considered one of the finest examples of early-19th-century neoclassical architecture in London) is the headquarters for one of the most distinguished gentlemen's clubs in Britain, the Athenaeum Club.

Notice, within Waterloo Place, the:

7. Statue of Edward VII. It was crafted in 1921 by Sir Bertram Mackennal in honor of the man who gave the world the

Edwardian Age and much of the grand neighborhood to the northeast of Buckingham Palace. The son of the long-lived Victoria, he ascended the throne at the age of 60, only 9 years before his death. As if to balance the position of his statue, a statue dedicated to the victims of the Crimean War, part of which honors Florence Nightingale, stands at the opposite end of Waterloo Place.

History buffs will appreciate Carlton House Gardens, which runs into Carlton House Terrace's western end. Lovers of France and French history especially appreciate the plaques that identify the facade of:

8. No. 4 Carlton House Gardens. This was the London headquarters during World War II of Charles de Gaulle's French government-in-exile and site of many of his French-language radio broadcasts to the French underground. (Another facade of this same building faces The Mall, on the opposite side of the block.)

One of the streets intersecting Waterloo Place is an avenue rich in the headquarters of many exclusive private clubs. Not to be confused with the longer and broader expanse of The Mall, this is:

9. Pall Mall. Despite its variant pronunciation in different parts of the Empire, Londoners usually pronounce it "pell mell" (not "paul mawl"). Membership in many of these clubs is both prestigious and desirable, with waiting lists of up to a decade for the best of them.

Walk west for a block along Pall Mall (beware of the speeding one-way traffic, which can be deadly) and take the first right (north) turn into the elegant 18th-century precincts of:

10. St. James's Square. Laid out in the 1660s, it was built on land donated by the first Earl of St. Albans, Henry Jermyn, a friend of the widow of Charles I and a friend of the future king Charles II. It was originally designed with very large private houses on all sides, probably with artistic input by Sir Christopher Wren, for noble families who wanted to live near the seat of royal power at nearby St. James's Palace. Buildings upon the square that are of special interest include no. 10 (Chatham House), private residence of three British prime ministers, the last of whom was Queen Victoria's nemesis, William Gladstone. At no. 32, General Eisenhower and his subordinates planned the 1942 invasion of North Africa and the 1944 Allied invasion of Normandy. At no. 16, the announcement of the climactic defeat by Wellington of Napoleon's forces at Waterloo was delivered (along with the captured eagle-shaped symbols of Napoleon's army) by a blood-stained officer, Major Percy, to the Prince Regent.

Circumnavigate the square, eventually exiting at its northern edge via Duke of York Street. One block later, turn left onto what might be the most prestigious shopping street in London:

11. Jermyn Street. Expensive, upscale, with shop attendants who are usually very polite, the street offers shops whose windows and displays show a mixture of what is considered inviolable British tradition mingled with the perceived necessities of "the good life."

REFUELING STOP **Green's Champagne and Oyster Bar,** 36 Duke St., SW1 (tel. 071/930-4566). Much about its facade and paneled decor might remind you of the many gentlemen's clubs you've already passed within the surrounding neighborhood. This one, however, welcomes nonmembers, and a healthy dose of the clientele is female. There's a battered bar for the consumption of "spirits" and glasses of wine. Also offered are platters of oysters, dollops of caviar, shrimp, and crabmeat (which you can consume either standing at the bar or sitting at a table), plus a wide variety of English-inspired appetizers and main courses. The place is especially popular at lunchtime.

Exit from Duke Street onto Jermyn Street, turn right (west) and continue to enjoy the shops. Two blocks later, turn left onto:

12. St. James's Street. As you have by now grown to expect, it contains its share of private clubs, the most fashionable of which is, arguably, White's, at no. 37. (Its premises were designed in 1788 by James Wyatt.) Prince Charles celebrated his stag party here with friends the night before his marriage to Lady (later, Princess) Diana. Past members included Evelyn Waugh (who received refuge here from his literary "hounds of modernity"). Even if you're recommended for membership (which is unlikely), the waiting list is 8 years.

At the bottom (southern end) of St. James's Street is one of the most historic buildings of London:

13. St. James's Palace. Birthplace of many British monarchs, it served as the principal royal residence from 1698 (when White-hall Palace burned down) until the ascent of Victoria (who moved into Buckingham Palace) in 1837. Originally enlarged from a Tudor core built by Henry VIII for one of his ill-fated queens, it was altered by Sir Christopher Wren in 1703. The palace, rich in history, gave its name to the entire neighborhood. After your visit, walk southwest along Cleveland Row, then turn left (southeast) onto Stable Yard Row. On your left rises the side of:

14. Clarence House. Designed in 1829 by John Nash, it is the official London home of the Queen Mother. On the opposite side of Stable Yard Row rises the side of the very formal:

15. Lancaster House. Designed in 1827 by Benjamin Wyatt, it has, during its lifetime, been known variously as York House and Stafford House. Chopin performed his ballads and noc-turnes for Victoria here. During the upsetting renunciation of his throne as a precondition for his marriage to Wallis Warfield Simpson, Edward VIII lived here during his tenure as Prince of Wales. Heavily damaged by World War II bombings, it has been gracefully restored, furnished in the French Louis XV style, and now serves as a setting for state receptions and dinners.

Within a few steps, when you arrive at the multiple plane trees of The Mall, turn right for a vista of the front of:

16. Buckingham Palace. The official London residence of every British monarch since Victoria, it exerts a pull and an allure that are at once mystical, magical, carefully cultivated, and vital. Its present occupant is Elizabeth II.

WALKING TOUR 4 —— CHELSEA

Start: Chelsea Embankment at Battersea Bridge. *Tube:* Sloane Sq.
Finish: Chelsea's Old Town Hall, or any of the nearby pubs. *Tube:* Sloane Sq.
Time: About 2 hours, not counting stops.
Best Time: Almost anytime.
Worst Time: A rainy day.

Historically, Chelsea has been one of the most artistically creative districts of London. Today, it's home to some of the most prosperous residents of the capital and is considered one of the most complete, perfect, and attractively scaled "villages within the city." Its residents have included Margaret Thatcher, Mick Jagger, Oscar Wilde, Thomas Carlyle, J. M. W. Turner, John Singer Sargent, Henry James, and Henry VIII. Begin your tour above the massive masonry buttresses known as the Chelsea Embankment, at the northern terminus of:

1. **Battersea Bridge.** Although not the most famous bridge in London, it will align and orient you to an understanding of Chelsea's vital link to the Thames. Here begins a beautiful walk eastward through a historic neighborhood marred only by the roar of the riverside traffic. Across the water rises the district of Battersea, a rapidly gentrifying neighborhood.

   The street that rambles beside the Thames eventually is identified as Cheyne Walk. Rich with Georgian and Victorian architecture (and containing some of the most expensive houses of a very expensive neighborhood), it is considered an architectural treasurehouse. Although the bulk of your exploration along this street will be eastward, for the moment detour from the base of Battersea Bridge westward to 119 Cheyne Walk, which is:

2. **Turner's House.** Its tall and narrow premises sheltered one of England's greatest painters, J. M. W. Turner (1775–1851), during the last years of his life. His canvases, although predating those of the French impressionists, are distinctly different and uniquely recognizable for the shimmering quality of their colors. When he died within one of the bedrooms of this house, his very appropriate final words were, "God is Light."

   Just to the east at nos. 96–100, is a building considered one of Chelsea's most beautiful, completed in the 1670s:

3. **Lindsey House.** Built by the Swiss-born physician to two British kings (James I and Charles II), it became the British headquarters of the Moravian Church around 1750. Later divided and sold as four separate residences, it housed the American-born painter James Whistler (at no. 96 between 1866 and 1879). The gardens of no. 99 and no. 100 were designed by Britain's most celebrated Edwardian architect, Sir Edwin Lutyens (1869–1944).

   At this point, retrace your steps eastward to Battersea Bridge and begin what will become a long eastwardly ramble along Cheyne Walk. Midway between the heavy traffic of Beaufort Street and the much quieter Danvers Street, you'll see:

4. **Crosby Hall.** Designated by no identifying street number, its original brick-and-stone construction (resembling a chapel) is prefaced with a modern wing of gray stone added in the 1950s. It

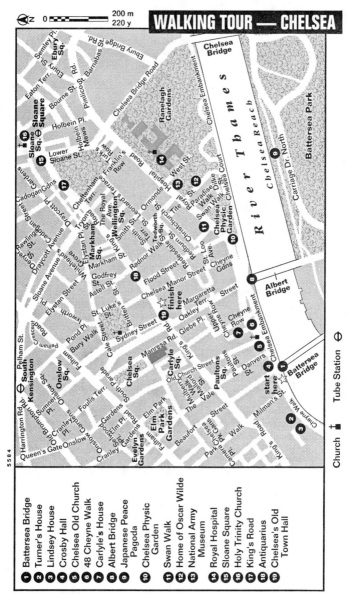

0 ━━━ 200 m
      220 y

Chelsea Bridge

Chelsea Embankment

Ranelagh Gardens

R i v e r   T h a m e s

Chelsea Reach

Battersea Park

Carriage Dr. North

Ebury Sq.

Semley Pl.

Ebury St.

Ebury Bridge Rd.

Eaton Terr.

Bourne St.

Barnabas St.

Pimlico Rd.

Chelsea Bridge Road

Sloane Square

Sloane St.

Holbein Pl.

Lower Sloane St.

Holbein Mews

Cadogan Gdns

Turks Row

Franklin's Row

Cheltenham Terr.

St. Leonard's Terr.

Ormonde Gate

West St.

Hospital Road

Royal Hospital Road

Tite St.

Dilke St.

Swan Walk

Chelsea Embankment

Albert Bridge

Chelsea Physic Garden

Rawlings Street

Cadogan Gardens

Draycott Pl.

Draycott Avenue

Whitehead's Grove

Tryon St.

The Ave.

Wellington Sq.

Markham Sq.

Smith St.

Smith Terr.

Redburn St.

Christchurch St.

Tedworth Sq.

Radnor Walk

Flood Street

Redesdale St.

St. Loo Ave.

Chelsea Manor Street

Cheyne Gdns

Margaretta Terr.

Oakley St.

Glebe Pl.

Cheyne Row

Upper Cheyne Row

Cheyne Walk

Danvers St.

Chelsea Embankment

Milman's St.

Beaufort St.

Paultons Sq.

Manresa Rd.

Old Church Street

Paultons St.

Margaretta Terr.

King's Road

Sloane Avenue

Elystan St.

Elystan Pl.

Markham St.

Godfrey St.

Astell St.

St. Luke's St.

Ixworth Pl.

Pond Pl.

Bury Walk

Sydney Street

Britten St.

Cale Street

South Parade

Chelsea Sq.

Carlyle Sq.

The Vale

Mallord St.

Mulberry Walk

Elm Park Gardens

Evelyn Gardens

Fulham Road

Foulis Terr.

Onslow Gardens

Cranley Gardens

Cranley Pl.

Onslow Sq.

Pelham St.

Sumner Pl.

Onslow Pl.

Bramerton St.

Cheyne Walk

Park Walk

Lamont Rd.

Limerston St.

Gunter Grove

Crescent

Pelham Crescent

Harrington Rd.

Queen's Gate

Onslow Cres.

Thurloe Pl.

South Kensington

Albert Bridge

Battersea Bridge

Chelsea Bridge

start here

finish here

Church ✝■

Tube Station ⊖

5584

① Battersea Bridge
② Turner's House
③ Lindsey House
④ Crosby Hall
⑤ Chelsea Old Church
⑥ 48 Cheyne Walk
⑦ Carlyle's House
⑧ Albert Bridge
⑨ Japanese Peace Pagoda
⑩ Chelsea Physic Garden
⑪ Swan Walk
⑫ Home of Oscar Wilde
⑬ National Army Museum
⑭ Royal Hospital
⑮ Sloane Square
⑯ Holy Trinity Church
⑰ King's Road
⑱ Antiquarius
⑲ Chelsea's Old Town Hall

was built in the early 1400s and owned successively by both Richard III and Sir Thomas More. It was transported in the early 1900s stone by stone from Bishopsgate, partly under the financial incentive of American-born Lady Nancy Astor. Today, it provides apartments and dining facilities for the British Federation of University Women. Parts of its interior (which contains paintings by Holbein, a gracefully trussed roof, and some Jacobean furniture) are open free to the public (Mon–Sat 10am–noon and 2:15–5pm).

After your visit, continue walking eastward on Cheyne Walk. After crossing both Danvers and Church Streets, if you detour a few buildings away from the river onto Old Church Street, you'll reach the parish church of the late Sir Thomas More:

5. Chelsea Old Church. Its beauty is diminished only by the masses of traffic outside and the fact that it and its neighborhood were heavily damaged by Nazi bombs during World War II. Gracefully repaired, it contains a chapel partly designed by Hans Holbein; an urn containing the earthly remains of a man who owned most of Chelsea during the 1700s, Sir Hans Sloane; and a plaque commemorating the life of American novelist Henry James, a longtime Chelsea resident who died nearby in 1916. The building's Lawrence Chapel is reputed to have been the scene of Henry VIII's secret marriage to Jane Seymour several days before their official marriage in 1536.

Continue walking eastward along Cheyne Walk. Within about a block, the pavement will branch to form a verdant swath of trees and lawn, behind which stand some of the most expensive and desirable town houses of Chelsea. Occupants of these elegantly proportioned buildings have included some very famous people, including Mick Jagger, who purchased:

6. No. 48 Cheyne Walk. Jagger lived here for a while, brushing elbows with neighbors like guitarist Keith Richards, publishing magnate Lord Weidenfeld, and the grandson of oil industry giant J. Paul Getty. Artistic denizens of an earlier age included George Eliot, who lived for part of her flamboyant life (and later died) at no. 41. The star of the Pre-Raphaelite movement, Dante Gabriel Rossetti, lived in what is considered the street's finest building, no. 16.

Branch inland from the Thames, heading north along Cheyne Row, where, within a short walk, at no. 5, stands:

7. Carlyle's House. Considered one of the most interesting houses in London, particularly to literary enthusiasts, it is one of the neighborhood's few houses open to the public. The former home of "the sage of Chelsea" and his wife, Jane, it offers a fascinating insight into the Victorian decor of its time. Notice the small gravestone in the garden marking the burial place of the author's favorite dog.

After your visit, retrace your steps to Cheyne Walk and continue east. The bridge that looms into view is:

8. Albert Bridge. Matched only by Tower Bridge and Westminster Bridge, this might be the most-photographed bridge in London. Created at the height of the Victorian fascination with cast iron, it was designed in 1873 by R. M. Ordish.

Continue walking eastward beneath the trees of Cheyne Walk, eventually branching inland, away from the river, along Royal Hospital Road. Before you leave the banks of the Thames, however, look on the opposite end of the Thames for the:

9. Japanese Peace Pagoda. Containing a massive statue of Buddha covered in gold leaf and unveiled in 1985, it was crafted by 50 Japanese nuns and monks. Set at the riverside edge of Battersea Park, according to plans by the Buddhist leader Nichidatsu Fugii, it was offered to Britain by the Japanese government.

Continue walking northeast along Royal Hospital Road. The turf on your right (its entrance is at 66 Royal Hospital

Rd.) belongs to the oldest surviving botanic garden in Britain, the:

10. **Chelsea Physic Garden** (also known as Chelsea Botanic Garden). Established in 1673 on four acres of riverfront land that belonged to Charles Cheyne, it was founded by the Worshipful Society of Apothecaries, and later (1722) funded permanently by Sir Hans Sloane, botanist and physician to George II. The germ of what later became international industries began in the earth of these gardens, greenhouses, and botanical laboratories.

Now, continue your walk northeast along Royal Hospital Road, but turn right at the first cross street onto:

11. **Swan Walk.** Known for its 18th-century row houses, it's a charming and obscure part of Chelsea. Walk down it, turning at the first left onto Dilke Street, and at its dead end, turn left onto Tite Street. (From here, your view of the Japanese Peace Pagoda on the opposite bank of the Thames might be even better than before.) At 34 Tite St., you'll see a plaque commemorating the:

12. **Home of Oscar Wilde.** Here, Wilde wrote many of his most charming plays, including *The Importance of Being Earnest* and *Lady Windermere's Fan.* After Wilde was arrested and imprisoned, following the most famous trial for homosexuality in British history, the house was sold to pay his debts. The plaque was presented in 1954, a century after Wilde's birthday. A few steps away on the same street are houses that once belonged to two of America's most famous expatriates. No. 31 was the home of John Singer Sargent (and the studio where he painted many of his most famous portraits), and no. 35 was the home of James McNeill Whistler.

At the end of Tite Street, turn right onto Royal Hospital Road. Within a block are the fortresslike premises of the:

13. **National Army Museum.** Its premises contain galleries devoted to weapons, uniforms, and art, with dioramas of famous battles and such memorabilia as the skeleton of Napoleon's favorite horse.

Next door to the museum, a short distance to the northeast, is the building that contains the world's most famous horticultural exhibition, the Chelsea Flower Show, which is held every year amid the vast premises of the:

14. **Royal Hospital.** Designed in 1682 in the aftermath of the Great Fire of London by Sir Christopher Wren (and considered, after St. Paul's Cathedral, his masterpiece) it might have been built to compete with Louis XIV's construction of Les Invalides in Paris. Both were designed as a home for wounded or aging soldiers, and both are grandiose.

Pass the Royal Hospital, eventually turning left (northeast) four blocks later at Chelsea Bridge Road. This street will change its name in about a block to Lower Sloane Street, which leads eventually to:

15. **Sloane Square.** Considered the northernmost gateway to Chelsea, it was laid out in 1780 on land belonging to Sir Hans Sloane. His collection of minerals, fossils, and plant specimens was the core of what eventually became the British Museum. Detour half a block north of Sloane Square (its entrance is on Sloane Street) to visit a church known as a triumph of the late 19th century's arts-and-crafts movement:

16. **Holy Trinity Church.** Completed in 1890, it contains windows by William Morris following designs by Sir Edward Burne-Jones and embellishments in the Pre-Raphaelite style.

Exit from Sloane Square's southwestern corner and stroll down one of the most variegated and interesting commercial streets in London:

17. **King's Road.** Laden with antiques stores, booksellers, sophisticated and punk clothiers, restaurants, coffeehouses, tearooms, and diehard adherents of the "Sloane Ranger" mystique, it is a delightful area in which to observe the human comedy. Dozens of possibilities for food, sustenance, and companionship exist.

REFUELING STOP **Henry J. Bean's (But His Friends All Call Him Hank) Bar & Grill,** 195–197 King's Rd. (tel. 071/352-9255), lures the homesick Yankee. It's been compared to a *Cheers*-style bar. Big burgers and meaty dogs are part of the American fare, and you can order such drinks as Tequila Sunrise. In summer, you can eat and drink in the rose garden in the back. Happy hour with reduced drink prices is daily from 5:30 to 7:30pm.

After your refreshment (which can be repeated at any of the neighborhood's other pubs and cafés along the way), continue walking southwest along King's Road. Midway between Shawfield Street and Flood Street lies a warren of antiques sellers, all clustered together into a complex known as:

18. **Antiquarius,** 135–141 King's Rd., SW3. Browse at will— maybe you'll buy an almost-heirloom or perhaps even something of lasting value.

As you continue down King's Road, oval-shaped blue-and-white plaques will identify buildings of particular interest. One that you should especially watch for is:

19. **Chelsea's Old Town Hall.** Set on the south side of King's Road, midway between Chelsea Manor and Oakley Street, it's the favorite hangout of everyone from punk rockers to soon-to-be-married couples applying for a marriage license. Many wedding parties are photographed in front of its Georgian grandeur.

The energetic and/or still curious participants in this walking tour might transform its finale into a pub crawl, as the neighborhood is filled with many enticing choices.

WALKING TOUR 5 — DICKENS'S LONDON

Start: Russell Square. *Tube:* Russell Square.
Finish: The Old Deanery. *Tube:* St. Paul's.
Time: 2½ hours.
Best Time: Any daylight hours. Early Saturday or anytime Sunday might have the least amount of traffic.
Worst Time: Monday through Friday morning and afternoon rush hours.

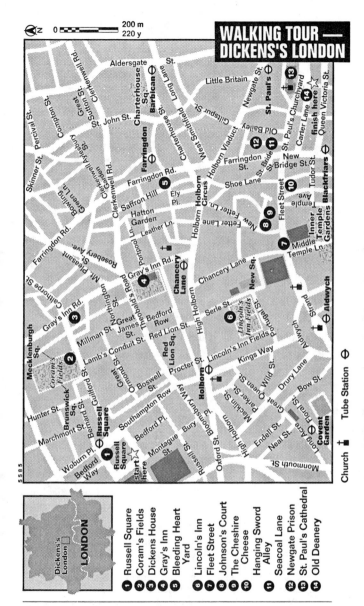

WALKING TOUR — DICKENS'S LONDON

0 — 200 m
0 — 220 y

Tube Station Φ

Church ✝

LONDON

Dickens's London

1 Russell Square
2 Coram's Fields
3 Dickens House
4 Gray's Inn
5 Bleeding Heart Yard
6 Lincoln's Inn
7 Fleet Street
8 Johnson's Court
9 The Cheshire Cheese
10 Hanging Sword Alley
11 Seacoal Lane
12 Newgate Prison
13 St. Paul's Cathedral
14 Old Deanery

London settings are very important in works of the great writer Charles Dickens, such as *Little Dorrit, The Pickwick Papers,* and *David Copperfield.* Follow this walking tour and try to recapture an earlier era of overcrowded alleys and grimy buildings; working conditions heavily polluted from the constant stream of coal smoke and dust; and streets littered with the waste of thousands of horses pulling passengers and freight.

Begin amid the regular symmetry of a neighborhood in the shadow of the British Museum:

1. **Russell Square.** In addition to inspiring Dickens, this square and its side streets were inhabited by other major writers like Ralph Waldo Emerson, T.S. Eliot, and young Edgar Allan Poe. From the square's eastern edge, walk east along Guildford Street, where to the left, you'll see:

2. **Coram's Fields.** This is the site where the Foundling Hospital stood in Victorian times (before it was moved to another part of London). Several Dickens characters, including a rebellious servant named Tattycoram in *Little Dorrit,* were raised there. Of the Foundling Hospital, established around 1740, only the ornate gateway survives to remind passersby of the formerly influential organization that brought up many of London's abandoned children.

   Turn right onto Doughty Street (not Doughty Mews, which you'll reach first). At no. 48 Doughty Street, you'll find one of London's most potent homages to Dickens:

3. **Dickens House.** The writer rented it between 1837 and 1839, producing within its walls three of his most famous novels, *The Pickwick Papers, Oliver Twist,* and *Nicholas Nickleby.* Today, it's the headquarters of the Dickens Fellowship, and contains a collection of Dickens memorabilia, including one of his writing desks. In the cellar is a construction of a kitchen described in *The Pickwick Papers.*

   Doughty Street soon changes its name to John Street. Continue south until it dead-ends at Theobald's Road, where you turn left. Two blocks later, turn right on Gray's Inn Road. The complex of buildings that has been on your right is:

4. **Gray's Inn.** Theoretically, the loosely defined official function of this sprawling collection of buildings was to provide offices and residential flats for lawyers, and to admit applicants to the practice of law in England. In *The Uncommercial Traveller,* Dickens called this warren of offices, residences, and dark cubbyholes, "one of the most depressing institutions in brick and mortar known to the children of men." This description was probably inspired by Dickens's unhappy experience at age 15, when he worked as a clerk in no. 1. Later, other addresses at Gray's Inn were used as settings for *David Copperfield* and served as inspiration for similarly depressing locales in other novels.

   Continue south on Gray's Inn Road until you reach wide and busy High Holborn (or just Holborn). Turn left, walking eastward, along the left-hand (northern) edge of the avenue, turning left very soon again onto Brooke Street. At this point, you'll be in a warren of alleys and narrow streets whose original layout was altered by the erection of several modern buildings after World War II. If you can imagine these streets teeming with residents and permeated with coal smoke, you'll have a feel for settings described by Dickens.

   In one short block, turn right onto Fox Court, which soon changes its name to Greville Street (the narrow streets run into one another at about this point), and walk eastward until, on your right, you reach a dignified courtyard stained black by industrial grime:

5. **Bleeding Heart Yard.** This opening in the neighborhood's mass of masonry was made famous by Dickens in *Little Dorrit* as

the locale of Doyce and Clennam's factory and the grimy home of the Plornish family. Its evocative name was attributed to a very old inn whose trademark was a brokenhearted virgin, but the place was also associated with a certain Lady Hatton. She entered into alliance with the Devil, who—when the fun was over—came to claim her embodied as a dashing swain dressed entirely in black. Spiriting her off to hell, he left only her bleeding heart beside the pump in a courtyard later known as Bleeding Heart Yard.

Although street urchins of a century ago were able to shortcut through the winding hallways and cellars of the district's slums, you'll have to walk almost completely around the block to reach your next objective. Exit from Bleeding Heart Yard onto Greville, turning right (east). Two blocks later, turn right (south) onto Farringdon St. and walk a block. Then, turn right (west) onto Charterhouse St. Walk a block on the right-hand side of the street until you reach a small and narrow street known as Ely Place. Herein lies a:

REFUELING STOP **Ye Old Mitre,** Ely Place, EC1 (tel. 071/405-4751). Some kind of inn has stood beside the dingy brick-lined sides of this alleyway since 1547, but the incarnation you'll see today has dark-stained Victorian paneling and battered wooden floors, tables, and benches well worn by characters who might have filled the pages of Dickens. Filled today with a clientele of City financiers and salespeople from the nearby jewelry district, the place serves uncomplicated food (place your order at the bar) and more mugs of Burton's ale than almost anywhere else in the City.

After your tipple, continue south along Ely Place, then turn right into the roundabout known as Holborn Circus, which will funnel into High Holborn Street. Proceed westward, walking along the south (left) side of the street for six blocks to Chancery Lane. On the junction's southwest corner lies another group of weathered buildings, used a century ago as a complex of Victorian apartments and legal offices:

6. **Lincoln's Inn.** Originally built during the 1400s, it has many associations with Dickens. Its Old Hall was the setting for the opening scene of *Bleak House*. Some 2½ labyrinthine blocks to the west is an open space, Lincoln's Inn Fields. Betsey Trotwood of *David Copperfield* took lodgings in a building that flanked it. On Lincoln's Inn Fields' western border sits no. 58, a town house that belonged to John Foster, who entertained Dickens from time to time.

Retrace your steps eastward to Chancery Lane, then head south past several narrow alleyways and covered passageways until you reach the traditional headquarters of British publishing and journalism:

7. **Fleet Street.** Although its grip on British journalism is now just a memory, many Dickens characters met or interacted with one another along Fleet Street. At no. 1, you'll find the Williams and Glyn Bank, which in an earlier incarnation was Child's Bank, a model for Tellson's Bank in *A Tale of Two Cities*. Fleet Street was crucially important to the author's career. In 1833, Chapman & Hall, the owners of *Monthly Magazine,* published

his first manuscript. To see the offices that launched one of England's greatest writers, turn north off Fleet Street into the postage-stamp-size confines of:

8. **Johnson's Court.** Farther along, from an entrance located at 145 Fleet St. (near the corner of Wine Office Court), is a restaurant and pub familiar to Dickens, and which provided a setting for some of his scenes:

9. **The Cheshire Cheese.** One of the greatest of the old City chophouses, it's been in business since 1667. It claims to be the place where Samuel Johnson dined and entertained friends.

Now cross to the south side of Fleet Street, and retrace your steps, walking west for a block. Extending south of Fleet Street is Whitefriars Street, which, if you'll enter, soon provides access to:

10. **Hanging Sword Alley.** Here, Dickens housed Jerry Cruncher, one of the more gruesome characters of *A Tale of Two Cities.*

Fleet Street soon empties into a traffic circle known as Ludgate Circus. Continue your walk eastward, onto a street identified as Ludgate Hill. The first street on your left is:

11. **Seacoal Lane.** This street contained one of the Victorian era's most feared and loathed prisons, long-ago demolished Fleet Prison, where Mr. Pickwick was incarcerated for debt. Continue northeast on Seacoal Lane, which merges after about a block with Old Bailey, where you turn left. There, a grim-looking judicial building, the Central Criminal Court, occupies the site of an even more famous Victorian jail:

12. **Newgate Prison.** Incarceration in its dank cells was perhaps the greatest fear of Fagin and his band of adolescent pickpockets in *Oliver Twist,* and the despair that reigned here was later portrayed by Dickens in sections of *Great Expectations.* Although Newgate was demolished in 1902, memories of this truly horrible prison linger in the neighborhood even today.

Turn south along Old Bailey for about a block, then go left (eastward) along Ludgate Hill until you come to a monument rich in connections both for Dickens and for dozens of other writers:

13. **St. Paul's Cathedral.** Dickens set some of the pivotal scenes of *David Copperfield* here, including episodes where Betsey Trotwood meets secretly with a man whom readers later learn is her estranged husband. To the south of the cathedral, in a very short alley that signs will identify as Dean's Court, stands the:

14. **Old Deanery,** where Dickens worked for a brief period as a legal reporter in 1829.

WALKING TOUR 6 — BRITISH MUSEUM

Start: Assyrian Transept.
Finish: The King's Library.
Tube: Holborn, Tottenham Court Rd., or Russell Sq.
Time: 2½ hours.
Best Time: Monday through Friday, when the museum opens at 10am.
Worst Times: Saturday and Sunday, when it's overcrowded.

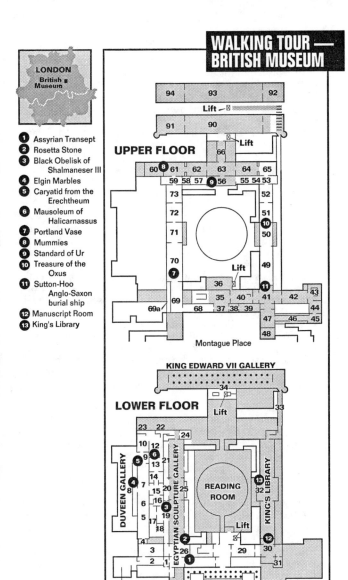

WALKING TOUR — BRITISH MUSEUM

LONDON
British
Museum

1. Assyrian Transept
2. Rosetta Stone
3. Black Obelisk of Shalmaneser III
4. Elgin Marbles
5. Caryatid from the Erechtheum
6. Mausoleum of Halicarnassus
7. Portland Vase
8. Mummies
9. Standard of Ur
10. Treasure of the Oxus
11. Sutton-Hoo Anglo-Saxon burial ship
12. Manuscript Room
13. King's Library

UPPER FLOOR

Lift
Lift
Lift
Lift

Montague Place

KING EDWARD VII GALLERY

LOWER FLOOR

Lift
Lift

DUVEEN GALLERY

EGYPTIAN SCULPTURE GALLERY

READING ROOM

KING'S LIBRARY

Cafeteria   Great Russell Street

As you enter the front hall of the British Museum, Great Russell Street, WC1 (tel. 071/636-1555), head immediately for one of its most monumental vistas, Room 26. Set near the main entrance, it's better known as the:

1. **Assyrian Transept.** There, you'll find the human-headed winged bulls that once guarded the gateways to the palaces of Assyrian kings. From here, you can continue north into the long and echoing Hall of Egyptian Sculpture (Room 25) to see the:

2. **Rosetta Stone,** whose discovery during one of Napoleon's campaigns led to the deciphering of hieroglyphs, explained in a wall display behind the stone. Within a parallel room to the east (Room 19, the Nimrud Gallery) rises the:

3. **Black Obelisk of Shalmaneser III** (858–824 B.C.), an ancient tribute from Jehu, king of Israel. Several galleries to the west of the Nimrud Gallery is one of the largest and most famous rooms of the British Museum, the Duveen Gallery (Room 8), containing the:

4. **Elgin Marbles,** which include some of the finest sculpture ever produced in ancient Greece, most notably fragments from the frieze of the Parthenon in Athens. Of the 92 metopes from the Parthenon, 15 are housed today in the British Museum. They depict the struggle-to-the-death between handsome Lapiths and grotesque, drunken Centaurs. The head of the horse from the chariot of Selene, goddess of the moon, is one of the pediment sculptures. Directly northeast of the Duveen Gallery in Room 9 (Room of the Caryatid) is:

5. **Caryatid from the Erechtheum** (421 B.C.), a gracefully robed depiction of a maiden whose body supported part of a temple dedicated to Athena and Poseidon. Displayed nearby, in Room 12, are sculptures from the:

6. **Mausoleum at Halicarnassus,** which, after its construction around 350 B.C., was considered one of the Seven Wonders of the World. It was intended to house the remains of Mausollus, ruler of Caria. Funneling off from Room 12 rise the museum's West Stairs. Climb them to reach the upper floor, then walk south through four galleries until you reach Room 70. There, you'll find the:

7. **Portland Vase,** considered the finest example of ancient cameo carving. Carved around 25 B.C. following techniques imported to Rome from Egypt, it's named after the Dowager Duchess of Portland, who acquired it from related Italian cardinals (the Barberinis) in 1784. Smashed to pieces by a British vandal in 1845, it has been expertly repaired and dismantled twice since then, most recently in 1985 using advanced techniques and epoxy resins.

   Now, retrace your steps through room 71 (site of a recently refurbished gallery of Etruscan artifacts) and continue straight past the entrance to the West Stairs. In rooms 61 and 60, note the collection of:

8. **Mummies,** ghoulish and mysterious reminders of the hopes for an afterlife of the ancient Egyptians. Adjacent, in room 63, are Egyptian exhibits resembling the props for the movie *Cleopatra:* cosmetics, domestic utensils, toys, and tools. Walk east to room 56, devoted to objects from early Mesopotamia and Sumeria (southern Iraq). Look for the jewellike:

9. **Standard of Ur.** Crafted from lapis-lazuli mosaics as the soundbox for an ancient stringed instrument in 2,500 B.C., it's considered one of the most remarkable objects in its collection. Other objects include a depiction in gold and lapis lazuli of a goat standing on two legs in a thicket, a queen's bull-headed harp (the oldest ever discovered), and a reconstruction from fragments of a queen's sledge (the oldest-known example of a land vehicle in the world). Walk east and south through rooms

devoted to artifacts from the Hittites and the ancient Anatolians. In Room 51, you'll find the:

10. Treasure of the Oxus, a temple deposit from ancient Persia whose objects range in date from the 6th to the 3rd century B.C.; included is a unique collection of goldsmith's work: votive plaques, signet rings, sculptures of a nude youth, and a fish-shaped pedestal. Several galleries to the south, in Room 41, are the artifacts unearthed from the:

11. Sutton-Hoo Anglo-Saxon burial ship, discovered in Suffolk. It is, in the words of one expert, "the richest treasure ever dug from English soil," containing gold jewelry, armor, weapons, bronze bowls and cauldrons, silverware, and the inevitable drinking horn of Norse culture. No body was found, although the tomb was believed to be that of a king of East Anglia who died in the 7th century A.D. You'll also see the 12th-century bulging-eyed Lewis chessmen fashioned from walrus ivory and Romanesque carvings in Scandinavian style and the Ilbert collection of clocks and watches.

You have now completed a tour of the museum's upper floor. Head for the Main Stairs, a very short walk west, and descend to street level. (Signs and personnel sometimes identify it as the Lower Floor.) Pass the museum's gift shop and information desk and head for Room 30, the:

12. Manuscript Room, where you'll find one of the richest depositories of documents in the world. They include an original of the Magna Carta and the Lindisfarne Gospels, an outstanding example of the work of Northumbrian artists in an early period (about 698) of English Christianity. Almost every major literary figure is represented with signatures, including Shakespeare, Dickens, Jane Austen, Charlotte Brontë, and Yeats. Also on display is Nelson's last letter to Lady Hamilton and the journals of Captain Cook. Other notable exhibits in the library include the Benedictional (in Latin) of St. Ethelwold, Bishop of Winchester (963–984); the Luttrell Psalter; and the Harley Golden Gospels (about 800). Head north into Room 32, the very large:

13. King's Library, where you'll find a copy of the magnificent Gutenberg Bible (1455), perhaps the first book printed in Europe with movable type. Other exhibits include Asian illuminated manuscripts, George III's personal library, and early postage stamps, notably the 1840 Great British Penny Black and the rare 1847 Post Office issues of Mauritius. Also on display is the Diamond Sutra, block printed in 868 by the Moghuls.

REFUELING STOP   The Museum Tavern, 49 Great Russell St., WC1 (tel. 071/242-8987), is a turn-of-the-century pub opposite the British Museum. Follow in the footsteps of Karl Marx (who used to drink and dine there) and join the museum visitors and students from the University of London for traditional English food or pub grub. Ever had English cider? It's served here.

CHAPTER 8

LONDON SHOPPING

1. THE SHOPPING SCENE

2. SHOPPING A TO Z

When Prussian Field Marshal Blücher, Wellington's stout ally at Waterloo, first laid eyes on London, he allegedly slapped his thigh and exclaimed, "Herr Gott, what a city to plunder!" He was gazing at what, for the early 19th century, was a phenomenal mass of shops and stores, overwhelming to Herr Blücher's unsophisticated eyes. Since those days, other cities have drawn level with London as shopping centers, but none has ever surpassed it.

1. THE SHOPPING SCENE

London's shopping world today is a superbly balanced mixture of luxury and utility, of small personalized boutiques and giant department stores, of junk-heaped market stalls and breathtakingly elegant specialty shops. As for bargains—that magic word in every traveler's dictionary—they are everywhere.

TAXES AND SHIPPING Many London shops will help you beat the whopping **value added tax (VAT)** levied on much of England's merchandise. By presenting your passport, you can frequently purchase goods tax free, but only on condition that you either have your purchase sent directly to your home address or have it delivered to the plane you're taking back. Because airlines usually charge a great deal for excess luggage, it's cheaper to have it shipped independently. Try **London Baggage Company,** 115 Buckingham Palace Rd., Desk 18, SW1 (tel. 071/834-9411, ext. 41; tube: Victoria Station). Their main office is at Gatwick Village South Terminal, Gatwick Airport, West Sussex (tel. 0293/543-853).

If you don't send goods, you can still have the VAT refunded by filling out a form available at many shops and then either presenting the form and the goods at a Cash VAT Refund desk at a major airport when you leave Great Britain or sending the form to the specified address.

Note: Many stores that assist foreigners in avoiding the VAT display a prominent sign—"TAX FREE Shopping/European VAT Refund Network."

BARGAINS When bargain hunting, zero in on those goods that are manufactured in England and liable to cost much more when exported. These are—above all—men's and women's suits, woolens, tweeds, overcoats, scarves, tartans, bone china, cutlery, and prints, plus specialties such as antiques, rare books, and those magnificent old-world and city maps in most bookstores.

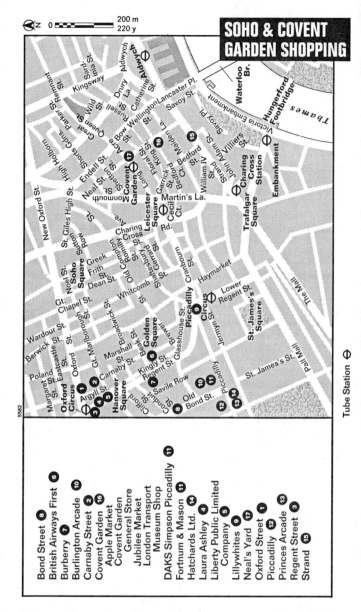

SOHO & COVENT GARDEN SHOPPING

200 m
220 y

Tube Station ⊕

Bond Street ⑧
British Airways First ⑥
Burberry ⑦
Burlington Arcade ⑩
Carnaby Street ②
Covent Garden ⑯
  Apple Market
  Covent Garden
    General Store
  Jubilee Market
  London Transport
    Museum Shop
DAKS Simpson Piccadilly ⑪
Fortnum & Mason ⑪
Hatchards Ltd. ⑭
Laura Ashley ④
Liberty Public Limited
  Company ⑤
Lillywhites ⑨
Neal's Yard ⑰
Oxford Street ①
Piccadilly ⑫
Princes Arcade ⑬
Regent Street ③
Strand ⑮

SALES Some savvy British shoppers don't buy anything until January. After the busy Christmas season, when business lags, stores revive shopping fever by offering a series of sales. Discounts can range from 25% to 50% at leading department stores such as Harrods and Selfridges (see below), along with many other smaller shops. But let's not paint too rosy a picture: Some shopkeepers deliberately display merchandise of lesser quality so they can discount it heavily just for these sales.

HOURS   London keeps fairly uniform **store hours,** mostly shorter than American equivalents. The norm is a 5:30pm closing, with a late Wednesday or Thursday night, until 7pm. Most central shops close Saturday around 1pm. They don't, however, observe a French-style lunch-hour closing.

MAIN SHOPPING STREETS   London's retail stores tend to cluster in certain areas, a phenomenon that evolved in the era when each guild or craft had its own street. This is what gives a London shopping spree its special flavor: You head in a certain direction to find a certain type of merchandise.

   Beauchamp Place (tube: Knightsbridge), pronounced like "Beecham," is a block off Brompton Road, near Harrods department store. Whatever you're looking for—from a pâté de marcassin to a carved pine mantelpiece—you are likely to find it here. Rejects of china, crystal, pottery, secondhand silver, old alligator bags, collages, custom-tailored men's shirts—whatever. It's pure fun even if you don't buy anything.

   Divided into New and Old, **Bond Street** (tube: Bond Street) connects Piccadilly with Oxford Street and is synonymous with the luxury trade. Here are found the very finest—and most expensive—of antiques shops, hatters, jewelers, milliners, tailors, shoe stores, and sporting goods establishments.

   Burlington Arcade (tube: Piccadilly Circus), the famous glass-roofed, Regency-style passage leading off Piccadilly, looks like a period exhibition and is lined with intriguing shops and boutiques. Lit by wrought-iron lamps, decorated with clusters of ferns and flowers, the small, smart stores specialize in fashion, jewelry, Irish linen, camera equipment, stationery, pipes and smoking accessories, and model soldiers.

   If you linger in the arcade until 5:30pm, you can watch the beadles, those ever-present attendants in their black-and-yellow livery and top hats, ceremoniously put in place the iron grills that block off the arcade until 9 the next morning, at which time they just as ceremoniously remove them to mark the start of a new business day. Also at 5:30pm, a hand bell called the Burlington Bell is sounded, signaling the end of trading. It's rung by one of the beadles. (There are only three of these constables remaining, the last London representatives of Britain's oldest police force.)

   Just off Regent, **Carnaby Street** (tube: Oxford Circus) no longer dominates the world of pacesetting fashion as it did in the 1960s, but it is still visited by the young, especially punks, and some of its shops display claptrap and quick-quid merchandise.

   Kensington High Street (tube: High Street Kensington) has been called "the Oxford Street of West London." Stretching for about 1½ miles, it includes numerous shops, such as the House of Fraser. Many establishments are on adjacent side streets, including **Earls Court** and **Abingdon roads. Thackeray** and **Victoria streets** retain some of the old village atmosphere. From Kensington High Street, you can walk up **Kensington Church Street,** which, like **Portobello Road,** is one of the city's main shopping avenues, selling everything from antique furniture to impressionist paintings.

   King's Road (tube: Sloane Square), the main street of Chelsea, which starts at Sloane Square, will forever remain a symbol of London in the "swinging sixties." Today, the street is still frequented by young people, but perhaps there are fewer Mohican haircuts,

"Bovver boots," and Edwardian ballgowns than before. More and more in the 1990s, King's Road is a lineup of markets and "multistores," large or small conglomerations of in- and outdoor stands, stalls, and booths within one building or enclosure. They spring up so fast that it's impossible to keep them tabulated, but few thorough shopping strollers in London can afford to omit King's Road from their itineraries.

Together with Kensington and Brompton roads, **Knightsbridge** (tube: Knightsbridge) forms an extremely busy shopping district south of Hyde Park. It's patronized for furniture, antiques, jewelry, and **Harrods** department store.

Oxford Street (tube: Tottenham Court Road), the main shopping artery of London, runs from St. Giles Circus to Marble Arch. It's an endless, faceless, totally uninspiring but utility-crammed strip of stores, stores, and yet more stores. It contains six of London's major department stores, along with just about every kind of retailing establishment under the sun.

Unlike the circus, the street **Piccadilly** (tube: Piccadilly Circus) is distinctly in the upper bracket, specializing in elegant automobile showrooms, travel offices, and art galleries, plus London's poshest grocery store, **Fortnum & Mason.**

If you like one-stop shopping, you may be drawn to the **Princes Arcade** (tube: Piccadilly Circus), opened by Edward VII in 1883, when he was still Prince of Wales. Situated between Jermyn Street and Piccadilly in the heart of London, the arcade has been restored. Wrought-iron lamps light your way as you search through some 20 bow-fronted shops, looking for that special curio (say, a 16th-century nightcap) or a pair of shoes made by people who have been satisfying royal tastes since 1847. A small sign hanging from a metal rod indicates what kind of merchandise a particular store sells.

Curving down elegantly from Oxford Circus to Piccadilly Circus, **Regent Street** (tube: Piccadilly Circus) is crammed with fashionable stores selling everything from silks to silverware. This stylish thoroughfare has both department stores and boutiques, but the accent is on the medium-size establishment in the upper-medium price range.

Saint Christopher's Place (tube: Bond Street), one of London's most interesting shopping streets (and lesser known to the foreign visitor), lies just off Oxford Street; walk down Oxford Street from Selfridges toward Oxford Circus, ducking north along Gees Court across Barrett Street. There you'll be surrounded by antiques markets and shops for women's clothing and accessories.

Stately, broad, and dignified, **The Strand** (tube: Charing Cross Station) runs from Trafalgar Square into Fleet Street. It's lined with hotels and theaters, and a selection of specialty stores you could spend a whole day peeking into.

2. SHOPPING A TO Z

ART

BERKELEY SQUARE GALLERY, 23A Bruton St., W1. Tel. 071/493-7939.
Established as a branch office of Christie's specializing in limited-

edition prints, it broke away from its illustrious owner in 1987. Now selling etchings, lithographs, and screen-prints by up-and-coming artists, it also offers major works by such masters as Moore, Chagall, Hockney, and Matisse. The gallery is considered innovative and creative even within the competitive world of London galleries. Open: Mon–Fri 10am–6pm, Sat 10am–4pm. Tube: Green Park.

BOOKS, MAPS & ENGRAVINGS

HATCHARDS LTD., 187–188 Piccadilly, W1. Tel. 071/ 439-9921.

On the south side of Piccadilly, Hatchards offers books ranging from popular fiction to specialized reference. There are shelves of guidebooks, atlases, cookbooks, paperbacks, puzzle books. Open: Mon–Fri 9am–6pm, Sat 9am–5pm. Tube: Piccadilly Circus.

HISTORY BOOKSHOP, 2 Broadway, N11. Tel. 081/368-8568.

This shop for history buffs stands at the corner of Friern Barnet Road and MacDonald Road. Behind an 1890s facade is one of London's largest repositories of secondhand books, some 40,000 on three floors. It specializes in military history and issues catalogs at regular intervals. Open: Wed–Fri 10am–4pm. Tube: Arnos Grove.

MAP HOUSE, 54 Beauchamp Place, SW3. Tel. 071/589-4325.

An ideal place to find an offbeat souvenir, Map House was established in 1907 and sells antique maps and engravings and a vast selection of old prints of London and England, original and reproduction. An original engraving, guaranteed to be more than a century old, can cost as little as £5 ($7.50), although some rare or historic items sell for as much as £50,000 ($75,000). Open: Mon–Fri 9:45am–5:45pm, Sat 10:30am–5pm. Tube: Knightsbridge.

STANFORDS, 12–14 Long Acre, WC2. Tel. 071/836-1321.

The world's largest map shop, Stanfords was established in 1852. Many of its maps, which include worldwide touring and survey maps, are unavailable elsewhere. It's also the best travel-book store in London (naturally, the staff has the good judgment to carry a complete selection of Frommer guides, in case you're going on to some other country after a tour of Britain). Open: Mon and Sat 10am–6pm, Tues–Wed and Thurs–Fri 9am–7pm. Tube: Leicester Sq. or Covent Garden.

W. & G. FOYLE, LTD., 113–119 Charing Cross Rd., WC2. Tel. 071/439-8501.

Claiming to be the world's largest bookstore, W. & G. Foyle, Ltd., has an impressive array of hardcovers and paperbacks, as well as travel maps. The stock also includes records, videotapes, and sheet music. Open: Mon–Wed and Fri–Sat 9am–6pm, Thurs 9am–7pm. Tube: Leicester Sq.

BRASS RUBBING

LONDON BRASS RUBBING CENTRE, St. Martin-in-the-Fields Church, Trafalgar Sq., WC2. Tel. 071/437-6023.

In the big brick-vaulted 1720s crypt, London Brass Rubbing Centre stands alongside a brasserie restaurant, a bookshop, and a crafts market. In the crypt is a small art gallery. The center has 88 exact copies of bronze portraits of medieval knights, ladies, kings, and merchants waiting for visiting aficionados to use. Paper, rubbing materials, and instructions on how to begin are furnished, and classical music plays as visitors work away. The charges range from £1.50 ($2.30) for a small copy to £11.50 ($17.30) for the largest, a life-size Crusader knight. A gift area sells British products with a historical theme, including Celtic jewelry. The center has a selection of more than a thousand handmade brass rubbings for sale. Even beginners who have never made a rubbing take home impressive artworks for themselves. For those who wish to make brass rubbings in countryside churches, the center offers instructions and sells the necessary materials. Open: Mon–Sat 10am–6pm, Sun noon–6pm. Tube: Charing Cross.

CHINA, SILVER & GLASS

GLASSHOUSE, 65 Long Acre, WC2. Tel. 071/836-9785.
This craftshop sells hand-blown studio glass. Visitors can watch the craftspeople produce the work on the premises. Open: Mon–Fri 10am–6pm, Sat 11am–5pm. Tube: Covent Garden.

LAWLEYS, 154 Regent St., W1. Tel. 071/734-3184.
A wide range of English bone china, as well as crystal and giftware, is sold here. The firm specializes in Royal Doulton, Minton, Royal Crown Derby, Wedgwood, and Aynsley china; Royal Doulton, Stuart, Waterford, and Swarovski; Lladró figures; David Winter Cottages, Border Fine Arts, and other famous giftware names. Lawleys also sells cutlery. Open: Mon–Wed and Fri–Sat 9:30am–6pm, Thurs 9:30am–7pm. Tube: Piccadilly Circus or Oxford Circus.

THOMAS GOODE, 19 S. Audley St., Grosvenor Sq., W1. Tel. 071/499-2823.
Thomas Goode was established in 1827, 10 years before Victoria came to the throne, and with three Royal Warrants this is perhaps the most famous china and glass shop in the world. Minton majolica elephants grace its front windows, and the main entrance, with its famous mechanical doors, gives access to the china, glass, and silverware displayed in 14 showrooms. You can choose a small gift or purchase a unique dinner service with cresting and monogram. A Thomas Goode catalog is available. Open: Mon and Wed–Fri 9am–5:30pm, Tues 10am–5:30pm, Sat 9:30am–5:30pm. Tube: Hyde Park Corner.

CLOCKS

STRIKE ONE ISLINGTON LIMITED, 33 Balcombe St., NW1. Tel. 071/224-9710.
Selling clocks, music boxes, and barometers, this store clearly dates and prices each old clock—from Victorian dial clocks to early English long-case timepieces—and every purchase is guaranteed worldwide for a year against faulty workmanship. Strike One specializes in Act of Parliament clocks. It also issues an illustrated catalog, which is mailed internationally to all serious clock collectors. The firm also undertakes to locate any clock a customer might request if no suitable example is in stock. Open: By appointment only. Tube: Baker St.

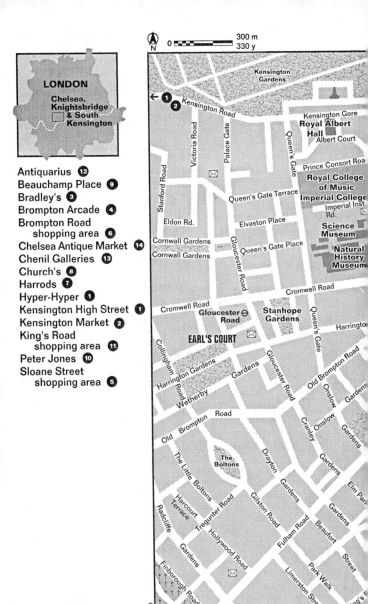

CRAFTS

CONTEMPORARY APPLIED ARTS, 43 Earlham St., WC2. Tel. 071/836-6993.
  This association of craftspeople sells and displays contemporary artwork, both traditional and progressive. The galleries at the center contain a diverse retail display of members' work that includes glass, rugs, lamps, ceramics, fabric, clothing, paper, metalwork, and

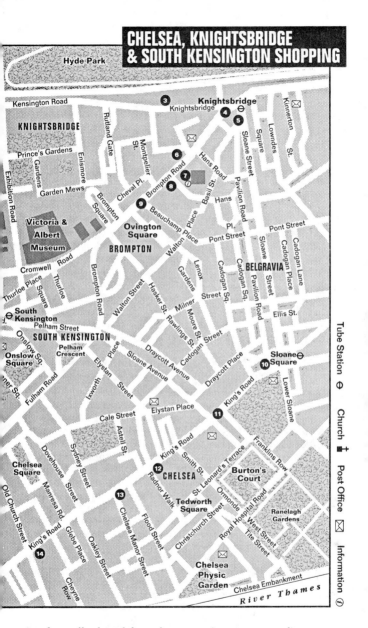

CHELSEA, KNIGHTSBRIDGE & SOUTH KENSINGTON SHOPPING

Hyde Park

Kensington Road

KNIGHTSBRIDGE

Prince's Gardens

Knightsbridge
Knightsbridge

Garden Mews

Victoria &
Albert
Museum

Cromwell Road

Thurloe Place

South
Kensington

Pelham Street

SOUTH KENSINGTON

Pelham
Crescent

Onslow
Square

BROMPTON

Ovington
Square

Beauchamp Place

Pont Street

BELGRAVIA

Ellis St.

Sloane
Square

King's Road

Chelsea
Square

CHELSEA

Tedworth
Square

Burton's
Court

Ranelagh
Gardens

Chelsea
Physic
Garden

Chelsea Embankment

River Thames

Tube Station ⊖   Church ■✝   Post Office ⊠   Information ⊙

jewelry—all selected from the country's most outstanding contemporary artisans. There is also a program of special exhibitions that focuses on innovations in the various crafts. Open: Mon–Wed and Fri–Sat 10am–6pm, Thurs 10am–7pm. Tube: Covent Garden.

CRAFTS COUNCIL, 44a Pentonville Rd. Islington, N1. Tel. 071/278-7700.
This is the national body for promoting fine craftsmanship,

encouraging high standards and public awareness of contemporary crafts. Here you can discover some of the most creative work in Britain today, plus a shop selling craft objects, books, and magazines. There are also a picture library, an information center, education workshops, and a café. Open: Tues–Sat 11am–6pm, Sun 2–6pm. Tube: Angel.

NATURALLY BRITISH, 13 New Row, WC2. Tel. 071/240-0551.

This shop has a traditional British ambience with old wooden floors and antique furniture. A wide range of English, Welsh, and Scottish goods are sold, including toys, cloths, ceramics, jewelry, and food. Many items can be made to order, including rocking horses, painted christening spoons, and furniture. Open: Mon–Sat 11am–7pm, Sun noon–5pm. Tube: Leicester Sq. or Covent Garden.

NEAL STREET EAST, 5 Neal St., WC2. Tel. 071/240-0135.

In this vast shop devoted to Asian and Asian-inspired merchandise, you can find dried and silk flowers, pottery, baskets, chinoiserie, and toys, as well as calligraphy, modern and antique clothing, textiles, and ethnic jewelry. There are also an extensive cookware department and a bookshop. Open: Mon–Sat 10am–7pm, Sun noon–6pm. Tube: Covent Garden.

DEPARTMENT STORES

DAKS SIMPSON PICCADILLY, 203 Piccadilly, W1. Tel. 071/734-2002.

Opened in 1936 as the home of DAKS clothing, Simpson's has been going strong ever since. It is known for menswear—its basement-level men's shoe department is a model of the way quality shoes should be fitted—as well as women's fashions, perfume, jewelry, and lingerie. Many of the clothes are lighthearted, carefully made, and well suited to casual elegance. More formal clothing is also sold by the always polite and thoughtful staff. A restaurant serves fine English food. Open: Mon–Wed and Fri–Sat 9am–6pm, Thurs 9am–7pm. Tube: Piccadilly Circus.

HARRODS, 87–135 Brompton Rd., Knightsbridge, SW1. Tel. 071/730-1234.

London's—indeed Europe's—top store, Harrods is an institution, and visitors have come to view it as a sightseeing attraction, like the Tower of London. Some of the goods displayed for sale are works of art, and so are the 300 departments displaying them. The sheer range, variety, and quality of merchandise is dazzling—from silver and pewter to clothing, from food to fabrics, from pianos to delicatessens. The store was recently refurbished to restore it to the elegance and luxury of the 1920s and '30s.

The whole fifth floor is devoted to sports and leisure, with a wide range of equipment and attire. Toy Kingdom is on the fourth floor, along with children's wear. The Egyptian Hall, which opened in 1991 on the ground floor, sells crystal from Lalique and Baccarat; porcelain; and antique Egyptian artifacts of the 18th dynasty, including carved stone pillars, sphinx heads, and a frieze with hieroglyphics. There's also a men's grooming room, an enormous jewelry department, and the "Way In" department for younger customers. You have a choice of 11 restaurants and bars at Harrods.

One of the highlights is Food Hall, stocked with a huge variety of foods. In the basement you'll find a bank, a theater-booking service, a travel bureau, and Harrods Shop, offering a range of souvenirs, including its famous green-and-gold bag. Open: Mon–Tues and Sat 10am–6pm, Wed–Fri 10am–7pm. Tube: Knightsbridge.

LIBERTY PUBLIC LIMITED COMPANY, 210–220 Regent St., W1. Tel. 071/734-1234.

This major department store is renowned worldwide for selling high-quality, stylish merchandise in charming surroundings. Its flagship store on Regent Street houses six floors of fashion, china, and home furnishings. In addition to Liberty Print fashion fabrics, upholstery fabrics, scarves, ties, luggage, and gifts, the shop sells top-drawer goods from all over the world. Liberty offers a personal "corner shop" service, with helpful and informed assistants selling its often unique merchandise. Open: Mon–Tues and Fri–Sat 9:20am–6pm, Wed 10am–6pm, Thurs 9:20–7:30pm. Tube: Tottenham Court Road.

PETER JONES, Sloane Sq., SW1. Tel. 071/730-3434.

Founded in 1877 and rebuilt in 1936, Peter Jones is known for fashion and household goods, including perfume, china, glass, soft furnishings, and linens. The store also displays a constantly changing selection of antiques. There's an abundance of gift items. The store also has a coffee shop and first-class licensed restaurant, both with extensive views. Open: Mon–Tues and Fri–Sat 9am–5:30pm, Wed 9:30am–7pm. Tube: Sloane Sq. Bus: 11, 19, 137, 210, or C1.

SELFRIDGES, 400 Oxford St., W1. Tel. 071/629-1234.

One of the largest department stores in Europe, Selfridges has more than 500 divisions selling everything from artificial flowers to groceries. The specialty shops are particularly enticing, with good buys in Irish linens, Wedgwood china, leather goods, silver-plated goblets, cashmere items, and woolen scarves. There's also the Miss Selfridge Boutique.

To help you travel light, the Export Bureau will air-freight purchases anywhere in the world, tax free. In the basement Services Arcade, the London Tourist Board will help you find your way around London's sights with maps and advice. Open: Mon–Wed and Fri–Sat 9:30am–6pm, Thurs 9:30am–8pm. Tube: Bond St. or Marble Arch.

FASHION

AQUASCUTUM, 100 Regent St., W1. Tel. 071/734-6090.

The magazine *Time Out* said this about Aquascutum: "It is about as quintessentially British as you'll get this side of Savile Row, and it's a popular stop-off for American tourists wanting to look more British than the Brits." On four floors, this classic shop offers only high-quality British and imported clothing (including leisure wear) for men and women. The Seasons Café is on three. Open: Mon–Wed and Fri 9:30am–6pm, Thurs 9am–7pm, Sat 9:30am–6:30pm. Tube: Piccadilly Circus.

AUSTIN REED, 103–113 Regent St., W1. Tel. 071/734-6789.

Offering both British and international designers, Austin Reed has long stood for quality clothing. The suits of Chester Barrie, for example, are said to fit like bespoke (custom-made) clothing. The polite employees are unusually honest about telling you what looks good. The store always has a wide variety of topnotch jackets and suits, and men can outfit themselves from dressing gowns to overcoats. The third floor is devoted to women's clothing, with carefully selected suits, separates, coats, shirts, knitwear, and accessories. Open: Mon–Wed and Fri–Sat 9:30am–6pm, Thurs 9:30am–7pm. Tube: Piccadilly Circus.

BERK, 46 Burlington Arcade, Piccadilly, W1. Tel. 071/493-0028.

Berk is one of those irresistible "fancy shops" for which London is famous. The store is believed to have one of the largest collections of cashmere sweaters in London—at least the top brands. Open: Mon–Fri 9am–5:30pm, Sat 9am–5pm. Tube: Piccadilly Circus.

BURBERRY, 18–22 Haymarket, SW1. Tel. 071/930-3343.

The name Burberry has been synonymous with raincoats ever since Edward VII publicly ordered his valet to "bring my Burberry" when the skies threatened. An impeccably trained staff sells the famous raincoat, along with excellent men's shirts, sportswear, knitwear, and accessories. Raincoats are available in women's sizes and styles as well. Prices are high, but you get quality and prestige. Open: Mon–Wed and Fri–Sat 9am–6pm, Thurs 9:30am–7pm. Tube: Piccadilly Circus.

HILDITCH & KEY, 37 and 73 Jermyn St., SW1. Tel. 071/930-4707.

Perhaps the finest name in men's shirts, Hilditch & Key has been in business since 1899. There are two shops on this street, with no. 37 specializing in womenswear and no. 73 offering men's clothing (including a bespoke shirt service). Hilditch also has an outstanding tie collection. Open: Mon–Wed and Fri 9:30am–6pm, Thurs 9:30am–7pm, Sat 9:30am–5:30pm. Tube: Piccadilly Circus or Green Park.

HYPER-HYPER, 26–40 Kensington High St., W8. Tel. 071/938-4343.

Hyper-Hyper has been showcasing young designers since 1983, and the work of nearly 70 is on display at all times. The range is sportswear to evening wear, with plenty of accessories, including shoes. Menswear is also sold. Hyper-Hyper will thrill and intrigue. Open: Mon–Wed and Fri–Sat 10am–6pm, Thurs 10am–7pm. Tube: High Street Kensington.

SCOTCH HOUSE, 84 Regent St., SW1. Tel. 071/734-5966.

For top-quality woolen fabrics and garments, go to Scotch House, renowned worldwide for its comprehensive selection of cashmere and wool knitwear for both men and women. Also available is a wide range of tartan garments and accessories, as well as Scottish tweed classics. The children's collection covers ages 2 to 13 and similarly offers excellent value and quality. Open: Mon–Wed 10am–6pm, Thurs 10am–7pm, Fri 10am–6:30pm, Sat 9am–6:30pm. Tube: Piccadilly Circus.

THOMAS PINK, 35 Dover St., W1. Tel. 071/493-6775.

IMPRESSIONS

London . . . a kind of Emporium for the whole Earth.
—JOSEPH ADDISON, *SPECTATOR* (1711)

This Dover Street shirtmaker, named after an 18th-century Mayfair tailor, gave the world the phrases "hunting pink" and "in the pink." It has a prestigious reputation for well-made cotton shirts, for both men and women. The shirts are created from the finest two-fold pure-cotton poplin, coming in a wide range of patterns, stripes, and checks, as well as in plain colors. Some patterns are classic, others new and unusual. All are generously cut, with extra-long tails, and finished with a choice of double cuffs or single-button cuffs. Open: Mon–Fri 9:30am–5:30pm, Sat 9:30am–5pm. Tube: Green Park.

WESTAWAY & WESTAWAY, 62–65 Great Russell St., WC1. Tel. 071/405-4479.

Opposite the British Museum, this is a substitute for a shopping trip to Scotland. Here you'll find a large range of kilts, scarves, waistcoats, capes, dressing gowns, and rugs in authentic clan tartans. The salespeople are knowledgeable about intricate clan symbols. They also sell superb—and untartaned—cashmere, camel-hair, and Shetland knitwear, along with Harris tweed jackets, Burberry raincoats, and cashmere overcoats for men. Open: Mon–Sat 9am–5:30pm. Tube: Tottenham Court Rd.

CHILDREN'S FASHION

The best buys—in both quality and price—are generally found at the leading department stores, notably:

LIBERTY & COMPANY LIMITED, 210–220 Regent St., W1. Tel. 071/734-1234.

Children's clothing and toys are found on the first floor (second floor to Americans) of this prestigious store, which is mainly known for its famous Liberty prints. There is also a baby-changing area on the same floor. Open: Mon–Tues and Fri–Sat 9:20am–6pm: Wed 10am–6pm, Thurs 9:20am–7:30pm. Tube: Oxford St.

SELFRIDGES, 400 Oxford St., W1. Tel. 071/629-1234.

Clothing for both babies and children can be found on the third floor. There's also a baby-changing area there. Open: Mon–Wed and Fri–Sat 9:30am–6pm, Thurs 9:30am–8pm. Tube: Bond St. or Marble Arch.

MEN'S FASHION

BURTON STORE, 311 Oxford St., W1. Tel. 071/491-0032.

Ready-made suits here—where a man first selects his jacket, then the trousers to match in his size—are among the most reasonably priced in London. The store also sells "Champion Sport" sportswear. Open: Mon–Tues and Sat 9am–6pm, Wed and Fri 9:30am–7pm, Thurs 9:30am–8pm. Tube: Oxford Circus.

GIEVES & HAWKES, 1 Savile Row, W1. Tel. 071/434-2001.

This place has a prestigious address and a list of clients that includes the Prince of Wales, yet its prices are not the lethal tariffs of other stores on this street. It's expensive, but you get good quality, as befits a supplier to the British Royal Navy since the days of Lord Nelson. Cotton shirts, silk ties, Shetland jumpers (sweaters), and exceptional ready-to-wear and tailormade (bespoke) suits are sold. Open: Mon–Sat 9am–5:30pm. Tube: Piccadilly Circus.

WOMEN'S FASHION

BRADLEY'S, 85 Knightsbridge, SW1. Tel. 071/235-2909.
Bradley's is the best-known lingerie specialty store in London, selling only items made and designed exclusively for it. Some members of the royal family shop here. Established in the 1950s and very fashionable today, Bradley's fits "all sizes" in silk, cotton, lace, polycotton, whatever. You'll love the fluffy slippers, and the satin or silk nightgowns will make you feel like a well-accessorized movie star. Open: Mon–Tues and Thurs–Fri 9:30am–6pm, Wed 9:30am–7pm, Sat 10–6pm. Tube: Knightsbridge.

THE CHANGING ROOM, 10a Gees Court, St. Christopher's Place, W1. Tel. 071/408-1596.
This small but well-staffed shop stocks the clothing and accessories of at least a dozen designers. The establishment's expertise lies in its ability to coordinate items from different lines to create unique fashion statements for all types of women. Among the designers featured are Issey Mikaye, Betty Jackson, and Helen Storey. Open: Mon–Wed and Fri–Sat 10:30am–6:30pm, Thurs 10:30am–7:30pm. Tube: Bond St.

FENWICK OF BOND STREET, 63 New Bond St., W1. Tel. 071/629-9161.
Fenwick is a small department store that offers an excellent collection of womenswear, ranging from moderately priced ready-to-wear items to designer fashions. A wide range of lingerie (in all price ranges) is also sold here. The store dates from 1891. Open: Mon–Wed and Fri–Sat 9:30am–6pm, Thurs 9:30am–7:30pm. Tube: Bond St.

LAURA ASHLEY, 256–258 Regent St., W1. Tel. 071/437-9760.
This famous store will outfit you with flower-print Victorian dresses and easy-to-wear jersey and knitwear. Also for sale: a wide range of accessories, including belts and handbags. Open: Mon–Wed and Fri 9:30am–6pm, Thurs 9:30am–8pm, Sat 9am–6pm. Tube: Oxford Circus.

SECONDHAND DESIGNER CLOTHING

PANDORA, 16–22 Cheval Place, SW7. Tel. 071/589-5289.
A London institution since the 1940s, Pandora stands in fashionable Knightsbridge, a stone's throw from Harrods. Several times a week, chauffeurs will drive up with bundles packed anonymously by the gentry of England. One woman voted best dressed at Ascot several years ago was wearing a secondhand dress acquired at Pandora. Identities of former owners are strictly guarded, but many buyers are titillated at the thought that they might be wearing a hand-me-down of a royal person, perhaps Princess Di. Prices are

generally one-third to one-half the retail value. Chanel and Anne Klein are among the designers represented. Outfits are usually no more than two seasons old. Open: Mon–Sat 10am–6pm. Tube: Knightsbridge.

FOOD

CHARBONNEL ET WALKER LTD., One, The Royal Arcade, 28 Old Bond St., W1. Tel. 071/491-0939.

What may be the finest chocolates in the world are made here. The firm will send messages of thanks or love spelled out on the chocolates themselves. The staff of this bow-fronted shop will help you choose from the variety of centers. Ready-made presentation boxes are also available. Open: Mon–Fri 9am–5:30pm, Sat 9:30am–5pm. Tube: Green Park.

FORTNUM & MASON LTD., 181 Piccadilly, W1. Tel. 071/734-8040.

The world's most elegant grocery store, down the street from the Ritz, Fortnum & Mason, with its swallow-tailed attendants, is a British tradition dating back to 1707. In fact, the establishment likes to think that Mr. Fortnum and Mr. Mason "created a union surpassed in its importance to the human race only by the meeting of Adam and Eve."

The chocolate-and-confectionery department is on the ground floor, while the upper floors will tempt you with china and glass, leather goods and stationery, antiques of all kinds, and more.

In the Mezzanine Restaurant, you can mingle at lunch with caviar-and-champagne shoppers; the pastries are calorie-loaded but divine. The Fountain Restaurant has both store and street entrances (Jermyn Street), and is open late for the benefit of theatergoers. The St. James's Room Restaurant on the fourth floor is open during normal store hours. Open: Store, Mon–Sat 9:30am–6pm; Fountain Restaurant, Mon–Sat 9:30am–11:30pm. Tube: Piccadilly Circus or Green Park.

TEA HOUSE, 15A Neal St., WC2. Tel. 071/240-7539.

This shop sells everything associated with tea, tea drinking, and teatime. It boasts more than 70 quality teas and ptisans (tisanes), including whole-fruit blends, the best tea of China (Gunpowder, jasmine with flowers), India (Assam leaf, choice Darjeeling), Japan (Genmaicha green), and Sri Lanka (pure Ceylon), plus such longtime English favorites as Earl Grey. The shop also offers novelty teapots and mugs, among other items. Open: Mon–Sat 10am–7pm. Tube: Covent Garden.

IRISH WARES

IRISH SHOP, 11 Duke St., W1. Tel. 071/935-1366.

For more than 25 years, this small family business has been selling a wide variety of articles shipped directly from Ireland. The staff will be happy to welcome you and answer any questions on the selection of out-of-the-ordinary tweeds, traditional linens, hand-knit Aran fisherman's sweaters, and Celtic jewelry. Merchandise includes Belleek and Royal Tara china, tapes of Irish music, souvenirs, and gift items. Waterford crystal in all styles and types is a specialty. Open: Mon–Wed and Fri–Sat 9:30am–5:30pm, Thurs 9:30am–7pm. Tube: Bond St.

JEWELRY

SANFORD BROTHERS LTD., 3 Holborn Bars, Old Elizabeth Houses, EC1. Tel. 071/405-2352.
A family firm, Sanford Brothers Ltd. has been in business since 1923. It sells all manner of jewelry, both modern and Victorian; silver of all kinds; and a fine selection of clocks and watches. The Old Elizabethan buildings that house the shop are among the sights of old London. Open: Mon–Fri 10am–4:30pm. Tube: Chancery Lane.

MARKETS

STREET MARKETS

Markets are considerably more ancient than shops as a retailing medium. Most of the Old World's large cities began as market towns, and in London you still have a few thriving survivors of the open-air trading tradition. They're great fun to visit, even if you don't plan on buying anything. But you'll probably go home with something.

Berwick Street Market (tube: Oxford Circus or Tottenham Court Road) may be the only street market in the world that is flanked by two rows of strip clubs, porno stores, and adult-movie dens. Don't let that put you off, however. Humming six days a week in the scarlet heart of Soho, this array of stalls and booths sells probably the best and cheapest fruit and vegetables in town. It also sells ancient records that may turn out to be collectors' items, tapes, books, and old magazines. It's open Monday to Saturday from 8am to 5pm.

After four centuries **Covent Garden,** the most famous market in all England—possibly all Europe—has gone suburban. It followed the lead of Les Halles in Paris and shifted to more contemporary but less colorful quarters south of the River Thames. The move relieves some of the wild congestion it generated, but a lot of memories have been left behind. The new Covent Garden (tube: Covent Garden) has developed into an impressive array of shops, pubs, and other attractions, such as smaller markets where you can buy just about anything.

Jubilee Market Hall, Covent Garden Piazza, WC2, is open seven days a week, offering antiques and bric-a-brac on Monday from 7am to 5pm. General goods (not necessarily antique) are featured Tuesday through Friday from 9am to 5pm. Items range from perfumes to household goods. London's largest craft market is held here every Saturday and Sunday, usually from 9am to 5pm.

The **Apple Market,** Covent Garden Piazza, WC2, almost qualifies as street entertainment. A fun, bustling place, it is filled with traders selling . . . well, everything. Much is what the English call "collectible nostalgia." Some items are generally worthless (of the type you capriciously give to "the man who has everything"), while other pieces are genuinely worthy, such as interesting brass door knockers. Wander through the market and keep your sales resistance up. Some of the vendors are mighty persuasive. It is open for antiques on Monday from 9am to 5pm and for crafts on Tuesday through Saturday from 9am to 5pm.

Off Neal Street runs a narrow road leading to **Neal's Yard** (tube: Covent Garden), a mews of warehouses that seem to retain some of the old London atmosphere. The open warehouses display such goods as vegetables, health foods, fresh-baked breads, cakes, sandwiches, and, in an immaculate dairy, the largest variety of flavored cream cheeses you are likely to encounter.

While in the area, you can pick up a copy of *In and Around Covent Garden,* which not only has a map but also will help you quickly locate the type of merchandise you might be seeking—everything from crafts to herbalists, from fashion to antique watches. Beauty salons, hairdressers, health clubs, chemists, and the like are listed here, along with a selection of restaurants and news of special exhibitions.

Open Monday through Friday from 11am to 5pm, the lively **Leather Lane Market** (tube: Chancery Lane) offers a good variety of items for sale: fruit from carts, vegetables, books, men's shirts and sweaters, and women's clothing. There are no try-ons at this outdoor market.

New Caledonian Market is commonly known as the **Bermondsey Market** because of its location on the corner of Long Lane and Bermondsey Street (tube: London Bridge, then bus 78 or walk down Bermondsey Street); at the extreme east end, it begins at Tower Bridge Road. It is one of Europe's outstanding street markets in the number and quality of the antiques and other goods offered. The stalls are well known, and many dealers come into London from the country. Prices are generally lower here than at Portobello Road and the other street markets. This market gets under way on Friday at 7am and—with the bargains gone by 9am—closes at noon.

Petticoat Lane (tube: Liverpool Street) still functions only on Sunday from 9am to 2pm. There's furious bargaining for every conceivable kind of object, from old clothing to just plain junk, and the air vibrates with voices, canned and human. In spite of the market's famous reputation, many readers have found that a Sunday-morning trip here is no longer worth the effort.

A magnet for collectors of virtually anything, **Portobello Market** (tube: Ladbroke Grove or Notting Hill Gate) is mainly a Saturday happening from 6am (it's best to go early) to 5pm. Once known mainly for fruit and vegetables (still sold, incidentally, throughout the week), Portobello in the past four decades has become synonymous with antiques. But don't take the stallholder's word for it that the mildewed fiddle he's holding is a genuine Stradivarius left to him in the will of his Italian great-uncle. It might just as well have been "nicked" from an East End pawnshop.

The market is divided into three major sections. The most crowded is the antiques section, running between Colville Road and Chepstow Villas to the south. (*Warning:* A great concentration of pickpockets is in this area.) The second section (and the oldest part) is the "fruit and veg" market, lying between Westway and Colville Road. In the third and final section, Londoners operate a flea market, selling bric-a-brac and lots of secondhand goods they didn't really want in the first place. But it still makes interesting fun for a look-around.

From many of the stores, the serious collector can pick up a copy of helpful official guide, *Saturday Antique Market: Portobello Road & Westbourne Grove,* published by the Portobello Antique Dealers Association. It lists where to find what, ranging from music boxes to militaria, from lace to 19th-century photographs. The serious collector can visit any of some 90 antiques and art shops during the week when the temporary market is closed.

ANTIQUES MARKETS

ALFIES ANTIQUE MARKET, 13–25 Church St., NW8. Tel. 071/723-6066.

This is the biggest and one of the cheapest covered markets in London, and it's where many dealers come to buy. It contains more than 370 stalls, showrooms, and workshops on 35,000 square feet of floorspace, plus an enormous 70-unit basement area. Open: Tues–Sat 10am–6pm. Tube: Marylebone.

ANTIQUARIUS, Antiques Centre, 131–141 King's Rd., SW3. Tel. 071/351-5353.

Antiquarius echoes the artistic diversity of King's Road. More than 120 dealers offer specialized merchandise, usually of the small, domestic variety. In the main, merchandise tends to run to period clothing, porcelain, silver, first-edition books, boxes, clocks, prints, and paintings, with an occasional piece of antique furniture. You'll also find a lot of items from the 1950s. Open: Mon–Sat 10am–6pm. Tube: Sloane Sq.

BOND STREET ANTIQUES CENTRE, 124 New Bond St., W1.

In the heart of London's finest shopping district, the stores grouped together in this center enjoy a reputation for being London's finest center for antique jewelry, silver, watches, porcelain, glass, and Asian antiques and paintings. Open: Tues–Sat 10am–6pm. Tube: Bond St. or Green Park.

CHENIL GALLERIES, 181–183 King's Rd., SW3. Tel. 071/351-5353.

The permanent exhibition of an Epstein statue reflects the artistic nature of this establishment, opened in 1979. The operators seem to specialize in art nouveau and art deco objects, along with plenty of jewelry, but the various galleries have a wide range of merchandise, including Asian carpets, collectors' dolls and teddy bears, as well as prints and maps, fine porcelain, chess sets, some period furniture, and 17th- and 18th-century paintings. Open: Mon–Sat 10am–6pm. Tube: Sloane Sq.

GRAYS and **GRAYS IN THE MEWS,** 58 Davies St. and 1–7 Davies Mews, W1. Tel. 071/629-7034.

These antiques markets are housed in two old buildings that have been converted into walk-in stands with independent dealers. The term *antique* here covers items from oil paintings to, say, the 1894 edition of the Encyclopaedia Britannica. Also sold here are exquisite antique jewelry; silver; gold; antiquarian books; maps and prints; drawings; bronzes and ivories; arms and armor; Victorian and Edwardian toys; furniture; art nouveau and art deco items; antique luggage; antique lace; scientific instruments; craftsmen's tools; and Asian, Persian, and Islamic pottery, porcelain, miniatures, and antiquities. There is also a whole floor of repair workshops and a Bureau de Change, plus a café-restaurant. Open: Mon–Fri 10am–6pm. Tube: Bond St.

MALL AT CAMDEN PASSAGE, Islington, N1.

This mall contains one of Britain's greatest concentration of antiques businesses. Here, housed in individual shop units, you'll find some 35 dealers specializing in fine furniture, porcelain, and silver. Open: Tues and Thurs–Fri 10am–5pm, Wed 7:30am–5pm, Sat 9am–6pm. Tube: Angel.

MUSIC

VIRGIN MEGASTORE, 14–16 Oxford St., W1. Tel. 071/ 631-1234.

If a recording has just been released—and if it's worth hearing in the first place—chances are this store carries it. It's like a giant "grocery store" of recordings, and you get to hear the release on a headphone before making a purchase. Even the rock stars themselves come here on occasion to pick up new releases. A large selection of classical and jazz recordings is also sold as are computer software and games. In between selecting your favorites, you can enjoy a coffee at the café, perhaps purchase an airline ticket from the Virgin Atlantic office. Another Megastore is at 527 Oxford St. Open: Mon–Sat 9:30am–8pm. Tube: Tottenham Court Rd.

OLD SILVER & PLATE

STANLEY LESLIE, 15 Beauchamp Place, SW3. Tel. 071/ 589-2333.

Behind the cramped and black-painted, big-windowed storefront of Stanley Leslie lies a staggering array of Georgian, Victorian, and early 20th-century silver. It's just the place to spend hours ferreting around for a special present. The quality is high—and the owner, Gary Hyams, knows just what he's got and what constitutes a fair price. Open: Mon–Fri 9am–5pm, Sat 9am–1pm. Tube: Knightsbridge.

PHILATELY

NATIONAL POSTAL MUSEUM, King Edward Building, King Edward St. (without number), EC1. Tel. 071/ 239-5420.

The museum houses a magnificent collection of postage stamps and allied material. It also sells postcards illustrating the collection and has a distinctive Maltese cross postmark first used on the Penny Black. Open: Mon–Thurs 9:30am–4:30pm, Fri 9:30am–4pm. Tube: St. Paul's.

POSTERS

LONDON TRANSPORT MUSEUM SHOP, Covent Garden (without number), WC2. Tel. 071/379-6344.

This museum carries a wide range of reasonably priced posters. The London Underground maps in their original size as seen at every tube station can be purchased here. This unique shop also carries books, cards, T-shirts, and other souvenirs. Open: Daily 10am–5:45pm. Closed: Dec 24–26. Tube: Covent Garden.

SHOES

CHARLES JOURDAN, 39–43 Brompton Rd., SW3. Tel. 071/581-3333.

Charles Jourdan carries one of the largest range of women's shoes in London, including a variety of styles. Shoe fanatics could run wild here, especially if they see some of the more unusual designs. Open: Mon–Tues and Thurs–Sat 10am–6:30pm, Wed 10am–7pm. Tube: Knightsbridge.

CHURCH'S, 143 Brompton Rd., SW3. Tel. 071/589-9136.

Top-quality shoes have been turned out by these famous shoemakers since 1873, when the company was founded at Northampton. A trio of brothers (Alfred, Thomas, William) started what has become a tradition among well-outfitted English gents who stamp around London in their Church's shoes. Of course, the company, always a bastion of English tradition, has changed with the tides of style and now offers more modern selections along with their traditional footwear. There is also a fashionable selection of shoes for women. Open: Mon–Fri 9am–5:30pm, Sat 9am–5pm. Tube: Knightsbridge.

LILLEY & SKINNERS, 360 Oxford St., W1. Tel. 071/629-6381.

Lilley & Skinners is the biggest shoe store in the world, displaying its merchandise throughout four floors. It markets shoes under its own label as well as those of famous designers. All sizes are fitted here, including extra-small and extra large, for both men and women. Prices, likewise, are wide-ranging. Open: Mon–Wed and Fri 9:30am–6:30pm, Thurs 9:30am–8pm, Sat 9am–6pm. Tube: Bond St.

NATURAL SHOE STORE, 21 Neal St., WC2. Tel. 071/836-5254.

This store sells all manner of comfort and quality footwear, from Birkenstock to the best of the British classics, for men, women, and children. It will also repair shoes. Open: Mon–Tues and Sat 10am–6pm, Wed–Fri 10am–7pm. Tube: Covent Garden.

SOUVENIRS

COVENT GARDEN GENERAL STORE, 111 Long Acre, WC2. Tel. 071/240-0331.

The General Store offers thousands of ideas for gifts and souvenirs at reasonable prices. It is ideally situated in Covent Garden, and because of the entertainment nature of the area, the store offers extended trading hours. It also features the Covent Garden General Store Restaurant, serving salads from a salad bar, jacket potatoes, chili con carne, and macaroni and cheese, among other items. The restaurant is located downstairs. Open: Store, Mon–Sat 10am–midnight, Sun 11am–7pm; restaurant, Mon–Sat 10am–7pm, Sun noon–6pm. Tube: Covent Garden.

SPORTING GOODS

LILLYWHITES LTD., 24–26 Lower Regent St., Piccadilly Circus, SW1. Tel. 071/915-4000.

Britain's biggest and most famous sports store, Lillywhites has floor after floor of sports clothing, equipment, and footwear. Established in 1863, it also offers new and exciting ranges of stylish and fashionable leisurewear for both men and women. Open: Mon–Fri 9:30am–7pm, Sat 9:30am–6pm. Tube: Piccadilly Circus.

TOILETRIES

FLORIS, 89 Jermyn St., SW1. Tel. 071/930-2885.

A variety of toilet articles and fragrances can be found in the floor-to-ceiling mahogany cabinets that line Floris's walls and are considered architectural curiosities in their own right. They were installed relatively late in the establishment's history (that is, 1851), long after the shop had received its Royal Warrants as suppliers of toilet articles to the king and queen. The business was established in 1730 by a Minorcan entrepreneur, Juan Floris, who brought from his Mediterranean home a technique for extracting fragrances from local flowers. Fashionable residents of St. James's flocked to his shop, purchasing his soaps, perfumes, and grooming aids. Today, you can buy essences of flowers grown in English gardens, like stephanotis, rose geranium, lily of the valley, and carnation. Other items are men's cologne and badger-hair shaving brushes. Open: Mon–Fri 9:30am–5:30pm, Sat 9:30am–4pm. Tube: Piccadilly Circus.

PENHALIGONS's, 41 Wellington St., WC2. Tel. 071/836-2150.

This Victorian perfumery was established in 1870, holding Royal Warrants to HRH Duke of Edinburgh and HRH Prince of Wales. All items sold are exclusive to Penhaligon's. It offers a large selection of perfumes, after-shaves, soaps, and bath oils for women and men. Gifts include antique-silver scent bottles, grooming accessories, and leather traveling requisites. Open: Mon–Fri 10am–6pm, Sat 10am–5:30pm. Tube: Covent Garden.

TRAVEL CENTER

BRITISH AIRWAYS FIRST, 156 Regent St., W1. Tel. 071/434-4700.

The retail flagship of British Airways, housed on three floors, offers not only worldwide travel and ticketing but also a wide range of services and shops, including a clinic for immunization, a pharmacy, a Bureau de Change, a passport and visa service, and a theater-booking desk. The ground floor offers luggage and other quality goods. There are various other services and a coffee shop. Passengers with hand baggage only can check in here for a BA flight. Open: Mon–Fri 9am–7pm, Sat 9am–5pm. Tube: Piccadilly Circus.

LONDON NIGHTS

The London nightlife establishments cover the entire social spectrum of the city, from the sleekest haunts to the plainest proletarian strongholds, from overstuffed Victorian plush palaces to re-creations of the decor of the Edwardian era, often in formerly dilapidated buildings. The range of entertainment is equally wide: from graveyard silence to blasting rock bands, nude female performers, and even lunchtime and evening theater performances. Also popular in London are drag shows featuring female impersonators.

Geographically, about 90% of the bright lights burn in the area roughly defined as the **West End.** The core of this region is **Piccadilly Circus,** which, with Coventry Street running down to Leicester Square, resembles New York's Broadway. To the north lies **Soho,** chockablock with entertainment in various hues of scarlet. To the northeast is the theaterland of **Covent Garden,** to the east **Trafalgar Square,** and to the west the fashionable and expensive night world of **Mayfair.**

Two weekly publications, *Time Out* and *What's On in London,* give full entertainment listings. They are available at newsstands and contain information on restaurants and nightclubs, as well as theaters. Daily newspapers, notably *The Times* and *The Telegraph,* also provide listings.

Nightlife in London can be divided into pre- and postmidnight. This "midnight curtain" operates against simple nighttime pleasures. It prevents you, for instance, from just dropping into a place for a drink (you must have something to eat with a drink served after 11pm). It doesn't prevent you, after hours, from paying a cover charge (frequently disguised as a membership fee) and enjoying a stage show, taking a spin on a dance floor, trying your luck at a gambling table, eating a five-course meal, or drinking yourself into oblivion.

Many of the places I'll describe in this chapter have some kind of front-door policy that passes as membership enrollment. What it amounts to is a so-called temporary membership, which satisfies the letter (if not the spirit) of the law and enables you to get in without delay. In many cases the temporary membership fee is deducted from the cost of dinner. There is, however, no hard-and-fast rule.

At this point I'd better add a word for the benefit of male travelers. London's club world is full of "hostesses." Their purpose is to make you buy things—from drinks to dolls and cigarettes—and they can shoot up your tab to much more than you intended to spend. However, London's recognized meeting spots, especially for the younger set, are ballrooms and dance clubs, neither of which employ hostesses.

1. THE PERFORMING ARTS

SOUTH BANK CENTRE, Royal Festival Hall, South Bank, SE1. Tel. 071/928-8800.

In recent years, London's musical focus has shifted to a uniquely specialized complex of buildings across Waterloo Bridge called South Bank Centre. There are three of the most stylish, comfortable, and acoustically perfect concert structures in the world—Royal Festival Hall, Queen Elizabeth Hall, and Purcell Room. More than 1,200 performances a year are presented, including classical music, ballet, jazz, popular music, and contemporary dance. Also here is the internationally famous Hayward Gallery, both contemporary and historical art. Recent exhibitions have included work by Andy Warhol, Pierre Auguste Renoir, Jasper Johns, Leonardo da Vinci, Diego Rivera, and Le Corbusier.

Royal Festival Hall opens at 10am every day and offers an extensive range of things to see and do. There are free exhibitions in the foyers and free lunchtime music at 12:30pm. The Poetry Library is open from 11am to 8pm, as well as shops providing a wide selection of books, records, and crafts.

The Festival Buffet offers a wide variety of food at reasonable prices, and there are numerous bars throughout the foyers. The Review Restaurant provides both lunch and dinner as well as a spectacular view of the River Thames. A preconcert menu is available; reservations are recommended by calling 071/921-0800.

Tickets: £5–£30.50 ($7.50–$45.80); credit cards accepted.
Open: Box office, daily 10am–9pm. **Tube:** Waterloo and Embankment Station.

LONDON COLISEUM, St. Martin's Lane (without number), WC2. Tel. 071/836-3161 (reservations), 071/240-5258 (inquiries and credit-card bookings).

The home of the **English National Opera,** this is the city's largest and most splendid theater, built in 1904 as a variety theater and converted into an opera house in 1968. The ENO performs a wide range of works, from great classics to operetta to world premieres, and every performance is in English. With a repertory of 18 to 20 productions, it plays five or six nights a week.

Tickets: £6–£10 ($9–$15) balcony, £10.50–£42.50 ($15.80–$63.80) upper dress circle or stalls.
Open: Performances usually Aug–June. **Tube:** Charing Cross or Leicester Square.

BARBICAN CENTRE, Silk St. (without number), the City, EC2. Tel. 071/638-8891.

Barbican Centre is said to be Western Europe's largest arts complex. It was created to make a perfect setting in which to enjoy good music and theater from comfortable and roomy seating. In addition to the theater, which is the London home of the Royal Shakespeare Company, the concert hall is the permanent home of the **London Symphony Orchestra** and host to visiting musicians from all over the world. There are also a studio theater known as The Pit; the Barbican Art Gallery, a showcase for the visual arts; exhibition spaces; Cinemas One and Two, showing recent mainstream films; and The Barbican Library, a general lending library with strong emphasis on the arts. In addition, you'll find one of London's largest plant houses, The Conservatory. There are four restaurants and a handful of bars.

Tickets: £5–£28 ($7.50–$42.00).
Open: Box office, Mon–Sat 9am–11pm, Sun noon–11pm.
Tube: Barbican or Moorgate.

ROYAL ALBERT HALL, Kensington Gore (without number), SW7. Tel. 071/589-8212.

Opened in 1871 and dedicated to the memory of Victoria's consort, Prince Albert, the building encircles one of the world's largest auditoriums, with a seating capacity of 5,200. Home since 1941 to the **BBC Promenade Concerts,** the famous eight-week festival of classical music, it is also a popular venue for music by such stars as Eric Clapton and Shirley Bassey, or perhaps the latest in rock and pop. Sporting events figure strongly here, including boxing and tennis.

Tickets: £2.50–£3 ($3.75–$4.50), depending on show.
Open: Box office, daily 9am–9pm. **Tube:** South Kensington.

LONDON PALLADIUM, Argyll St. (without number), W1. Tel. 071/494-5100.

This is a show-business legend. Performers from Britain, Europe, and America have "arrived" when they've appeared here. In days of yore, the Palladium has starred Frank Sinatra, Judy Garland, Shirley MacLaine, Andy Williams, Perry Como, Julie Andrews, Tom Jones, Sammy Davis, Jr., and many others.

Tickets: Prices depend entirely on show.
Open: Show times vary. **Tube:** Oxford Circus.

ROYAL OPERA HOUSE, Bow St. (without number), Covent Garden, WC2. Tel. 071/240-1911.

The central shrine of London opera and ballet is the Royal Opera House, a classical building on Bow Street (actually the northeast corner of Covent Garden) and the home of the Royal Opera and the Royal Ballet, the capital's leading international opera and ballet companies. Newspapers give details on performances. The Opera House's box office is at 48 Floral St., WC2 (tel. 071/240-1066).

Tickets: £3.30–£124 ($5–$186) ballet, £1.65–£54 ($2.50–$81) opera.
Open: Box office, Mon–Sat 10am–8pm. **Tube:** Covent Garden.

SADLER'S WELLS, Rosebery Ave. (without number), EC1. Tel. 071/278-8916.

Sadler's Wells is in a theater that has stood here since 1683, on the site of a well that was once known for the healing powers of its waters. Today, the theater is a showcase for British and foreign ballet and modern dance companies and international opera.

Tickets: £5–£35 ($7.50–$52.50)
Open: Performances usually 7:30pm. **Tube:** Angel.

WIGMORE HALL, 36 Wigmore St., W1. Tel. 071/935-2141.

An intimate auditorium, Wigmore Hall is where you'll hear excellent recitals and concerts. After an expansion of its facilities, it reopened in 1992. There are regular series of song recitals, piano and chamber music, early and baroque music, and concerts featuring composers or themes. A free list of the month's programs is available from Wigmore.

Tickets: £4.50–£40 ($6.75–$60).

Open: Performances nightly, plus Sun Morning Coffee Concerts and also concerts on Sun at 4 or 7pm. **Tube:** Bond Street.

THE LONDON THEATER
HOURS & TICKETS

London theaters generally start and finish earlier than their American cousins. Evening performances start between 7:30 and 8:30pm, midweek matinees at 2:30 and 3pm, Saturday matinee at 5:45pm. Many theaters offer additional trimmings in the shape of licensed bars on the premises and hot coffee during intermissions, called "intervals."

Matinees are performed Tuesday through Saturday and they are cheaper, of course, than regular performances. Prices for London shows vary widely—usually from £10 to £35 ($15 to $52.50), depending on the seat.

Many theaters will accept telephone bookings at regular prices if you have a credit card. They will hold the tickets for you at the box office, where you present your credit card when you pick them up at show time.

Finally, there's economy. London theater prices are—by U.S. standards—very reasonable. The **Leicester Square Half-Price Ticket Booth,** Leicester Square, WC2 (tube: Leicester Square), sells theater tickets on the day of a performance for half price (cash only), plus up to a £1.50 ($2.25) service charge. It's open Monday through Saturday from noon for matinee performances and from 2:30 to 6:30pm for evening performances. The shows for which tickets are available are displayed at the booth, so you can make up your mind on what to see as you wait in line.

Visitors interested in ordering theater tickets days, weeks, or months in advance can contact **Edwards & Edwards,** 156 Shaftesbury Ave., WC2 (tel. 071/379-5822). Tickets to almost anything in London can be arranged in advance by telephone. (In most cases, a personal visit is not necessary.) Tickets will be mailed or delivered to the box office of any particular theater, usually with a service charge of 10% to 20% added. Some North Americans opt to order tickets for London plays through Edwards & Edwards' New York office, 1 Times Square Plaza, New York, NY 10036 (tel. 212/944-0290 in New York City, or toll free 800/223-6108 from the rest of the U.S.).

On the day of any particular London performance, tickets are sometimes reduced in price and sold through discount outlets like **Theatre Tonight** (tel. 071/753-0333), a division of Edwards & Edwards. Personal visits to Theatre Tonight are not encouraged or necessary, and only tickets for performances that day are sold, but with a telephone and a credit card (VISA or MasterCard), you'll pay only the cost of the ticket and sometimes less, depending on the popularity of the show. Tickets are picked up at the theater before the show begins. Theatre Tonight's switchboard is open Monday to Saturday from 11am to 5:45pm. This company has a somewhat greater range of seats than the Leicester Square Half-Price Ticket Booth (see above), which only rarely has tickets for the big musicals.

If you want to see specific shows, particularly hits, you'll have to reserve in advance through one of the many London ticket agencies, including **Keith Prowse/First Call** (tel. 071/836-9001). For various locations near you, look under "Keith" in the telephone book. This agency has an office in the United States, where you can reserve weeks or even months in advance for hit shows. Contact Keith Prowse, 234 W. 44th St., New York, NY 10036 (tel. 212/398-1430, or toll free 800/669-8687). The fee for booking a ticket is £2.30 to £7 ($3.45 to $10.50) in London or $10 to $20 in New York.

One of the most sure-fire ticket agents is **British Airways,** which has some of the best seats available for London productions (including musicals), Stratford-upon-Avon, and the Edinburgh Festival. The reservation service is available only to BA customers. For information and reservations, call toll free 800/AIRWAYS in the U.S.

Warning: Beware of "scalpers" who hang out in front of hit shows at London theaters. Even if their tickets are valid—and there are many reports of forged tickets—they charge very high prices.

MAJOR CONCERT & PERFORMANCE HALLS

Barbican Centre (tel. 071/638-8891)
London Coliseum (tel. 071/836-3161 or 240-5258)
London Palladium (tel. 071/494-5100)
Royal Albert Hall (tel. 071/589-8212)
Royal National Theatre (tel. 071/928-2033)
Royal Opera House (tel. 071/240-1911)
South Bank Centre (including Royal Festival Hall; tel. 071/928-8800)

THEATERS

BARBICAN THEATRE, in the Barbican Centre, Silk St. (without number), Barbican, EC2. Tel. 071/638-8891.
This is the London home of the Royal Shakespeare Company, one of the world's finest theater companies. The central core of its work remains, of course, the plays of William Shakespeare. It also presents a wide-ranging program of three different productions each week in the Barbican Theatre—the 1,200-seat main auditorium, with excellent sightlines throughout, thanks to a raked orchestra—and in The Pit, the small studio space where much of the company's new writing is presented.

Tickets: Barbican Theatre, £7–£21.50 ($10.50–$32.25); The Pit, £11.50 ($17.25) matinees, £13.50 ($20.25) evening performances.

Open: Box office, Mon–Sat 9am–11pm, Sun noon–11pm.
Tube: Barbican or Moorgate.

FORTUNE, Russell St. (without number), Covent Garden, WC2. Tel. 071/836-2238.
A part of the ancient and odd theater concentration around Covent Garden, the Fortune is an intimate house of 440 seats.

Tickets: £7–£18 ($10.50–$27).
Open: Evening performances Mon–Sat 8pm; matinees Tues 3pm and Sat 4pm. **Tube:** Covent Garden.

GLOBE, 33 Shaftesbury Ave., W1. Tel. 071/494-5065.
The Globe has only a nominal connection with Shakespeare's playhouse (which was by the Thames); this is one of a row of theaters on the same street, leading off Piccadilly Circus. Dramas and comedies are presented here.

Tickets: £7.50–£20 ($11.25–$30).

Open: Check daily press for shows and times of performances. **Tube:** Piccadilly Circus.

HER MAJESTY'S, Haymarket (without number), W1. Tel. 071/494-5400.

Big, plush, and ornate, this is one of London's traditional homes for top musicals—located on what used to be "the street for scarlet women."

Tickets: £8.50–£28 ($12.75–$42).

Open: Evening performances Mon–Sat 7:45pm; matinees Wed and Sat 3pm. **Tube:** Piccadilly Circus.

OLD VIC, Waterloo Rd. (without number), SE1. Tel. 071/928-2651, or 071/928-7616 (box office).

The facade and some of the interior of this 170-year-old theater has been restored to its original early 19th-century style. Also, the proscenium arch has been moved back, the stage has been trebled in size, and more seats and stage boxes have been added. It is air-conditioned and contains five bars. It presents short seasons of varied plays, and several subscription offerings have been introduced.

Tickets: Plays £5–£20 ($7.50–$30); musicals £8–£30 ($12–$45). **Tube:** Waterloo.

OPEN AIR, Inner Circle, Regent's Park, NW1. Tel. 071/486-2431.

As the name indicates, this is an outdoor theater, right in Regent's Park. The setting is idyllic, and the longest theater bar in London provides both drink and food. Presentations are mainly Shakespeare, usually in period costume. Both seating and acoustics are excellent. If it rains, you're given tickets for another performance.

Tickets: £6.50–£15.50 ($9.75–$23.25).

Open: Performances May 28–Sept 11, evenings 8pm, matinees Wed, Thurs, and Sat 2:30pm. **Tube:** Baker St.

ROYAL COURT THEATRE, Sloane Sq. (without number), Chelsea, SW1. Tel. 071/730-1745.

This is the place that caused a sensation at the turn of the century by presenting plays by George Bernard Shaw. In the 1950s it ushered in, with no less of a stir, the New Wave of British plays by presenting John Osborne's *Look Back in Anger*. As home to the English Stage Company, it still presents "fringe productions" in its experimental theater upstairs; call the theater for programs and hours. The main theater downstairs features plays by better-known authors and new interpretations of the classics, among other offerings.

Tickets: £5 ($7.50) all seats upstairs; downstairs £5 ($7.50) all seats Mon, £9–£12 ($13.50–$18) Tues–Sat, £5–£18 ($7.50–$27) Sat matinees.

Open: Main theater, evening performances Mon–Sat 8pm, matinees Sat 4pm. **Tube:** Sloane Sq.

ROYAL NATIONAL THEATRE, South Bank (without number), SE1. Tel. 071/928-2033.

Home of one of the world's greatest stage companies, the Royal National Theatre is not one but three theaters—the Olivier, reminiscent of a Greek amphitheater with its open stage; the more traditional Lyttelton; and the Cottesloe, with its flexible stage and seating. The National presents the finest in world theater from classic drama to award-winning new plays, from comedy to musicals to shows for young people, offering the choice of at least six plays at any one time. The National is also a full-time theater center, featuring an unrivaled selection of bars, cafés, and restaurants, free foyer music and exhibitions, short early-evening performances, bookshops, backstage tours, riverside walks, and terraces. You can have a three-course meal in Ovations, the National's restaurant; enjoy a light meal in the brasserie-style Terrace Café; or have a snack in one of the coffee bars.

Tickets: £9–£20 ($13.50–$30); midweek matinees, Sat matinees, and previews cheaper. **Tube:** Waterloo, Embankment, or Charing Cross.

THEATRE ROYAL DRURY LANE, Catherine St. (without number), Covent Garden, WC2. Tel. 071/494-5060.

Drury Lane is one of the oldest and most prestigious establishments in town, crammed with traditions, not all of them venerable. This is the fourth theater on this site, dating from 1812. The first was built in 1663, and Nell Gwynne, the rough-tongued cockney lass who became Charles II's mistress, used to sell oranges under the long colonnade in front. Nearly every star of the London stage has played here at some time. It has a wide-open repertoire but leans toward musicals, including long-running hits. Guided tours may be arranged through George Hoare, the theater historian, call 071/836-3352.

Tickets: £8.50–£28.50 ($12.75–$42.75).

Open: Box office, Mon–Sat 10am–8pm. Evening performances Mon–Sat 7:45pm; matinees Wed and Sat 3pm. **Tube:** Covent Garden or Holborn.

YOUNG VIC, 66 The Cut, Waterloo, SE1. Tel. 071/928-6363.

The Young Vic presents classical and modern plays for theatergoers of all ages and backgrounds, but primarily for young people between 16 and 25. Recent productions have included Shakespeare, Ibsen, Arthur Miller, and specially commissioned plays for children.

Tickets: £14 ($21) adults, £7 ($10.50) students and children.

Open: Performances usually 7:30pm. **Tube:** Waterloo.

DINNER THEATER

GILBERT AND SULLIVAN EVENINGS, Mansion House at Grim's Dyke, Old Redding, Harrow Weald, Middlesex HA3 6SH. Tel. 071/954-4227.

The English Heritage Singers present Gilbert and Sullivan programs in the context of a dinner event. You arrive for cocktails in the Library Bar of the house where Gilbert once lived and worked on his charming operettas. Sullivan once visited the premises. A full Edwardian-style dinner is served, with costumed performances of the most beloved of Gilbert and Sullivan songs both during and after the meal. You can request your favorite melodies.

Prices: £32 ($48) per person.

Open: Dinner/performance every other Sun 8pm in winter; usually each Sun 8pm rest of year.

TALK OF LONDON, New London Theatre, Parker St. (without number) (off Drury Lane), WC2. Tel. 071/568-1616.

A unique theater restaurant in a unique setting, Talk of London is

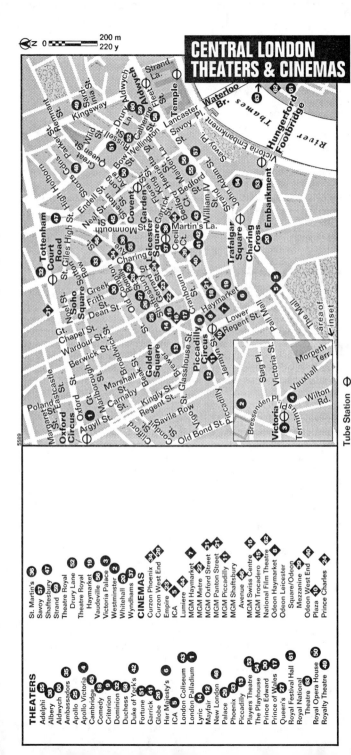

CENTRAL LONDON THEATERS & CINEMAS

Tube Station ⊖

THEATERS

Adelphi 55
Albery 57
Aldwych 60
Ambassadors 35
Apollo 7
Apollo Victoria 4
Cambridge 18
Comedy 9
Criterion 32
Dominion 32
Duchess 58
Duke of York's 56
Fortune 51
Garrick 53
Globe 21
Her Majesty's 6
ICA 5
London Coliseum 43
London Palladium 1
Lyric 42
Mayfair 12
New London 49
Palace 14
Phoenix 13
Piccadilly 53
Players Theatre 54
The Playhouse 38
Prince Edward 47
Prince of Wales 61
Queen's 27
Royal Festival Hall 58
Royal National Theatre 50
Royal Opera House 49
Royalty Theatre

St. Martin's 36
Savoy 57
Shaftesbury 47
Strand 59
Theatre Royal 52
Drury Lane
Theatre Royal 19
Haymarket
Vaudeville 56
Victoria Palace 2
Westminster 20
Whitehall 37
Wyndhams

CINEMAS

Curzon Phoenix
Curzon West End 28
Empire 23
ICA 5
Lumiere 44
MGM Haymarket 47
MGM Metre
MGM Oxford Street 31
MGM Panton Street 41
MGM Piccadilly
MGM Shaftesbury
Avenue
MGM Swiss Centre 16
MGM Trocadero 15
National Film Theatre 62
Odeon Haymarket 8
Odeon Leicester
Square/Odeon
Mezzanine 39
Odeon West End 40
Plaza
Prince Charles 24

situated in the heart and soul of London theaterland. Sitting in a circular layout on varying floor levels, everyone has an uninterrupted view of the show. Talk of London offers a complete evening's entertainment—three-course dinner, dancing to a show band, and international cabaret at 9:45pm. Only drinks are not included in the price. Reservations are essential.

Admission: (including dinner): £36 ($54) Sun–Thurs, £39 ($58.50) Fri–Sat.

Open: Six nights a week (different nights each week—so call) 7:30pm–midnight.

2. THE CLUB & MUSIC SCENE

NIGHTCLUBS/CABARETS

CAMDEN PALACE, 1A Camden High St., NW1. Tel. 071/ 387-0428.

Camden Palace is housed in what was originally a theater. It draws an over-18 crowd who flock in various costumes and energy levels according to the night of the week. Since it offers a variety of music styles, it's best to phone in advance to see if that evening's musical genre appeals to your taste. Styles range from rhythm and blues to what young rock experts call "boilerhouse," "garage music," "acid funk," "hip-hop," and "twist and shout." A live band performs only on Tuesday. There's a restaurant if you get the munchies. Open: Tues–Wed and Fri–Sat 9pm–2:30am. Prices: Bottle of lager £2.20 ($3.30). Tube: Camden Town or Mornington Crescent.

Admission: £5 ($7.50) Tues–Wed, £10 ($15) Fri–Sat.

CSAR RICARDO, 9 Young St., W8. Tel. 071/937-9403.

Just off Kensington High Street, this is a good place to go for a widely varied repertoire of music, including rock. Patrons come from many countries and backgrounds and span a wide age spectrum. Open: Mon–Sat 10pm–12:30am, Sun 9pm–2am. Prices: Beer £2.50 ($3.75). Tube: High St. Kensington.

Admission: £3–£6 ($4.50–$9).

L'HIRONDELLE, 99–101 Regent St., W1. Tel. 071/734-6666.

L'Hirondelle stands in the heart of the West End and puts on some of the most lavish floor shows in town. What's more, you can dine, drink, and dance without a "temporary membership" or an entrance fee. The shows are full-scale revues and go on at 11pm and 1am. Dancing to one of the few live bands in London begins at 9:30pm. Dancing-dining partners are available. The club offers a three-course dinner for £30 ($45) per person, including VAT and service charges, or you can choose from their very large à la carte menu; a bottle of wine costs from £23 ($34.50). Open: Mon–Sat 8:30pm–3:30am. Tube: Piccadilly Circus.

Admission: £10 ($15) cover charge for nondiners.

RHEINGOLD CLUB, Sedley Place, off 361 Oxford St., W1. Tel. 071/629-5343.

Founded in 1959, Rheingold is the oldest and most successful "singles club" in London, existing long before the term had been coined. Both couples and singles are welcome here. Set in a century-old wine cellar, the Rheingold has a restaurant, two bars, and a good-size dance floor. The main attraction is a top-class band playing Monday through Saturday (except bank holidays). There is also an occasional cabaret, usually with big-time guest stars. The club offers a tasty German dish called *Champignonschnitzel,* tender Dutch veal served with rice and peas in cream-and-mushroom sauce, costing £9 ($13.50). Excellent French and German wines are available from £10 ($15) for an *appellation contrôlée.* Open: Mon–Tues 7:30pm–1:30am, Wed–Thurs and cabaret nights 7:30pm–2am, Fri–Sat 7:30pm–2:30am. Prices: German beer £1.50 ($2.25) per half pint. Tube: Bond St.

Admission: £6 ($9) temporary membership.

TIDDY DOLS, 55 Shepherd Market, Mayfair, W1. Tel. 071/499-2357.

Housed in nine small atmospheric Georgian houses that were built around 1741, this club is named after the famous gingerbread baker and eccentric. Guests come to Tiddy Dols to enjoy such dishes as jugged hare, cock-a-leekie, plum pudding, and the original gingerbread of Tiddy Dol. While dining, they are entertained with madrigals, Noël Coward and Gilbert and Sullivan music, music-hall songs, and a town crier. In summer, there is a large pavement café with parasols and a view of the "village" of Shepherd Market; in winter, there are open fires. An à la carte dinner costing from £28 ($42) is served nightly. Dancing is restricted to special evenings. All year there is a café/wine bar serving a full menu, at lower prices, and offering sandwiches as well. Open: Mon–Sun 6pm–1am (11:30pm last arrivals); café/wine bar, noon–midnight. Prices: Drinks from £2.75 ($4.13). Tube: Green Park.

Admission: £1.55 ($2.33) cover charge.

COMEDY CLUB

THE COMEDY STORE, corner of Coventry St. and Oxendon, off Leicester Sq., W1. Tel. 0426/914433.

Set in the heart of the city's nighttime district, this is London's most visible showcase for established and rising comic talent. A prerecorded telephone message announces the various performers scheduled during the upcoming week. Even if their names are unfamiliar (highly likely), you will enjoy the spontaneity of live comedy performed before a British audience. Visitors must be more than 18; dress is casual. Reservations are accepted, and the club opens 1½ hours before each show. Open: Wed–Thurs and Sun shows at 8pm; Fri–Sat shows at 8pm and midnight. Tube: Leicester Sq. or Piccadilly Circus.

Admission: £8 ($12).

ROCK

GULLIVER'S, 15–21 Ganton St., W1. Tel. 071/499-0760.

Established 20 years ago at another location, this well-rooted club now sits within a very modern black-and-gold cellar off Carnaby Street. It specializes in American and British soul music, although an appealing blend of other styles is presented. The format ranges from "old soul" night to evenings that include swing, beat, and rap music, with doses of calypso, reggae, and soca music thrown in. Open:

Thurs 10pm–3:30am, Fri–Sat 10pm–4:30am, Sun 7pm–midnight.
Prices: Beer £2.50 ($3.75). Tube: Oxford Circus.
   Admission: £6–£8 ($9–$12).

MARQUEE, 105 Charing Cross Rd., WC2. Tel. 071/437-6603.

Marquee is considered one of the best-known centers for rock in the world. Its reputation goes back to the 1950s and another location, but it remains forever young. Groups like the Rolling Stones played at the Marquee long before they achieved world celebrity. Live bands perform Monday through Thursday from 7pm to midnight. On Friday, live bands perform from 7 to 10:30pm, then disco takes over until 3am. On Saturday, you get only recorded music from 10:30pm to 3:30am. Sunday night is for comedy, with live comedians performing from 7pm to midnight. That's when a £18 ($27) cover charge is imposed. Fortunately, you don't have to be a member—you just pay at the door. Those 18 or older can order hard drinks. Well-known musicians frequent the place regularly on nights off. Open: Mon–Thurs 7pm–midnight, Fri 7pm–3am, Sat 10:30pm–3:30pm. Tube: Leicester Sq. or Tottenham Court Rd.
   Admission: £5.50–£18 ($8.25–$27).

ROCK GARDEN RESTAURANT & ROCK MUSIC VENUE, 6–7 The Piazza, Covent Garden, WC2. Tel. 071/836-4052.

This is the place where new bands are launched, where such renowned groups as Dire Straits, Police, U2, and Stanglers all played before becoming famous. In summer, the restaurant offers outside seating in the heart of Covent Garden. A wide range of meals is offered, costing from £7 ($10.50). Both the Restaurant and the Venue are licensed for drinks. Open: Restaurant, Mon–Thurs and Sun noon–midnight, Fri–Sat noon–1am; Venue, Mon–Sat 7:30pm–3am, Sun 7:30pm–midnight. Prices: Drinks from £2 ($3). Tube: Covent Garden. Bus: Night buses from neighboring Trafalgar Sq.
   Admission: £3–£6 ($4.50–$9) at Venue.

JAZZ & BLUES

THE BASS CLEF/THE TENOR CLEF, 58 Hoxton Sq. Tel. 071/729-2476.

Both clubs are in the same sprawling brick-fronted building that was an important hospital in the early 20th century. Bass Clef is a multimusic venue, whereas Tenor Clef (located one floor above street level) presents traditional jazz and a style labeled fusion jazz. Both are the kind of smoke- and ambience-filled places beloved by London's nighttime crowds. Weeknights, a complicated series of stairs and hallways interconnect the two clubs, although on Friday and Saturday, each club is considered a fiscally separate entity. Both contain restaurants, where full meals cost around £12 ($18). Open: Mon–Sat 7:30pm–2am; Sunday 8pm–midnight. Call for show times. Prices: Drinks from £2.50 ($3.75). Tube: Old St.
   Admission: £3.50–£7 ($5.25–$10.50).

BULL'S HEAD, 373 Lonsdale Rd., Barnes, SW13. Tel. 081/876-5241.

Bull's Head has presented live modern jazz every night of the week for more than 30 years. One of the oldest hostelries in the area, in the mid-19th century it was a staging post where travelers on their way to Hampton Court and beyond could eat, drink, and rest while coach horses were changed. Today, the place is known for its jazz, performed by musicians from all over the world. Jazz concerts are presented on Sunday from 12:30 to 3pm and 8:30 to 10:30pm. Monday through Saturday, you can hear music from 8:30 to 11pm. You can order good food at the Carvery in the Saloon Bar daily or dine in the 17th-century Stable Restaurant. The latter, in the original, restored stables, specializes in steak, fish, and other traditional fare; meals cost £7.50 ($11.25) and up. Open: Mon–Sat 11am–11pm, Sun noon–3pm and 7–10:30pm. Prices: Wine by the glass from £1.40 ($2.10). Transportation: Tube to Hammersmith, then bus 9A rest of way; or take Hounslow Look train from Waterloo Station and get off at Barnes Bridge Station, then walk five minutes to club.

Admission: £4–£7 ($6–$10.50).

100 CLUB, 100 Oxford St., W1. Tel. 071/636-0933.

Although less plush and cheaper, 100 Club is considered a serious rival to the above among many dedicated jazz fans. Its cavalcade of bands includes the best British jazz musicians, as well as many Americans. Open: Fri 8:30pm–3am, Sat 7:30pm–1am, Sun 7:30–11:30pm. Prices: Drinks from £1.80 ($2.70). Tube: Tottenham Court Rd. or Oxford Circus.

Admission: Fri £7 ($10.50) members and nonmembers; Sat £7 ($10.50) members, £8 ($12) nonmembers; Sun £5 ($7.50) members, £6 ($9) nonmembers.

RONNIE SCOTT'S, 47 Frith St., W1. Tel. 071/439-0747.

Mention the word *jazz* in London and people immediately think of Ronnie Scott's, long the European citadel of modern jazz, where the best English and American groups are booked. Featured on almost every bill is an American band, often with a top-notch singer. In the heart of Soho, the place is a 10-minute walk from Piccadilly Circus along Shaftesbury Avenue—and worth an entire evening. You don't have to be a member, although you can join if you wish. In the Main Room you can either stand at the bar to watch the show or sit at a table, where you can order dinner. The Downstairs Bar is more intimate, a quiet rendezvous where you can meet and talk with the regulars, often some of the world's most talented musicians. The separate Upstairs Room has a disco called Club Latino. Open: Main Room, Mon–Sat 8:30pm–3am; Upstairs Room, Mon–Sat 8:30pm–3am. Prices: Drinks from £2.50 ($3.75); half-pint beer £1.20 ($1.80). Tube: Tottenham Court Rd. or Leicester Sq.

Admission: From £12 ($18), depending on the performers; with student ID, £6 ($9) Mon–Thurs.

DANCE CLUBS/DISCOS

BARBARELLA 2, 43 Thurloe St., SW7. Tel. 071/584-2000.

IMPRESSIONS

London is a bad habit one hates to lose.
—ANONYMOUS SAYING, QUOTED IN
BLUE SKIES BROWN STUDIES (1961)

This place combines a first-class Italian restaurant with a carefully controlled disco. The electronic music and flashing lights of the disco are separated from the dining area by thick sheets of glass, so diners can converse in normal tones. Full meals, costing from £20 ($30), include an array of Neapolitan-inspired dishes. Only clients of the restaurant are allowed into the disco. Open: Mon–Sat 7:30pm–3am (last food orders 12:45am). Prices: Drinks from £2.50 ($3.75), beer £1.80 ($2.70). Tube: South Kensington.

Admission: Free.

EQUINOX, Leicester Square, WC2. Tel. 071/437-1446.

New and flashy, Equinox opened in 1992, rising from the ashes of the old London Empire. The club has now established itself as a firm favorite among London nightlifers, and it was recently awarded "Club of the Year" by Disco International. Equinox features nine well-stocked bars, a unique 1950s-style diner, and one of the capital's biggest lighting rigs. Open: Tues–Sat 9pm–4am; closed on Christmas night. Prices: Drinks begin at £2.30 ($5.25). Tube: Leicester Square.

Admission: £5–£12 ($7.50–$18), depends on night of week.

HIPPODROME, corner of Cranbourn St. and Charing Cross Rd., WC2. Tel. 071/437-4311.

Here you will find one of London's greatest discos, an enormous place where light and sound beam in on you from all directions. Revolving speakers even descend from the roof to deafen you in patches, and you can watch yourself on closed-circuit video. Golden Scan lights are a spectacular treat. Lasers and a hydraulically controlled stage highlight visiting international performers. There are six bars, together with an à la carte balcony restaurant. Open: Mon–Sat 9pm–3:30am. Prices: Drinks from £3 ($4.50). Tube: Leicester Sq.

Admission: £5–£12 ($7.50–$18).

ROYAL ROOF RESTAURANT, in the Royal Garden Hotel, 2–24 Kensington High St., W8. Tel. 071/937-8000.

Situated on the top floor of the hotel, the elegant and refined Royal Roof Restaurant overlooks Kensington Gardens and Hyde Park. From your table you will see the lights not only of Kensington but of Knightsbridge, with a view of London's West End skyline. In a romantic candlelit aura, you can dance to the resident band on Thursday, Friday, and Saturday and enjoy a five-course set dinner costing £35 ($52.50). On other nights, there's a live pianist. Reservations are vital. Open: Mon–Sat 7pm–1am (last order 10:30pm Mon–Fri and 11:30pm Sat). Tube: High St. Kensington.

Admission: Free.

SMOLLENSKY'S ON THE STRAND, 105 the Strand, WC2. Tel. 071/497-2101.

This American eatery and drinking bar is a cousin of Smollensky's Balloon at 1 Dover Street (see below). At the Strand location, there is dancing on Friday and Saturday nights. On Sunday nights there is a special live jazz session, in association with Jazz FM, a radio station devoted to jazz. Many visit just for drinks, ordering everything from house cocktails to classic cocktails to deluxe cocktails. Beer costs from £2.05 ($3.08), drinks from £3.95 ($5.93). Meals, ranging from

barbecue loin of pork to corn-fed chicken, cost from £12 ($18).
Open: Mon–Sat noon–midnight and Sun noon–10:30pm.
   Admission: Free, except charge of £3 ($4.50) imposed when live
music is offered. Tube: Charing Cross or Embankment.

STRINGFELLOWS, 16–19 Upper St. Martin's Lane, WC2. Tel. 071/240-5534.

   This is one of London's most elegant nighttime rendezvous spots.
It is said to have nearly $2-million worth of velvet and high-tech gloss
and glitter. In theory, it's a members-only club, but—and only at the
discretion of management—nonmembers may be admitted. It offers
two lively bars and a first-class restaurant. Its disco has a glass dance
floor and a dazzling sound-and-light system. Open: Dinner Mon–Sat
8pm–3am; dancing 11pm–3am. Prices: Drinks £3.25 ($4.88), beer
£2.25 ($3.38). Tube: Leicester Sq.
   Admission: Mon–Wed £8 ($12); Thurs £10 ($15); Fri–Sat
£11–£15 ($16.50–$22.50).

WAG CLUB, 35 Wardour St., W1. Tel. 071/437-5534.

   This popular dance club is set behind an innocuous-looking brick
facade in one of the most congested neighborhoods of London's
entertainment districts. Its two levels are decorated with unusual
murals, some with themes from ancient Egypt, others with snakes.
Clients all seem to love to dance, and hail from throughout Europe
and the rest of the world. Live bands are sometimes presented on the
street level, while the upstairs is reserved for highly danceable
recorded music. Open: Mon–Thurs 10:30pm–3:30am; Fri–Sat
10:30pm–6am. Prices: Drinks £2.20 ($3.30). Tube: Piccadilly Circus
or Leicester Sq.

GAY CLUBS

The most reliable source of information on gay clubs and activities is
the **Lesbian and Gay Switchboard** (tel. 071/837-7324). The
staff runs a 24-hour service for information on places and activities
catering to homosexual men and women.

HEAVEN, The Arches, Craven St., WC2. Tel. 071/839-3852.

   Heaven is the biggest gay venue not only in Great Britain but
perhaps in Europe as well. It also has the most sophisticated
sound-and-laser system of any European gay club. A London
landmark, set within the vaulted cellars of Charing Cross Railway
Station and painted black inside, Heaven is divided into at least four
distinctly different areas, each of these connected by a labyrinth of
catwalks, stairs, and hallways, allowing for different activities within
the club at the same time. It features different theme nights. For
example, Wednesday is for gay men and lesbians; Thursday is
"straight night;" and Saturday leaves you guessing, as clients are
about 50% straight, 50% gay. Open: Tues–Sat 10:30pm–3:30am.
Tube: Charing Cross or Embankment.
   Admission: £5–£9 ($7.50–$13.50).

MADAME JO JO'S, 8 Brewer St., W1. Tel. 071/734-2473.

   Set side by side with some of Soho's most explicit girlie shows,
Madame Jo Jo's also presents "girls," but they are in drag. This is

London's most popular transvestite showplace, with revues staged nightly at 12:15am and 1:15am. There is also a popular piano bar. Open: Mon–Sat 10pm–3am. Prices: Drinks from £2.75 ($4.13). Tube: Piccadilly Circus.

Admission: £8–£10 ($12–$15).

ROY'S, 306B Fulham Rd., SW10. Tel. 071/352-6828.

Roy's is the leading gay restaurant of London. People come here not only for the good food but also for the entertaining and relaxing ambience. The set menu of freshly prepared ingredients is only £17.50 ($26.25) at this basement restaurant. Open: Mon–Sat 7:30–11:30pm, Sun 1:30–3pm and 7:30–11pm. Tube: Earls Court or South Kensington.

STEPH'S, 39 Dean St., W1. Tel. 071/734-5976.

Looking like a stage set for *Pink Flamingos,* Steph's is one of the most charming restaurants of Soho, near the exclusive Groucho Club. Owner Stephanie Cooke, a much-traveled former British schoolteacher, is today the sophisticated hostess of this well-run little restaurant. A theatrical crowd, among others, is attracted to the place. Overall, the clientele is mixed—straight, gay, lesbian, bi, or whatever.

You conceivably could go here just to have fun, but the food is worthy in its own right. Everything is cooked fresh, so sit back, relax, and enjoy such specialties as Snuffy's chicken, beef-and-oyster pie, or else selections from the charcoal grill, including filet steak with barbecue sauce. Steph might even suggest her own "diet"—a plate of wild Scottish smoked salmon and a bottle of champagne. The ubiquitous burger also appears on the menu, as do salads and even a vegetarian club sandwich (how fashionable can you get?). Meals cost from £15 ($22.50). Open: Mon–Thurs noon–3pm and 5:30–11:30pm, Fri noon–3pm and 5:30pm–midnight, Sat 5:30pm–midnight. Tube: Piccadilly Circus.

WILD ABOUT OSCAR, in the Philbeach Hotel, 30–31 Philbeach Gardens, SW5. Tel. 071/373-1244.

Catering to a mostly gay clientele, this French restaurant lies on the garden level of an interconnected pair of Victorian row houses. Decorated in blues and greens, with portraits of Oscar Wilde (the restaurant's namesake), the establishment overlooks a view of the brownstone's garden. There's a small cocktail bar open only to restaurant patrons and residents of the gay hotel that contains it. Reservations are required. Three-course fixed price meals cost £13–£20 ($19.50–$30). Open: Dinner only, Mon–Sat 7–10:30pm (last order); brunch only, Sun 1:30–4pm. Tube: Earl's Court.

---

3. THE BAR SCENE

PUBS, WINE BARS & BARS

AMERICAN BAR, in the Savoy Hotel, The Strand (without number), WC2. Tel. 071/836-4343.

At the American Bar, still one of the most sophisticated places in London, the bartender is known for such special concoctions as Royal Silver and Savoy 90. Monday through Saturday evenings, a jazz and piano music. The après-theater crowd flocks here (it's near many

West End theaters) to listen to show tunes. Men should wear jackets and ties. Open: Mon–Sat 11am–3pm and 5:30–11pm, Sun noon–3pm and 7–10:30pm. Prices: Drinks from £5 ($7.50). Tube: Charing Cross or Embankment.

BRACEWELL'S BAR, in the Park Lane Hotel, Piccadilly (without number), W1. Tel. 071/499-6321.

Chic, nostalgic, and elegant, it's the kind of bar where Edward VII and his stylish companion, Mrs. Langtry, might have felt very much at home. The plush, comfortable decor has touches of Chinese lacquer, upholstered sofas, soft lighting, and an ambience like that of an elegant private club. The bar adjoins Bracewell's (see Chapter 5), one of the finest hotel restaurants in London. Open: Mon–Sat 11am–3pm and 5:30–11pm, Sun noon–2:30pm and 7–10:30pm. Prices: Mixed drinks from £5 ($7.50), beer from £2.50 ($3.75). Tube: Green Park.

COCKTAIL BAR, in the Café Royal, 68 Regent St., W1. Tel. 071/437-9090.

In business since 1865, this bar was once patronized by Oscar Wilde, James McNeill Whistler, and Aubrey Beardsley. Decorated in a 19th-century rococo style, it is one of the more glamorous places in London to order a drink. Café Royal cocktails, including Golden Cadillac and Prince William, begin at £5.50 ($8.25). Nonalcoholic drinks are also served, and you can order wine by the glass from the superb wine cellars. A traditional English tea, served between 3 and 5pm, costs £9.50 ($14.25). Open: Mon–Sat noon–11:30pm, Sun noon–10:30pm. Prices: Drinks from £2.40 ($3.60). Tube: Piccadilly Circus.

THE DORCHESTER BAR, in the Dorchester, Park Lane. Tel. 071/629-8888.

This is a fun and sophisticated modern hideaway on the lobby level of one of the most lavishly decorated hotels in the world. Amid its champagne-colored premises, you'll find a clientele derived from everywhere in the world and commonly shared assumptions about the pleasures that only taste and lots of money can buy. You can order upscale bar snacks, lunches, and suppers throughout the day and evening, including lobster cream soups, Scottish smoked salmon, fried filet of sea bass with seasonal salads, and "fine chocolate layers with a chocolate mousse." Otherwise, the bartender can make any drink ever conceived on the planet. A pianist performs highly drinkable music every evening after 6:30pm. Open: Mon–Sat 11:30am–11pm, Sun noon–3pm, 6:30pm–10:30pm. Entrance: Free, drinks from £6 ($9). Tube: Hyde Park Corner.

LILLIE LANGTRY BAR, in the Cadogan Hotel, Sloane St. (without number), SW1. Tel. 071/235-7141.

This bar, next to Langtry's Restaurant, exudes a 1920s aura and epitomizes the charm and elegance of the Edwardian era. Lillie Langtry, actress and society beauty at the turn of the century (notorious as the mistress of Edward VII), used to live here. Oscar Wilde, who was arrested in this bar, is honored on the drinks menu with Hock and Selzer, his favorite libation here, according to Sir John Betjeman's poem "The Arrest of Oscar Wilde at the Cadogan Hotel." The most popular drink is a Cadogan Cooler. Open: Daily 11am–11pm. Prices: Drinks from £3.75 ($5.63); glass of wine from £2.75 ($4.13). Tube: Sloane Sq.

RUMOURS, 33 Wellington St., WC2, Tel. 071/836-0038.

Rumours is the kind of place where you expect Tom Cruise to turn up as bartender. Called the "granddaddy of modern American cocktail-style bars," it is a spacious pillared bar, enveloped by mirrors. Once this was a flower market in the heyday of Covent Garden, but today it dispenses about 10 pages of cocktail suggestions; at least three dozen of these are considered originals and worthy of carrying a copyright. On Friday and Saturday nights, the place is packed. Cocktails with generous measures cost £3.75 ($5.63) and up. Open: Mon–Sat 5–11pm and Sun 7–10:30pm. Tube: Covent Garden.

SMOLLENSKY'S BALLOON, 1 Dover St., W1. Tel. 071/491-1199.

A basement restaurant, this American eatery and drinking bar is packed during happy hour (5:30 to 7pm) with Mayfair office workers fortifying themselves before heading home. The place has a 1930s piano bar atmosphere, with polished wood and a mirrored ceiling. Steaks and french fries are favorite fare, though you can also order well-prepared vegetarian dishes. Meals start at £12 ($18); house cocktails (good measures), at £2.85 ($4.28); beer, at £2.05 ($3.08). A pianist/singer entertains Monday through Saturday evenings. Open: Mon–Sat noon–midnight and Sun noon–10:30pm. Tube: Green Park.

SPECIALTY BARS

BOUZOUKI

ELYSÉE, 13 Percy St., W1. Tel. 071/636-4804.

Elysée is for *Never on Sunday* devotees who like the reverberations of bouzouki and the smashing of plates. The domain of the Karegeorgis brothers—Michael, Ulysses, and the incomparable George—it offers hearty fun at moderate tabs. You can dance nightly to the music by Greek musicians. Two different cabaret shows are presented (last one at 1am), highlighted by brother George's altogether amusing art of balancing wine glasses (I'd hate to pay his breakage bill). You can book a table on either the ground floor or the second floor, but the Roof Garden is a magnet in summer. The food is good, too, including the house specialty, the classic moussaka, and kebabs from the charcoal grill. A complete meal with wine costs £30 ($45). Open: Mon–Sat 7pm–2:45am. Tube: Goodge St. or Tottenham Court Rd.

Admission: £3 ($4.50) cover charge.

GAY & LESBIAN BARS

BRIEF ENCOUNTER, 41 St. Martin's Lane, WC2. Tel. 071/240-2221.

This place stands across from the Duke of York's Theatre, in the very heart of West End theaterland. In fact, it's the most frequented West End gay pub. Bars are on two levels, but even so it's hard to find room to stand up, much less drink. The crowd's costumes vary. Some men are in jeans, leather, whatever, whereas others are dressed in business suits. Open: Mon–Sat 11am–11pm, Sun noon–3pm and 7–10:30pm. Prices: Lager from £1.72 ($2.58). Tube: Leicester Sq. or Charing Cross.

COLEHERNE, 261 Old Brompton Rd., SW5. Tel. 071/373-9859.

This leather-and-denim bar must have been featured in every guide to the gay scene in Europe ever written. As a consequence, it's often jammed. Lunch and afternoon tea are served upstairs. Open: Mon–Sat 11am–11pm, Sun noon–3pm and 7–10:30pm. Prices: Lager from £1.72 ($2.58). Tube: Earls Court.

THE DUKE OF WELLINGTON, 119 Balls Pond Rd., N1. Tel. 071/249-3729.

Originally built in the late 19th-century, this pub is perhaps the most popular lesbian bar in London. The outer bar is open to gay men. An inner room, "The Women's Room," is wheelchair accessible, containing a pool table, a bar, and art deco lighting. Live bands perform every Friday and Saturday, and many special events are often staged here (check the local gay press for details). Open: Outer bar, Mon–Sat 6pm–midnight, Sun 7–10:30pm; inner bar, Mon–Sat 8pm–midnight, Sun 7–10:30pm. Prices: Pints of lager from £1.70 ($2.55), vegetarian meals from £2 ($3). Tube: Highbury.

HALFWAY TO HEAVEN, 7 Duncannon St., WC2. Tel. 071/930-8312.

Contained within a century-old structure whose beamed ceiling is straight out of a novel by Charles Dickens, this is perhaps the most popular and least frenetic gay bar in the Trafalgar Square neighborhood. Most clients wear jackets and ties. Open: Mon–Sat 3–11pm, Sun 7:30–10:30pm. Prices: Lager from £1.72 ($2.58). Tube: Charing Cross or Embankment.

4. MORE ENTERTAINMENT

CASINOS

London was a gambling metropolis long before anyone had ever heard of Monte Carlo or Las Vegas. Victoria's reign changed all that, as usual, by jumping to the other extreme. For more than a century, games of chance were so rigorously outlawed that no bartender dared to keep a dice cup on the counter. However, according to the 1960 Betting and Gaming Act, gambling was again permitted in "bona fide clubs" by members and their guests.

There are at least 25 such clubs in the West End alone, with many more scattered throughout the suburbs. But under a new law, casinos aren't allowed to advertise, which in this context would mean appearing in a guidebook. Nonetheless, most hall porters can tell you where you can gamble in London.

You will be required to become a member of your chosen club, and in addition you must wait 24 hours before you can play at the tables . . . then strictly for cash. The most common games are roulette, blackjack, punto banco, and baccarat.

MOVIES

MGM CINEMA, Panton St. (without number) (off Leicester Sq.), SW1. Tel. 071/930-0631.

This streamlined black-and-white block houses four superb

theaters. They share one sleekly plush lobby, but each runs a separate program, including at least one Continental film, along with the latest releases, often from the United States. Tube: Piccadilly Circus or Leicester Sq.

Tickets: £2.50 ($3.75) all day Mon; £3.50 ($5.25) Tues–Fri before 6pm; otherwise £5 ($7.50).

NATIONAL FILM THEATRE, South Bank (without number), Waterloo, SE1. Tel. 071/928-3232.

This cinema is in the South Bank complex. More than 2,000 films a year from all over the world are shown here, including features, shorts, animation, and documentaries. Tube: Waterloo.

Admission: 40p (60¢) daily membership, £4.35 ($6.53) screenings with membership.

ODEON LEICESTER SQUARE AND ODEON MEZZANINE, Leicester Sq. (without number), WC2. Tel. 0426/915-683.

The Odeon is another major London film theater, with one main screen and a mezzanine complex comprising another five screens. All screens feature the latest international releases. Tube: Leicester Sq.

Tickets: £6.50–£9 ($9.75–$13.50).

STRIP SHOWS

Soho has many strip clubs, located mainly along Frith Street, Greek Street, Old Compton Street, Brewer Street, Windmill Street, Dean and Wardour streets, and the little courts and alleys in between.

RAYMOND REVUEBAR, Walker's Court, Brewer St., W1. Tel. 071/734-1593.

The Revuebar dates from 1958. Proprietor Paul Raymond is considered the doyen of strip society and his young, beautiful, hand-picked strippers are among the best in Europe. This strip theater occupies the much-restored premises of a Victorian dance hall, with a decor of red velvet. There are two bars, which allow clients to take their drinks to their seats. Open: Nightly shows at 8 and 10pm. Drinks: Whisky £3 ($4.50) for a large measure. Tube: Piccadilly Circus.

Admission: £17 ($25.50).

STORK CLUB, 99 Regent St., W1. Tel. 071/734-3686.

This first-class nightclub incorporates good food, a Las Vegas-style cabaret with a lineup of attractive dancers who don't believe in overdressing, and an ambience noted for its good taste and theatrical flair. Located near the corner of Swallow Street in the upscale heart of Mayfair, it welcomes diners and drinkers to a decor of royal blue and peach with an art deco inspiration. Two shows are staged nightly, at 11:30pm and at 1am. Foreign visitors don't have to go through the tedium of obtaining membership. Open: Mon–Sat 8:30pm–3:30am. Prices: Drinks from £4 ($6). Tube: Piccadilly Circus.

Admission: Three-course dinner £35 ($52.50), or £10 ($15) cover charge for show only.

CHAPTER 10

EASY EXCURSIONS FROM LONDON

You could spend a year or more exploring London, but I still advise you to tear yourself away and visit one or two of the many resorts, historic sites, and cultural and religious shrines that are within comfortable commuting range. Most are close enough for a day trip—you could return to London in time for dinner and a night at the theater. The only real drawbacks of these excursions are that there are too many to choose from!

1. BRIGHTON

51 miles S of London

GETTING THERE **By Train** Fast trains leave often from Victoria Station or London Bridge Station, with the trip taking 55 minutes (tel. 071/730-3466).

By Bus Buses from Victoria Coach Station (tel. 071/283-0202) take around 2 hours.

By Car M23 (signposted from Central London) leads to A23, which will take you into Brighton.

Brighton's Asian-style **Royal Pavilion** represented fashionable wickedness when the Prince Regent built it in 1787. But today, the town is very much a family resort, boasting warm summer sunshine.

Although the beaches are pebbly and the water is cold, the seafront **promenade** and two **amusement piers** make Brighton a fun place to visit. It has waxworks, aquariums, three live theaters, every conceivable form of sport, and the annual London-Brighton Veteran Car Run.

Nonetheless, the town still exudes Regency elegance, and, at night, the floodlights play on the Royal Pavilion and the floral boulevard.

WHERE TO DINE

MODERATE

LANGAN'S BISTRO, 1 Paston Place. Tel. 0273/606933.
 Cuisine: FRENCH. **Reservations:** Required.

$ Prices: Appetizers £3.95–£5.50 ($5.90–$8.30); main courses £10.95–£13.50 ($16.40–$20.30); three-course fixed-price lunch £13.50 ($20.30). AE, DC, MC, V.
    Open: Lunch Sun and Tues–Fri 12:30–2:30pm; dinner Tues–Sat 7:30–10:30pm. **Closed:** 2 weeks in Aug.

Located near the waterfront, off King's Cliff, this is the latest branch of a well-known minichain of restaurants that gained fame in London. The limited menu is based on the freshest of market ingredients. You might, for example, begin with a salad made from tiger prawns and scallops, then follow with halibut meunière or a gigot of perfectly done lamb. Vegetarian meals are also available. Desserts are often sumptuous, as reflected by a crème brûlée flavored with Grand Marnier and orange.

2. CAMBRIDGE

55 miles NE of London

GETTING THERE By Train Trains depart frequently from Liverpool Street Station (tel. 071/283-7171) and King's Cross Station (tel. 071/278-7477), arriving an hour later. A same-day round-trip ticket is £13.50 ($20.30). A regular round-trip fare is £15.40 ($23.10).

By Bus National Express coaches (tel. 071/283-0202) run hourly between London's Victoria Coach Station and Drummer Street Station in Cambridge (trip time: 2 hrs.). A one-way or same-day round-trip ticket costs £8.50 ($12.80).

By Car Head north on M11 from London to Exit 11.

Cambridge is one of the world's great university towns, its oldest college, Peterhouse, having been founded in 1284. The town boasts 29 colleges for both men and women. A good starting point for your exploration is the corner of **Market Hill** and **King's Parade,** the heart of Cambridge. Nearby is **Great St. Mary's,** the university church. Here, too, is the most brilliant jewel in the Cambridge crown—15th-century **King's College Chapel,** considered one of the most perfect buildings in the world. From here, you can walk to most colleges along the various paths. **"The Backs,"** where the grounds of the colleges sweep down to the River Cam, are exciting to see.

WHERE TO DINE

MODERATE

MIDSUMMER HOUSE, Midsummer Common (without number). Tel. 0223/69299.
    Cuisine: FRENCH. **Reservations:** Required.
$ Prices: Appetizers £5.50 ($8.30); main courses £9.50–£15.50 ($14.30–$23.30); three-course fixed-price lunch £13.95 ($20.90); six-course fixed-price dinner £23–£38 ($34.50–$57.00). AE, MC, V.
    Open: Lunch Tues–Fri and Sun 12:30–2pm; dinner Tues–Sat 7–9:30pm.

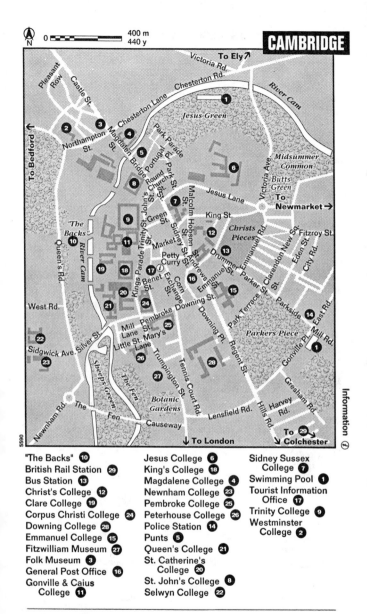

"The Backs" ⑩	Jesus College ⑥	Sidney Sussex College ⑦
British Rail Station ㉙	King's College ⑱	Swimming Pool ①
Bus Station ⑬	Magdalene College ④	Tourist Information Office ⑰
Christ's College ⑫	Newnham College ㉓	Trinity College ⑨
Clare College ⑲	Pembroke College ㉕	Westminster College ②
Corpus Christi College ㉔	Peterhouse College ㉖	
Downing College ㉘	Police Station ⑭	
Emmanuel College ⑮	Punts ⑤	
Fitzwilliam Museum ㉗	Queen's College ㉑	
Folk Museum ③	St. Catherine's College ⑳	
General Post Office ⑯	St. John's College ⑧	
Gonville & Caius College ⑪	Selwyn College ㉒	

★ Located near the River Cam, between Elizabeth Way and Victoria Avenue, Midsummer House is reached by towpath. The preferred dining area is in an elegant conservatory, but an upstairs dining room is also available. The menu is wisely limited. Chef Hans Schweitzer was schooled in French cuisine, and every dish bears his own special imprint.

TWENTY TWO, 22 Chesterton Rd. Tel. 0223/351880.
Cuisine: ENGLISH/CONTINENTAL. **Reservations:** Required.

$ Prices: Set menu £21.50 ($32.30). MC, V.
   Open: Dinner only, Tues–Sat 7:30–9:30pm.
Who would expect to find one of the best restaurants in Cambridge in this quiet residential and hotel district? In the vicinity of Jesus Green, it is jealously guarded by the locals. Decorated in pink-and-gray, Twenty Two offers an ever-changing fixed-price menu based on fresh produce. Owners David Carter and Louise Crompton use time-tested recipes along with their own inspiration. Typical dishes include Stilton-and-bacon soup; pan-fried local venison with cranberry sauce; and, for dessert, perhaps homemade ice cream served in a confectioner's basket made from a recipe for brandy snaps.

3. CANTERBURY

56 miles E of London

GETTING THERE   By Train   Frequent trains from Victoria, Charing Cross, Waterloo, or London Bridge stations take 1½ hours (tel. 071/730-3466).

By Bus   Buses leave twice daily from Victoria Coach Station (tel. 071/283-0202), taking 2 to 3 hours.

By Car   From London take A2, then M2. Canterbury is signposted along the way.

When Thomas à Becket was murdered there in 1170,   ✪ **Canterbury Cathedral,** 11 The Precincts (tel. 0227-762862), was already a century old. Then, as now, it dominates the town with its gentle beauty and touching simplicity. The art treasures it houses include stained-glass windows and the opulent tomb of Edward the Black Prince, hero of the "Longbow Battle" of Crécy during the Hundred Years War. The original church on the site was erected by St. Augustine in 597 and became the cradle of English Christianity among the pagan folk of Kent.

WHERE TO DINE

INEXPENSIVE

GEORGE'S BRASSERIE, 71–72 Castle St. Tel. 0227/ 765658.
   Cuisine: FRENCH/MEDITERREAN. **Reservations:** Recommended.
$ Prices: Appetizers £2.50–£6.50 ($3.80–$9.80); main courses £6.50–£14 ($9.80–$21). AE, DC, MC, V.
   Open: Mon–Thurs 11am–10pm, Fri–Sat 10am–10:30pm (with last-order time extended for theatergoers). **Closed:** Dec 25 and Jan 1.
This attractive establishment in the town center, east of Stour Street, is run by brother and sister Simon Day and Beverley Holmes, who serve everything from coffee and croissants to gourmet meals. The numerous appetizers include fresh anchovy salad and George's terrines. Main dishes change with the season but always include fish and meat dishes served with new potatoes or french fries. Vegetarian meals are available.

SULLYS, County Hotel, High St. (without number). Tel. 0227/766266.
  Cuisine: ENGLISH/CONTINENTAL. **Reservations:** Recommended.
$ **Prices:** Appetizers £2.50–£5.50 ($3.80–$8.30); main courses £8.50–£15.50 ($12.80–$23.30); fixed-price lunch £14.50 ($21.80). AE, DC, MC, V.
  Open: Lunch daily 12:30–2:30pm; dinner daily 7–10pm.

The most distinguished restaurant in Canterbury is centrally located in its most distinguished hotel. Considering the quality of ingredients, the menu offers good value. You can always count on a selection of traditional English dishes, but you might try a more imaginative platters like the chef's specialty, civet of venison.

4. CHARTWELL

2 miles S of Westerham off B2026; 26 miles E of London

GETTING THERE By Train From London's Victoria Station (tel. 071/730-3466), trains run daily to Westerham, where you can take a taxi to Chartwell.

By Car From London, head east along M25, taking the exit to Westerham, where B2026 leads to Chartwell (road is signposted).

For many years, former prime minister Winston Churchill lived at his fairly modest home two miles south of Westerdam in Kent. Maintained by the National Trust, **Churchill's house** (tel. 0732/866-368) is open to the public. From April to October, the house, gardens, and studio are open on Tuesday through Thursday from noon to 5pm and on Saturday and Sunday from 11am to 5pm. In March and November, only the house is open, on Wednesday, Saturday, and Sunday from 11am to 4pm. Admission to the house only in March and November is £2.30 ($3.50); to the house and gardens from April to October, £4.20 ($6.30); to the gardens only, £2.20 ($3.30); and to Churchill's studio only, 60p (90¢). Children pay half price. A restaurant on the grounds operates from 10:30am to 5pm on days the house is open.

5. HAMPTON COURT

13 miles W of London

GETTING THERE By Train Frequent trains from Waterloo Station (Network SouthEast) go to Hampton Court Station. Round-trip tickets cost £3.10 ($4.70).

By Bus London Regional Transport buses no. 111, 131, 216, 267, and 461 make the trip, as do Green Line coaches (ask at the nearest London Country Bus office) on routes 715, 716, 718, and 726.

By Boat Waterbus service in summer is offered to and from Westminster Pier four times daily. Take the tube to Westminster.

Round-trips take 3 to 4 hours, depending on water conditions. Call 071/930-4721 for schedules.

By Car   From London, take A308 to the junction with A309 on the north side of Kingston Bridge over the Thames.

On the north side of the Thames is   ✪ **Hampton Court** (tel. 081/781-9500; or write to Superintendent, Hampton Court Palace, East Molesey, Surrey KT8 9AU). Set amid rolling green country by the riverside, this ranks as the grandest of all the great palaces built in England during the Tudor period. It was intended as the home of Cardinal Wolsey, chancellor (meaning prime minister) to Henry VIII. But the wily cardinal presented it as a gift to his royal master, who then added a few luxurious touches of his own.

Walk in and see the fantastic and still-working **Astronomical Clock,** made by Nicholas Oursian in 1540; it was regarded as one of the mechanical miracles of its period. Wander through the royal kitchens (restored as in the 1530s), where an ox could be roasted whole, and lounge on the original lawn where Henry VIII once serenaded Anne Boleyn—whom he eventually married and subsequently beheaded.

Later, baroque additions were made by Sir Christopher Wren for William of Orange and Queen Mary. Wren built the formal **Fountain Court** and the great **East Front** facing the gardens. Still standing is the **Great Vine** (mentioned in Ripley's "Believe It or Not"), which was planted in 1769 and has a main branch now more than 100 feet long. You can also lose yourself in the **Maze.**

The gardens are open daily year round from 7am until dusk, but not later than 9pm, and can be visited free. The cloisters, maze, courtyards, state apartments, great kitchen, cellars, Hampton Court exhibition, and Mantegna paintings gallery are open mid-March to mid-October, daily from 9:30am to 6pm; and mid-October to mid-March, daily from 9:30am to 4:30pm. The Tudor tennis court and banqueting house are open the same hours as above, but only from mid-March to mid-October. Admission to all these attractions is £5.90 ($8.90) for adults and £3.90 ($5.90) for children (children under 5 are free). A garden café/restaurant is in Tiltyard Gardens.

---

6. OXFORD

57 miles NW of London

GETTING THERE   By Train   Hourly trains from Paddington Station (tel. 071/262-6767) reach Oxford in 1¼ hours. A same-day round-trip ticket costs £13.20 ($19.80).

By Bus   Oxford City Link provides coach services from London's Victoria Coach Station (tel. 071/730-0202) to the Oxford Bus Station. Three buses per hour leave daily, taking 1½ hours. A day return ticket costs £6.50 ($9.80).

By Car   Take M40 west from London and follow signs.

Oxford is well over a thousand years old, and the earliest of the colleges—St. Edmund Hall, Merton, and Balliol—date from the

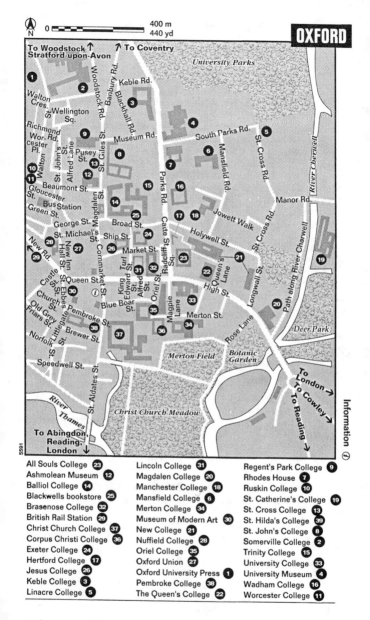

OXFORD

To Woodstock ↑ ↑ To Coventry
Stratford-upon-Avon

University Parks

College	No.	College	No.	College	No.
All Souls College	23	Lincoln College	31	Regent's Park College	9
Ashmolean Museum	12	Magdalen College	20	Rhodes House	7
Balliol College	14	Manchester College	18	Ruskin College	10
Blackwells bookstore	25	Mansfield College	6	St. Catherine's College	19
Brasenose College	32	Merton College	34	St. Cross College	13
British Rail Station	29	Museum of Modern Art	30	St. Hilda's College	39
Christ Church College	37	New College	21	St. John's College	8
Corpus Christi College	36	Nuffield College	28	Somerville College	2
Exeter College	24	Oriel College	35	Trinity College	15
Hertford College	17	Oxford Union	27	University College	33
Jesus College	26	Oxford University Press	1	University Museum	4
Keble College	3	Pembroke College	38	Wadham College	16
Linacre College	5	The Queen's College	22	Worcester College	11

13th century. The two main streets, known as **The High** and **The Broad,** are perhaps the most beautiful period thoroughfares in England, set off by the **Sheldonian Theatre;** the **University Church of St. Mary;** and the **Bodleian Library,** one of the most important book collections in the world.

On Broad Street, you'll see a cross marking the spot where England's martyr bishops, Latimer, Ridley, and Cranmer, were burned at the stake during the reign of "Bloody Mary" in 1557.

WHAT TO SEE & DO

Because there are so many well-known buildings in Oxford, I have narrowed the sights to a representative list of a few colleges.

CHRIST CHURCH, St. Aldates. Tel. 0865/276-499.

Begun by Cardinal Wolsey as Cardinal College in 1525, Christ Church, familiarly known as The House, was founded by Henry VIII in 1546 and has the largest quadrangle of any college in Oxford. **Tom Tower** houses Great Tom, the 18,000-pound bell that rings at 9:05 nightly, signaling the closing of the college gates (it originally signified the number of students in residence). In the 16th-century **Great Hall,** with its hammer-beam ceiling, portraits by Gainsborough, Reynolds, and others depict prime ministers for whom Christ Church was training ground. There is also another picture gallery.

The **cathedral,** dating from the 12th century, is not only the college chapel but also the cathedral of the diocese of Oxford. The Norman pillars and the vaulting of the choir date from the 15th century.

Admission: £1.50 ($2.30) adults, 50p (80¢) children.

Open: College and cathedral, daily 9:30am–noon and 2–6pm in summer (until 4:30pm in winter).

MAGDALEN COLLEGE, High St. Tel. 0865/276-000.

Pronounced "MAWD-len," this college was founded in 1458 by William of Waynflete, bishop of Winchester and later chancellor of England. Its alumni range from Wolsey to Wilde. Opposite the **botanic garden,** the oldest in England, is the **bell tower,** where the choristers sing in Latin at dawn on May Day. The grounds of Magdalen are the most extensive of any Oxford college and even contain a deer park. A favorite pastime is to take **Addison's Walk** through the water meadows—a stroll named after former alumnus Joseph Addison, the 18th-century essayist and playwright noted for his contributions to *The Spectator* and *The Tatler*.

Admission: Free.

Open: Daily 2–6:15pm; inquire about opening times for hall and other attractions.

MERTON COLLEGE, Merton St. Tel. 0865/276310.

Founded in 1264, Merton is one of the three oldest at the university. It is noted for its **library,** which is said to be the oldest college library in England, built between 1371 and 1379. One of its treasures is an astrolabe (astronomical instrument used for measuring the altitude of the sun and stars), thought to have belonged to Chaucer. There is also a 13th-century **chapel.**

Admission: £1 ($1.50) to visit ancient library, as well as Max Beerbohm Room (English caricaturist and parodist, 1872–1956).

Open: Mon-Fri 2–4pm (until 4:30pm Mar–Oct), Sat-Sun 10am–4pm. **Closed:** Christmas to mid-Feb; one week at Easter.

UNIVERSITY COLLEGE, High St. Tel. 0865/276602.

Located on The High, University College traces its history back to 1249, when money was donated by an ecclesiastic, William of Durham. More fanciful is the old claim that the real founder was Alfred the Great. The original structures have all disappeared, and what remains today is essentially a Gothic-like structure from the 17th century, with subsequent additions in Victoria's day, as well as in more recent times. The Goodhart Quadrangle was added as late as

1962. Shelley was originally "sent down" for collaborating on a pamphlet on atheism, but the poet is nonetheless honored by a memorial erected in 1894.

Admission: £1.25 ($1.90) adults, 50p (80¢) children.
Open: During vacations, daily 2–4pm.

WHERE TO DINE

MODERATE

CHERWELL BOATHOUSE RESTAURANT, Bardwell Rd. (without number). Tel. 0865/52746.
    Cuisine: FRENCH. **Reservations:** Recommended.
$ Prices: Main courses £8–£12 ($12–$18); set dinner from £15.75 ($23.60); set lunch £11.75 ($17.60). MC, V.
    Open: Lunch Sun 12:30–2pm: dinner Tues–Sat 7:30–11:30pm.
This Oxford landmark is owned by Tony Verdin, who at each meal, offers two fixed-price menus that change every two weeks according to the availability of fresh vegetables, fish, and meat. Main dishes include casseroles, pies, and hotpots. Appetizers aren't served separately. There is a very reasonable, even exciting, wine list. Children are granted half price. Before dinner, you can rent a punt and try punting on the Cherwell since the restaurant is beside the river, north of the town center.

INEXPENSIVE

MUNCHY MUNCHY, 6 Park End St. Tel. 0865/245710.
    Cuisine: SOUTHEAST ASIAN. **Reservations:** Recommended.
$ Prices: Main courses £4.35–£6.85 ($6.50–$10.30). No credit cards.
    Open: Lunch Tues–Sat noon–2pm; dinner Tues–Sat 5:30–10pm. **Closed:** 2 weeks Sept; 2 weeks Dec.
Some Oxford students claim that this restaurant near the railroad station offers the best food value in the city. Ethel Ow is adept at herbs and seasoning and often uses fresh fruit inventively, as reflected by such dishes as scallops sautéed with ginger and lamb with passion-fruit sauce. Indonesian and Malaysian dishes are also popular. Appetizers aren't served. Sometimes, especially on Friday and Saturday, long lines form at the door. Children under 6 are not allowed on Friday and Saturday evenings.

---

7. STRATFORD-UPON-AVON

91 miles NW of London

GETTING THERE   By Train   Frequent trains from Paddington Station take 2¼ hours. Call 071/262-6767 for schedules. Standard round-trip tickets cost £25 ($37.50).

By Bus   Eight National Express (tel. 071/730-0202) coaches a day leave from Victoria Station, with a trip time of 2¾ hours. A single-day round-trip ticket costs £12.75 ($19.10).

By Car Take M40 toward Oxford and continue to Stratford-upon-Avon on A34.

The **Tourist Information Centre,** Bridgefoot (without number; tel. 0789/293127), will provide any details you might wish about the Shakespeare properties. It's open March to October on Monday through Saturday from 9am to 5:30pm, on Sunday from 2 to 5pm. From November to February, it's open on Monday through Saturday from 10:30am to 4pm.

WHAT TO SEE & DO

It's recommended that you go first to **Shakespeare's Birthplace,** on Henley Street. The Elizabethan dramatist was born there on April 23, 1564, the son of a "whittawer," or fine leather worker. Since 1847, when fans of the Bard raised money to purchase the property, the house has been operated as a national shrine. Built to honor the 400th anniversary of the writer's birth, the **Shakespeare Centre** next door was dedicated as a library and study center in 1964.

For many, the chief attraction here is ✪ **Anne Hathaway's Cottage,** in the small hamlet of Shottery outside of Stratford. Anne resided here as a child and while her husband went to London in 1587 to pursue his career as a playwright and actor at the Blackfriars and Globe theaters. Of the furnishings remaining, the "courting settle" evokes the most interest. If the weather is good, the best way to reach Shottery is from Evesham Place in town (the strolling path is marked), traversing a meadow. Otherwise, a bus leaves from Bridge Street in Stratford.

At the so-called **New Place,** on Chapel Street, Shakespeare retired in comfort in 1610. The house itself was later destroyed, but you can walk through the gardens (entered through the home of Thomas Nash, a man who married Shakespeare's granddaughter, Elizabeth Hall). The mulberry tree is said to have been rooted from a cutting of a tree that Shakespeare planted.

Although often ignored by the casual visitor, **Mary Arden's House** is a delight, built in the charming Tudor style. Shakespeare's mother, who like his wife was the daughter of a yeoman farmer, lived here in Wilmcote, a village about 3 miles outside Stratford. A farming museum is accommodated in the barns.

In the Old Town is the **Hall's Croft,** not far from the parish church. It was here that Shakespeare's daughter, Susanna, lived with her husband, Dr. John Hall. It is a Tudor house with a beautiful walled garden. Visitors are welcome to use the adjoining **Hall's Croft Club,** which serves morning coffee, lunch, and afternoon tea. The house is only a short walk from the Royal Shakespeare Theatre, about a block from the river.

Although not administrated by the Trust, the **Holy Trinity Church,** one of England's most beautiful parish churches, on the banks of the Avon, is also much visited. Shakespeare was buried here, his tombstone bearing the words "and curst be he who moves my bones." A contribution is requested from adults wishing to view Shakespeare's tomb.

From April to October, all Shakespeare properties are open Monday through Saturday from 9am to 6pm, on Sunday from 10am to 6pm. In the winter season, they remain open from 9am to 4:30pm.

On off-season Sundays, only the two most visited attractions, **Shakespeare's Birthplace** and **Anne Hathaway's Cottage,** remain open; the hours are 1:30 to 4:30pm. Last admissions are 30 minutes before closing time.

You can purchase a comprehensive ticket admitting you to all five **Shakespeare Birthplace Trust** properties at any of the sights. The cost is £7.50 ($11.30) for adults and £3.25 ($4.90) for children.

Nearly every visitor to Stratford wants to attend at least one performance at the **Royal Shakespeare Theatre,** Waterside (tel. 0789/295623), designed in 1932 to stand right on the Avon. The long season begins in April and lasts until January. Each season, five of the Bard's dramas and comedies are usually performed in repertory at the Royal Shakespeare Theatre; and five additional plays by Shakespeare, his great contemporaries, and later playwrights are staged at the small **Swan Theatre Waterside.** Ticket prices at the RST are £6 to £39 ($9 to $58.50), and at the Swan are £8 to £27 ($12 to $40.50). Reservations should be made in advance.

WHERE TO DINE
MODERATE

BOX TREE RESTAURANT, in the Royal Shakespeare Theatre, Waterside (without number). Tel. 0789/293226. Cuisine: FRENCH/ITALIAN/ENGLISH. **Reservations:** Required.

$ Prices: Dinner Mon–Thurs £21.70 ($32.60), Fri–Sat £22.70 ($34.10); matinee lunch £13.50 ($20.30). AE, MC, V.
Open: Matinee lunch Thurs–Sat noon–2:30pm; dinner Mon–Sat 5:45pm–midnight.

Box Tree is in the best location in town, right in the theater itself, with walls of glass providing an unobstructed view of the Avon and its swans. During intermission, there is a snack feast of smoked salmon and champagne. After each evening's performance, you can dine by flickering candlelight. There's a special phone for reservations in the theater lobby.

8. WINDSOR
21 miles W of London

GETTING THERE   By Train   The train from Paddington Station (tel. 071/262-6767) takes 30 minutes. More than a dozen trains per day make the run, costing £4 ($6) for a same-day round trip.

By Bus   Green Line coaches (tel. 071/688-7261) no. 704 and 705 from Hyde Park Corner in London take about 1½ hours. A same-day round trip costs £3.80 ($5.70).

By Car   Take M4 west from London.

Windsor means two things to an English person: a castle and a college. Windsor Castle, the largest inhabited castle in the world, has been the home of English sovereigns for just over 900 years. And nearby Eton College has been educating future sovereigns, along with lesser fry, for more than 500.

✪ **Windsor Castle** (tel. 0753/86826 for public visiting hours) was built by William the Conqueror. The **State Apartments** are still used at certain times by the present monarch, Elizabeth II. The apartments can be visited unless the Royal Standard is up. Admission is £4.20 ($6.30) for adults and £1.60 ($2.40) for children. In November 1992 a fire swept through part of Windsor Castle, severely damaging it. It has since been reopened, but until restoration is complete visitors can't see all the rooms they could before. In January, February, November, and December, hours are daily from 10:30am to 3pm; in March and October, daily from 10:30am to 4pm; and April through September, daily from 10:30am to 5pm. For periods in April, June, and December, when the royal family is in residence, the castle is closed to the public.

Eton College, founded in 1440 by Henry VI, is still the most illustrious "public" (meaning private) school in Britain, and its pupils still wear Edwardian garb—top hat and collar—that makes them look like period fashion plates and carries massive snob appeal. You can visit the schoolyard and cloisters free daily from 2 to 5pm.

Two miles beyond Windsor lies the meadow of **Runnymede,** where King John, chewing his beard in fury, signed the Magna Carta. Runnymede is also the site of the **John F. Kennedy Memorial,** an acre of hallowed ground presented to the United States by the people of Great Britain.

WHERE TO DINE
MODERATE

HOUSE OF THE BRIDGE, 71 High St. Tel. 0753/860914.
  Cuisine: ENGLISH/INTERNATIONAL. **Reservations:** Recommended.
$ **Prices:** Appetizers £3.26–£24.50 ($4.90–$36.80); main courses £11.50–£16.95 ($17.30–$25.40). AE, DC, MC, V.
  Open: Lunch daily noon–2:30pm; dinner daily 6–11pm.

This restaurant, in a charming Victorian house of red brick and terra cotta, is set beside the river and adjacent to the bridge, at Windsor's border with Eton. Near the handful of outdoor tables is an almost vertical garden whose plants cascade into the Thames. Some of the well-prepared main dishes are crispy duckling with Calvados and Seville oranges, chicken suprême flavored with tarragon and served with mushrooms, and chateaubriand. Specialties like roast rack of herb-flavored lamb are served only for two. Desserts, such as flambées and crêpes Suzette, are elaborate.

9. WOBURN ABBEY

44 miles N of London; 8½ miles NW of Dunstable

GETTING THERE   By Bus   In summer, travel agents can book you on organized coach tours from London.

By Car   Take M1 north to the junction of 12 or 13, where Woburn Abbey directions are signposted.

The great 18th-century Georgian mansion of ✪ **Woburn Abbey,** Woburn, Bedfordshire (tel. 0525/290666), is the traditional seat of the dukes of Bedford and the most publicized of England's Stately Homes. A wondrous repository of art gems, it contains works by Rembrandt, Holbein, Van Dyck, and Gainsborough, plus antique furniture, silver, and tapestries. Guests have included Queen Victoria as well as Marilyn Monroe.

The **Stately Antique Market** consists of three streets of period shops selling objets d'art. Surrounding it is a 3,000-acre park containing the **Wild Animal Kingdom,** with herds of rare deer, European bison, and a pets corner, as well as amusement rides and a light railway. Light meals are available at the Flying Duchess Pavilion Coffee Shop.

From January 1 to March 28, the house and park are open only on Saturday and Sunday. Visiting times for the house are from 11am to 4:45pm; for the park, 10:30am to 3:45pm. From March 29 to October 31, the abbey is open daily, and the house can be visited on Monday through Saturday from 11am to 6:15pm. The park is open on Monday through Saturday from 10am to 4:45pm and on Sunday from 10am to 5:45pm. Admission is £6 ($9) for adults and £2 ($3) for children.

APPENDIX

METRIC MEASURES

LENGTH

1 millimeter (mm)	=	0.04 inches (*or* less than 1/16 in.)
1 centimeter (cm)	=	0.39 inches (*or* under 1/2 in.)
1 meter (m)	=	39 inches (*or* about 1.1 yd.)
1 kilometer (km)	=	0.62 miles (*or* about 2/3 of a mile)

To convert kilometers to miles, multiply the number of kilometers by 0.62. Also use to convert kilometers per hour (kmph) to miles per hour (m.p.h.).

To convert miles to kilometers, multiply the number of miles by 1.61. Also use to convert from m.p.h. to kmph.

CAPACITY

1 liter (l)	=	33.92 fluid ounces = 2.1 pints = 1.06 quarts
	=	0.26 U.S. gallons
1 Imperial gallon	=	1.2 U.S. gallons

To convert liters to U.S. gallons, multiply the number of liters by 0.26.

To convert U.S. gallons to liters, multiply the number of gallons by 3.79.

To convert Imperial gallons to U.S. gallons, multiply the number of Imperial gallons by 1.2.

To convert U.S. gallons to Imperial gallons, multiply the number of U.S. gallons by 0.83.

WEIGHT

1 gram (g)	=	0.035 ounces (*or* about a paperclip's weight)
1 kilogram (kg)	=	35.2 ounces
	=	2.2 pounds
1 metric ton	=	2,205 pounds (1.1 short ton)

To convert kilograms to pounds, multiply the number of kilograms by 2.2.

To convert pounds to kilograms, multiply the number of pounds by 0.45.

AREA

1 hectare (ha)	=	2.47 acres		
1 square kilometer (km²)	=	247 acres	=	0.39 square miles

To convert hectares to acres, multiply the number of hectares by 2.47.

INDEX

GENERAL INFORMATION

SIGHTS & ATTRACTIONS

LONDON

Note An asterisk (*) indicates an Author's Favorite.

EXCURSION AREAS

ACCOMMODATIONS

RESTAURANTS

LONDON

Key to Abbreviations *B* = Budget; *E* = Expensive; *I* = Inexpensive; *M* = Moderate; * = Author's Favorite; \$ = Super-Value Choice.

EXCURSION AREAS

Now Save Money on All Your Travels by Joining
FROMMER'S ™ TRAVEL BOOK CLUB
The World's Best Travel Guides at Membership Prices

FROMMER'S TRAVEL BOOK CLUB is your ticket to successful travel! Open up a world of travel information and simplify your travel planning when you join ranks with thousands of value-conscious travelers who are members of the FROMMER'S TRAVEL BOOK CLUB. Join today and you'll be entitled to all the privileges that come from belonging to the club that offers you travel guides for less to more than 100 destinations worldwide. Annual membership is only $25 (U.S.) or $35 (Canada and foreign).

The Advantages of Membership

1. Your choice of three FREE travel guides. You can select any **two** FROMMER'S COMPREHENSIVE GUIDES, FROMMER'S $-A-DAY GUIDES, or FROMMER'S FAMILY GUIDES—plus **one** FROMMER'S CITY GUIDE or FROMMER'S CITY $-A-DAY GUIDE.
2. Your own subscription to **TRIPS AND TRAVEL** quarterly newsletter.
3. You're entitled to a **30% discount** on your order of any additional books offered by FROMMER'S TRAVEL BOOK CLUB.
4. You're offered (at a small additional fee of $6.50) our **Domestic Trip-Routing Kits.**

Our quarterly newsletter **TRIPS AND TRAVEL** offers practical information on the best buys in travel, the "hottest" vacation spots, the latest travel trends, world-class events and much, much more.
Our **Domestic Trip-Routing Kits** are available for any North American destination. We'll send you a detailed map highlighting the best route to take to your destination—you can request direct or scenic routes.

Here's all you have to do to join:
Send in your membership fee of $25 ($35 Canada and foreign) with your name and address on the form below along with your selections as part of your membership package to **FROMMER'S TRAVEL BOOK CLUB, P.O. Box 473, Mt. Morris, IL 61054-0473.** Remember to select any **two** FROMMER'S COMPREHENSIVE GUIDES, FROMMER'S $-A-DAY GUIDES, or FROMMER'S FAMILY GUIDES—plus **one** FROMMER'S CITY GUIDE or FROMMER'S CITY $-A-DAY GUIDE.
If you would like to order additional books, please select the books you would like and send a check for the total amount (please add sales tax in the states noted below), plus $2 per book for shipping and handling ($3 per book for all foreign orders) to:

FROMMER'S TRAVEL BOOK CLUB
P.O. Box 473
Mt. Morris, IL 61054-0473
(815) 734-1104

[ ] **YES.** I want to take advantage of this opportunity to join FROMMER'S TRAVEL BOOK CLUB.
[ ] **My check is enclosed.** Dollar amount enclosed_____*

Name_____
Address_____
City_____ State_____ Zip

To ensure that all orders are processed efficiently, please apply sales tax in the following areas: CA, CT, FL, IL, NJ, NY, TN, WA and CANADA.

*With membership, shipping and handling will be paid by FROMMER'S TRAVEL BOOK CLUB for the three free books you select as part of your membership. Please add $2 per book for shipping and handling for any additional books purchased ($3 per book for foreign orders).

Allow 4–6 weeks for delivery. Prices of books, membership fee, and publication dates are subject to change without notice.

AC1

Please Send Me the Books Checked Below:

FROMMER'S COMPREHENSIVE GUIDES
(Guides listing facilities from budget to deluxe,
with emphasis on the medium-priced)

	Retail Price	Code		Retail Price	Code
☐ Acapulco/Ixtapa/Taxco 1993–94	$15.00	C120	☐ Jamaica/Barbados 1993–94	$15.00	C105
☐ Alaska 1994–95	$17.00	C130	☐ Japan 1992–93	$19.00	C020
☐ Arizona 1993–94	$18.00	C101	☐ Morocco 1992–93	$18.00	C021
☐ Australia 1992–93	$18.00	C002	☐ Nepal 1994–95	$18.00	C126
☐ Austria 1993–94	$19.00	C119	☐ New England 1993	$17.00	C114
☐ Belgium/Holland/ Luxembourg 1993–94	$18.00	C106	☐ New Mexico 1993–94	$15.00	C117
☐ Bahamas 1994–95	$17.00	C121	☐ New York State 1994–95	$19.00	C132
☐ Bermuda 1994–95	$15.00	C122	☐ Northwest 1991–92	$17.00	C026
☐ Brazil 1993–94	$20.00	C111	☐ Portugal 1992–93	$16.00	C027
☐ California 1993	$18.00	C112	☐ Puerto Rico 1993–94	$15.00	C103
☐ Canada 1992–93	$18.00	C009	☐ Puerto Vallarta/ Manzanillo/Guadalajara 1992–93	$14.00	C028
☐ Caribbean 1994	$18.00	C123	☐ Scandinavia 1993–94	$19.00	C118
☐ Carolinas/Georgia 1994–95	$17.00	C128	☐ Scotland 1992–93	$16.00	C040
☐ Colorado 1993–94	$16.00	C100	☐ Skiing Europe 1989–90	$15.00	C030
☐ Cruises 1993–94	$19.00	C107	☐ South Pacific 1992–93	$20.00	C031
☐ DE/MD/PA & NJ Shore 1992–93	$19.00	C012	☐ Spain 1993–94	$19.00	C115
☐ Egypt 1990–91	$17.00	C013	☐ Switzerland/ Liechtenstein 1992–93	$19.00	C032
☐ England 1994	$18.00	C129	☐ Thailand 1992–93	$20.00	C033
☐ Florida 1994	$18.00	C124	☐ U.S.A. 1993–94	$19.00	C116
☐ France 1994–95	$20.00	C131	☐ Virgin Islands 1994–95	$13.00	C127
☐ Germany 1994	$19.00	C125	☐ Virginia 1992–93	$14.00	C037
☐ Italy 1994	$19.00	C130	☐ Yucatán 1993–94	$18.00	C110

FROMMER'S $-A-DAY GUIDES
(Guides to low-cost tourist accommodations and facilities)

	Retail Price	Code		Retail Price	Code
☐ Australia on $45 1993–94	$18.00	D102	☐ Israel on $45 1993–94	$18.00	D101
☐ Costa Rica/Guatemala/ Belize on $35 1993–94	$17.00	D108	☐ Mexico on $45 1994	$19.00	D116
☐ Eastern Europe on $30 1993–94	$18.00	D110	☐ New York on $70 1992–93	$16.00	D016
☐ England on $60 1994	$18.00	D112	☐ New Zealand on $45 1993–94	$18.00	D103
☐ Europe on $50 1994	$19.00	D115	☐ Scotland/Wales on $50 1992–93	$18.00	D019
☐ Greece on $45 1993–94	$19.00	D100	☐ South America on $40 1993–94	$19.00	D109
☐ Hawaii on $75 1994	$19.00	D113	☐ Turkey on $40 1992–93	$22.00	D023
☐ India on $40 1992–93	$20.00	D010	☐ Washington, D.C. on $40 1992–93	$17.00	D024
☐ Ireland on $40 1992–93	$17.00	D011			

FROMMER'S CITY $-A-DAY GUIDES
(Pocket-size guides with an emphasis on low-cost tourist accommodations and facilities)

	Retail Price	Code		Retail Price	Code
☐ Berlin on $40 1994–95	$12.00	D111	☐ Madrid on $50 1992–93	$13.00	D014
☐ Copenhagen on $50 1992–93	$12.00	D003	☐ Paris on $45 1994–95	$12.00	D117
☐ London on $45 1994–95	$12.00	D114	☐ Stockholm on $50 1992–93	$13.00	D022

FROMMER'S WALKING TOURS
(With routes and detailed maps, these companion guides point out the places and pleasures that make a city unique)

	Retail Price	Code		Retail Price	Code
☐ Berlin	$12.00	W100	☐ Paris	$12.00	W103
☐ London	$12.00	W101	☐ San Francisco	$12.00	W104
☐ New York	$12.00	W102	☐ Washington, D.C.	$12.00	W105

FROMMER'S TOURING GUIDES
(Color-illustrated guides that include walking tours, cultural and historic sights, and practical information)

	Retail Price	Code		Retail Price	Code
☐ Amsterdam	$11.00	T001	☐ New York	$11.00	T008
☐ Barcelona	$14.00	T015	☐ Rome	$11.00	T010
☐ Brazil	$11.00	T003	☐ Scotland	$10.00	T011
☐ Florence	$ 9.00	T005	☐ Sicily	$15.00	T017
☐ Hong Kong/Singapore/			☐ Tokyo	$15.00	T016
Macau	$11.00	T006	☐ Turkey	$11.00	T013
☐ Kenya	$14.00	T018	☐ Venice	$ 9.00	T014
☐ London	$13.00	T007			

FROMMER'S FAMILY GUIDES

	Retail Price	Code		Retail Price	Code
☐ California with Kids	$18.00	F100	☐ San Francisco with		
☐ Los Angeles with Kids	$17.00	F002	Kids	$17.00	F004
☐ New York City with Kids	$18.00	F003	☐ Washington, D.C. with		
			Kids	$17.00	F005

FROMMER'S CITY GUIDES
(Pocket-size guides to sightseeing and tourist accommodations and facilities in all price ranges)

	Retail Price	Code		Retail Price	Code
☐ Amsterdam 1993–94	$13.00	S110	☐ Montreál/Québec		
☐ Athens 1993–94	$13.00	S114	City 1993–94	$13.00	S125
☐ Atlanta 1993–94	$13.00	S112	☐ New Orleans 1993–		
☐ Atlantic City/Cape			94	$13.00	S103
May 1993–94	$13.00	S130	☐ New York 1993	$13.00	S120
☐ Bangkok 1992–93	$13.00	S005	☐ Orlando 1994	$13.00	S135
☐ Barcelona/Majorca/			☐ Paris 1993–94	$13.00	S109
Minorca/Ibiza 1993–			☐ Philadelphia 1993–94	$13.00	S113
94	$13.00	S115	☐ Rio 1991–92	$ 9.00	S029
☐ Berlin 1993–94	$13.00	S116	☐ Rome 1993–94	$13.00	S111
☐ Boston 1993–94	$13.00	S117	☐ Salt Lake City 1991–		
☐ Cancún/			92	$ 9.00	S031
Cozumel 1991–92	$ 9.00	S010	☐ San Diego 1993–94	$13.00	S107
☐ Chicago 1993–94	$13.00	S122	☐ San Francisco 1994	$13.00	S133
☐ Denver/Boulder/			☐ Santa Fe/Taos/		
Colorado			Albuquerque 1993–94	$13.00	S108
Springs 1993–94	$13.00	S131	☐ Seattle/		
☐ Dublin 1993–94	$13.00	S128	Portland 1992–93	$12.00	S035
☐ Hawaii 1992	$12.00	S014	☐ St. Louis/Kansas		
☐ Hong Kong 1992–93	$12.00	S015	City 1993–94	$13.00	S127
☐ Honolulu/Oahu 1994	$13.00	S134	☐ Sydney 1993–94	$13.00	S129
☐ Las Vegas 1993–94	$13.00	S121	☐ Tampa/St.		
☐ London 1994	$13.00	S132	Petersburg 1993–94	$13.00	S105
☐ Los Angeles 1993–94	$13.00	S123	☐ Tokyo 1992–93	$13.00	S039
☐ Madrid/Costa del			☐ Toronto 1993–94	$13.00	S126
Sol 1993–94	$13.00	S124	☐ Vancouver/		
☐ Miami 1993–94	$13.00	S118	Victoria 1990–91	$ 8.00	S041
☐ Minneapolis/St.			☐ Washington,		
Paul 1993–94	$13.00	S119	D.C. 1993	$13.00	S102

Other Titles Available at Membership Prices

SPECIAL EDITIONS

	Retail Price	Code		Retail Price	Code
☐ Bed & Breakfast North America	$15.00	P002	☐ Marilyn Wood's Wonderful Weekends (within a 250-mile radius of NYC)	$12.00	P017
☐ Bed & Breakfast Southwest	$16.00	P100	☐ National Park Guide 1993	$15.00	P101
☐ Caribbean Hideaways	$16.00	P103	☐ Where to Stay U.S.A.	$15.00	P102

GAULT MILLAU'S "BEST OF" GUIDES
(The only guides that distinguish the truly superlative from the merely overrated)

	Retail Price	Code		Retail Price	Code
☐ Chicago	$16.00	G002	☐ New England	$16.00	G010
☐ Florida	$17.00	G003	☐ New Orleans	$17.00	G011
☐ France	$17.00	G004	☐ New York	$17.00	G012
☐ Germany	$18.00	G018	☐ Paris	$17.00	G013
☐ Hawaii	$17.00	G006	☐ San Francisco	$17.00	G014
☐ Hong Kong	$17.00	G007	☐ Thailand	$18.00	G019
☐ London	$17.00	G009	☐ Toronto	$17.00	G020
☐ Los Angeles	$17.00	G005	☐ Washington, D.C.	$17.00	G017

THE REAL GUIDES
(Opinionated, politically aware guides for youthful budget-minded travelers)

	Retail Price	Code		Retail Price	Code
☐ Able to Travel	$20.00	R112	☐ Kenya	$12.95	R015
☐ Amsterdam	$13.00	R100	☐ Mexico	$11.95	R128
☐ Barcelona	$13.00	R101	☐ Morocco	$14.00	R129
☐ Belgium/Holland/ Luxembourg	$16.00	R031	☐ Nepal	$14.00	R018
☐ Berlin	$13.00	R123	☐ New York	$13.00	R019
☐ Brazil	$13.95	R003	☐ Paris	$13.00	R130
☐ California & the West Coast	$17.00	R121	☐ Peru	$12.95	R021
☐ Canada	$15.00	R103	☐ Poland	$13.95	R131
☐ Czechoslovakia	$15.00	R124	☐ Portugal	$16.00	R126
☐ Egypt	$19.00	R105	☐ Prague	$15.00	R113
☐ Europe	$18.00	R122	☐ San Francisco & the Bay Area	$11.95	R024
☐ Florida	$14.00	R006	☐ Scandinavia	$14.95	R025
☐ France	$18.00	R106	☐ Spain	$16.00	R026
☐ Germany	$18.00	R107	☐ Thailand	$17.00	R119
☐ Greece	$18.00	R108	☐ Tunisia	$17.00	R115
☐ Guatemala/Belize	$14.00	R127	☐ Turkey	$13.95	R027
☐ Hong Kong/Macau	$11.95	R011	☐ U.S.A.	$18.00	R117
☐ Hungary	$14.95	R118	☐ Venice	$11.95	R028
☐ Ireland	$17.00	R120	☐ Women Travel	$12.95	R029
☐ Italy	$18.00	R125	☐ Yugoslavia	$12.95	R030